EYEWITNESS TRAVEL
WASHINGTON, DC

PENN QUARTER
Pages 86–103
Street Finder maps 3, 4

CAPITOL IIILL
Pages 42–53
Street Finder map 4

PENN
QUARTER

THE MALL

CAPITOL
HILL

Washington Channel

Anacostia River

THE MALL
Pages 54–85
Street Finder maps 3, 4

| 0 meters | 750 |
| 0 yards | 750 |

EYEWITNESS TRAVEL
WASHINGTON, DC

MAIN CONTRIBUTORS:
SUSAN BURKE AND ALICE L. POWERS

LONDON, NEW YORK,
MELBOURNE, MUNICH AND DELHI
www.dk.com

PROJECT EDITOR Claire Folkard
ART EDITORS Tim Mann, Simon J.M. Oon
SENIOR EDITOR Helen Townsend
EDITORS Emily Anderson, Felicity Crowe
US EDITOR Mary Sutherland
DESIGNERS Gillian Andrews, Eli Estaugh,
Elly King, Rebecca Milner
DTP Sam Borland, Maite Lantaron
PICTURE RESEARCHERS Brigitte Arora, Katherine Mesquita
PRODUCTION Mel Allsop

CONTRIBUTORS
Susan Burke, Alice L. Powers, Jennifer Quasha, Kem Sawyer

PHOTOGRAPHERS
Philippe Dewet, Kim Sayer, Giles Stokoe, Scott Suchman

ILLUSTRATORS
Stephen Conlin, Gary Cross, Richard Draper, Chris Orr & Associates,
Mel Pickering, Robbie Polley, John Woodcock

Reproduced by Colourscan, Singapore
Printed and bound by South China Printing Co. Ltd., China

First American Edition, 2000
11 12 13 14 10 9 8 7 6 5 4 3 2 1

Published in the United States by DK Publishing, 375 Hudson Street,
New York 10014

**Reprinted with revisions 2002, 2003, 2004, 2005, 2006, 2008,
2009, 2010, 2011**

Copyright © 2000, 2011 Dorling Kindersley Limited, London

Published in Great Britain by Dorling Kindersley Limited.

A CATALOGING IN PUBLICATION RECORD IS AVAILABLE
FROM THE LIBRARY OF CONGRESS.

ISSN 1542-1554
ISBN 978-0-75666-916-4

Front cover main image: View across Jefferson Memorial lake

MIX
Paper from
responsible sources
FSC™ C018179

**The information in this DK Eyewitness
Travel Guide is checked regularly.**

Every effort has been made to ensure that this book is as up-to-date
as possible at the time of going to press. Some details, however,
such as telephone numbers, opening hours, prices, gallery hanging
arrangements and travel information are liable to change. The
publishers cannot accept responsibility for any consequences arising
from the use of this book, nor for any material on third party
websites, and cannot guarantee that any website address in this
book will be a suitable source of travel information. We value the
views and suggestions of our readers very highly. Please write to:
Publisher, DK Eyewitness Travel Guides, Dorling Kindersley,
80 Strand, London, WC2R 0RL, or email travelguides@dk.com.

◁ **The White House**

CONTENTS

Fountain in Dumbarton Oaks

INTRODUCING
WASHINGTON, DC

**View toward the Lincoln Memorial
from Arlington National Cemetery**

Columns from the US Capitol building, now in the National Arboretum

Map seller outside the National Gallery of Art on the Mall

Maryland crab cakes

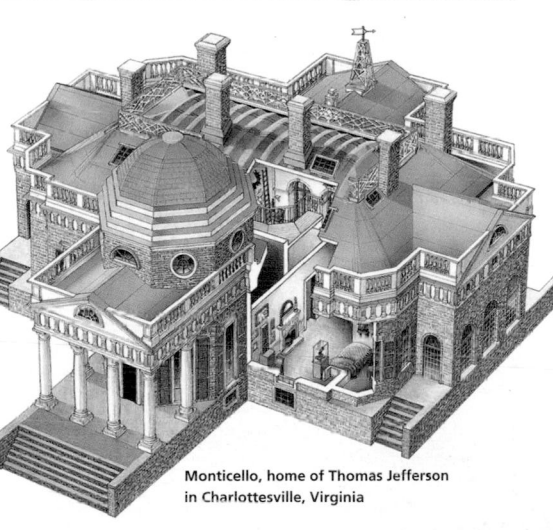

Monticello, home of Thomas Jefferson in Charlottesville, Virginia

HOW TO USE THIS GUIDE

This guide helps you to get the most from your stay in Washington, DC. It provides detailed practical information and expert recommendations. *Introducing Washington, DC* maps the city and the region, sets it in its historical and cultural context, and gives an overview of the main attractions. *Washington, DC Area By Area* is the main sightseeing section, giving detailed information on all the major sights, with photographs, illustrations and maps. *Farther Afield* looks at sights outside the city center, and *Beyond Washington, DC* explores other places within easy reach of the city. Carefully researched suggestions for restaurants, hotels, entertainment, and shopping are found in the *Travelers' Needs* section, while the *Survival Guide* contains useful advice on everything from changing money to traveling on Washington's Metrorail system.

FINDING YOUR WAY AROUND WASHINGTON, DC

The center of Washington has been divided into five sightseeing areas, each with its own chapter, color-coded for easy reference. All sights are numbered and plotted on an area map for each chapter.

1 Area Introduction *This describes the history and character of the area and has a map on which the sights have been plotted. Other key information is also given.*

Each area has color-coded thumb tabs.

Locator Map

The area shaded pink is shown in greater detail on the Street-by-Street map on the following pages.

2 Street-by-Street map *This gives a bird's-eye view of the heart of each sightseeing area. Interesting features are labeled. There is also a list of "star sights" that no visitor should miss.*

The Visitors' Checklist provides detailed practical information.

A suggested route takes in the most interesting and attractive streets in the are

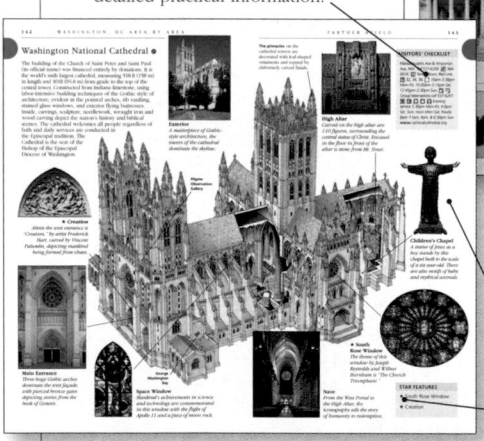

3 Star sight map *These are given two or more full pages. Historic buildings a dissected to reveal their interiors. Wher necessary, sights are color-coded to hel you locate the most interesting areas.*

Stars indicate the sights that no visitor should miss.

WASHINGTON, DC AREA MAP

The colored areas shown on this map (inside the front cover) are the five main sight-seeing areas used in this guide. Each is covered in a full chapter in *Washington, DC Area by Area (pp40–127)*. They are highlighted on other maps throughout the book. In *Washington, DC at a Glance (see pp30–35)*, they help you to locate the top sights. The *Street Finder (see pp224–229)* shows you the sights from these five areas on a detailed street map of Washington.

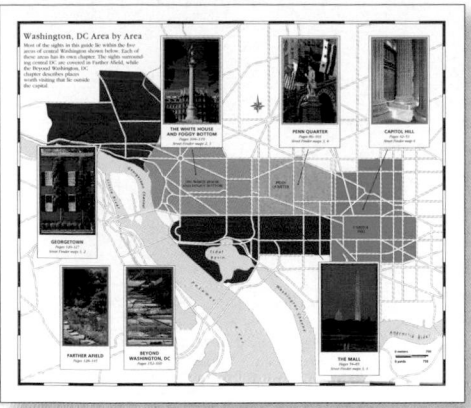

---

4 Detailed information *All the important sights are described individually. They are listed in order, following the numbering on the area map.*

Practical information is provided in an information block. The key to the symbols used is on the back flap.

The Introduction outlines the areas covered in this section and their historical context.

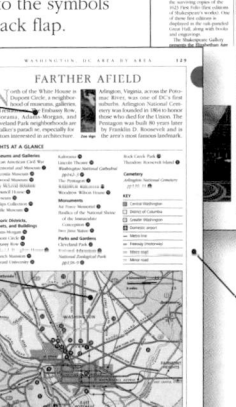

A map of the city shows the location of the Farther Afield sights in relation to the city center.

5 Farther Afield *This section covers those sights that lie just outside central Washington and are easily accessible from the city center.*

6 Beyond Washington *Places worth visiting that are situated within a day's travel of Washington are described here. They include interesting cities, historic towns, and national parks.*

Special sights, such as this national park, are highlighted with maps or detailed illustrations.

INTRODUCING WASHINGTON, DC

FOUR GREAT DAYS IN WASHINGTON, DC

Although many of the capital's highlights are easily recognized, these great days in Washington, DC will introduce visitors to its unexpected treasures. The city boasts not only world-renowned works of art and majestic monuments, but picturesque

Lincoln Memorial

neighborhoods and beautiful gardens. All the sights can be reached on foot or by public transportation. Feel free to dip into the itineraries as you wish. Price guides show the daily cost for two adults or for a family of two adults and two children including lunch.

The White House, the Presidential residence

MONUMENTAL CITY

- Lincoln Memorial
- World War II Memorial
- Corcoran Gallery of Art
- The White House

TWO ADULTS allow at least $40

Morning
Start your day at the **Lincoln Memorial** *(see pp84–5)*, six blocks south of the Foggy Bottom Metro stop. Inside, on the north and south walls, you will find inscriptions of President Lincoln's **Gettysburg Address** *(see p163)*. In front of the memorial, to the left of the Reflecting Pool, is the moving **Vietnam Veterans Memorial** *(see p83)*. Engraved on black granite are the names of Americans who died in the war. Then make your way through the shady Constitution Gardens back to the Reflecting Pool. To the right is the **Korean War Veterans Memorial** *(see p83)* and nearby is the **World War II Memorial** *(see p82)*. Here you can see the Freedom Wall, its inscriptions, and the bas-reliefs showing the US at war. After this memorial,

move on to 17th Street where there are several historic buildings including the **Organization of American States** and the **Daughters of the American Revolution** *(see p114)*. Drop into the **Corcoran Gallery of Art**, one of the country's first art galleries *(see p113)*. Have lunch here, or head to a café near Pennsylvania Avenue.

Afternoon
Stroll down Pennsylvania Avenue, passing the red brick Renwick Gallery, Blair House (where presidential guests stay), and **The White House** *(see pp108–9)*. Walk around the White House to the Visitor Center at 1450 Pennsylvania Avenue. Afterwards, visit the **US National Archives** *(see p90)* to see historic documents including the *Declaration of Independence* and the *Bill of Rights*. End your day with a tour of **Ford's Theater** *(see p96)* where Lincoln was shot,

followed by a meal in **Chinatown** *(see pp96–7)* or **Penn Quarter** *(see pp86–103)*.

BLACK HISTORY

- **Frederick Douglass House**
- **Mary McLeod Bethune Site**
- **U Street landmarks**
- **African American Civil War Museum and Memorial**

TWO ADULTS allow at least $20

Morning
Spend the morning at the **Frederick Douglass House**, a 15-acre estate in Anacostia *(see p145)*. Douglass was a fugitive slave who became a famous abolitionist. Almost all of the furnishings at the house are original (look out for the walking stick collection). Cross the river to **The Shaw Neighborhood** *(see p141)* with its lovely Victorian houses. This is where prominent African-Americans lived in the 1940s. Visit the **Mary McLeod Bethune Council House** *(see p140)*, home of the civil rights leader and founder of the National Council of Negro Women.

Lincoln Theatre, the venue for many of Duke Ellington's performances

Georgetown's pretty gardens and houses, a delightful neighborhood to stroll through

Lunch at **Ben's Chili Bowl** on U Street, a delightful place that was once the Minnehaha silent movie theater.

Afternoon
Stroll along U Street, once known as Black Broadway. Audiences went wild when Duke Ellington performed at the **Lincoln Theatre** *(see p140)*. He lived nearby at numbers 1805 and 1816 13th Street. Visit the **African American Civil War Museum and Memorial**, honoring black soldiers *(see p133)*. End the day in style in Georgetown with dinner and jazz at **Blues Alley** *(see pp202–3)*.

ART AND SHOPPING

- **National Gallery of Art**
- **Lunch on the Mall**
- **Georgetown Shopping**
- **Washington Harbor**

TWO ADULTS allow at least $35

Morning
To experience the full scope of art covered at the **National Gallery of Art** *(see pp58–61)*, visit both the West Building (13th–19th century European and American art) and the East Building (modern and contemporary art). Don't miss the Matisse Cut-Outs in the tower of the East Building. Have a coffee break at the Espresso Bar on the Concourse level. Outside, in the Garden Court (north side of East Building), find the Andy Goldsworthy installation entitled *Roof*, a study of domes. Wander through the enchanting Sculpture Garden to the Pavilion Café, a charming spot for lunch.

Afternoon
Now head to cobblestoned **Georgetown** *(see pp120–27)*. You could take the 90-minute walk *(see p148–9)*, but if shopping is your ultimate goal, go to M Street or Wisconsin Avenue for an impressive number of galleries and shops and a range of stylish goods – lamps, Italian ceramics, antiques, and prints, as well as cutting-edge fashion. To finish, have tea in the Garden Terrace at the **Four Seasons Hotel** *(see p177)*, or have a drink at **Washington Harbor** while watching the boats *(see p122)*.

A FAMILY DAY

- **Visit the National Zoo**
- **National Air and Space Museum**
- **Washington Monument**

FAMILY OF FOUR allow at least $55

Morning
Start early at the **National Zoo** *(see pp138–9)*, checking at its Visitor Center for feeding times, talks, and training sessions (entry is free). See Clouded Leopards and Giant Pandas on the Asia Trail and the great cats on Lion-Tiger Hill. At the Great Ape House orangutans scale a 400-ft (130-m) "O Line." Have lunch at the Mane Restaurant or at one of the snack bars.

Afternoon
Go by metro to the **National Air and Space Museum** *(see pp64–5)*. Discover facts such as the cruising speed of the *Spirit of St. Louis*, or the reason Skylab was covered with a coating of gold. Catch a film at the IMAX theatre, where you can experience flying without leaving the ground. Then head for the **Washington Monument** *(see p78)* and take the elevator to the top for the spectacular view (advance booking required). Finish off at the **Kennedy Center** *(see pp118–19)* in Foggy Bottom, for free entertainment on the Millennium Stage at 6pm.

Washington Monument, for a fabulous view of the city

Putting Washington, DC on the Map

Washington, DC is situated near the East Coast of North America, surrounded by the state of Maryland and separated from Virginia by the Potomac River. It covers an area of 108 sq km (67 sq miles) and has a population of 591,000. As the capital of the United States, and seat of federal government, the city is a major focus of American life. It is a very popular tourist destination, attracting millions of visitors each year. The beautiful countryside of Maryland and Virginia is also easily reached from the capital city.

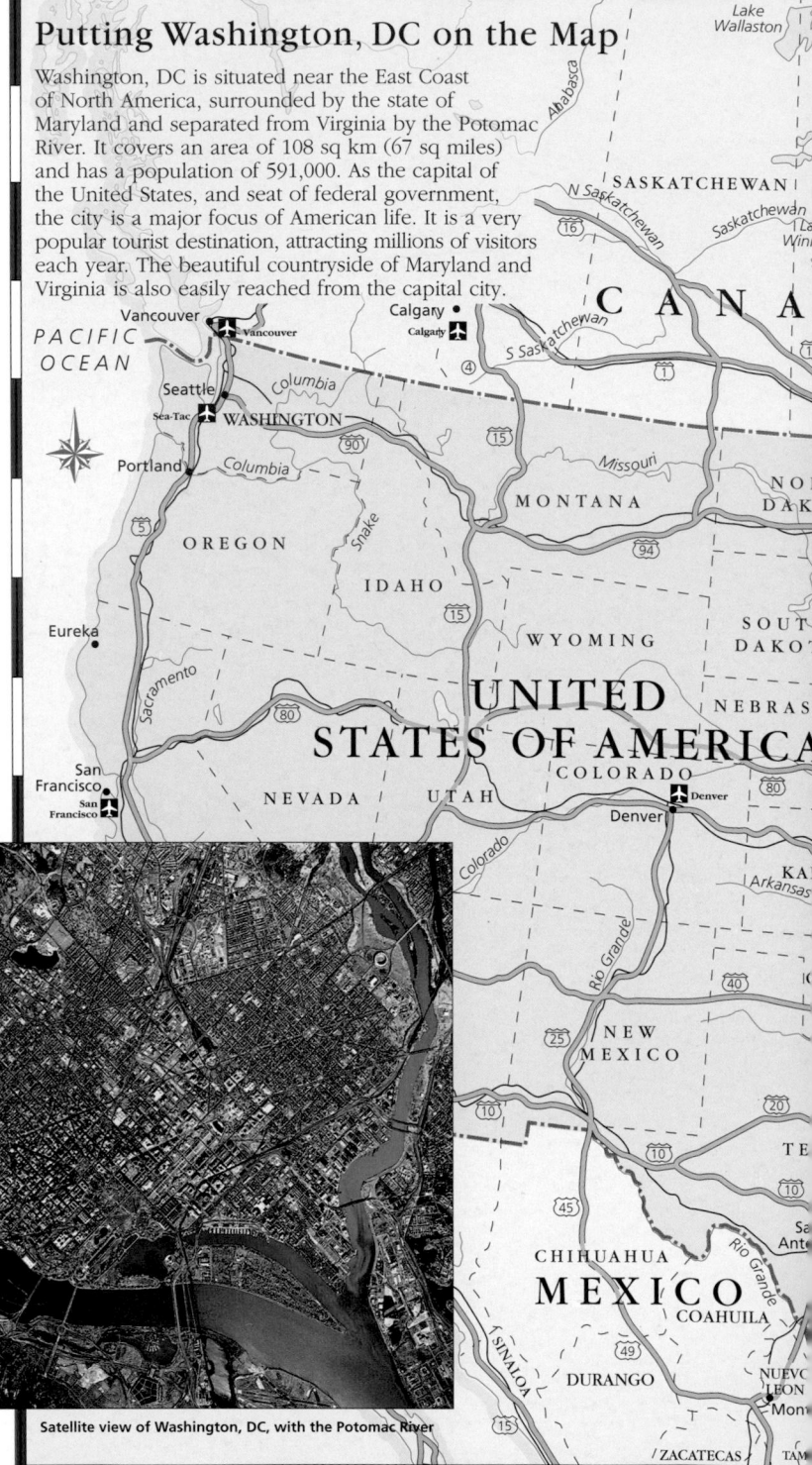

Satellite view of Washington, DC, with the Potomac River

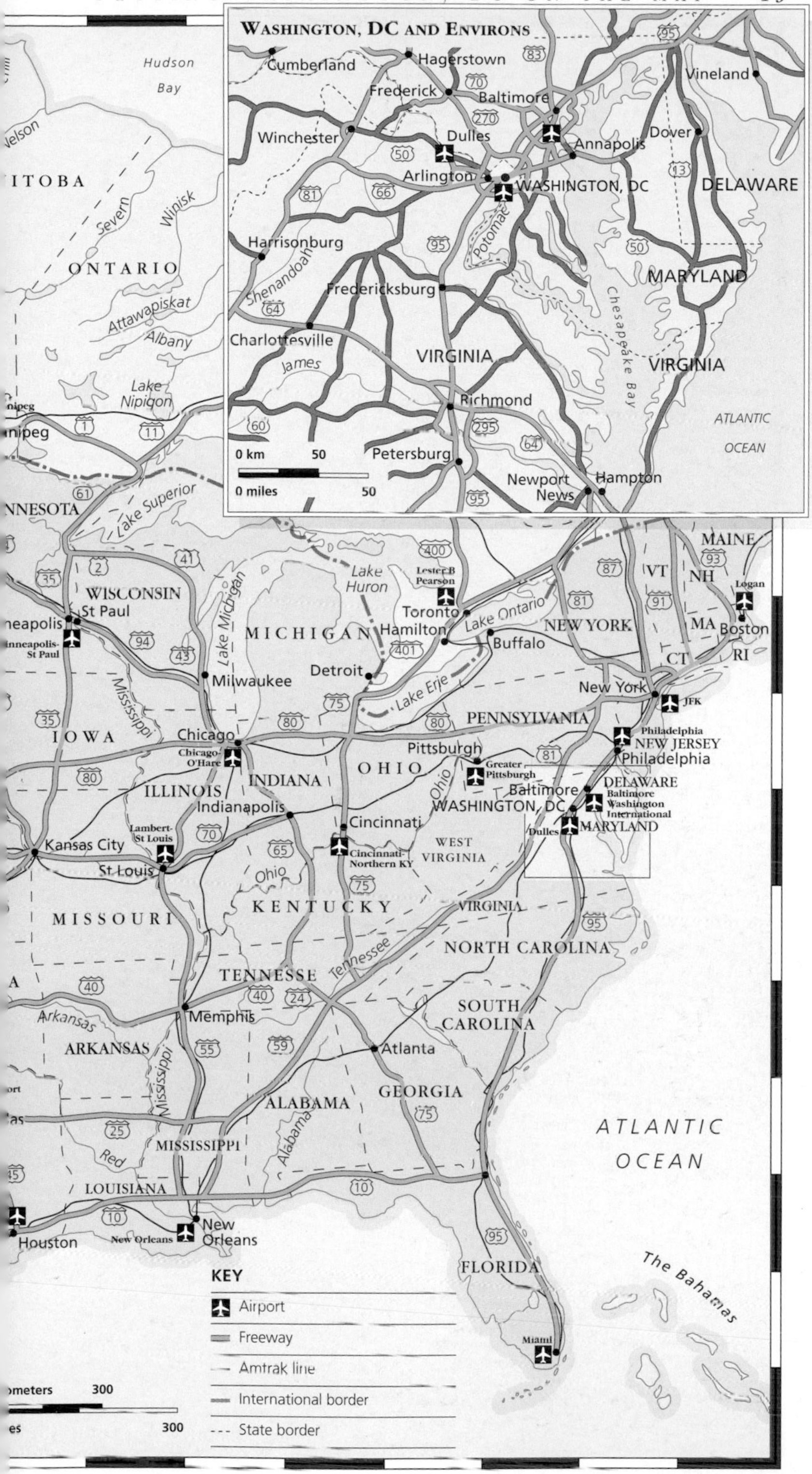

WASHINGTON, DC AND ENVIRONS

Hudson
Bay

Cumberland
Hagerstown
Frederick
Baltimore
Winchester
Dulles
Annapolis
Dover
Arlington
WASHINGTON, DC
DELAWARE
Harrisonburg
Shenandoah
Fredericksburg
MARYLAND
Charlottesville
James
VIRGINIA
VIRGINIA
Richmond
Chesapeake Bay
Petersburg
ATLANTIC
OCEAN
Newport
News
Hampton

0 km   50
0 miles   50

ITOBA

ONTARIO

Severn
Winisk
Attawapiskat
Albany

Lake
Nipigon

nipeg
nipeg

NNESOTA

Lake Superior

WISCONSIN
St Paul

Lake Michigan

Lake
Huron

Lester B
Pearson
Toronto
Hamilton
Lake Ontario
Buffalo

MAINE

VT   NH   Logan

NEW YORK

MA   Boston

CT   RI

neapolis
nneapolis-
St Paul

MICHIGAN

Milwaukee

Detroit

Lake Erie

New York
JFK

IOWA

Mississippi

Chicago
Chicago
O'Hare
INDIANA

ILLINOIS
Indianapolis

Pittsburgh

OHIO

Ohio

PENNSYLVANIA

Greater
Pittsburgh

NEW JERSEY
Philadelphia
Philadelphia

DELAWARE
Baltimore
Baltimore
Washington
International
WASHINGTON, DC

Kansas City

Lambert-
St Louis
St Louis

Cincinnati

Cincinnati-
Northern KY

WEST
VIRGINIA

Dulles
MARYLAND

MISSOURI

Ohio

KENTUCKY

VIRGINIA

NORTH CAROLINA

A

Arkansas

TENNESSE

Tennessee

Memphis

SOUTH
CAROLINA

ARKANSAS

Atlanta

ort

as

MISSISSIPPI

ALABAMA   GEORGIA

Alabama

Red

LOUISIANA

Houston
New Orleans
New
Orleans

ATLANTIC

OCEAN

FLORIDA

The Bahamas

KEY

✈ Airport

— Freeway

--- Amtrak line

— International border

---- State border

Miami

ometers   300

es   300

Greater Washington, DC

The city of Washington was created not only as a new capital for the United States but also as the seat of government, independent from the other states. It was laid out in a diamond-shaped area with a grid system of roads. One side of the square was lost after land was ceded back to Virginia in 1846. Although the city has sprawled beyond its original limits, officially the District of Columbia remains within the boundaries indicated. Washington is an easy city to get around, with an efficient modern metro system.

KEY

- Central Washington
- District of Columbia
- Built-up area
- ✈ Domestic airport
- Freeway
- Major road
- 🚆 Train station
- Train line
- Metro line/station
- State border

0 kilometers 2.5

0 miles 2.5

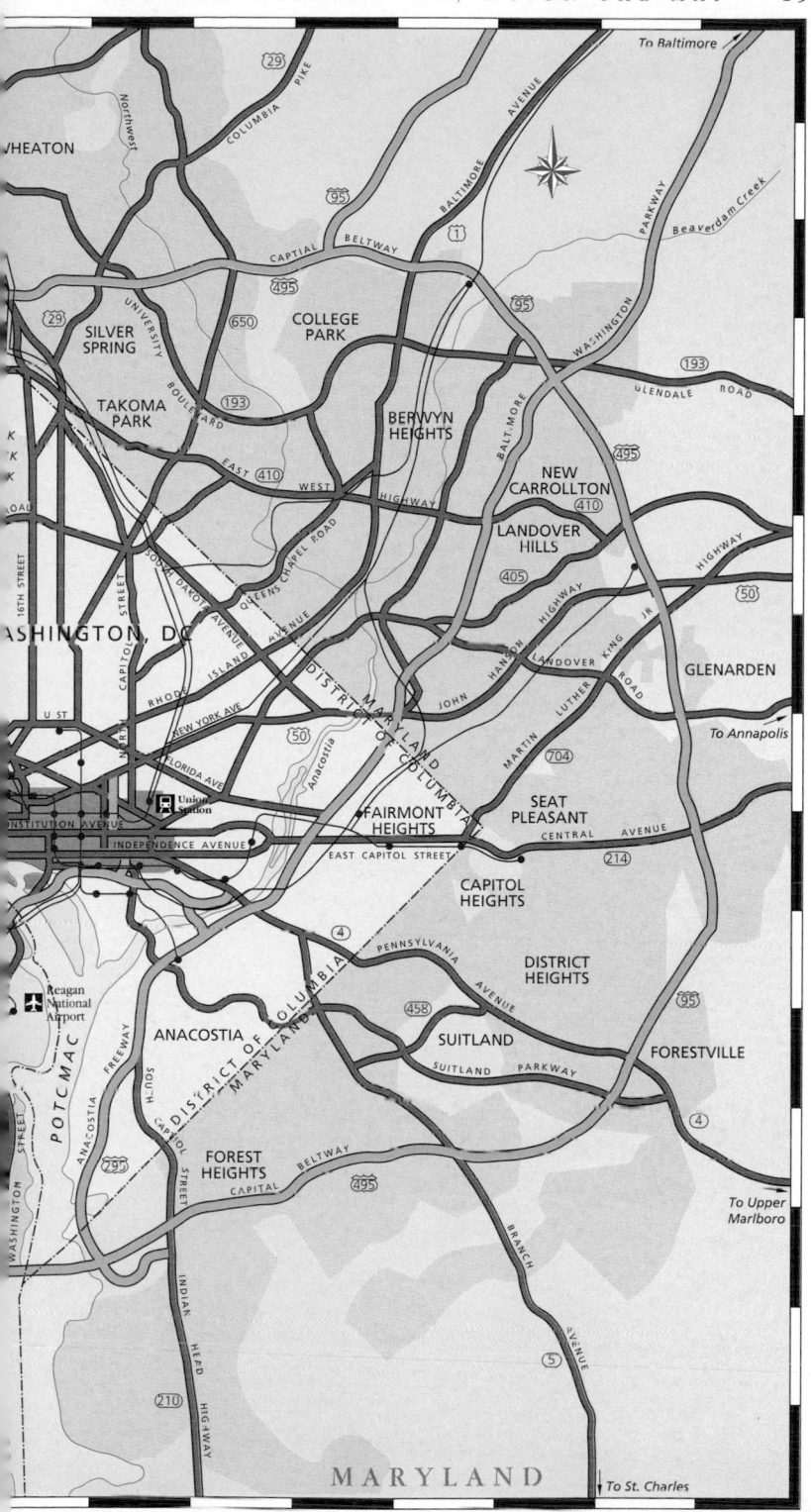

THE HISTORY OF WASHINGTON, DC

Native Americans settled in what is now the District of Columbia as long as 6,000 years ago. Archeologists have discovered traces of three villages in the area; the largest was called Nacotchtanke. Its people, the Anacostines, settled along the Potomac River and a smaller tributary now named the Anacostia River.

ENGLISH SETTLEMENT

In December 1606 Captain John Smith of the Virginia Company, under the charge of King James I of England, set sail fromEngland for the New World. Five months later he arrived in the Chesapeake Bay and founded the Jamestown colony. A skilled cartographer, Smith was soon sailing up the Potomac River. In 1608 he came to the area that would later become Washington.

The English settlers who followed supported themselves through the fur trade, and later cultivated tobacco and corn (maize). The marriage in 1614 between John Rolfe, one of the settlers, and Pocahontas, daughter of the Indian chief Powhatan, kept the peace between the English and the Indians for eight years. Struggles over land ownership led to massacres in 1622. The English finally defeated the Indians in 1644, and a formal peace agreement was made in 1646.

The settlement of Jamestown, Virginia, in 1607

The first Africans arrived in the region in 1619 and worked as indentured servants on plantations. They were given food and lodging as payment for serving for a fixed number of years. However, within the next 40 years the practice changed so that blacks were purchased for life, and their children became the property of their master. As the number of plantations grew, so did the number of slaves.

In the late 1600s another group of settlers, this time Irish-Scottish, led by Captain Robert Troop, established themselves here. Along the Potomac River two ports, George Town (later Georgetown) and Alexandria, soon became profitable centers of commerce. Here planters had their crops inspected, stored, and shipped. In both towns streets were laid out in rectangular patterns. With rich soil, plentiful land, abundant labor, and good transportation, the region rapidly grew in prosperity.

TIMELINE

1607 Captain John Smith founds Jamestown settlement in Virginia

1619 The first Africans arrive in American colonies

Captain John Smith (1580–1631)

1751 George Town is established

1600	1650	1700	1750

1646 The Indians and the English reach a peace agreement in the Tidewater and Potomac region

1634 Lord Baltimore founds Catholic colony in Maryland

1748 Tobacco merchants granted land for the town of Alexandria

◁ George Washington by Rembrandt Peale, painted 1824–5

REVOLUTIONARY YEARS

Some 100 years after the first settlers arrived, frustration over British rule began to grow, both in the Potomac region and elsewhere in the 13 American colonies. In 1775, the colonies began their struggle for independence. On April 19, shots were fired at Lexington, Massachusetts by American colonists who wanted "no taxation without representation," thus beginning the War of Independence.

On July 4, 1776, the Declaration of Independence was issued as colonists attempted to sever ties with Britain. Revolt led to revolution, and the newly formed United States won an important victory at Saratoga, New York in 1777. The French came to the aid of the Americans and finally, on October 19, 1781, the British, led by Lord Cornwallis, surrendered at Yorktown, Virginia. This ended the war and assured the independence of the United States. The peace treaty was signed in Paris on September 3, 1783. Britain agreed to boundaries giving the US all territory to the south of what is now Canada, north of Florida, and west to the Mississippi River.

The Continental Congress, a legislative body of representatives from the newly formed states, appointed a committee to draft the country's first constitution. The result was the Articles of Confederation, which established a union of the newly created states but provided the central government with little power. This later gave way to a stronger form of government, created

Meeting in New York of first delegates of Congress to discuss location for a new capital city

by the delegates of the Federal Constitutional Convention in Philadelphia in May, 1787. George Washington was unanimously chosen to be president. He took office on April 30, 1789.

A NEW CITY

The Constitution of the United States, ratified in 1788, allowed for the creation of a seat of government, not to exceed 10 square miles, which would be ruled by the United States Congress. This area was to be independent and not part of any state. At the first meeting of Congress in New York City in 1789, a dispute arose between northern and southern delegates over where the capital should be located. Secretary of the Treasury Alexander Hamilton and Secretary of State Thomas Jefferson worked out an agreement whereby the debts incurred by northern states

Lord Cornwallis

TIMELINE

1781 The British surrender at Yorktown

1783 The US and Britain sign the Treaty of Paris

1787 The Federal Constitutional Convention meets in Philadelphia

1793 Preside Washington the Capitol's cornerstone

| 1775 | 1780 | | 1785 | 1790 | |

1775 The first battles of the American Revolution are fought at Lexington and Concord

Articles of Confederation

1789 Delegates gather in New York City to discuss a location for the capital

1791 President Washington obtains land for the capital city

1792 Construction on the President's (later the White H

during the Revolution would be taken over by the government, and in return the capital would be located in the south. George Washington chose an area that incorporated land from both Maryland and Virginia, and included the towns of Alexandria and Georgetown. It was to be known as the city of Washington. At Suter's Tavern in Georgetown, Washington convinced local residents to sell their land for £25 an acre. He chose a surveyor, Andrew Ellicott, and his assistant Benjamin Banneker, a free African-American, to lay out the streets and lots. Washington also invited Major Pierre Charles L'Enfant to create a grand design for the new capital city *(see p67)*.

In 1800 the government was moved to Washington. President John Adams and his wife Abigail took up residence in the new President's House, designed by James Hoban, which was later renamed the White House by Theodore Roosevelt. The city remained empty of residents for many years while the building works took place.

Ellicott's engraved map of 1792, based on L'Enfant's plan

WAR OF 1812

Tension with Britain over restrictions on trade and freedom of the seas began to escalate during James Madison's administration. On June 18, 1812, the US declared war on Britain. In August 1814, British troops reached Washington and officers at the Capitol fled, taking the Declaration of Independence and the Constitution with them. First Lady Dolley Madison escaped from the White House with Gilbert Stuart's portrait of George Washington.

On August 24, the British defeated the Americans at Bladensburg, a suburb of Washington. They set fire to the War Department, the Treasury, the Capitol, and the White House. Only a night of heavy rain prevented the city's destruction. The Treaty of Ghent, which finally ended the war, was signed on February 17, 1815 in the Octagon.

The British attack on Washington, DC in August 1814

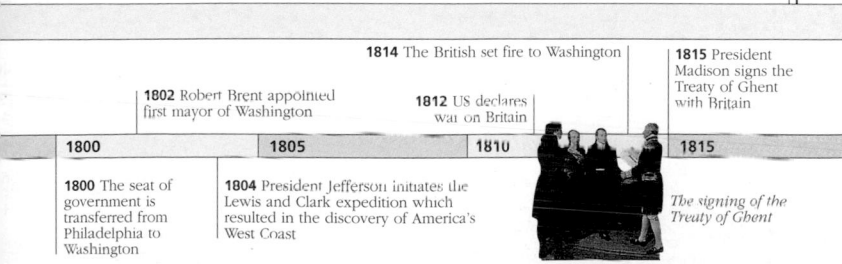

1814 The British set fire to Washington

1802 Robert Brent appointed first mayor of Washington

1812 US declares war on Britain

1815 President Madison signs the Treaty of Ghent with Britain

| 1800 | 1805 | 1810 | 1815 |

1800 The seat of government is transferred from Philadelphia to Washington

1804 President Jefferson initiates the Lewis and Clark expedition which resulted in the discovery of America's West Coast

The signing of the Treaty of Ghent

The Baltimore and Ohio Railroad's "Tom Thumb" locomotive racing a horse-drawn car

REBIRTH

With the end of the War of 1812 came a period of renewed optimism and economic prosperity in Washington. Washingtonians wanted to make their city a bustling commercial capital. They planned to build the Chesapeake and Ohio Canal to connect Washington to the Ohio River Valley and thus open trade with the west.

Construction on the Baltimore and Ohio Railroad line also got under way. As the population grew, new hotels and boarding-houses, home to many of the nation's congress-men, opened up. Newspapers, such as the *National Intelligencer*, flourished.

In 1829 an Englishman called James Smithson bequeathed a collection of minerals, books, and $500,000 in gold to the United States, and the Smithsonian Institution was born.

Construction began on three important government buildings, each designed by Robert Mills (1781–1855): the Treasury Building, the Patent Office, and the General Post Office building. Also at this time, the Washington National Monument Society, led by George Watterston, chose a 600-ft obelisk to become the Washington Monument, again designed by the architect Robert Mills.

Chained slaves walking past the unfinished Capitol building

SLAVERY DIVIDES THE CITY

Racial tension was beginning to increase around this time, and in 1835 it erupted into what was later known as the Snow Riot. After the attempted murder of the widow of architect William Thornton, a botany teacher from the North was arrested for inciting blacks because plant specimens had been found wrapped in the pages of an abolitionist newspaper. A riot ensued, and in the course of the fighting a school for black children was destroyed as well as the interior of a restaurant owned by Beverly Snow, a free black. As a result, and to the anger of many people, black and white, laws were passed denying free blacks licenses to run saloons or eating places.

Nothing has been more divisive in Washington's history than the issue of slavery. Many Washingtonians were slaveholders; others became ardent abolitionists. The homes of several

TIMELINE

1828 President John Quincy Adams breaks ground for the Chesapeake and Ohio Canal	*James Smithson (1765–1829)*		**1844** The invention of the telegraph speeds the distribution of news from Washington
1825	1830	1835	1840
	1829 James Smithson leaves a fortune worth more than $500,000 to the United States	**1835** Baltimore and Ohio Railroad links Washington and Baltimore. Racial tension leads to the Snow Riot	**1846** Construction the Smithsonian C begins. Alexand retroceded to Vir
	1827 The Washington Abolition Society is organized		

abolitionists and free blacks, as well as black churches, were used as hiding places for fugitive slaves. On an April night in 1848, 77 slaves attempted to escape the city, and boarded a small schooner on the Potomac River. But the following night they were captured and brought back to Washington, where they were sold at auction. The incident served only to heighten the tension between pro-slavery and anti-slavery groups. Slavery was abolished in Washington in 1862.

THE CIVIL WAR

In 1860, following the election of President Abraham Lincoln, several southern states seceded from the Union in objection to Lincoln's stand against slavery. Shots were fired on Fort Sumter in Charleston, South Carolina on April 12, 1861, and the Civil War began. By the summer, 50,000 volunteers arrived in Washington to join the Army of the Potomac under General George B. McClellan. Washington suddenly found itself in the business of housing, feeding, and clothing the troops, as well as caring for the wounded. Buildings and churches became makeshift hospitals.

Black residents of Washington celebrating the abolition of slavery in the District of Columbia

Many people came to nurse the wounded, including author Louisa May Alcott and poet Walt Whitman.

Thousands of northerners came to help the war effort. They were joined by hordes of black people heading north to escape slavery, so that by 1864 the population of Washington had doubled that of 1860, reaching 140,000.

After skirmishes on July 12, 1864, witnessed by Lincoln himself at Fort Stevens, the Confederates retreated. By March 1865 the end of the war appeared to be close at hand. Parades, speeches, and band concerts followed Confederate General Robert E. Lee's surrender on April 9, 1865. Yet the celebratory mood was short-lived. Disturbed by the Union Army's victory, John Wilkes Booth assassinated President Lincoln at Ford's Theatre during the third act of *Our American Cousin* on April 14, 1865. Lincoln was taken to the house of tailor William Petersen, across the street from the theater, where he died the next morning (see p96).

Victory parade through Washington, DC to celebrate the end of the Civil War in April 1865

POST CIVIL WAR

The Freedmen's Bureau was created to help provide African Americans with housing, food, education, and employment. In 1867 General Oliver Otis Howard, commissioner of the bureau, used $500,000 of the bureau's funds to purchase land to establish a university for African Americans. He was president of this institution, later named Howard University, from 1869 to 1873.

On February 21, 1871, a new "territorial government" was formed to unite George-town, the city of Wash-ington, and the County of Washington into the District of Columbia. A governor and a board of public works were appointed by President Ulysses S. Grant. Alexander "Boss" Shepherd, a member of the board of public works, paved streets, installed streetlights, laid sidewalks, planned parks, and designed an advanced sewerage system. But the District's debts

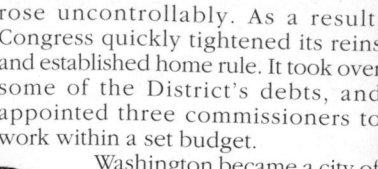

Frederick Douglass

rose uncontrollably. As a result, Congress quickly tightened its reins and established home rule. It took over some of the District's debts, and appointed three commissioners to work within a set budget.

Washington became a city of contrasts, attracting both rich and poor. One of the most distinguished literati in the city was Henry Adams, best known for his autobiographical work, *The Education of Henry Adams*. He lived on Lafayette Square next door to John Hay, Secretary of State and also a man of letters. One of Washington's most prominent African Americans, Frederick Douglass, lived at Cedar Hill, across the river in Anacostia. Born a slave in Maryland, he escaped north to freedom where he started an abolitionist newspaper. During the Civil War he became an adviser to President Lincoln.

Many lived well, including the growing middle class, which moved to the new suburbs of Mount Pleasant and LeDroit Park, yet a large number of the poor made their home in Washington's hidden alleys.

A NEW CENTURY

In 1901 Senator James McMillan of Michigan spearheaded a plan to improve the design of Washington by partaking in the "city beautiful" movement, in vogue at the time. L'Enfant's plan was finally completed, and the Mall between the Washington Monument and the US Capitol was laid out. Architects Daniel Burnham,

The Library of Congress under construction

TIMELINE

1867 Howard University is established

1877 Frederick Douglass moves to Cedar Hill. First issue of the *Washington Post*

1884 Washington Monument is completed

1901 Senator James McMillan spearheads "city beautiful" movement

1889 Construction on the Library of Congress begins

1870   1880   1890   190(

1871 Territorial government is formed

Oliver Otis Howard (1830–1909)

1878 First telephone service in Washington becomes a municipal corporation

1897 First automobile in the District of Columbia

1899 The Height of Buildings Act puts vertical limitations on all construction in DC

Suffragettes demanding a hearing for imprisoned leader Alice Paul

attracted small businesses, theaters, nightclubs, and restaurants. It became home to many successful musicians and writers; Duke Ellington and the opera star Madame Evanti lived here, as did poets Langston Hughes and Paul Dunbar. Alain Locke, a professor of philosophy at Howard, and Jean Toomer, author of *Cane,* were also residents.

Charles F. McKim, and others planned the building of a memorial to honor President Abraham Lincoln.

When the US entered World War I in 1917, growing numbers of women came to Washington to fill the posts vacated by men. Suffragists took to the streets to campaign for the right to vote. The National Women's Party, led by Alice Paul, picketed the White House to urge President Wilson to endorse a constitutional amendment to give women the vote.

African Americans in Washington were not only banned from voting but also faced discrimination in housing and education. After a local black battalion was excluded from a World War I victory parade, tension mounted. On July 20, 1919, riots erupted on the streets and did not stop for four days. Although discrimination continued, the 1920s were a period of commercial, artistic, and literary success for the black community. The area around U Street and Howard University

ROOSEVELT USHERS IN A NEW DEAL

Following the stock market crash of 1929, federal workers received salary cuts, and many other Washingtonians lost their jobs. As a result, President Roosevelt created the "New Deal," an ambitious public works program to reduce unemployment. People were paid to do a range of tasks, from planting trees on the Mall to completing some of the city's edifices, such as the Supreme Court, the government office buildings of the Federal Triangle, and the National Gallery of Art.

Roosevelt's wife, Eleanor, was a champion of the poor and a tireless reformer. In 1939, when Marian Anderson, the African American singer, was denied permission by the Daughters of the American Revolution to perform at Constitution Hall, Eleanor Roosevelt arranged for her to sing at the Lincoln Memorial instead, to a crowd of 75,000.

President Franklin D. Roosevelt with First Lady Eleanor

Marian Anderson (1897–1993)

Teddy Roosevelt's daughter, is married in the White House	**1918** Washington celebrates Armistice Day		
1908 Opening of Union Station, designed by Daniel Burnham	**1919** Race riots continue for four days		
1910	**1920**	**1930**	**1940**
1917 US enters World War I	**1929** The Great Depression begins	**1939** Marian Anderson performs at the Lincoln Memorial	
1920 The 19th amendment, granting suffrage to women, is ratified	**1933** New Negro Alliance is formed to improve the status of blacks		

After the US entered World War II in December 1941, Washington's population soared. Women from all across the country arrived in the capital, eager to take on government jobs while the men were overseas. They faced housing shortages, and long lines as they waited to use rationing coupons for food and services. The city also offered a respite for soldiers on leave. Actress Helen Hayes, a native Washingtonian, opened the Stage Door Canteen where celebrities provided food and entertainment.

Soldiers on patrol after the death of Martin Luther King, Jr.

THE CIVIL RIGHTS MOVEMENT

In 1953 the Supreme Court's ruling in the Thompson Restaurant case made it illegal for public places to discriminate against blacks. With the passage of other anti-discrimination laws, life in Washington began to change. In 1954, the recreation department ended its public segregation. In the same year, on May 17, the Supreme Court ruled that "separate educational facilities are inherently unequal."

On August 28, 1963, more than 200,000 people arrived in the capital for the "March on Washington" to support civil rights. From the steps of the Lincoln Memorial, Marian Anderson sang again and Reverend Martin Luther King, Jr. shared his dream in words that would echo for generations (see p91).

In November 1963, the nation was stunned by the assassination of President John F. Kennedy in Dallas, Texas. An eternal flame was lit at his funeral in Arlington Cemetery by his widow, Jaqueline. Five years later, on April 4, 1968, Martin Luther King was shot. Killed at the age of 39, he is revered as a hero and a martyr.

The opening of the Kennedy Center for Performing Arts in 1971 indicated the growing international character of the city. Several art museums

Anti-Vietnam protesters in Washington in 1969

with impressive collections (the East Wing of the National Gallery of Art, the Hirshhorn, the National Museum of American Art, and the National Portrait Gallery) also opened to enrich the city's cultural life. The construction of the Metro helped alleviate traffic problems. The embassies, the foreign banking community (the World Bank,

John F. Kennedy, Jr. salutes his father's casket at Arlington Cemetery in 1963

TIMELINE

1940	1950	1960	1970	
1940 First plane lands at National Airport	**1945** The first atomic bomb is dropped on Hiroshima, ending World War II	**1973** Washingtonians gain the right to elect a mayor		**1976** Metro of National Air Space Museum opens
		1963 Martin Luther King gives "I Have a Dream" speech	**1969** 250,000 anti-Vietnam War protesters march	
1941 The National Gallery of Art opens. After Japan attacks Pearl Harbor, the US enters World War II	*Dr. Martin Luther King, Jr. (1929–68)*	**1964** Washington residents vote in a presidential election for the first time	**1974** President Richard Nixon resigns following criminal investigation	**1978** Marion Barry elected mayor for the first of four terms

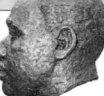

the International Monetary Fund, and the Inter-American Development Bank), and the increasing number of immigrants, provided a cosmopolitan flavor.

HOME RULE

Residents of the District of Columbia have never been given full representation in American politics, as they have no congressman. (Until the 23rd Amendment of 1961 they could not even vote for president – the 1964 election was the first in which they took part.) In 1967, with people clamoring for a greater say in local government, President Lyndon Johnson replaced the system of three commissioners, set up by Congress in 1871, with an appointed mayor and a city council with greater responsibility in policy and budget issues. The result was the city's first elected mayor in over 100 years, Walter E. Washington. Residents were permitted to elect a non-voting delegate to Congress in 1971, and the Home Rule Act of 1973 allowed the people to elect both mayor and city council.

Walter E. Washington campaigning for re-election

In 1978 Marion Barry succeeded as mayor. Born in Mississippi and raised in Tennessee, he came to Washington in 1965 to work for civil rights. He was the city's mayor for 16 of the next 20 years, but toward the end of his tenure, a large deficit and dissatisfaction with city politics developed. Middle-class families, both white and black, were beginning to flee the increasingly crime-ridden city for the safety of the suburbs.

In 1995 Congress stripped the mayor of much of his power and appointed a five-person "financial control board" to oversee the city's affairs. The election in 1998 was won by Anthony Williams, an outsider who offered a fresh outlook and financial stability. Congress returned to the mayor much of the authority it had taken away. Within months of taking his new office it appeared that Mayor Williams was turning the city around. The budget was operating with a surplus, the population had stabilized, and unemployment was down.

The new administration under Adrian Fenty, elected in 2006, has transformed the city's image. No longer dubbed the crime capital of the US, Washington, DC has once again become a mecca for tourists and a safer, cleaner place for its residents.

In 2009 Barack Obama became the first African-American president in US history – a momentous occasion. During his time in office, he aims to create a new direction in politics.

Fireworks lighting the Washington Monument during the 2000 celebrations

President Bill Clinton (1946–)

1993 Opening of the US Holocaust Memorial Museum

2005 George W. Bush inaugurated for a second term as US president

1990	2000	2010	2020

...edication of the Vietnam ...s Memorial, designed by ...ing Lin

1998 Anthony Williams elected mayor

2001 September 11 Terrorist attack on the Pentagon

2009 Barack Obama becomes the first African-American elected president

The American Presidents

The presidents of the United States have come from all walks of life; at least two were born in a log cabin – Abraham Lincoln and Andrew Jackson. Others, such as Franklin D. Roosevelt and John F. Kennedy, came from privileged backgrounds. Millard Fillmore attended a one-room schoolroom and Jimmy Carter raised peanuts. Many, including Ulysses S. Grant and Dwight D. Eisenhower, were military men, who won public popularity for their great achievements in battle.

Benjamin Harrison
(1889–93)

Chester A. Arthur
(1881–5)

Millard Fillmore
(1850–53)

Zachary Taylor
(1849–50)

Franklin Pierce
(1853–7)

James K. Polk
(1845–9)

W.H. Harrison
(1841)

Rutherford B. Hayes
(1877–81)

Andrew Johnson
(1865–9)

George Washington
(1789–97) was a Revolutionary War general. He was unanimously chosen to be the first president of the United States.

James Madison
(1809–17), known as the Father of the Constitution, was co-author of the Federalist Papers.

| 1775 | 1800 | 1825 | 1850 | 1875 |

| 1775 | 1800 | 1825 | 1850 | 1875 |

John Adams
(1797–1801), a lawyer and historian, was the first president to live in the White House.

James Monroe
(1817–25)

John Quincy Adams
(1825–9)

John Tyler
(1841–5)

Martin Van Buren
(1837–41)

James A. Garfield
(1881)

Ulysses S. Grant
(1869–77)

Grover Cleveland
(1885–9)

Thomas Jefferson
(1801–9), architect, inventor, landscape designer, diplomat, and historian, was the quintessential Renaissance man.

James Buchanan
(1857–61)

Andrew Jackson
(1829–37) defeated the British at the Battle of New Orleans in the War of 1812.

Abraham Lincoln
(1861–5) won the epithet, the Great Emancipator, for his role in the abolition of slavery. He led the Union through the Civil War.

Grover Cleveland (1893–

William McKinley (1897–

Harry S. Truman
(1945–53) made
the decision to
drop the atomic
bombs on
Hiroshima
and Nagasaki
in 1945.

Woodrow Wilson
(1913–21) led the country
through World War I and
paved the way for the
League of Nations.

John F. Kennedy (1961–3)
was one of the most popular
presidents. He sent the first
astronaut into space, started the
Peace Corps, and created the
Arms Control and Disarmament
Agency. His assassination
rocked the nation.

Richard Nixon
(1969–74) opened up China and
sent the first men to the moon.
He resigned after the Watergate
scandal *(see p117)*.

**Franklin D.
Roosevelt** (1933–45)
started the New
Deal, a reform and
relief program,
during the Great
Depression. He was
elected to four terms.

Jimmy Carter
(1977–81)

George Bush
(1989–93)

George W. Bush
(2001–09)

1925	1950	1975	2000	2025

1925	1950	1975	2000	2025

**William
H. Taft**
(1909–13)

**Dwight D.
Eisenhower**
(1953–61)

Herbert Hoover
(1929–33)

Calvin Coolidge
(1923–9)

Warren Harding
(1921–3)

**Gerald
Ford**
(1974–7)

**William J.
Clinton**
(1993–2001)

Ronald Reagan (1981–9),
a one-time movie actor
and popular presi-
dent, cut taxes,
increased military
spending, and
reduced
government
programs.

Barack Obama
(2009–), a senator
from Illinois, is the
first African-American
president in the
history of the US.

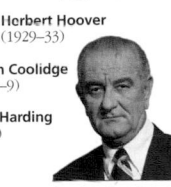

Lyndon B. Johnson
(1963–9) escalated the
Vietnam conflict, resulting
in widespread protests.

Theodore Roosevelt
(1901–9) created many
national parks and over-
saw the construction of
the Panama Canal.

THE ROLE OF THE FIRST LADY

In the 19th century, the First Lady acted primarily
as hostess and "behind-the-scenes" adviser. Later,
when Eleanor Roosevelt held her own press
conferences, the role of First Lady changed
greatly. Jackie Kennedy gave support to the
arts, Rosalynn Carter attended Cabinet
meetings, Barbara Bush promoted
literacy, and Hillary Clinton ran her
own political campaign. Michelle
Obama follows strongly in this vein,
delivering political speeches and
campaigning for charitable causes.

**Eleanor Roosevelt at a press
conference in the 1930s**

How the Federal Government Works

Great Seal of the United States

In September 1787, the Constitution of the United States of America was signed (see p91). It was created as "the supreme Law of the Land," to ensure that it would take precedence over state laws. The powers of the federal government were separated into three distinct areas: the legislative branch to enact the laws, the executive branch to enforce them, and the judicial branch to interpret them. No one branch, however, was to exert too much authority, and the system of checks and balances was instituted. Provisions were made for amending the Constitution, and by December 1791 the first ten amendments, called the Bill of Rights, were ratified.

CHECKS AND BALANCES

The system of checks and balances means that no one branch of government can abuse its power.

The Executive Branch: The President can recommend and veto legislation and call a special session of Congress. The President appoints judges to the courts and can grant pardons for federal offenses.

The Judicial Branch: The Supreme Court interprets laws and treaties and can declare an act unconstitutional. The Chief Justice presides at an impeachment trial of the President.

The Legislative Branch: Congress can override a presidential veto of a bill with a two-thirds majority. Presidential appointments and treaties must be approved by the Senate. Congress also oversees the jurisdiction of the courts and can impeach and try the President and federal judges.

The Senate, *sitting in session in the US Capitol.*

THE EXECUTIVE BRANCH

The President, together with the Vice President, is elected for a four-year term. The President suggests, approves, and vetoes legislation. The Executive also develops foreign policy and directs relations with other countries, serves as Commander-in-Chief of the armed forces, and appoints ambassadors. Secretaries to the Cabinet, composed of various heads of departments, meet regularly to advise the President on policy issues. Several agencies and councils, such as the National Security Council and the Office of Management and Budget, help determine the executive agenda.

Seal of the President

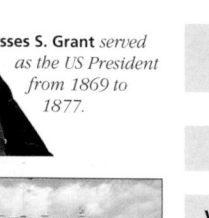

Ulysses S. Grant *served as the US President from 1869 to 1877.*

EXECUTIVE BRANCH

PRESIDENT

VICE PRESIDENT

CABINET

Henry A. Wallace *served as Vice President under Franklin D. Roosevelt, from 1941 to 1945.*

The White House *is the official residence of the US President.*

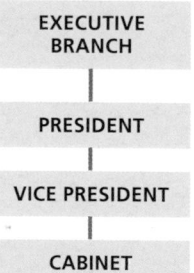

Madeleine Albright, *the first woman to serve as Secretary of State, was appointed in 1997.*

THE JUDICIAL BRANCH

The Supreme Court and other federal courts determine the constitutionality of federal, state, and local laws. They hear cases relating to controversies between states and those affecting ambassadors or citizens of different states. They also try cases on appeal. The Supreme Court consists of nine justices appointed for life by the President.

JUDICIAL BRANCH

The Supreme Court *is the highest court in the United States and is the last stop in issues of constitutionality.*

9 SUPREME COURT JUSTICES

OF WHOM ONE IS CHIEF SUPREME COURT JUSTICE

Thurgood Marshall *was the first African American to be a Supreme Court Justice. He held the position from 1967 to 1991.*

Oliver Wendell Holmes, *Supreme Court Justice from 1902 to 1932, was a strong advocate of free speech.*

Earl Warren *was Supreme Court Justice from 1953 to 1969. He wrote the unanimous opinion in Brown v. Board of Education (1954). (See p48).*

THE LEGISLATIVE BRANCH

The Congress of the United States consists of two bodies, the House of Representatives and the Senate. Representatives to the House are elected by the voters in each state for a two-year term. The number of Representatives for each state is determined by the state's population. The Senate is composed of two Senators from each state, elected for six-year terms. Congress regulates commerce and is empowered to levy taxes and declare war. This branch also makes the laws: bills discussed, written, and revised in legislative committees must be passed first by the House and by the Senate before being approved by the President.

Daniel Webster *served both in the House of Representatives (1813–17) and in the Senate (1822–41).*

LEGISLATIVE BRANCH

HOUSE OF REPRESENTATIVES

SENATE

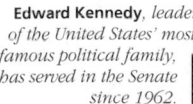

Sam Rayburn *was a popular and distinguished Speaker of the House.*

Edward Kennedy, *leader of the United States' most famous political family, has served in the Senate since 1962.*

The US Capitol *is home to both the House of Representatives and the Senate.*

WASHINGTON, DC AT A GLANCE

Washington is more than just the political capital of the United States. It is also the home of the Smithsonian Institution, and as such is the cultural focus of America. Its many superb museums and galleries have something to offer everyone. Always one of the most popular sights, the president's official residence, the White House, attracts millions of visitors each year. Equally popular is the National Air and Space Museum, which draws vast numbers of visitors to its awe-inspiring displays of air and spacecraft. Also unique to Washington are its many monuments and memorials. The huge Washington Monument, honoring the first US president, dominates the city skyline. In contrast, the war memorials, dedicated to the thousands of soldiers who died in battle, are quietly poignant.

WASHINGTON'S TOP TEN ATTRACTIONS

The White House *See pp102–111*

National Air and Space Museum
See pp62–5

National Gallery of Art
See pp58–61

Kennedy Center
See pp118–19

Vietnam Veterans Memorial
See p83

Washington National Cathedral *See pp142–3*

Arlington National Cemetery
See pp130–31

Washington Monument
See p78

Lincoln Memorial
See p84

US Capitol
See pp50–51

◁ View from the US Capitol looking down Pennsylvania Avenue

Museums and Galleries in Washington, DC

Few cities can claim to have as many museums and galleries in such a concentrated area as Washington. The Mall forms the main focus because it is lined with museums, most of which are owned by the Smithsonian Institution *(see p72)*. They cover a wide range of exhibits, from great works of art to space shuttles to mementos of major events in American history. Admission to most of the museums and galleries is free.

National Museum of American History
This statue of a toga-clad George Washington is one of millions of artifacts in this museum of American history (see pp74–7).

GEORGETOWN

THE WHITE HOUSE AND FOGGY BOTTOM

Tidal Basin

Potomac River

Corcoran Gallery of Art
This Beaux Arts building houses a collection of American and European art and sculpture, including some of the best works by US artists of the 19th and 20th centuries (see p113).

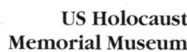

US Holocaust Memorial Museum
Photographs, videos, and re-created concentration camp barracks bring to life the brutality of the Holocaust and illustrate the terrible fate of Jews and others in World War II Nazi Germany (see pp80–81).

National Museum of Natural History
A huge African elephant is the focal point of the building's main foyer. The museum's fascinating exhibits trace the evolution of animals and explain the creation of gems and minerals (see pp70–71).

0 meters 500
0 yards 500

Smithsonian American Art Museum and the National Portrait Gallery
This Neoclassical building houses the world's largest collection of American paintings, sculpture, photographs, and crafts (see pp98–101).

PENN QUARTER

CAPITOL HILL

E MALL

National Gallery of Art
The futuristic East Building houses the 20th-century art in this collection, while the 1930s West Building is home to older works (see pp54–61).

National Air and Space Museum
...shington's most popular ...useum has exhibits from ...ation and space history, including the Wright ...hers' first airborne plane and the Apollo 14 space module (see pp62–5).

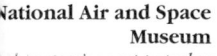

Monuments and Memorials in Washington, DC

As the political center of the United States, and home of its president, Washington has a great number of monuments and memorials honoring America's key figures and historic events. The most well-known among these are the Washington Monument and the Lincoln Memorial – sights of great interest to all who visit the city. For those who wish to remember the countless men and women who lost their lives fighting for their nation, there are poignant monuments, set in tranquil parks, where visitors can reflect in peace.

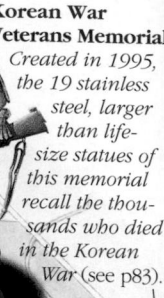

Korean War Veterans Memorial
Created in 1995, the 19 stainless steel, larger than life-size statues of this memorial recall the thousands who died in the Korean War (see p83).

GEORGETOWN

Lincoln Memorial
This emotive and inspirational marble figure has often been the focus of civil rights protests (see p85).

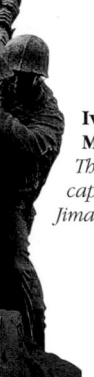

Iwo Jima Statue (US Marine Corps Memorial)
This iconic memorial depicts US Marines capturing the Japanese island of Iwo Jima at the end of World War II (see p134).

Potomac River

Vietnam Veterans Memorial
Visitors to this dramatic memorial are confronted by a sobering list of names on the V-shaped granite walls (see p83).

Washington Monument
One of the most enduring images of Washington, this 555-ft (170-m) marble obelisk can be seen from all over the city. Built in two stages, the monument was finally completed in 1884 (see p78).

Jefferson Memorial
This Neoclassical building houses a bronze statue of President Jefferson, the key player in America's struggle for independence (see p79).

WHITE SE AND GGY TTOM

PENN QUARTER

THE MALL

CAPITOL HILL

0 meters 500

0 yards 500

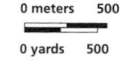
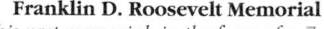

Franklin D. Roosevelt Memorial
This vast memorial, in the form of a 7-acre park, includes statuary, waterfalls, and ornamental gardens (see pp84–5).

WASHINGTON, DC THROUGH THE YEAR

A wide variety of events takes place in Washington, DC all through the year. In late March or early April, when the famous cherry blossoms bloom, the city really comes to life. Parades and outdoor festivals begin, and continue through the summer as more and more people come to explore the DC

Patriotic member of the public celebrating Independence Day

area in June, July, and August. The White House is a focus for many visitors, and it plays host to annual events such as the Easter Egg Roll in the spring and the Garden Tours in the spring and fall. Some of the more popular events are listed below; for further details on these and other events in the city, contact the Destination DC tourist office *(see p211)*.

SPRING

The air is clear in springtime in Washington, DC, with crisp mornings and warm, balmy days. The cherry tree blossoms surrounding the Tidal Basin are world famous and should not be missed, although the area does get very busy. Memorial Day is a big event in DC; it marks the official beginning of summer, and is celebrated in many ways.

MARCH

Washington Home and Garden Show, Walter E. Washington DC Convention Center, 801 Mount Vernon Place, NW (7th St and New York Ave, NW). *Tel 249-3000*. A vast array of garden items.
St. Patrick's Day *(Mar 17)*, Constitution Ave, NW. Parade celebrating Irish culture. There are also celebrations in Old Town Alexandria.

Smithsonian Kite Festival *(last Saturday)*, Washington Monument. *Tel 633-1000*. Kite designers fly their best models and compete for prizes.

APRIL

National Cherry Blossom Festival *(late Mar–early Apr)*, Constitution Ave, NW. *Tel 877-44BLOOM*. Parade and concerts to celebrate the blooming of Washington's famous trees.
White House Egg Roll *(Easter Mon)*, White House Lawn. *Tel 456-2200*. Children roll eggs in a race across the lawn.
White House Spring Garden Tours *(second weekend)*, White House gardens. *Tel 456-7041*. Tour of the Jacqueline Kennedy Garden and more.
Thomas Jefferson's Birthday *(Apr 13)*, Jefferson Memorial. *Tel 619-7222*. Military drills, speeches, and wreath-laying.
Shakespeare's Birthday Celebration *(end of Apr)*, Folger Shakespeare Library,

Mother-and-daughter team in the Easter Egg Roll at the White House

201 E Capitol St, SE. *Tel 544-4600*. A day of music, plays, food, and children's events.

MAY

Flower Mart *(first Fri & Sat)*, Washington National Cathedral. *Tel 537-6200*. Flower booths, music, and crafts.
Memorial Day Weekend Concert *(last Sun)*, West Lawn of Capitol. *Tel 619-7222*. National Symphony Orchestra performs. **Memorial Day** *(last Mon)*, Arlington National Cemetery. *Tel (703) 607-8000*. US Navy Memorial. *Tel 737-2300*. Vietnam Veterans Memorial. *Tel 619-7222*. Wreath-laying, speeches, and music to honor war veterans.
Memorial Day Jazz Festival *(last Mon)*, Old Town Alexandria. *Tel (703) 883-4686*. Live, big-band jazz music.
Twilight Tattoo Military Pageant *(7pm every Wed, May & Jun)*, Fort McNair. *Tel 685-2888*. Military parade presenting the history of the US Army.

Cherry tree blossoms surrounding Jefferson Memorial at the Tidal Basin

AVERAGE DAYS OF SUNSHINE PER MONTH

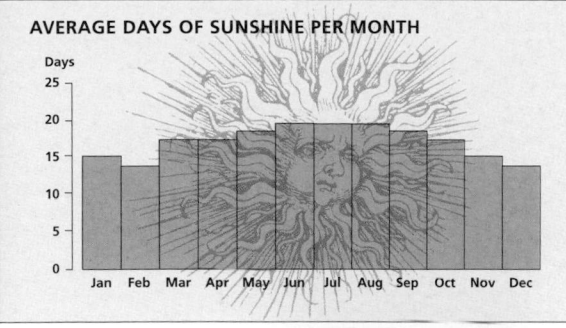

Days
25
20
15
10
5
0
Jan Feb Mar Apr May Jun Jul Aug Sep Oct Nov Dec

Sunshine Chart
The amount of sunshine per month in Washington does not vary greatly – even in winter months half the days will enjoy blue skies. In summer the sunshine is at its most persistent, although it is best to be prepared for the occasional rainstorm. The chart gives the number of days per month with little or no cloud.

SUMMER

In June, July, and August, visitors come to Washington, DC from far and wide. The streets and parks are packed with people enjoying the sunshine. Many attractions become overcrowded, so it is important to call ahead and make reservations at this time of year.

The summer months can also be extremely hot and humid; even so, parades and outdoor fairs are usually very popular. Independence Day on July 4 is particularly exciting, with a parade during the day and fireworks at night.

JUNE

Shakespeare Free for All *(throughout Jun)*, Carter Barron Amphitheater, Rock Creek Park. *Tel (202) 426-0486.* Nightly performances by the Shakespeare Theater Company, free of charge.
Alexandria Waterfront Festival *(first or second weekend)*, Oronoco Bay Park, Alexandria. *Tel (703) 838-4200.* Tall ships, games, and music celebrating maritime history.
Smithsonian Festival of American Folklife *(late Jun–early Jul)*, The Mall. *Tel 633-1000.* A huge celebration of folk culture, including music, dance, games, and food.
Washington National Cathedral Summer Festival of Music *(mid-Jun–mid-Jul)*, Washington National Cathedral. *Tel 537-6200.* A varied program of modern and classical concerts.
Capitol Pride *(mid-Jun)*, Pennsylvania Ave, NW. Street festival and parade celebrating the gay communities of DC.

Fireworks over Washington, DC on the Fourth of July

JULY

Independence Day *(Jul 4)*, Constitution Ave & US Capitol, other areas. Concert on west front of the Capitol. A parade along Constitution Avenue, with fireworks from the base of the Washington Monument. Other areas such as Old Town Alexandria and Mount Vernon have parades and fireworks.
Bastille Day *(Jul 14)*. A celebration involving food, music, and dance. Events are held in the French Embassy and selected cafés and restaurants.

Mary McLeod Bethune Celebration *(Jul 10)*, Bethune Statue, Lincoln Palk, E Capitol St, SE, between 11th St & 13th St. *Tel 673-2402.* Memorial wreath-laying, gospel music, and speeches.
Screen on the Green *(Mon evening Jul–Aug)*, The Mall. Classic movies shown on giant screens.
Hispanic-Latino Festival *(late Jul)*, Washington Monument. *Tel 619-7222.* Music, food, and celebration of 40 Latin American Nations.

AUGUST

Arlington County Fair *(mid-Aug)*, Thomas Jefferson Center, Arlington, VA. *Tel (703) 920-4556.* Food, crafts, music, and fairground rides.
Georgia Avenue Day *(end of Aug)*, Georgia Ave, NW. A parade plus food, stalls, rides, and music.
National Frisbee Festival *(late Aug)*, Washington Monument. *Tel 619-7222.* A weekend celebrating the game of Frisbee, including a free Frisbee contest for champions and amateurs alike.

A frenzy of Frisbee throwing at Washington's National Frisbee Festival

AVERAGE MONTHLY RAINFALL

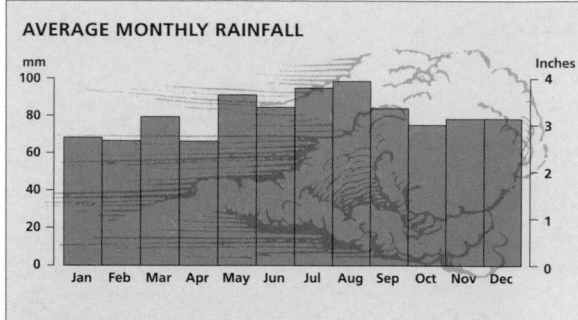

mm: 100, 80, 60, 40, 20, 0
Inches: 4, 3, 2, 1, 0

Jan Feb Mar Apr May Jun Jul Aug Sep Oct Nov Dec

Rainfall Chart
It is impossible to escape the rain completely in Washington. The heaviest rainfall occurs during the summer months of May through August, when rain can come as a welcome break from the humidity. Rainfall tails off in the fall months of September and October and reaches its lowest ebb in late winter. Rain rarely lingers for long in the city.

A school band performing in front of the Lincoln Memorial

FALL

With the air turning cooler, Labor Day (the first Monday in September) bids goodbye to the summer. The fall (autumn) season covers September, October, and November in Washington, when the temperatures steadily drop. A particularly enjoyable event at this time of year is Halloween, when children dress up as their favorite creatures or characters to go trick-or-treating.

Halloween Jack-O'-Lantern

SEPTEMBER

Labor Day Weekend Concert *(Sun before Labor Day)*, West Lawn of the US Capitol. *Tel 619-7222.* National Symphony Orchestra performs a concert.
Kennedy Center Prelude Festival *(throughout Sep).* *Tel 467-4600.* Performances of blues, rock, jazz, dance, comedy, drama, and film. Many concerts are free.

International Children's Festival, Wolf Trap Park, Vienna, VA. *Tel (703) 255-1900.* Performers come from around the world.
18th-century Fair, Mount Vernon, VA. *Tel (703) 780-2000.* Craft demonstrations and 18th-century entertainment.

OCTOBER

DC Open House *(first weekend)*, various venues. *Tel 889-7000.* Free walking tours and museum visits.
Taste of Georgetown *(second Sat)*, Wisconsin Ave, NW. *Tel 298-9222.* Washington's finest restaurants showcase their talents.
Columbus Day *(second Mon)*, Columbus Memorial, Union Station. *Tel 289-1908.* Speeches and wreath-laying for the man who discovered America.
National Book Fair *(early Oct)*, National Mall. *Tel 707-5000.*
White House Fall Garden Tours *(mid-Oct). Tel 456-2200.* A chance to walk the grounds of the President's home.

Halloween *(Oct 31)*. Young people appear on the streets trick-or-treating, dressed as ghosts, clowns, and witches. Dupont Circle and Georgetown are popular areas.

NOVEMBER

Thanksgiving Parades *(fourth Thu)*. Parades and festivals take place all around the DC area.
Veterans Day Ceremonies *(Nov 11)*, Arlington National Cemetery. *Tel (703) 607-8000.* Services, parades, and wreath-layings at various memorials around the city, commemorating United States military personnel who died in war. There are special Veterans Day ceremonies also at the Vietnam Veterans Memorial, *Tel 426-6841*, and at the US Navy Memorial, *(Tel 737-2300).*
Kennedy Center Holiday Festival *(late Nov–New Year's Eve). Tel 467-4600.* Musicals, ballet, and classical concerts for the holiday season.

Military guard on Veterans Day in Arlington National Cemetery

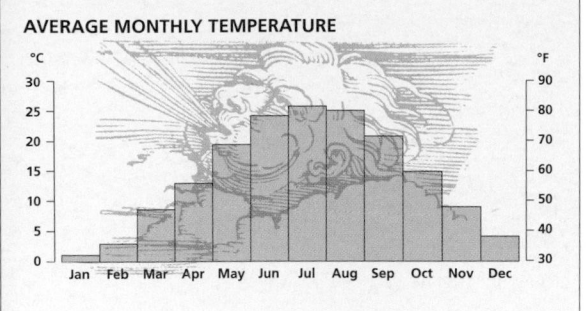

AVERAGE MONTHLY TEMPERATURE

Temperature Chart
Washington's climate varies greatly. In winter the air is bitterly cold, with temperatures rising little above freezing. In July and August, however, it becomes very hot and extremely humid. The best time to visit the city is in the spring or fall, when the weather is pleasantly mild and the air is clear.

WINTER

Temperatures can plummet below freezing during the winter months of December, January, and February. Hence the city is generally quieter at this time of year, making it a good time to see the most popular sights. Over the Christmas period, Washington becomes busy again with festive events to get people into the holiday spirit. Decorations are visible across the city, and many places offer Christmas tours.

Toward the end of winter, a number of famous birthdays are celebrated, including those of Martin Luther King Jr. and Presidents Abraham Lincoln and George Washington.

DECEMBER

National Christmas Tree Lighting *(mid-Dec)*, Ellipse south of the White House. **Tel** *456-2200*. The President turns on the lights on the National Christmas tree (advance tickets only).

Washington National Cathedral Christmas Services *(throughout Dec)*. **Tel** *537-6200*. Holiday celebrations with festive music.
Christmas at Mount Vernon *(weekends late Nov–mid-Dec)*, Mount Vernon, VA. **Tel** *(703) 780-2000*. Experience an 18th-century Christmas.

JANUARY

Robert E. Lee's Birthday *(mid-Jan)*. Tours of the Lee-Fendall house in Alexandria. **Tel** *(703) 548-1789*.
Martin Luther King Jr.'s Birthday *(third Mon)*, **Tel** *619-7222*.
Restaurant week *(mid-Jan)*, Many of Washington's top restaurants offer prix fixe lunch or dinner specials.

FEBRUARY

Chinese New Year *(first two weeks)*, N St, Chinatown. **Tel** *789-7000*. Parades, dancing, and live music.
African American History Month *(throughout Feb)*. Various events are held across the

city: contact the Smithsonian (**Tel** *633-1000*) and the National Park Service (**Tel** *619-7222*).
George Washington's Birthday Parade *(around Feb 15)*, Old Town Alexandria, VA. **Tel** *(703) 838-4200*.
Abraham Lincoln's Birthday, *(Feb 12)*, Lincoln Memorial. **Tel** *619-7222*. There is a wreath-laying ceremony which is followed by a reading of the Gettysburg Address.

Girl Scouts watching George Washington's Birthday Parade

The National Christmas tree outside a snow-covered White House

Jefferson Memorial ▷

WASHINGTON, DC
AREA BY AREA

CAPITOL HILL

Soon after the Constitution was ratified in 1788, America's seat of government began to take root on Capitol Hill. The site was chosen in 1791 from 10 acres that were ceded by the state of Maryland. Pierre L'Enfant (see p19) chose a hill on the east side of the area as the foundation for the Capitol building and the center of the new city.

In more than 200 years, Capitol Hill has developed into a bustling microcosm of modern America

Statue of Roman Legionnaire at Union Station

Symbols of the country's cultural development are everywhere, from its federal buildings to its centers of commerce, shops, and restaurants, as well as residential areas for a wide variety of people.

The Capitol Hill area is frequented by the most powerful people in the United States, yet at the same time, ordinary citizens are able to petition their congressional representatives here, or pose for a photograph with them on the steps of the Capitol building.

SIGHTS AT A GLANCE

Historic Buildings
Folger Shakespeare Library ❷
Library of Congress pp46–7 ❶
Sewall-Belmont House ❹
Union Station ❸
US Capitol pp50–51 ❺
US Supreme Court ❸

Museums and Galleries
National Postal Museum ❹

Market
Eastern Market ❷

Monuments and Memorials
National Japanese American Memorial ❼
Robert A. Taft Memorial ❻

Ulysses S. Grant Memorial ❽

Parks and Gardens
Bartholdi Park and Fountain ❿
US Botanic Garden ❾

Church
Ebenezer United Methodist Church ⓫

KEY

▨	Street-by-street map pp44–5
Ⓜ	Metro station
ⓘ	Tourist information
⌂	Police
⊠	Post office
☐	Train station

0 meters	500
0 yards	500

GETTING THERE
The best way to get to Capitol Hill is by Metro. Take the red line to Union Station, or the blue or orange line to Capitol South, Eastern Market, or Federal Center SW. Metrobuses 30, 32, 34, 35, and 36 stop at various points on Capitol Hill.

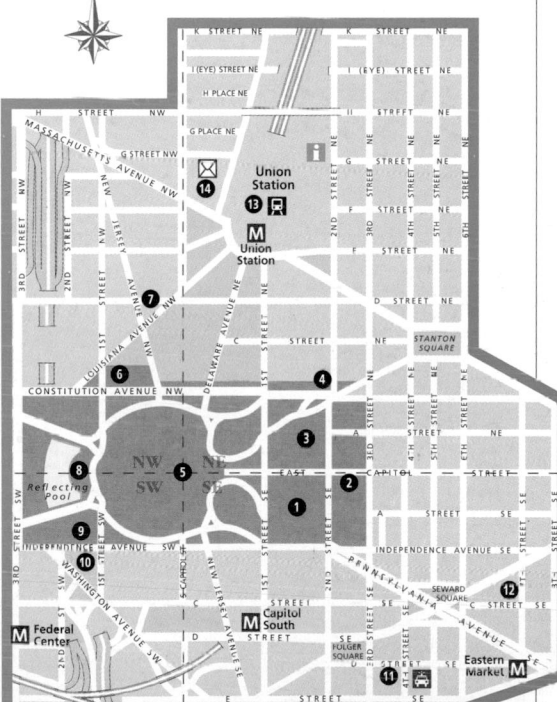

◁ The stunning front doors of the Supreme Court surrounded by Corinthian columns

Street-by-Street: Capitol Hill

The cityscape extending from the Capitol is an impressive combination of grand classical architecture and stretches of grassy open spaces. There are no skyscrapers here, only the immense marble halls and columns that distinguish many of the government buildings. The bustle and excitement around the US Capitol and US Supreme Court contrast with the calm that can be found by a reflecting pool or in a quiet residential street. Many of the small touches that make the city special can be found in this area, such as the antique lighting fixtures on Second Street, the brilliant bursts of flowers along the sidewalks, or the brightly painted façades of houses on Third Street near the Folger Shakespeare Library.

★ US Capitol
The famous dome of the nation's seat of government is one of the largest in the world 5

Robert A. Taft Memorial
A statue of Taft (1889–1953) stands in front of the bell tower that was erected to honor his principles and achievements 6

Ulysses S. Grant Memorial
General Grant (1822–85), the Union leader in the American Civil War, is the central figure in a remarkable group of bronze equestrian statuary 7

US Botanic Garden
Established in 1820, th Botanic Garden conta thousands of exotic an domestic plants 8

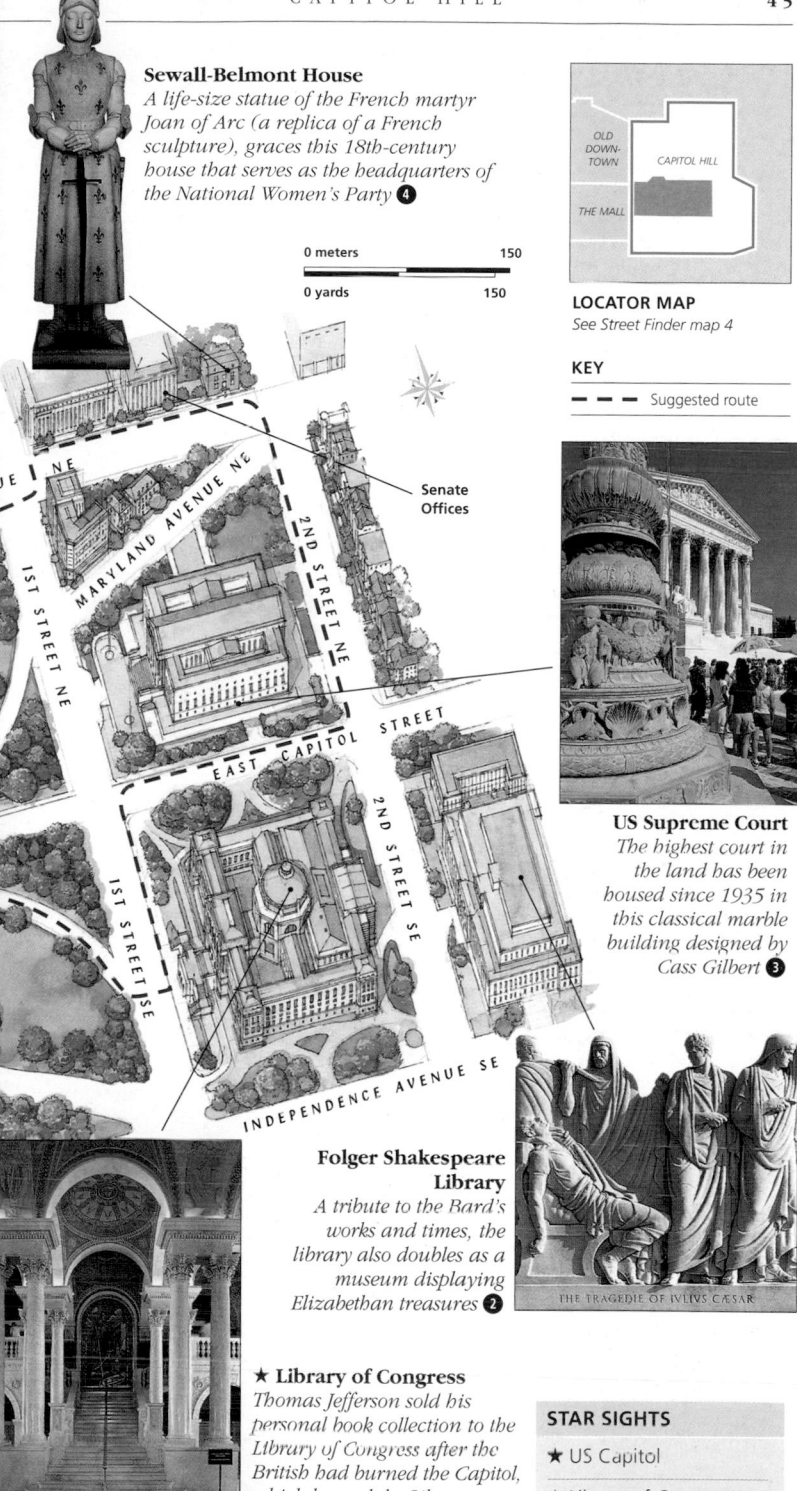

Sewall-Belmont House
A life-size statue of the French martyr Joan of Arc (a replica of a French sculpture), graces this 18th-century house that serves as the headquarters of the National Women's Party **4**

0 meters	150
0 yards	150

LOCATOR MAP
See Street Finder map 4

OLD DOWN-TOWN · CAPITOL HILL · THE MALL

KEY

– – – Suggested route

Senate Offices

US Supreme Court
The highest court in the land has been housed since 1935 in this classical marble building designed by Cass Gilbert **3**

Folger Shakespeare Library
A tribute to the Bard's works and times, the library also doubles as a museum displaying Elizabethan treasures **2**

THE TRAGEDIE OF IVLIVS CÆSAR

★ Library of Congress
Thomas Jefferson sold his personal book collection to the Library of Congress after the British had burned the Capitol, which housed the Library, using the books as kindling **1**

STAR SIGHTS

★ US Capitol

★ Library of Congress

Library of Congress ❶

Congress first established a reference library in the U.S. Capitol in 1800. When the Capitol was burned in 1814, Thomas Jefferson offered his own collection as a replacement, his belief in a universality of knowledge becoming the foundation for the Library's acquisition policy. In 1897 the Library of Congress moved to an Italian Renaissance-style building designed by John L. Smithmeyer and Paul J. Pelz. The main building, now known as the Thomas Jefferson Building, is a marvel of art and architecture, with its paintings, mosaics, exhibitions, such as Creating the United States, and the Thomas Jefferson's Library. The Library of Congress has the world's largest collection of books, with over 650 miles (1,050 km) of bookshelves.

Thomas Jefferson (1743–1826)

Front façade of the Jefferson Building

★ **Main Reading Room**
Eight huge marble columns and 10-ft (3-m) high female figures personifying aspects of human endeavor dwarf the reading desks in this room. The domed ceiling soars 160 ft (49 m) above the reading room floor.

STAR SIGHTS

★ Great Hall

★ Gutenberg Bible

★ Main Reading Room

African & Middle Eastern Reading Roo
This is one of 10 readi rooms in the Jefferson Building where visitor can use books from th Library's collections.

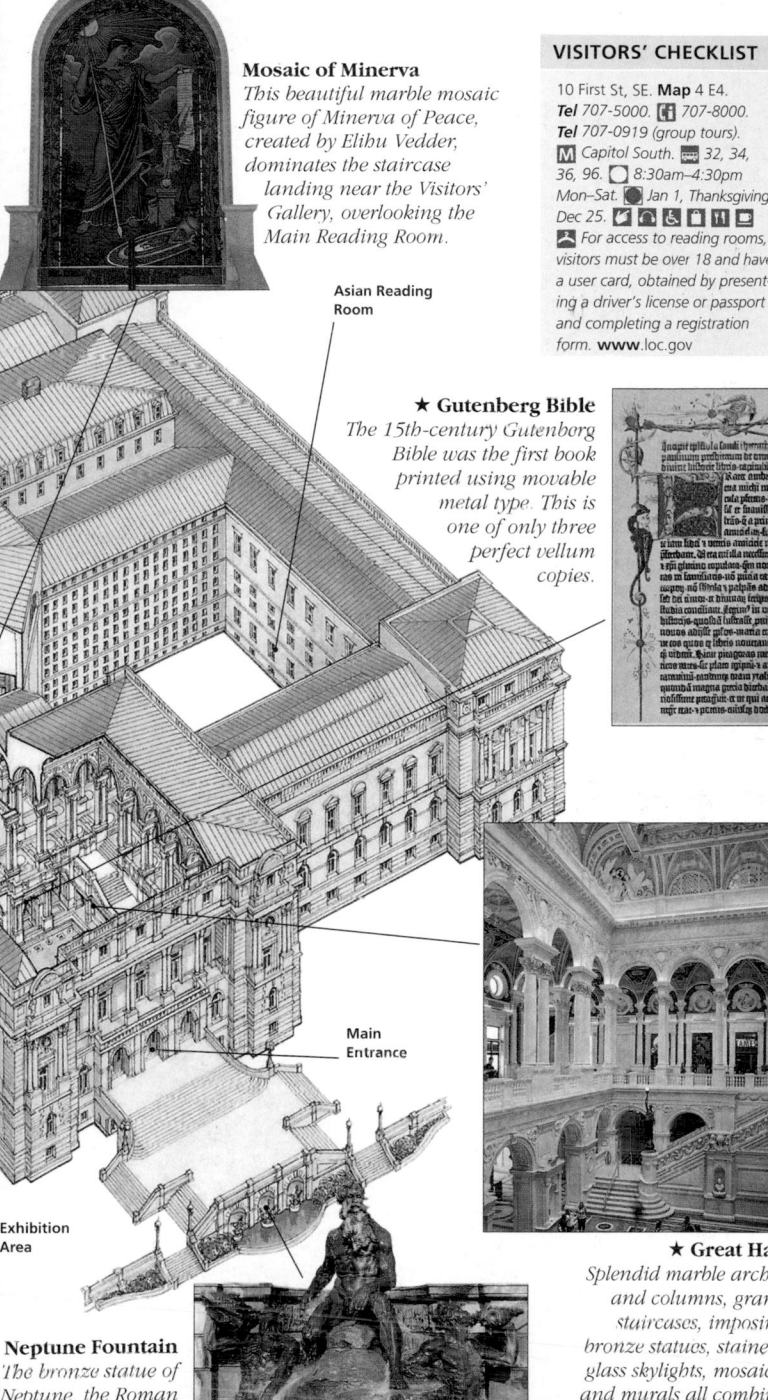

Mosaic of Minerva
This beautiful marble mosaic figure of Minerva of Peace, created by Elihu Vedder, dominates the staircase landing near the Visitors' Gallery, overlooking the Main Reading Room.

Asian Reading Room

★ Gutenberg Bible
The 15th-century Gutenberg Bible was the first book printed using movable metal type. This is one of only three perfect vellum copies.

Main Entrance

Exhibition Area

Neptune Fountain
The bronze statue of Neptune, the Roman god of the sea, forms a striking feature at the front of the Jefferson Building.

★ Great Hall
Splendid marble arches and columns, grand staircases, imposing bronze statues, stained-glass skylights, mosaics, and murals all combine to create a magnificent entrance hall.

Folger Shakespeare Library ❷

201 E Capitol St, SE. **Map** 4 F4.
Tel 544-4600. Ⓜ️ *Capitol South.*
⬜ *10am–5pm Mon–Sat.* ⬤ *Federal hols.* 🎫 ♿ *Tickets for plays, concerts, and readings available from box office.* **www**.folger.edu

Inspired by Shakespeare's own era, this library and museum celebrate the works and times of the Elizabethan playwright.

The research library was a gift to the American people in 1932 from Henry Clay Folger who, as a student in 1874, began to collect Shakespeare's works. Folger also funded the construction of this edifice, built specifically to house his collection. It contains 310,000 Elizabethan books and manuscripts, as well as the world's largest collection of Shakespeare's writings, including a third of the surviving copies of the 1623 First Folio (first editions of Shakespeare's works). One of these first editions is displayed in the oak-paneled Great Hall, along with books and engravings.

The Folger hosts many cultural events. For example, there are regular performances of Shakespeare's plays in the library's 250-seat reconstructoin of an Elizabethan theater. There is also an annual series of poetry readings, as well as numerous lectures and talks throughout the year. The acclaimed Folger Consort early music

The Great Hall in the Folger Shakespeare Library

ensemble, performs concerts of 12th- to 20th-century music.

In the grounds of the library, the Elizabethan Garden has been planted with the herbs, shrubs, and flowers that are featured in Shakespeare's plays.

US Supreme Court ❸

1st St between E Capitol St and Maryland Ave, NE. **Map** 4 E4.
Tel 479-3211. Ⓜ️ *Capitol South.*
⬜ *9am–4:30pm Mon–Fri.*
⬤ *Federal hols.* 📷 🖥️ ♿ *Lectures.*
www.supremecourtus.gov

The Supreme Court forms the judicial and third branch of the US government *(see pp28–9)*. It was established in 1787 at the Philadelphia Constitutional Convention and provides the last stop in the disposition of the nation's legal disputes and issues of constitutionality. Groundbreaking cases settled here include *Brown v. Board of Education*, which abolished racial segregation in schools, and *Miranda v. Arizona*, which declared crime suspects were entitled to a lawyer before

The impressive Neoclassical façade of the US Supreme Court

being interrogated. The Court is charged to guarantee "Equal Justice Under Law," the motto emblazoned over the entrance.

As recently as 1929 the Supreme Court was still meeting in various sections of the US Capitol building. Then, at Chief Justice William Howard Taft's urging, Congress authorized a separate building to be constructed. The result was a magnificent Corinthian edifice, designed by Cass Gilbert, that opened in 1935. Sculptures depicting the allegorical figures of the Contemplation of Justice and the Guardian of the Law stand beside the steps while on the pediment above the entrance are figures of Taft (far left) and John Marshall, the fourth Chief Justice (far right).

Visitors are permitted to watch the court in session Monday to Wednesday from October through April. Admission is on a first-come, first-served basis. When court is not in session, public lectures on the Supreme Court are held every hour on the half-hour in the Courtroom (contact for confirmation).

Sewall-Belmont House 4

144 Constitution Ave, NE. **Map** 4 E4. ***Tel*** *546-1210.* [M] *Capitol South, Union Station.* ◯ *noon–4pm Wed–Sun.* ● *Federal hols.* ***Donations welcome.*** 📷 🛍 **www**.sewallbelmont.org

Robert Sewall, the original owner of this charming 18th-century house, rented it out to Albert Gallatin, the Treasury Secretary under President Thomas Jefferson, in the early 1800s. It was here Gallatin entertained a number of wealthy contributors whose financial backing brought about the Louisiana Purchase in 1803, which doubled the size of the United States. During the British invasion in 1814, the house was the only site in Washington to resist the attack. While the US Capitol was burning, American soldiers took refuge in the house from where they fired upon the British.

Hallway of the 18th-century Sewall-Belmont House

The National Women's Party, who won the right to vote for American women in 1920, bought the house in 1929 with the help of feminist divorcee Alva Vanderbilt Belmont. Today, the house is still the headquarters of the Party, and visitors can admire the period furnishings and suffragist artifacts. The desk on which the, as yet unratified, Equal Rights Amendment of 1923 was written by Alice Paul, leader of the Party, is here.

US Capitol 5

See pp50–51.

Robert A. Taft Memorial 6

Constitution Ave and 1st St, NW. **Map** 4 E4. [M] *Union Station.* ♿

This statue of Ohio senator Robert A. Taft (1889–1953) stands in a park opposite the US Capitol. The statue itself, by sculptor Wheeler Williams, is dwarfed by a vast, white bell tower that rises up behind the figure of the politician. The memorial, designed by Douglas W. Orr, was erected in 1959 as a "tribute to the honesty, indomitable courage, and high principles of free government symbolized by his life." The son of President William Howard Taft, Robert Taft was a Republican, famous for sponsoring the Taft-Hartley Act, the regulator of collective bargaining between labor and management.

Statue of Robert Taft

National Japanese American Memorial 7

Louisiana and New Jersey Avenues at D St, NW. **Map** 4 E3. [M] *Union Station.*

This memorial, designed by Davis Buckley, commemorates the story of the 120,000 Japanese Americans interned during World War II and the more than 800 Japanese Americans who died in military service. The names of these servicemen are carved upon a curving granite wall, while etched on the top are the names of the ten detention camps where Japanese American civilians were confined. An 18-foot long aluminum gong may be rung by visitors, serving as a call to reflection and remembrance.

Ulysses S. Grant Memorial 8

Union Square, west side of US Capitol in front of Reflecting Pool. **Map** 4 E4. [M] *Capitol South, Union Station.* ♿

This dramatic memorial was sculpted by Henry Merwin Shrady and dedicated in 1922. With its 13 horses, it is one of the world's most complex equestrian statues. The bronze groupings around General Grant provide a graphic depiction of the suffering of the Civil War. In the artillery group, horses and soldiers pulling a cannon are urged on by their mounted leader, the staff of his upraised flag broken. The infantry group storms into the heat of battle, where a horse and rider have already fallen under the charge.

Shrady worked on the sculpture for 20 years, using soldiers in training for his models. He died two weeks before it was dedicated.

The artillery group in the Ulysses S. Grant Civil War Memorial

United States Capitol 5

The US Capitol is one of the world's best-known symbols of democracy. The center of America's legislative process for 200 years, its Neoclassical architecture reflects the democratic principles of ancient Greece and Rome. The cornerstone was laid by George Washington in 1793, and by 1800 the Capitol was occupied. The British burned it down in the War of 1812, but restoration began in 1815. Many architectural and artistic features, such as the Statue of Freedom and Brumidi's murals, were added later. An impressive Capitol Visitor Center, located below the East Plaza, offers improved visitor access and facilities.

The Dome
Originally a wood and copper construction, the current cast iron dome was designed by Thomas U. Walter.

★ **The Rotunda**
Completed in 1865, the 180-ft (55-m) high Rotunda is capped by The Apotheosis of Washington, *a fresco by Constantino Brumidi.*

The Hall of Columns
is lined with statues of notable Americans.

The House Chamber

Crypt wit
star deno
the city's
into quad

★ **National Statuary Hall**
In 1864 Congress invited each state to contribute two statues of prominent citizens to stand in this hall.

Old Senate Chamber
Occupied by the Senate until 1859, this chamber was subsequently home to the Supreme Court for 75 years.

VISITORS' CHECKLIST

Independence Mall, between 1st & 3rd Sts, and Independence and Constitution Aves.
Map 4 E4. **Tel** 224-3121.
Visitor Center Tel 226-8000.
225-6827. **M** Capitol South, Union Station, Federal Center.
32, 34, 36, 96.
8:30am–4:30pm Mon–Sat.
Call for further information.
Federal hols.
www.visitthecapitol.gov

The Senate Chamber has been the home of the US Senate since 1859.

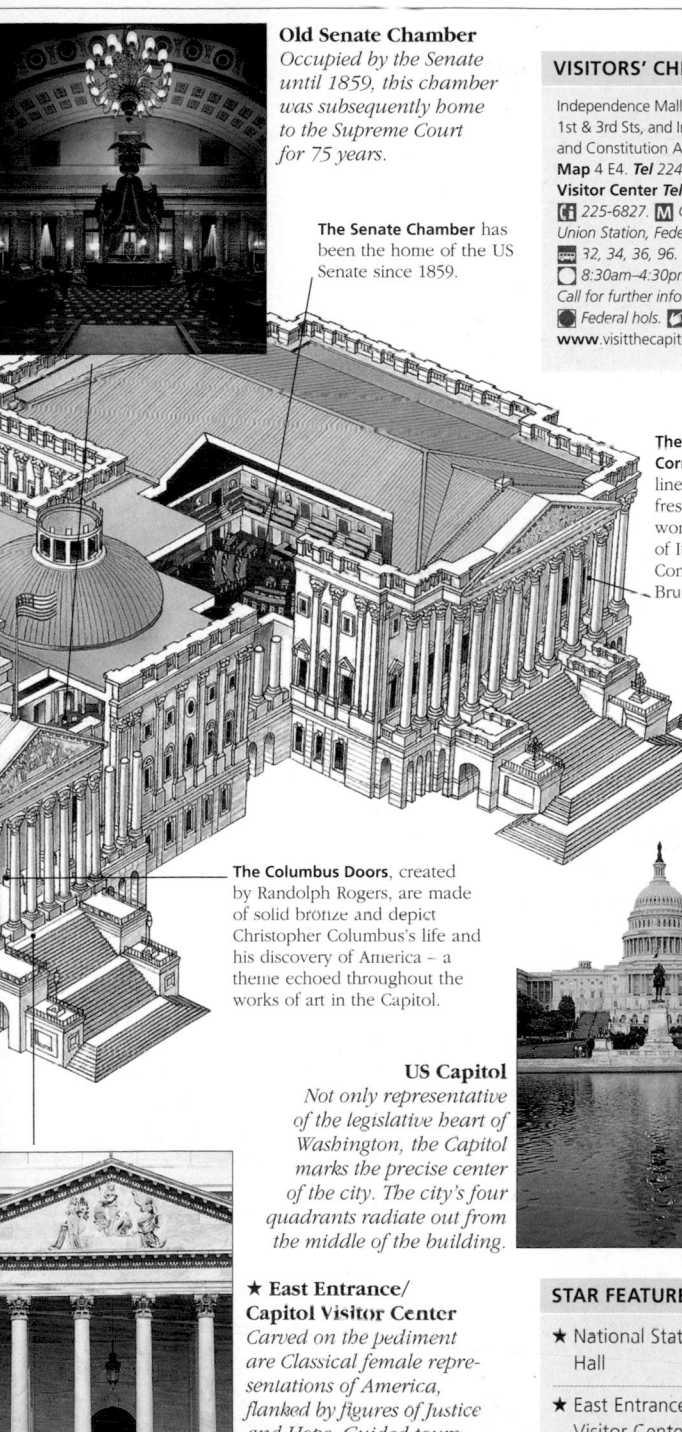

The Brumidi Corridors are lined with the frescoes, bronzework, and paintings of Italian artist Constantino Brumidi (1805–80).

The Columbus Doors, created by Randolph Rogers, are made of solid bronze and depict Christopher Columbus's life and his discovery of America – a theme echoed throughout the works of art in the Capitol.

US Capitol
Not only representative of the legislative heart of Washington, the Capitol marks the precise center of the city. The city's four quadrants radiate out from the middle of the building.

★ East Entrance/ Capitol Visitor Center
Carved on the pediment are Classical female representations of America, flanked by figures of Justice and Hope. Guided tours start from the Capitol Visitor Center, located below the East Plaza.

STAR FEATURES

★ National Statuary Hall

★ East Entrance/Capitol Visitor Center

★ The Rotunda

US Botanic Garden ❾

1st St and Independence Ave, SW.
Map 4 D4. **Tel** 225-8333.
Ⓜ *Federal Center SW.* ☐ *10am–5pm daily.* ♿ **www.**usbg.gov

The 80-ft (24-m) tall Palm House is the centerpiece of the Botanic Garden Conservatory. The appearance of the 1933 building has been preserved but modernized, creating a spacious venue for the collection of tropical and subtropical plants, and the comprehensive fern and orchid collections. Other specialties are plants native to deserts in the Old and New Worlds, plants of economic and healing value, and endangered plants rescued through an international trade program.

The Botanic Garden was originally established by Congress in 1820 to cultivate plants that could be beneficial to the American people. The garden was revitalized in 1842, when the Wilkes Expedition to the South Seas brought back an assortment of plants from around the world, some of which are still are on display.

A National Garden of plants native to the mid-Atlantic region was created on three acres west of the Conservatory. It includes a Water Garden, a Rose Garden, a Regional Garden, and a terraced lawn.

Bartholdi Park and Fountain ❿

Independence Ave and 1st St, SW. **Map** 4 D4. Ⓜ *Federal Center SW.* ♿ **www.**usbg.gov/gardens/bartholdi-park.cfm

The graceful fountain that dominates this jewel of a park was created by Frédéric August Bartholdi (sculptor of the Statue of Liberty) for the 1876 Centennial. Originally lit by gas, it was converted to electric lighting in 1881 and became a nighttime attraction. Made of cast iron, the symmetrical fountain is decorated

The elegant Bartholdi Fountain, surrounded by miniature gardens

with figures of nymphs and tritons. Surrounding the fountain are tiny model gardens, planted to inspire the urban gardener. They are themed, and include Therapeutic, Romantic, and Heritage plants, such as Virginia sneezeweed, sweet william, and wild oats.

Ebenezer United Methodist Church ⓫

4th St and D St, SE. **Tel** 544-1415.
Map 4 F5. Ⓜ *Eastern Market.*
☐ *10am–2pm Tue–Fri.*
⬤ *Federal hols.*

Ebenezer Church, established in 1819, was the first black church to serve Methodists in Washington. Attendance grew

rapidly, and a new church, Little Ebenezer, was built to take the overflow. After the Emancipation Proclamation in 1863 *(see p21)*, Congress decreed that black children should receive public education. In 1864, Little Ebenezer became the District of Columbia's first school for black children. The number of members steadily increased and another church was built in 1868, but this was badly damaged by a storm in 1896. The replacement church, which was constructed in 1897 and still here today, is Ebenezer United Methodist Church. A model of Little Ebenezer stands next to it.

Eastern Market ⓬

7th St and C St, SE. **Map** 4 F4.
Ⓜ *Eastern Market.* ☐ *7am–7pm Tue–Sat, 9am–5pm Sun.* ⬤ *Jan 1, Jul 4, Thanksgiving, Dec 25 & 26.*
♿ *at West end.* **www.**easternmarketdc.com

This block-long market hall has been a fixture in Capitol Hill since 1871, and the provisions sold today still have an Old World flavor. Big beefsteaks and fresh pigs' feet are plentiful, along with gourmet sausages and cheeses from all over the world. The aroma of fresh bread, roasted chicken, and flowers pervades the hall. On Saturdays, the covered

The redbrick, late 19th-century Ebenezer United Methodist Church

Flowers for sale on the sidewalk outside the Eastern Market

stalls outside are filled with crafts and farmers' produce, while on Sundays they host a flea market. The markets draw large crowds.

Eastern Market was designed by local architect Adolph Cluss. It is one of the few public markets left in Washington, and the only one that is still used for its original purpose.

Union Station

50 Massachusetts Ave, NE. **Map** 4 E3. **Tel** 289-1908. M Union Station. ○ daily. 🌢 🅷 🔳 ᠖ www.unionstationdc.com

When Union Station opened in 1908, its fine Beaux Arts design (by Daniel H. Burnham) set a standard that influenced architecture in Washington for 40 years. The elegantly proportioned white granite structure, its three main archways modeled on the Arch of Constantine in Rome, was the largest train station in the world. For half a century, Union Station was a major transportation hub, but as air travel became increasingly popular, passenger trains went into decline.

By the late 1950s, the size of the station outweighed the number of passsengers it served. For two decades, the railroad authorities and Congress debated its fate. Finally, in 1981, a joint public and private venture set out to restore the building.

Union Station reopened in 1988, and today is the second most visited tourist attraction

in Washington. Its 96-ft (29-m) barrel-vaulted ceiling has been covered with 22-carat gold leaf. There are around 100 specialty shops and a food court to visit, and the Main Hall hosts cultural and civic events throughout the year. The building still serves its original purpose as a station, however, and over 100 trains pass through daily.

National Postal Museum

1st St and Massachusetts Ave, NE. **Map** 4 E3. **Tel** 633-5555. M Union Station. ○ 10am–5:30pm daily. ● Dec 25. 🗱 🛍 ᠖ www.postalmuseum.si.edu

Opened by the Smithsonian in 1990, this fascinating museum is housed in the

Vintage stamp depicting Benjamin Franklin

former City Post Office building. Exhibits include a stagecoach and a postal rail car, showing how mail traveled before modern airmail.

The "Art of Cards and Letters" exhibit highlights the personal and artistic nature of correspondence. The Philatelic Gallery displays one of the best stamp collections in the world. "Binding the Nation" explains the history of the mail from the pre-Revolutionary era to the end of the 19th century. Other exhibits illustrate how the mail system works and how a stamp is created.

At postcard kiosks, you can address a postcard electronically, see the route it will take to its destination, and drop it in a mailbox on the spot.

Columbus Memorial, sculpted by Lorado Taft, in front of Union Station

THE MALL

In L'Enfant's original plan for the new capital of the United States, the Mall was conceived as a grand boulevard lined with diplomatic residences of elegant, Parisian architecture. L'Enfant's plan was never fully realized, but it is nevertheless a moving sight – this grand, tree-lined expanse is bordered on either side by the Smithsonian museums and features the Capitol at its eastern end and the Washington Monument at its western end. This dramatic formal version of the Mall did not materialize until after World War II. Until then the space was used for everything from a zoo to a railroad

Gold mirror back,
Sackler Gallery

terminal to a wood yard. The Mall forms a vital part of the history of the United States. Innumerable demonstrators have gathered at the Lincoln Memorial and marched to the US Capitol. The Pope said Mass here, African-American soprano Marian Anderson sang here at the request of first lady Eleanor Roosevelt, and Dr. Martin Luther King, Jr. delivered his famous "I have a dream" speech here. Every year on the Fourth of July (Independence Day), America's birthday party is held on the Mall, with a fireworks display. On summer evenings, teams of local employees play softball and soccer on its fields.

SIGHTS AT A GLANCE

Museums and Galleries
Arthur M. Sackler Gallery **9**
Arts and Industries Building **4**
Freer Gallery of Art **10**
Hirshhorn Museum **3**
National Air and Space Museum pp62–5 **2**
National Gallery of Art pp58–61 **1**
National Museum of African Art **5**
National Museum of American History pp74–7 **11**
National Museum of the American Indian **6**
National Museum of Natural History pp70–71 **7**
Smithsonian Castle **8**
United States Holocaust Memorial Museum pp80–81 **13**

Monuments and Memorials
Franklin D. Roosevelt Memorial **20**
Jefferson Memorial **15**
Korean War Veterans Memorial **19**
Lincoln Memorial **21**
Vietnam Veterans Memorial **18**
Washington Monument **12**
World War II Memorial **17**

Parks and Gardens
Tidal Basin **16**

Official Buildings
Bureau of Engraving and Printing **14**

GETTING THERE
Although visitors can park at the limited parking meters on the Mall, it is easier to get to the area by Metrobus (on routes 32, 34, 36, or 52) or by Metrorail. The nearest Metrorail stops are Smithsonian and Archives-Navy Memorial.

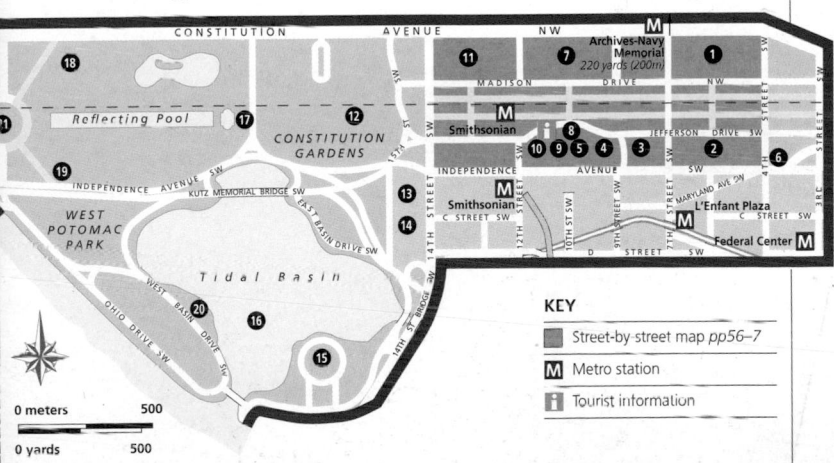

KEY

▓	Street-by-street map *pp56–7*
Ⓜ	Metro station
ⓘ	Tourist information

0 meters   500
0 yards   500

◁ **Night-time view of the Washington Monument with the US Capitol in the background**

Street-by-Street: The Mall

This 1-mile (1.5-km) boulevard between the Capitol and the Washington Monument is the city's cultural heart; the many different museums of the Smithsonian Institution can be found along this green strip. At the northeast corner of the Mall is the National Gallery of Art. Directly opposite is one of the most popular museums in the world – the National Air and Space Museum – a soaring construction of steel and glass. Both the National Museum of American History and the National Museum of Natural History, on the north side of the Mall, also draw huge numbers of visitors.

Smithsonian Castle
The main information center for all Smithsonian activities, this building once housed the basis of the collections found in numerous museums along the Mall **8**

★ National Museum of Natural History
The central Rotunda was designed in the Neoclassical style and opened to the public in 1910 **7**

★ National Museum of American History
From George Washington's uniform to this 1940s Tucker Torpedo, US history is documented here **11**

MADISON DRIVE

12TH STREET NW

JEFFERSON DRIVE SW

← Washington Monument

0 meters 100
0 yards 100

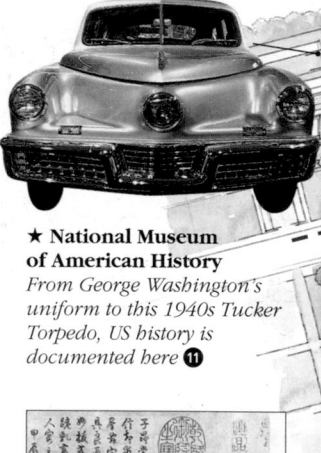

Freer Gallery of Art
Asian art, including this 13th-century Chinese silk painting, is a highlight, in addition to a superb Whistler collection **10**

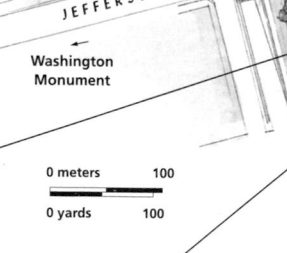

Arthur M. Sackler Gallery
This extensive collection of Asian art was donated to the nation by New Yorker Arthur Sackler **9**

National Museum of African Art
Founded in 1965 and situated underground, this museum houses a comprehensive collectic of ancient and modern African art **5**

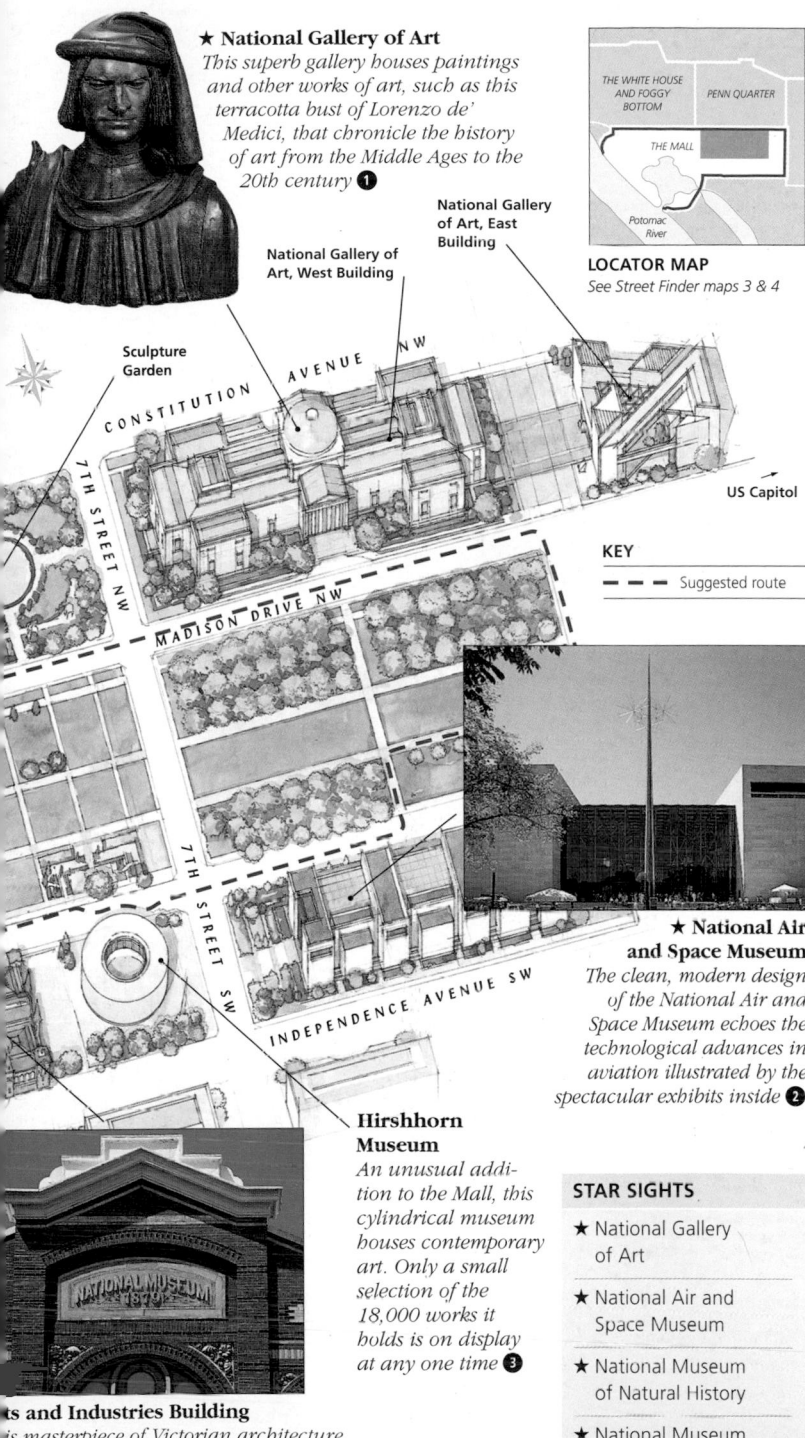

★ National Gallery of Art
This superb gallery houses paintings and other works of art, such as this terracotta bust of Lorenzo de' Medici, that chronicle the history of art from the Middle Ages to the 20th century ❶

National Gallery of Art, East Building

National Gallery of Art, West Building

LOCATOR MAP
See Street Finder maps 3 & 4

THE WHITE HOUSE AND FOGGY BOTTOM — PENN QUARTER

THE MALL

Potomac River

Sculpture Garden

CONSTITUTION AVENUE NW

7TH STREET NW

US Capitol

KEY
— — — Suggested route

MADISON DRIVE NW

7TH STREET SW

INDEPENDENCE AVENUE SW

★ National Air and Space Museum
The clean, modern design of the National Air and Space Museum echoes the technological advances in aviation illustrated by the spectacular exhibits inside ❷

Hirshhorn Museum
An unusual addition to the Mall, this cylindrical museum houses contemporary art. Only a small selection of the 18,000 works it holds is on display at any one time ❸

STAR SIGHTS

★ National Gallery of Art

★ National Air and Space Museum

★ National Museum of Natural History

★ National Museum of American History

NATIONAL MUSEUM 1879

ts and Industries Building
is masterpiece of Victorian architecture s originally built to contain exhibits from Centennial Exposition in Philadelphia ❹

National Gallery of Art ❶

In the 1920s, American financier and statesman Andrew Mellon began collecting art with the intention of establishing a new art museum in Washington. In 1936 he offered his collection to the country and offered also to provide a building for the new National Gallery of Art. Designed by architect John Russell Pope, the Neo-classical building was opened in 1941. Other collectors followed Mellon's example and donated their collections to the Gallery, and by the 1960s it had outgrown the West Building. I.M. Pei designed the innovative East Building, which was opened in 1978. The building was paid for by Andrew Mellon's son and daughter.

★ **Ginevra de' Benci**
This depiction of a thoughtful young Florentine girl by Leonardo da Vinci (c.1474) is his only painting in the US.

The Alba Madonna
Painted c.1510 by Raphael, this work is considered one of the major achievements of the Renaissance.

West Garden Court

Portrait of a Young Man and His Tutor
This charming work by French artist Nicolas de Largilliere (1656–1746) was painted in 1685.

KEY TO FLOOR PLAN

- ☐ 13th-15th-century Italian
- ☐ 16th-century Italian
- ☐ 17th-century Dutch and Flemish
- ☐ 17th-18th-century Spanish, Italian, and French
- ☐ 18th-19th-century Spanish and French
- ☐ 19th-century French
- ☐ 20th-century
- ☐ American paintings
- ☐ British paintings
- ☐ Sculpture and Decorative Arts
- ☐ Special exhibitions
- ☐ Non-exhibition space

Micro Gallery

Sculpture Garden

Ground Floor

★ **Woman with a Parasol – Mme Monet and Her Son**
(1875) This painting by Claude Monet of his wife hangs in the West Building.

Symphony in White, No. 1: The White Girl
(1862) James McNeill Whistler's painting of his mistress, Joanna Hiffernan.

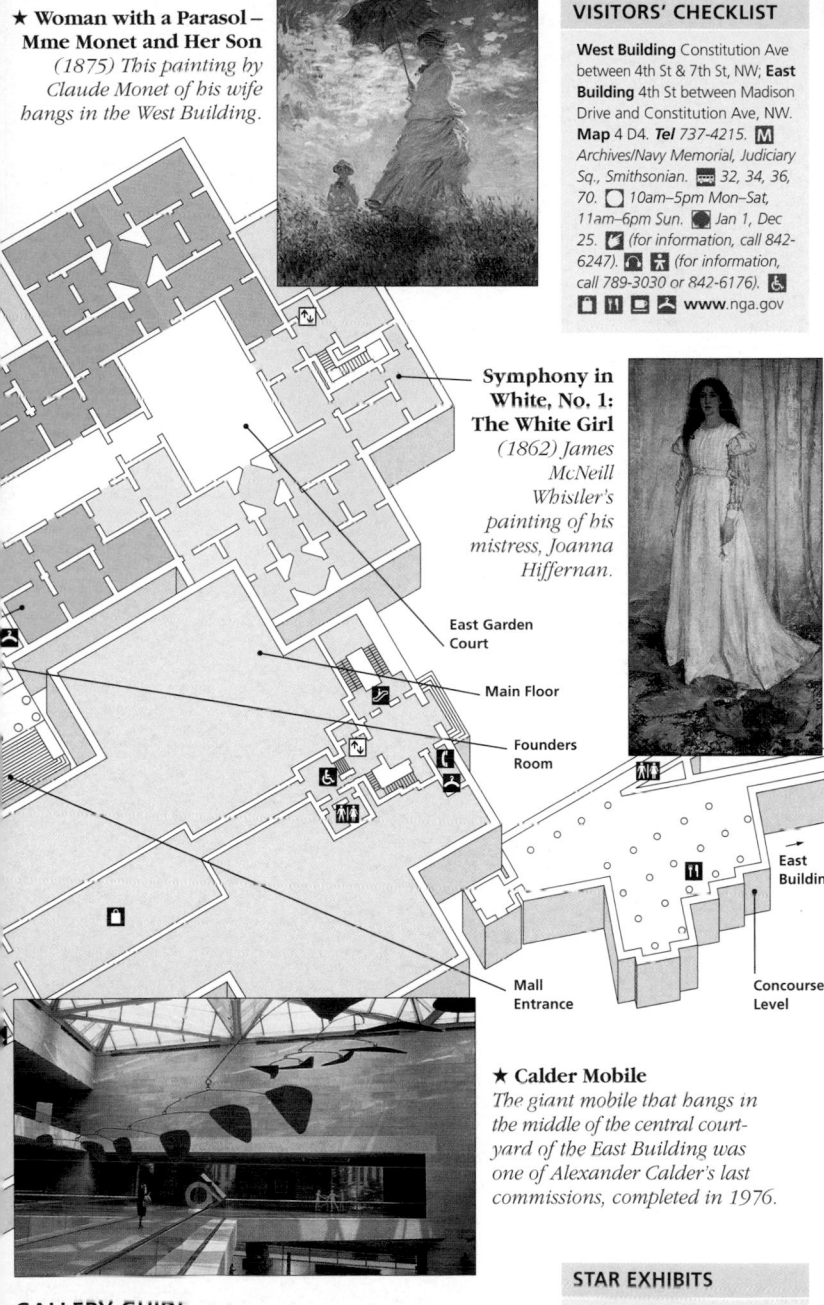

East Garden Court

Main Floor

Founders Room

East Building

Mall Entrance

Concourse Level

★ **Calder Mobile**
The giant mobile that hangs in the middle of the central courtyard of the East Building was one of Alexander Calder's last commissions, completed in 1976.

GALLERY GUIDE
The National Gallery of Art is divided into two main buildings. The West Building features European paintings and sculptures from the 13th to the 19th centuries, including American works, a substantial Impressionist collection, and Sculpture Gallery. The East Building features modern art. An underground concourse connects the two buildings.

STAR EXHIBITS

★ Calder Mobile

★ Ginevra de' Benci

★ Woman with a Parasol

Exploring the National Gallery of Art

The National Gallery's West and East Buildings are an unusual pair. The West Building, designed by John Russell Pope, is stately and Classical, with matching wings flanking its rotunda. Built of Tennessee marble, it forms a majestic presence on the Mall. Its collection is devoted to Western art from the 13th to the early 20th century. The East Building, completed in 1978, occupies a trapezoidal plot of land adjacent to the West Building. The triangular East Building is as audacious as the West one is conservative, but together they are harmonious. The interior of the East Building is a huge, fluid space, with galleries on either side housing works of modern art. The Sculpture Garden, adjacent to the West Building, has a fountain area that becomes an ice rink in winter.

Detail of *Christ Cleansing the Temple* (c.1570), by El Greco

Giotto's *Madonna and Child*, painted between 1320 and 1330

13TH- TO 15TH-CENTURY ITALIAN ART

The Italian galleries house paintings from the 13th to 15th centuries. The earlier pre-Renaissance works of primarily religious themes illustrate a decidedly Byzantine influence.

The Florentine artist Giotto's *Madonna and Child* (c.1320–30) shows the transition to the Classical painting of the Renaissance. *Adoration of the Magi*, painted around 1480 by Botticelli, portrays a serene Madonna and Child surrounded by worshipers in the Italian countryside. Around the same date Pietro Perugino painted *The Crucifixion with the Virgin, St. John, St. Jerome and St. Mary Magdalene*. Andrew Mellon bought the triptych from the Hermitage Gallery in Leningrad. Raphael's *The Alba Madonna* of 1510 was called

by one writer "the supreme compositional achievement of Renaissance painting." Leonardo da Vinci's *Ginevra de' Benci* (c.1474–8) is thought to be the first ever "psychological" portrait (depicting emotion) to be painted.

16TH-CENTURY ITALIAN ART

This collection includes works by Tintoretto, Titian, and Raphael. The 1500s were the height of Italian Classicism. Raphael's *St. George and the Dragon* (c.1506) typifies the perfection of technique for which this school of artists is known. Jacopo Tintoretto's *Christ at the Sea of Galilee* (c.1575/1580) portrays Christ standing on the shore while his disciples are on a storm-tossed fishing boat. The emotional intensity of the painting and the role of nature in it made Tintoretto one of the greatest of the Venetian artists.

17TH- TO 18TH-CENTURY SPANISH, ITALIAN, AND FRENCH ART

Among the 17th- and 18th-century European works are Jean-Honoré Fragonard's *Diana and Endymion* (c.1753–6), which was heavily influenced by Fragonard's mentor, François Boucher. El Greco's *Christ Cleansing the Temple* (pre-1570) demonstrates the influence of the 16th-century Italian schools. El Greco ("The Greek") signed his real name, Domenikos Theotokopoulos, to the panel.

17TH-CENTURY DUTCH AND FLEMISH ART

This collection holds a number of Old Masters including works by Rubens, Van Dyck, and Rembrandt. An example of Rembrandt's self-portraits is on display, which he painted

Oil painting, *Diana and Endymion* (c.1753), by Jean-Honoré Fragonard

in oils in 1659, ten years before his death.

Several paintings by Rubens in this section testify to his genius, among them *Daniel in the Lions' Den* (c.1615). This depicts the Old Testament prophet, Daniel, thanking God for his help during his night spent surrounded by lions. In 1617, Rubens exchanged this work for antique marbles owned by a British diplomat. Rubens also painted *Deborah Kip, Wife of Sir Balthasar Gerbier, and her Children* (1629–30). Not a conventional family portrait, the mother and her four children seem withdrawn and pensive, suggesting unhappiness and perhaps even foreboding tragedy. Van Dyck painted Rubens's first wife, *Isabella Brant* (c.1621) toward the end of her life. Although she is smiling, her eyes reveal an inner melancholy.

19TH-CENTURY FRENCH ART

This is one of the best Impressionist collections outside Paris. Works on display include Paul Cézanne's *The Artist's Father Reading "L'Evénement"* (1866), Auguste Renoir's *A Girl with a Watering Can* (1876), *Four Dancers* (c.1899) by Edgar Degas, and Claude Monet's *Woman with a Parasol – Madame Monet and Her Son* (1875) and *Palazzo da Mula, Venice* (1908). Post-Impressionist works include Seurat's pointillist *The Lighthouse at Honfleur* (c.1886), in which thousands of dots are used to create the image, and Van Gogh's *Self Portrait*. The latter was painted in St Rémy in 1889 when he was staying in an asylum and shows his mastery at capturing character and emotion. Toulouse-Lautrec's painting, *Quadrille at the Moulin Rouge* (1892), depicts a dancer provocatively raising her skirts above her ankles.

Geometric skylights in the plaza from the West Building to the East Building

AMERICAN PAINTING

This important collection of American artists shows evidence of European influence, but in themes that are resolutely American. James McNeill Whistler's *Symphony in White, No. 1: The White Girl* (1862) has a European sophistication. Mary Cassatt left America for exile in Europe and was heavily influenced by the Impressionists, especially Degas. *Boating Party* (1893–4) is an example of one of her recurrent themes: mother and child. *Children Playing on a Beach* (1884) is also a good example of her child paintings, and *Miss Mary Ellison* of her portraiture. Winslow Homer's *Breezing Up (A Fair Wind)* (1873–6) is a masterpiece by the American Realist. His painting is a charming depiction of three small boys and a fisherman.

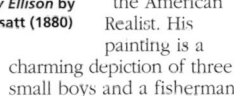

Miss Mary Ellison by Mary Cassatt (1880)

MODERN AND CONTEMPORARY ART

The enormous East Building houses modern and contemporary art. I.M. Pei's "H"-shaped building contains a vast atrium which is edged by four balconies and adjacent galleries. Architecturally, this space provides a dramatic focus and spatial orientation for visitors to the East Building.

Centered in the atrium is *Untitled*, a vast red, blue, and black creation by Alexander Calder. It was commissioned in 1972 for the opening of the museum in 1978. At the entrance to the East Building is Henry Moore's bronze sculpture *Knife Edge Mirror Two Piece* (1977–8).

Also in the East Building are a research center for schools, offices for the curators, a library, and a large collection of drawings and prints.

Both the East and West buildings also host traveling exhibits. These are not limited to modern art, but have included the art of ancient Japan, American Impressionists, and the sketches of Leonardo da Vinci. The East Building's galleries are surprisingly intimate.

SCULPTURE GARDEN

Located across the street from the West Building at 7th Street, the Sculpture Garden holds 17 sculptures. The late 20th-century works include pieces by Louise Bourgeois, Roy Lichtenstein, and Joan Miró. Although different, the sculptures do not compete with each other because they are spread out. Transformed into an ice rink in winter and a venue for free jazz concerts in summer, the garden functions both as an outdoor gallery and as a pleasant oasis within the city. The pavilion houses a year-round café.

National Air and Space Museum ❷

The Smithsonian's National Air and Space Museum opened on July 1, 1976, during the country's bicentennial. The soaring architecture of the building, designed by Hellmuth, Obata, and Kassabaum, is well suited to the airplanes, rockets, balloons, and space capsules of aviation and space flight. The Steven F. Udvar-Hazy Center, named after its primary benefactor, opened in 2003 to celebrate the 100th anniversary of the Wright brothers' first powered flight. With this facility, the museum is now the largest air and space museum complex in the world.

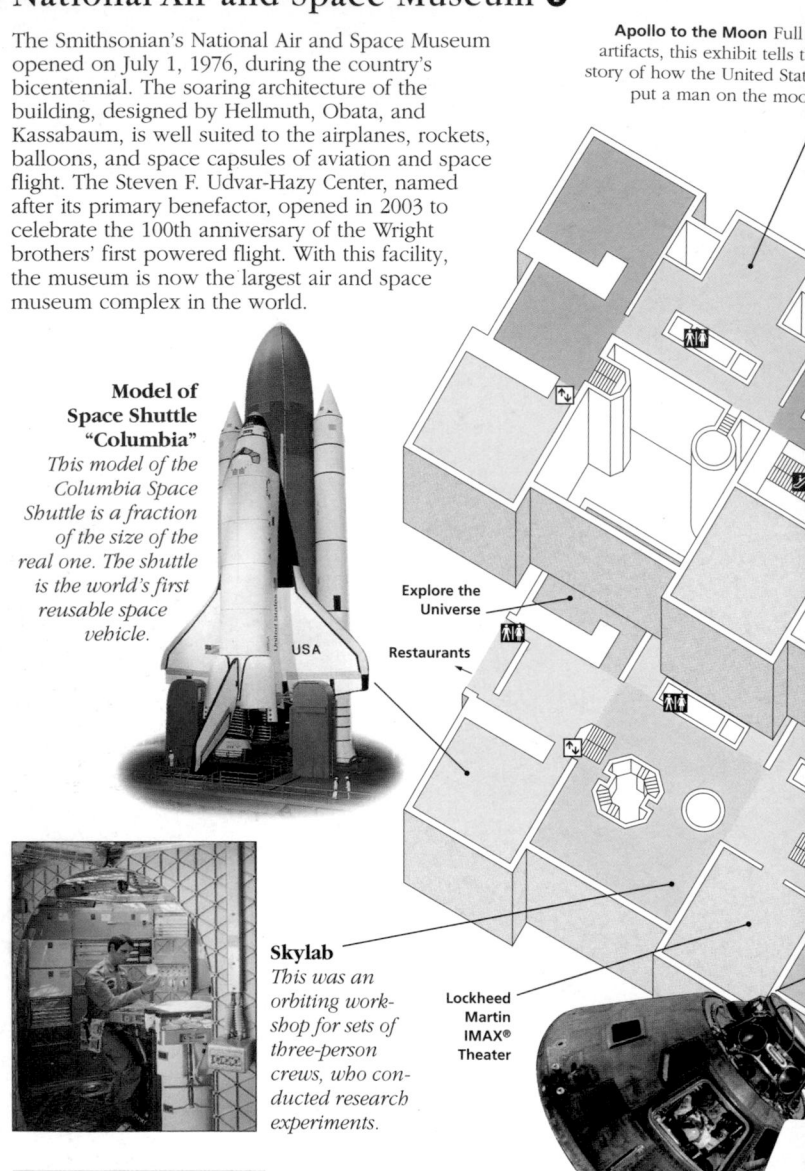

Apollo to the Moon Full of artifacts, this exhibit tells the story of how the United States put a man on the moon

Model of Space Shuttle "Columbia"
This model of the Columbia Space Shuttle is a fraction of the size of the real one. The shuttle is the world's first reusable space vehicle.

USA

Explore the Universe

Restaurants

Skylab
This was an orbiting work-shop for sets of three-person crews, who con-ducted research experiments.

Lockheed Martin IMAX® Theater

STAR EXHIBITS

- ★ 1903 Wright Flyer
- ★ Amelia Earhart's Red Vega
- ★ Apollo 11 Command Module
- ★ Spirit of St. Louis

GALLERY GUIDE

The first floor houses many themed displays, as well as the Lockheed Martin IMAX® theater and the Museum Store. The lofty second-floor ceilings show exhibits and models demonstrat-ing the history of flight from the early days to the space age.

Mall Entrance

★ Apollo 11 Command Module
This module carried astronauts Buzz Aldrin, Neil Armstrong, and Michael Collins on their historic mission to the moon in July 1969, when Neil Armstrong took his famous first steps.

★ 1903 Wright Flyer

This exhibit, along with others in the Wright Brothers and the Invention of the Aerial Age gallery, show the accomplishments of Orville and Wilbur Wright.

VISITORS' CHECKLIST

Independence Ave at 6th St, SW. **Map** 4 D4. **Tel** 633-1000. Ⓜ *Smithsonian.* 🚌 *32, 34, 36, 52.* ◯ *10am–5:30pm daily (to 7:30pm in summer).* ● *Dec 25.* 🎫 *10:15am, 1pm.* ⚫ 🚻 ⬜ 📷 🚻 🖥 www.nasm.si.edu

KEY TO FLOOR PLAN

⬜	Milestones of Flight
⬜	Developments in Flight
⬜	Aviation in World Wars I and II
⬜	The Space Race
⬜	Modern Space Exploration
⬜	Other exhibitions
⬜	Explore the Universe
⬜	Temporary exhibition space

Albert Einstein Planetarium

Supermarine Spitfire MK. VII

With more than 20,351 Spitfires built, these planes saw service on every major front and sucessfully defended England against Germany in WWII.

★ Amelia Earhart's Red Vega

Amelia Earhart was the first woman to make a solo transatlantic flight. She succeeded in her red Lockheed Vega, five years after Charles Lindbergh.

Second Floor

★ Spirit of St. Louis

At the age of 25, pilot Charles Lindbergh made the first solo transatlantic flight in this plane, landing in France on May 21, 1927.

Milestones of Flight
Many of the firsts in both aviation and space travel are on display in this gallery.

First Floor

Flight simulators

America by Air
Located near the museum store, this exhibit outlines the fascinating history of America's airline industry and its effect on the nation and the world.

Exploring the National Air and Space Museum

The National Air and Space Museum on the Mall has a massive exhibition space of 23 galleries. The most visited museum in the world, it has to cope not only with millions of visitors but also with the range and sheer size of its artifacts, which include hundreds of rockets, planes, and spacecraft. In 2003 the museum opened a sister exhibition space: a huge new state-of-the art facility, the Steven F. Udvar-Hazy Center, located near Dulles Airport. Now with two sites, more of NASM's historic collections are on display for the public to enjoy.

The Boeing F4B Navy fighter

MILESTONES OF FLIGHT

Entering the National Air and Space Museum from the Mall entrance, first stop is the soaring **Milestones of Flight** gallery, which gives an overview of the history of flight. The exhibits in this room are some of the major firsts in aviation and space technology, as they helped to realize man's ambition to take to the air.

The gallery is vast, designed to accommodate the large aircraft – many of which are suspended from the ceiling – and spacecraft. Some of these pioneering machines are surprisingly small, however. Charles Lindbergh's *Spirit of St. Louis*, the first aircraft to cross the Atlantic with a solo pilot, was designed with the fuel tanks ahead of the cockpit so Lindbergh had to use a periscope to look directly ahead. John Glenn's Mercury spacecraft, *Friendship 7*, in which he orbited the earth, is smaller than a sports car.

Near the entrance to the gallery is a moon rock – a symbol of man's exploration of space. Also in this gallery is the *Apollo 11* Command Module, which carried the first men to walk on the moon. The Wright brothers' *Flyer*, (in gallery 209) was the first plane to sustain powered flight on December 17, 1903, at Kitty Hawk, North Carolina.

DEVELOPMENTS IN FLIGHT

Travelers now take flying for granted – it is safe, fast, and, for many, routine. The National Air and Space Museum, however, displays machines and gadgets from an era when flight was new and daring.

The **Pioneers of Flight** gallery celebrates the men and women who have challenged the physical and psychological barriers faced when leaving the earth. Adventurer Cal Rogers was the first to fly across the United States, but it was not non-stop. In 1911 he flew from coast to coast in less than 30 days, with almost 70 landings. His early biplane is one of the exhibits. (Twelve years later, a Fokker T-2 made the trip in less than 27 hours.)

Amelia Earhart was the first woman to fly the Atlantic, just five years after Charles Lindbergh. Her red Lockheed Vega is displayed. Close by is *Tingmissartoq*, a Lockheed Sirius seaplane belonging to Charles Lindbergh. Its unusual name is Inuit for "one who flies like a bird." Some of the greatest strides in aviation were made in the period between the two world wars, celebrated in the **Golden Age of Flight** gallery. The public's intense interest in flight resulted in races, exhibitions, and adventurous exploration. Here a visitor can see planes equipped with skis for landing on snow, with short wings for racing, and a "staggerwing" plane on which the lower wing was placed ahead of the upper.

The F4B Navy fighter, used by US Marine Corps squadrons, was developed between the world wars and is on display in the **Sea-Air Operations** gallery. Flight then progressed from propeller propulsion to

The propeller-driven Douglas DC-3 aircraft in the America by Air gallery

Rockets on display in the Space Race gallery

jets. The **Jet Aviation** gallery has the first operational jet fighter, the German Messerschmitt Me 262A. *Lulu Belle*, the prototype of the first US fighter jet, was used in the Korean War of 1950–53.

America by Air traces the development of commercial air-travel, from the air mail age to the "glass cockpit", and beyond. This is a fun, family-friendly gallery with hands-on exhibits.

AVIATION IN WORLD WARS I AND II

One of the most popular parts of the museum is the **World War II Aviation** gallery, which has planes from the Allied and the Axis air forces. Nearby is an example of the Japanese Mitsubishi A6M5 Zero Model 52, which was a light, highly maneuverable fighter plane.

The maneuverability of the Messerschmitt Bf 109 made it Germany's most successful fighter. It was matched, and in some areas surpassed, by the Supermarine Spitfire of the Royal Air Force, which helped to win control of the skies over Britain in 1940–41.

THE SPACE RACE

The animosity that grew between the United States and the Soviet Union after World War II manifested itself in the Space Race. America was taken by surprise when

the Soviets launched *Sputnik 1* on October 4, 1957. The US attempt to launch their first satellite proved a spectacular failure when the *Vanguard* crashed in December 1957. The satellite is on display here.

In 1961, Soviet cosmonaut Yuri Gagarin became the first man to orbit the earth. The Americans countered with Alan Shepard's manned space flight in *Freedom 7* later the same year. The first space walk was from the *Gemini IV* capsule by American astronaut Edward H. White in 1965.

On July 20, 1969, the race reached a climax when the world watched as Neil Armstrong walked on the moon. His original spacesuit from the Apollo 11 mission is on display. Other exhibits from the Space Race include the *Skylab 4* command module, and *Gemini 7*, a two-person spacecraft that successfully orbited the earth in 1965.

Gemini IV capsule

The Space Hall gallery shows the result of the final détente between the superpowers with the Apollo-Soyuz Test Project. This was a purposefully collaborative space mission meant to symbolize a new era of cooperation. It was the last Apollo flight. When the American *Apollo* module docked alongside the Soviet *Soyuz* spacecraft in 1975, it was the start of the end of the Space Race.

PROGRESS IN AIR AND SPACE TECHNOLOGY

Mankind's fascination with flight is in part a desire to see the earth from a great distance and also to get closer to other planets. In the Independence Avenue lobby is artist Robert T. McCall's interpretation of the birth of the universe, the planets, and astronauts reaching the moon.

The Hubble Telescope, launched from the *Discovery* shuttle in April 1990, provides pictures of extremely distant astronomical objects. Launched in 1964, the *Ranger* lunar probe also took high-quality pictures of the moon, and then transmitted them to Cape Canaveral.

Beyond the Limits explains how computers have revolutionized flight technology and displays some of the recent achievements in aircraft design, a process that has been transformed by the arrival of CAD (Computer-Aided-Design).

The spacesuit worn by Apollo astronauts in 1969

Fountain in the central plaza of the Hirshhorn Museum

Hirshhorn Museum ❸

Independence Ave and 7th St, SW.
Map 3 C4. **Tel** 633-1000.
Ⓜ Smithsonian, L'Enfant Plaza.
⏲ 10am–5:30pm daily (Sculpture Garden: 7:30am–dusk).
⊘ Dec 25. 🎫 ♿ 🚻 ⛙
www.hirshhorn.si.org

When the Hirshhorn Museum was still in its planning stages, S. Dillon Ripley, then Secretary of the Smithsonian Institution, told the planning board that the building should be "controversial in every way" so that it would be fit to house contemporary works of art.

The Hirshhorn certainly fulfilled its architectural mission. It has been variously described as a doughnut or a flying saucer, but it is actually a four-story, not-quite-symmetrical cylinder. It is also home to one of the greatest collections of modern art in the United States.

The museum's benefactor, Joseph H. Hirshhorn, was an eccentric, flamboyant immigrant from Latvia who amassed a collection of 6,000 pieces of contemporary art. Since the museum opened in 1974, the Smithsonian has built on Hirshhorn's original donation, and the collection now consists of 3,000 pieces of sculpture, 4,000 drawings and photographs, and approximately 5,000 paintings. The works of art are arranged chronologically. The main, lower floor displays recent acquisitions. It is also home to the "Black Box," a space dedicated to film, video, and other digital works by emerging international artists. The second floor hosts temporary exhibitions, of which there are at least three a year. These are usually arranged thematically, or as tributes to individual artists, such as Lucien Freud, Alberto Giacometti, or Francis Bacon. The third floor houses the permanent collection, which includes works by artists such as Alexander Calder, Arshile Gorky, Willem de Kooning, and John Singer Sargent. In addition, visitors should not miss the outdoor sculpture garden, across the street from the museum. It includes pieces by Alexander Calder, Auguste Rodin, Henri Matisse, and many others.

An outdoor café in the circular plaza at the center of the building provides light lunches during the summer.

Arts and Industries Building ❹

900 Jefferson Drive, SW.
Map 3 C4. **Tel** 633-1000.
Ⓜ Smithsonian.
⦿ to the public. ♿ 🚻
www.si.edu

The ornate, vast galleries and the airy rotunda of the splendid Victorian Arts and Industries Building were designed by Montgomery Meigs, architect of the National Building Museum *(see p103)*. The Arts and Industries Building was extraordinary because of its expanse of open space, boasting 17 uninterrupted exhibition areas, and abundance of natural light.

The museum served a wide-ranging variety of functions after its completion on March 4, 1881. In its opening year, it was the

Arts and Industries Building's fountain

site of President James A. Garfield's inaugural ball; it also displayed artifacts from Philadelphia's 1876 Centennial Exposition, including a complete steam train; later, it was home to a collection of the First Ladies' Gowns, as well as Lindbergh's famous airplane the *Spirit of St. Louis*, before these exhibits were moved to other Smithsonian museums on the Mall. A pretty, working carousel is located in front of the building, on the Mall (closed in winter.)

Sadly, concerns over its deteriorating condition led to the building's closure in 2004, and for many years it has remained empty, facing an uncertain future. This period of doubt thankfully came to an end with the American Recovery and Reinvestment Act of 2009; it has allocated $25 million for much-needed renovation work.

The Burghers of Calais **(1884–1889) by Auguste Rodin, in the Hirshhorn garden**

Tribal masks at the National Museum of African Art

National Museum of African Art ❺

950 Independence Ave, SW. **Map** 3 C4. **Tel** 633-1000. **Ⓜ** Smithsonian. ☐ 10am–5:30pm daily. ⬤ Dec 25. www.nmafa.si.edu

The National Museum of African Art is one of the most peaceful spots on the Mall. Perhaps because it is mostly underground, with a relatively low above-ground presence, it is often missed by visitors. The entrance pavilion, situated in the Enid A. Haupt Garden directly in front of the Smithsonian Castle, leads to three subterranean floors, where the museum shares space with the adjacent Ripley Center and the Arthur M. Sackler Gallery (see pp72–3).

The museum was founded in 1964 by Warren Robbins, a former officer in the American Foreign Service (he was a cultural attaché and public affairs officer), and was the first museum in the US to concentrate entirely on the art and culture of the African continent. It was first situated in the home of Frederick Douglass (see p145), on Capitol Hill. For several years Robbins had to finance the museum himself, gradually acquiring more space in the form of a collection of town houses near the original building. Eventually financial support was forthcoming as the importance of the collection was recognized.

The Smithsonian Institution acquired Robbins' collection in 1979, and the works were finally moved to their current home on the Mall in 1987.

The 9,000-piece permanent collection includes both modern and ancient art from Africa, although the majority of pieces date from the 19th and 20th centuries. Traditional African art of bronze, ceramics, and gold are on display, along with an extensive collection of masks. There is also a display of *kente* cloth from Ghana – brightly colored and patterned cloth used to adorn clothing as a symbol of African nationalism. The Eliot Elisofon Photographic Archives (Eliot Elisofon was a famous photographer for *Life* magazine) contain 300,000 prints and some 120,000 ft of edited and unedited film footage, as well as videos and documentaries on African art

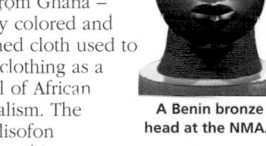

A Benin bronze head at the NMAA

and culture. The museum now also holds 525 pieces of the Walt Disney-Tishman African Art Collection. The Warren M. Robbins Library has approximately 32,000 books in its collection, mainly on African art, history, and culture. The library, however, also has children's literature and videos. It is open to the public by appointment only.

To display its vast archive of exhibits, the museum runs a rolling program of themed exhibitions. It also hosts performing arts events featuring dance, music, and spoken word. Year-round there is a full calendar of educational tours, lectures, and workshops, including many for children. At the bi-monthly Music of Africa workshop, children over six can play African musical instruments and learn about different rhythms and playing techniques.

HISTORY OF THE MALL

In September, 1789, French-born Pierre L'Enfant (1754–1825) was invited by George Washington to design the capital of the new United States While the rest of the city developed, the area planned by L'Enfant to be the Grand Avenue, running west from the Capitol, remained swampy and undeveloped. In 1850, landscape gardener Andrew Jackson Downing was employed to develop the land in accordance with L'Enfant's plans. However, the money ran out, and the work was abandoned. At the end of the Civil War in 1865, President Lincoln, eager that building in the the city should progress, instructed that work on the area should begin again, and the Mall began to take on the park-like appearance it has today. The addition of many museums and memorials in the latter half of the 20th century established the Mall as the cultural heart of Washington.

Aerial view, showing the Mall stretching down from the Capitol

National Museum of the American Indian ❻

Built from Minnesota Kasota limestone, the National Museum of the American Indian was established in collaboration with Native American communities throughout the western hemisphere. It is the only national museum dedicated to the Native peoples of the Americas, and is the eighteenth museum of the Smithsonian Institution. The original collections of artifacts were assembled by George Gustav Heye (1874–1957), a wealthy New Yorker, at the turn of the 20th century. The exhibitions showcase the spiritual and daily lives of diverse peoples and encourage visitors to look beyond stereotypes.

★ **Our Peoples**
American Indians, including the Blackfeet and Kiowa, tell their own stories and histories, focusing on both the destruction of their culture and their resilience.

George Heye (1874–1957)
Collector and world traveler George Gustav Heye and his wife, Thea, accompanied a Zuni delegation in New York c.1923.

★ **Lelawi Theater**
In this circular theater a spectacular multimedia presentation is shown every 15 minutes. "Who We Are" highlights the diversity of American Indian life from the Arctic, to the Northwest Coast, to Bolivia.

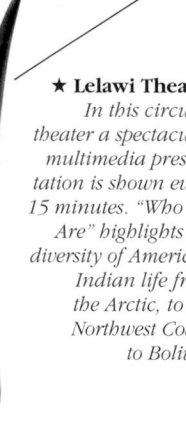

★ **Our Universes**
Eight groups of American Indians, from the Santa Clara Pueblo in New Mexico to the Lakota in South Dakota, share their world-views, philosophies of creation, and spiritual relationship with nature.

Window on Collections: Many Hands, Many Voices
Over 3,500 objects are on display, including dolls, beaded objects, and artwork.

VISITORS' CHECKLIST

4th St & Independence Ave,
SW. **Map** 4 D4. *Tel* 633-1000.
M L'Enfant Plaza (Maryland Ave
exit). ◯ 10am–5:30pm daily.
◉ Dec 25. 🚻 🚪 🔲 🔲
www.americanindian.si.edu

Exterior of Museum
*The museum's curvilinear limestone exterior gives it a
natural, weathered effect. It is set in a landscape of flow-
ing water, hardwood forest, meadowland, and croplands,
to reflect the American Indian's connection to the land.*

Window on Collections
*Interactive technology allows for
a self-guided tour of the exhibits. Shown here is a peace
medal that once belonged to
Powder Face, an Arapaho.*

4th Floor

Resource
Center

KEY TO FLOORPLAN

▢	Our Peoples
▢	Window on Collections
▢	Our Universes
▢	Lelawi Theater
▢	Education classrooms
▨	Contemporary Gallery
▢	Our Lives

3rd Floor

STAR SIGHTS

★ Our Universes

★ Our Peoples

★ Lewali Theater

GALLERY GUIDE
*Begin your visit with the
"Who We Are" multimedia
presentation at the Lelawi
Theater (4th floor). The three
permanent exhibitions on this
level are "Our Universes,"
"Our Peoples," and "Window
on Collections," while "Our
Lives" is on the 3rd floor. On
the ground level is a shop and
the Mitsitam café.*

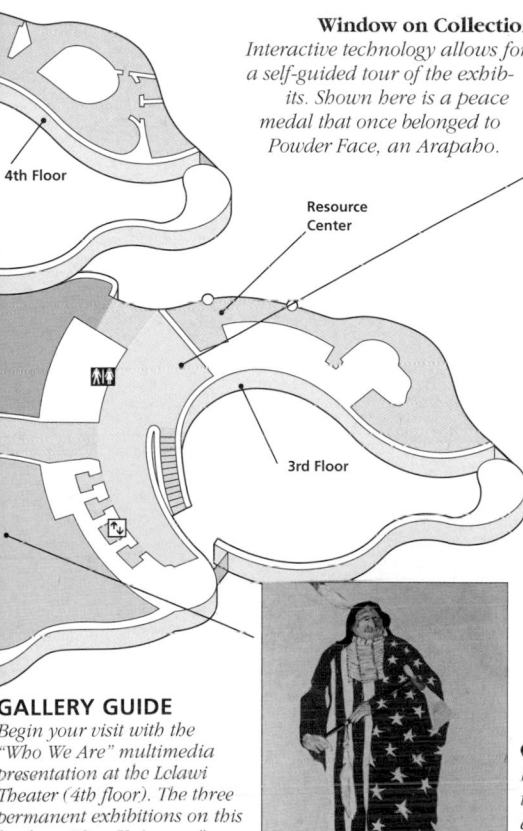

Our Lives
*Examines the lives and iden-
tities of Native Americans
and the consequences of
legal policies that determine
who is an American Indian.
Here Fritz Scholder (b.1937)
explores "nativeness" in this
work* The American Indian.

National Museum of Natural History ❼

Second Floor

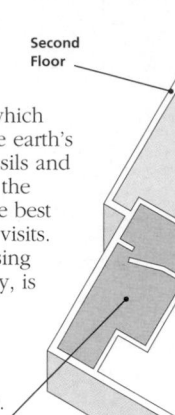

The National Museum of Natural History, which opened in 1910, preserves artifacts from the earth's diverse cultures and collects samples of fossils and living creatures from land and sea. Visiting the museum is a vast undertaking, so sample the best of the exhibits and leave the rest for return visits. The O. Orkin Insect Zoo, with its giant hissing cockroaches and large leaf-cutter ant colony, is popular with children, while the Dinosaur Hall delights young and old. The stunning Hall of Mammals displays 274 specimens, and looks at how they adapted to changes in habitat and climate over millions of years.

★ O. Orkin Insect Zoo
This popular exhibit explores the lives and habitats of the single largest animal group on earth and features many live specimens.

Butterflies+Plants: Partners in Evolution
This permanent exhibition innovatively combines traditional and experiential learning.

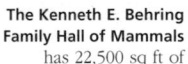

The Kenneth E. Behring Family Hall of Mammals
has 22,500 sq ft of displays explaining the diversity of mammals.

African Elephant
The massive African Bush Elephant is one of the highlights of the museum. It is the centerpiece of the Rotunda and creates an impressive sight as visitors enter the museum.

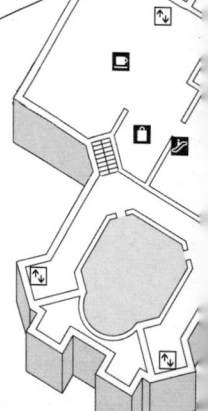

STAR SIGHTS

★ Dinosaur Hall

★ Insect Zoo

★ Hope Diamond

GALLERY GUIDE

The first floor's main exhibitions feature mammals and marine life from different continents. Dinosaurs and myriad cultural exhibits are also displayed on this level. The Gems and Minerals collection and the Insect Zoo are on the second floor.

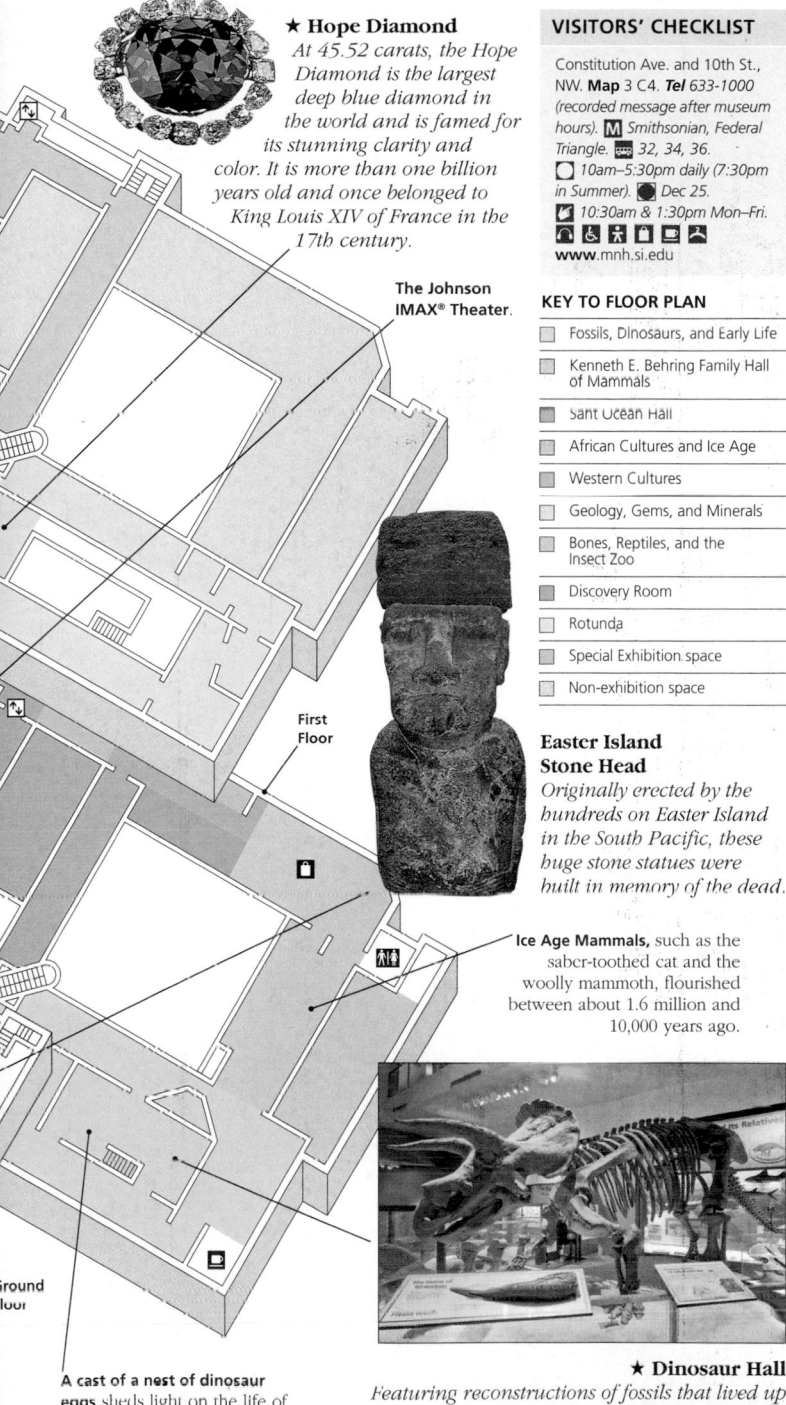

★ Hope Diamond

At 45.52 carats, the Hope Diamond is the largest deep blue diamond in the world and is famed for its stunning clarity and color. It is more than one billion years old and once belonged to King Louis XIV of France in the 17th century.

The Johnson IMAX® Theater.

First Floor

Ground Floor

VISITORS' CHECKLIST

Constitution Ave. and 10th St., NW. **Map** 3 C4. **Tel** 633-1000 *(recorded message after museum hours).* Ⓜ Smithsonian, Federal Triangle. 🚌 32, 34, 36. 🕙 *10am–5:30pm daily (7:30pm in Summer).* ⬤ *Dec 25.* 📷 *10:30am & 1:30pm Mon–Fri.* 🅿 ♿ 🚻 🏛 🖥 ☕ www.mnh.si.edu

KEY TO FLOOR PLAN

☐	Fossils, Dinosaurs, and Early Life
☐	Kenneth E. Behring Family Hall of Mammals
☐	Sant Ocean Hall
☐	African Cultures and Ice Age
☐	Western Cultures
☐	Geology, Gems, and Minerals
☐	Bones, Reptiles, and the Insect Zoo
☐	Discovery Room
☐	Rotunda
☐	Special Exhibition space
☐	Non-exhibition space

Easter Island Stone Head

Originally erected by the hundreds on Easter Island in the South Pacific, these huge stone statues were built in memory of the dead.

Ice Age Mammals, such as the saber-toothed cat and the woolly mammoth, flourished between about 1.6 million and 10,000 years ago.

A cast of a nest of dinosaur eggs sheds light on the life of *Maiasaura*, a kind of duck-billed dinosaur, who lived around 70 million years ago.

★ Dinosaur Hall

Featuring reconstructions of fossils that lived up to 230 million years ago, including this skeleton of Triceratops horridus, *the Dinosaur Hall is one of the most popular areas of the museum.*

The elegant Victorian façade of the Smithsonian Castle, viewed from the Mall

Smithsonian Castle **8**

1000 Jefferson Drive, SW. **Map** 3 C4.
Tel 633-1000. M *Smithsonian.*
☐ 8:30am–5:30pm daily. ● Dec
25. 🎫 ♿ 🏢 www.si.edu

This ornate Victorian edifice served as the first home of the Smithsonian Institution, and was also home to the first Secretary of the Smithsonian, Joseph Henry, and his family. A statue of Henry stands in front of the building.

Constructed of red sandstone in 1855, the Castle was designed by James Renwick,

The tomb of James Smithson

architect of the Renwick Gallery *(see p113)* and St Patrick's Cathedral in New York. It is an outstanding example of the Gothic Revival style. Inspired also by 12th-century Norman architecture, the Castle has nine towers and an elaborate cornice.

Today it is the seat of the Smithsonian administration and houses its Information Center. Visitors can visit the Crypt Room and see the tomb of James Smithson, who bequeathed his fortune to the United States. The South Tower Room was the first children's room in a Washington museum. The ceiling and colorful wall

stencils that decorate the room were restored in 1987.

Outside the castle is the Smithsonian rose garden, fille with beautiful hybrid tea roses The garden was a later additio that now connects the Castle to the equally ornate Arts and Industries Building *(see p66)*.

Arthur M. Sackler Gallery **9**

1050 Independence Ave, SW.
Map 3 C4. **Tel** 633-1000. M *Smith-sonian.* ☐ 10am–5:30pm daily.
● Dec 25. 🎫 12:15pm. ♿ 🏢
🖼 www.asia.si.edu

Dr. Arthur M. Sackler, a New York physician, started collecting Asian art in the 1950s. In 1982, he

JAMES SMITHSON (1765–1829)

Although he never once visited the United States, James Smithson, English scientist and philanthropist, and illegitimate son of the first Duke of Northumberland, left his entire fortune of half a million dollars to "found at Washington, under the name of the Smithsonian Institution, an establishment for the increase and diffusion of knowledge among men." However, this was only if his nephew and heir were to die childless. This did happen and hence, in 1836, Smithson's fortune passed to the government of the United States, which did not quite know what to do with such a vast bequest. For 11 years Congress debated various proposals, finally agreeing to set up a government-run foundation that would administer all national museums. The first Smithson-funded collection was shown at the Smithsonian Castle in 1855.

James Smithson

10th-century Indian sculpture of the goddess Parvati in the Arthur M. Sackler Gallery

donated more than 1,000 artifacts, along with $4 million in funds, to the Smithsonian Institution to establish this museum. The Japanese and Korean governments also contributed $1 million each toward the cost of constructing the building, and the museum was completed in 1987.

The entrance is a small pavilion at ground level that leads down to two sub-terranean floors of exhibits. The Sackler's 3,000-piece collection is particularly rich in Chinese works, and highlights include a stunning display of Chinese bronzes and jades, some dating back to 4000 BC. There are also 7th-century ceramics from the Ming dynasty and an extensive range of sculpture from India and southeast Asia.

Over the years the gallery has built on Arthur Sackler's original collection. In 1987 it acquired the impressive Vever Collection from collector Henri Vever, which includes such items as Islamic books from the 11th to the 19th centuries, 19th-and 20th century Japanese prints, Indian, Chinese, and Japanese paintings, and modern photography. The gallery also hosts international traveling exhibitions of Asian art from museums such as the Louvre in Paris.

The Sackler is one of two underground museums in this area; the other is the National Museum of African Art (see p67), which is part of the same complex. The Sackler is also connected by underground exhibition space to the Freer Gallery of Art. The two galleries share a director and

administrative staff as well as the Meyer Auditorium, which hosts dance performances, films, and chamber music concerts. There is also a research library in the Sackler devoted to Asian art.

Freer Gallery of Art ⓾

Jefferson Drive and 12th Street, SW.
Map 3 C4. **Tel** 633-1000.
Ⓜ Smithsonian. ⦿ 10am–5:30pm daily. ⦿ Dec 25. ⓮ ⓯ www.asia.si.edu

The Freer Gallery of Art is named after Charles Lang Freer, a railroad magnate who donated his collection of 9,000 pieces of American and Asian art to the Smithsonian, and funded the building of a museum to house the works. Freer died in 1919 before the building's completion. When the gallery opened in 1923 it became the first Smithsonian museum of art.

Constructed as a single-story building in the Italian Renaissance style, the Freer has an attractive courtyard with a fountain at its center. There are 19 galleries, most with skylights that illuminate a superb collection of Asian

Detail of a screen by Thomas Wilmer Dewing

and American art. Since Freer's original donation, the museum has tripled its holdings. In the Asian Art collection are examples of Chinese, Japanese, and Korean art, including sculpture, ceramics, folding screens, and paintings. The gallery also has a fine selection of Buddhist sculpture, and painting and calligraphy from India.

There is a select collection of American art in the Freer as well, most of which shows Asian influences. Works by the artists Childe Hassam (1859–1935), John Singer Sargent (1865–1925), and Thomas Wilmer Dewing (1851–1938) are all on display.

The most astonishing room in the museum is James McNeill Whistler's "The Peacock Room." Whistler (1834–1903) was a friend of Freer's who encouraged his art collecting. Whistler painted a dining room for Frederick Leyland in London, but Leyland found that it was not to his taste. Freer purchased the room in 1904; it was later moved to Washington and installed here after his death. In contrast to the subtle elegance of the other rooms, this room is a riot of blues, greens, and golds. Whistler's painted peacocks cover the walls and ceiling.

The attractive courtyard of the Freer Gallery of Art

National Museum of American History ⓫

The National Museum of American History preserves a collection of artifacts from the nation's past. Among the 3 million holdings are the First Ladies' gowns (including Michelle Obama's inaugural ball gown), a 280-ton steam locomotive, and the original Star-Spangled Banner that flew over Fort McHenry in 1814. The museum is undergoing a program of renovation, with new exhibitions opening regularly.

Second Floor

★ Star-Spangled Banner
This flag is the symbol of America. It inspired Francis Scott Key to write the poem that became the US national anthem. Visitors can view the flag through a window wall.

★ The First Ladies at the Smithsonian
Always a popular exhibition, this is a selection of gowns worn by America's First Ladies, such as this white-silk chiffon gown, worn by Helen Taft in 1909.

Mall Entrance

KEY TO FLOOR PLAN

- ☐ Transportation and technology
- ☐ Science and innovation
- ☐ American Ideals
- ☐ American lines
- ☐ American wars and politics
- ☐ Entertainment, sports and music
- ☐ Non exhibition space

STAR EXHIBITS

- ★ America on the Move
- ★ The Price of Freedom: Americans at War
- ★ The First Ladies at the Smithsonian
- ★ Star-Spangled Banner

Bon Appétit! Julia Child's Kitchen at the Smithsonian
Visitors can see chef and author Julia Child's legendary kitchen, which has been carefully packed and reassembled in the museum.

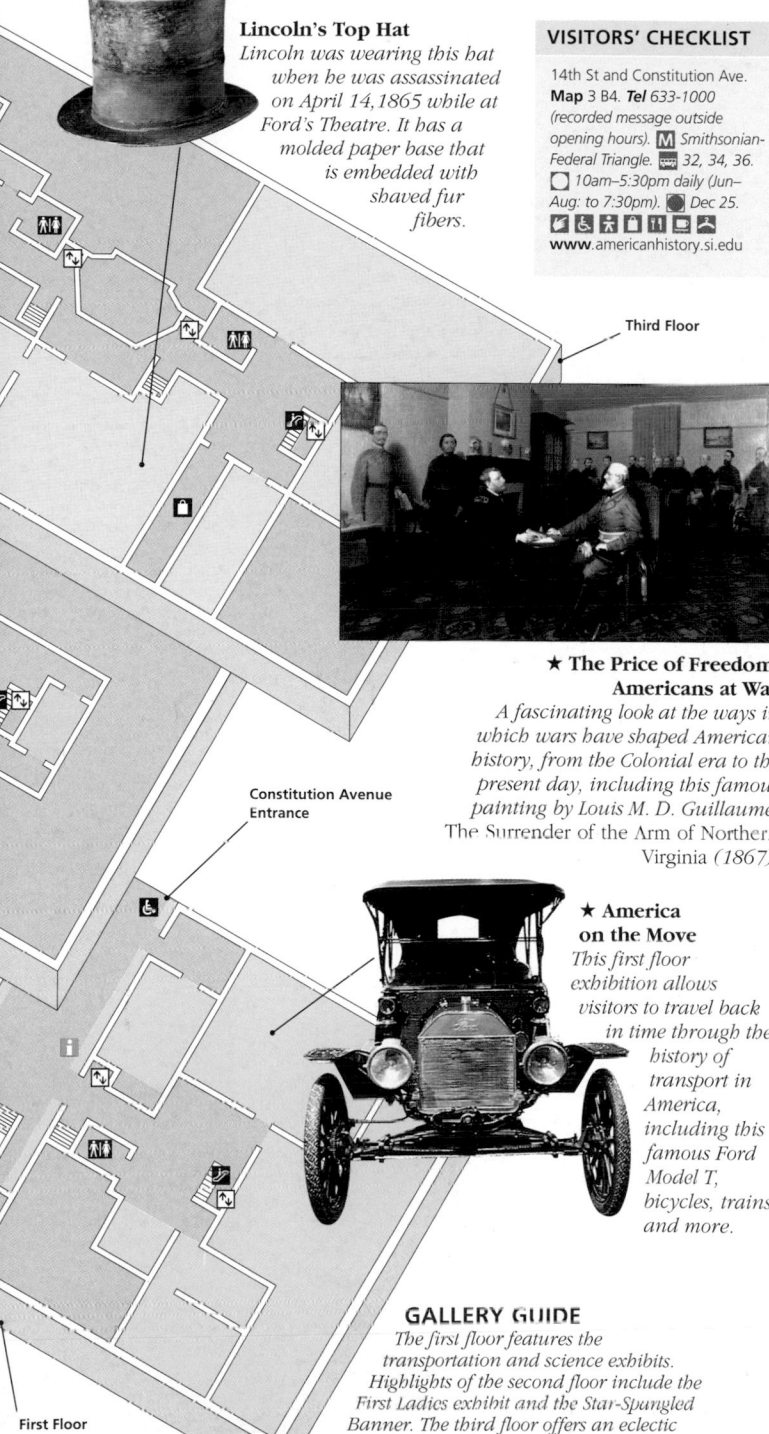

Lincoln's Top Hat
Lincoln was wearing this hat when he was assassinated on April 14, 1865 while at Ford's Theatre. It has a molded paper base that is embedded with shaved fur fibers.

Third Floor

★ The Price of Freedom: Americans at War
A fascinating look at the ways in which wars have shaped American history, from the Colonial era to the present day, including this famous painting by Louis M. D. Guillaume, The Surrender of the Arm of Northern Virginia (1867).

Constitution Avenue Entrance

★ America on the Move
This first floor exhibition allows visitors to travel back in time through the history of transport in America, including this famous Ford Model T, bicycles, trains, and more.

GALLERY GUIDE
The first floor features the transportation and science exhibits. Highlights of the second floor include the First Ladies exhibit and the Star-Spangled Banner. The third floor offers an eclectic selection including the American Presidency: A Glorious Burden, and military displays.

First Floor

Exploring the National Museum of American History

The collections at the National Museum of American History are so diverse that a visitor could ricochet from exhibit to exhibit, running out of time and patience before seeing the entire collection. The best approach is to be selective; there is simply too much to take in during one visit. Whether you head straight for the First Ladies' gowns or spend time viewing the collections of money, medals, musical instruments, and presidential artifacts, planning is the key to a successful visit.

The museum's modern façade on Madison Drive

FIRST FLOOR

Transported from its original location in Cambridge, Massachussetts, Julia Child's famous kitchen has been faithfully reassembled as **Bon Appétit! Julia Child's Kitchen at the Smithsonian**. When Child moved back to her home state of California in 2001, she donated the contents of her custom-designed kitchen including small utensils, personal cookbooks, copper pots, the stainless steel kitchen sink, and her six-burner Garland commercial range. The kitchen, which Child used as the set for three television shows and as the testing ground for many recipes featured in her cookbooks, comprises more than 1,200 individual pieces.

America on the Move is the museum's largest single exhibition and tells the story of how trains, streetcars, and automobiles have shaped American lives. Exhibits include the locomotive that pulled Franklin D. Roosevelt's funeral train, a 40-ft (12-m) section of pavement from the legendary Route 66, a 1903 Winton, Ford's *Model T*, and a Hot Rod.

The **Science in American Life** exhibition explores the impact of scientific discovery on everyday life, allowing visitors to explore concepts such as DNA fingerprinting and phenomena such as global warming and radioactivity.

One of the biggest draws in this exhibition is the **Spark! Lab**, which is popular with all ages. Here you can investigate various scientific subjects, such as the mysteries of DNA and radioactive hotspots, and learn how to use lasers for incredibly accurate measuring of distances, how to transmit the human voice, and all about the techniques used in the conservation of the Star-Spangled Banner. Activities correlate to exhibits in the rest of the museum. All children visiting the Spark! Lab must be accompanied by an adult. The Lab includes a section for children under five. Tickets are required on weekends and other busy times (it is best to check the times with the museum first).

Elsewhere on the first floor visitors can explore **Lighting a Revolution**, which looks at electricity and electrical invention in the 20th century, and illuminates the differences in the process of invention between Thomas Edison's time and our own.

For those with an interest in all things mechanical, the **Power Machinery Hall** is a must. This exhibition features examples of the machines that made America a world leader in industrial production, and contains models and actual examples of engines, turbines, pumps, and more. Perhaps the most famous machine of all is the **John Bull Locomotive** in the East Wing, the oldest operative self-propelled locomotive in the world. The **Invention at Play** exhibit explores the similarities between the way children and adults play, and the impact play has on invention.

SECOND FLOOR

Dominating the West Wing of the second floor is one of the museum's most popular

1950 Buick Super sedan displayed in America on the Move

The kitchen of 16 Elm Street, rebuilt in the museum as it was in the 1940s

exhibits, where fashion meets history: **The First Ladies at the Smithsonian** is a collection of gowns worn by some of the nation's most iconic presidential wives. The most recent addition is Michelle Obama's white chiffon gown worn to the 2009 inaugural ball. It was made by a relatively unknown designer, Jason Wu.

The West Wing also contains **Within These Walls...** This exhibition tells the story of American history through the domestic lives of the families who lived at 16 Elm Street in Ipswich, Massachusetts, from the mid-1760s to 1945. The walls of this extraordinary house saw American colonists forging a new way of living, the birth of a revolution, community activists united against slavery, a family on the home front in World War II, and more.

Communities in a Changing Nation: The Promise of 19th-Century America takes a look at America's history through the lives of different communities – industrial workers in Bridgeport, Connecticut; Jewish immigrants in Cincinnati, Ohio; and slaves and free blacks in South Carolina. Through hundreds of photographs, stories, objects, and illustrations, visitors can learn about the challenges and successes that made up the lives of these different groups of people.

In the East Wing of the second floor, visitors can see the legendary **Star-Spangled Banner** that flew over Fort McHenry in 1814 and inspired Francis Scott Key to write the poem that was later to become the national anthem. Also on the second floor is the **National Museum of African-American History and Culture Gallery**, which is dedicated to showcasing some of the exhibits that will feature in what will be the Smithsonian's newest museum, currently under construction.

Teddy Bear, dating from 1903

THIRD FLOOR

The largest exhibition on this floor is **The Price of Freedom: Americans at War** in the East Wing. It explores the nation's military history, from the French and Indian War in the 1750s to recent conflicts in Afghanistan and Iraq. The exhibition features a restored Vietnam-era Huey helicopter, uniforms from the Civil War, a World War II jeep, and General Colin Powell's battle dress uniform from Operation Desert Storm.

The gunboat *Philadelphia* is located on the third floor. Sunk by the British in 1776, the 54-ft (16-m), 29-ton timber boat rested on the bottom of Lake Champlain until it was found and recovered in 1935.

The **American Presidency: A Glorious Burden** displays over 400 objects that represent the lives and office of the presidency. Artifacts include the portable desk on which Thomas Jefferson wrote the Declaration of Independence, and the top hat worn by President Lincoln the night he was shot.

Also here is a delightful teddy bear. The name of the bear was inspired by President Theodore "Teddy" Roosevelt, who, while out hunting one day, refused to shoot a bear cub that had been captured for him. A cartoon appeared in the *Washington Post* the next day, which inspired the production of a range of bears, named Teddy Bears.

In the West Wing of the third floor, the **Treasures of Popular Culture** exhibition examines how sport, music, and entertainment have shaped American life. Highlights include a 1955 hand and rod puppet of Kermit the Frog created by Jim Henson and the ruby slippers worn by Judy Garland in the film *The Wizard of Oz*.

"We'll have lots to eat this winter, won't we Mother?"

Grow your own Can your own

Office of War information poster

Washington Monument ⑫

Constructed of 36,000 pieces of marble and granite, the Washington Monument remains one of the most recognizable monuments in the capital. Funds for this tribute to the first president of the United States initially came from individual citizens. A design by Robert Mills was chosen, and construction began in 1848. When the money ran out, the building work stopped for 25 years. Then, in 1876, President Ulysses S. Grant approved an act authorizing the completion of the project. (A slight change in the color of stone marks the point where construction resumed.) The Monument has been thoroughly cleaned, cracks have been sealed, chipped stone patched, and the 193 commemorative stones repaired.

VISITORS' CHECKLIST

Independence Ave at 17th St, SW. **Map** 2 F5 & 3 B4. **Tel** 42 6841. **M** Smithsonian. 13 52. 9am–5pm daily (free timed tickets are handed out from 8:30am, or can be ordered online). Jul 4, Dec 25. **www**.nps.gov/wamo

Viewing window

The Marble Capstone
The capstone weighs 3,300 pou (2,000 kg) and is topped by an aluminum pyramid. Restoratio the monument was carried out 1934 as part of President Roose Public Works Project (see p23).

Elevator taking visitors to top

The two-tone stonework indicates the point at which construction stopped in 1858 and then began again in 1876.

Commemorative stones inside the monument are donations from individuals, societies, states, and nations.

50 flagpoles surrounding monument

The Original Design
Although the original design included a circular colonnade around the monument, lack of funds prohibited its construction.

View of the Monument
The gleaming white stone of the restored monument makes it clearly visible from almost all over the city. The views from the top of the monument across Washington are stunning.

Restoration
Specially designe scaffolding encase the monument du its two year progr of repair and clea

The colonnaded domed Jefferson Memorial, housing the bronze statue

United States Holocaust Memorial Museum ⑬

See pp80–81.

Bureau of Engraving and Printing ⑭

14th and C St, SW. **Map** 3 B5.
Tel 874-2330. Ⓜ *Smithsonian.*
⏰ *8:30am–3:30pm Mon–Fri
(Apr–Aug: 8:30am–7:30pm).* ◗
Week after Christmas, Federal hols.
⑁ ⓘ www.moneyfactory.gov

Until 1863, individual banks were responsible for printing American money. A shortage of coins and the need to finance the Civil War led to the production of standardized bank notes, and the Bureau of Engraving and Printing was founded. Initially housed in the basement of the Treasury Building *(see p112)*, the bureau was moved to its present location in 1914. It prints over $140 billion a year, as well as stamps, federal documents, and White House invitations. Coins are not minted here, but in a federal facility in Philadelphia.

The 40-minute tour includes a short film, and a walk through the building to view the printing processes and checks for defects. Also on display are bills that are out of circulation, counterfeit money, and a special $100,000 bill. The Visitor Center has a gift shop, videos, and exhibits.

Jefferson Memorial ⑮

South bank of the Tidal Basin
Map 3 B5. *Tel 426-6841.*
Ⓜ *Smithsonian.* ◗ *24 hours daily.*
◗ *Dec 25. Interpretive talks.*
⑁ ⓘ www.nps.gov/thje

Thomas Jefferson *(see p166)* was a political philisopher, architect, musician, book collector, scientist, horticulturist, diplomat, inventor and the third American president, from 1801 to 1809. He also played a significant part in drafting the Declaration of Independence in 1776.

Statue of Jefferson

The idea for the memorial came from President Franklin Delano Roosevelt, who felt that Jefferson was as important as Lincoln. Designed by John Russell Pope, this Neo-Classical memorial was dedicated in 1943 and covers an area of 2.5 acres. At the time, metal was being strictly rationed so the standing statue of Jefferson had to be cast in plaster. After World War II, the statue was recast in bronze and the plaster version was moved.

Etched on the walls of the memorial are Jefferson's words from the Declaration of Independence as well as other writings. The impressive bronze statue of Jefferson is 19 ft (6 m) high and weighs 10,000 lb.

Tidal Basin ⑯

Boathouse: 1501 Maine Ave, SW.
Map 2 F5 & 3 A5. Ⓜ *Smithsonian.*
Paddle-boats: *Tel 479-2426.*
◗ *Mar–Oct: 10am 6pm.* ⑁
www.tidalbasinpaddleboats.com

The Tidal Basin was built in 1897 to catch the overflow from the Potomac River and prevent flooding. In 1912, hundreds of cherry trees, given by the Japanese government, were planted along the shores of the man-made lake. However, during the two weeks when the cherry trees bloom (between mid-March and mid-April) chaos reigns around the Tidal Basin. The area is filled with cars and busloads of people photographing the sight. The only way to avoid the gridlock is to see the blossoms at dawn. The Tidal Basin reverts to a relatively quiet park after the blossoms have fallen and the hordes depart. Paddle-boats can be rented from the boathouse on Maine Ave.

The banks of the Tidal Basin, with Jefferson Memorial in the distance

United States Holocaust Memorial Museum ⑬

The US Holocaust Memorial Museum, opened in 1993, bears witness to the systematic persecution and murder in Europe of six million Jews and others deemed undesirable by the Third Reich, including homosexuals and the disabled. The exhibition space ranges from the intentionally claustrophobic to the soaringly majestic. The museum contains 2,500 photographs, 1,000 artifacts, 53 video monitors, and 30 interactive stations that contain graphic and emotionally disturbing images of violence, forcing visitors to confront the horror of the Holocaust. While Daniel's Story is suitable for children of eight years and up, the permanent exhibition is not recommended for the under 12s.

★ **Hall of Remembrance**
The Hall of Remembrance house an eternal flame that pays homage to the victims of the Holocaust.

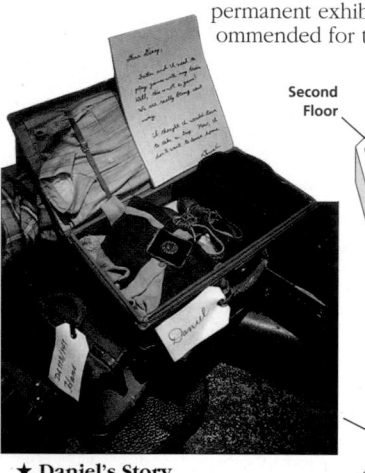

★ **Daniel's Story**
This exhibit, aimed at children between the ages of eight and 12, tells the history of the Holocaust from the point of view of an eight-year-old Jewish boy in 1930s Germany.

Second Floor

First F

14th Entra

KEY TO FLOOR PLAN

▦	Concourse Level
▦	First Floor
▦	Second Floor
▦	Third Floor
▦	Fourth Floor

GALLERY GUIDE

The Holocaust Museum is meant to be experienced, not just seen. Starting from the top, footage, artifacts, photographs, and testimonies of survivors can be seen from the fourth to the second floors. The first floor has an interactive display, and the Concourse Level houses the Children's Tile Wall.

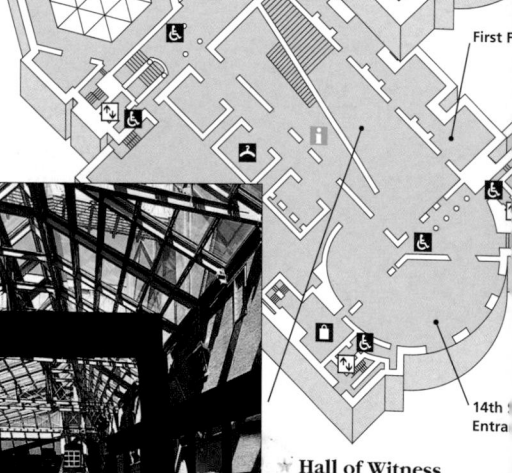

✳ **Hall of Witness**
The soaring central atrium features the Hall of Witness. The Museum aims to preser the memory of those who di

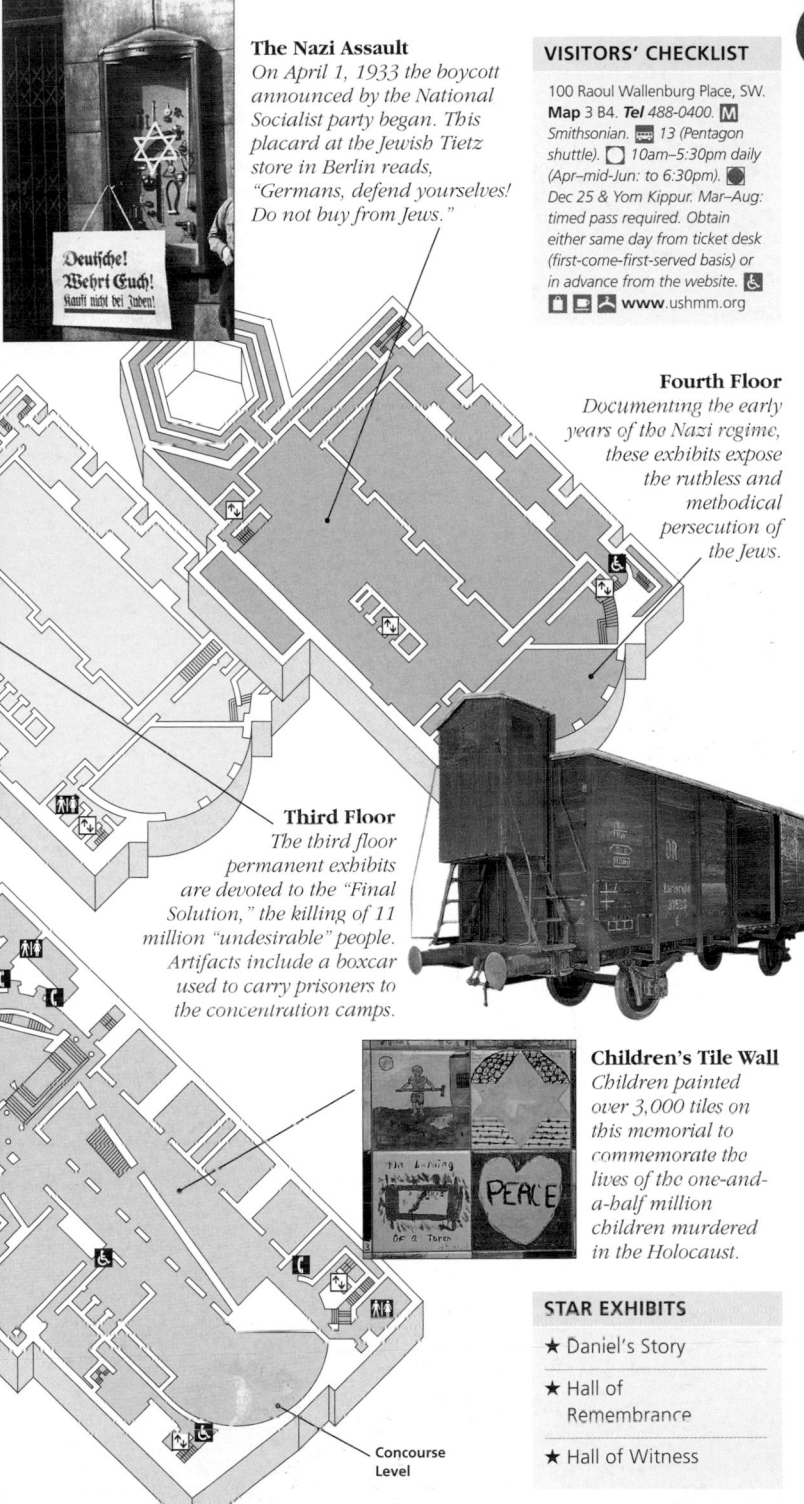

The Nazi Assault
On April 1, 1933 the boycott announced by the National Socialist party began. This placard at the Jewish Tietz store in Berlin reads, "Germans, defend yourselves! Do not buy from Jews."

VISITORS' CHECKLIST

100 Raoul Wallenburg Place, SW. **Map** 3 B4. *Tel* 488-0400. [M] Smithsonian. [bus] 13 (Pentagon shuttle). [clock] 10am–5:30pm daily (Apr–mid-Jun: to 6:30pm). [closed] Dec 25 & Yom Kippur. Mar–Aug: timed pass required. Obtain either same day from ticket desk (first-come-first-served basis) or in advance from the website. [access] [icons] www.ushmm.org

Fourth Floor
Documenting the early years of the Nazi regime, these exhibits expose the ruthless and methodical persecution of the Jews.

Third Floor
The third floor permanent exhibits are devoted to the "Final Solution," the killing of 11 million "undesirable" people. Artifacts include a boxcar used to carry prisoners to the concentration camps.

Children's Tile Wall
Children painted over 3,000 tiles on this memorial to commemorate the lives of the one-and-a-half million children murdered in the Holocaust.

STAR EXHIBITS

★ Daniel's Story

★ Hall of Remembrance

★ Hall of Witness

Concourse Level

The National WWII Memorial looking west towards the Lincoln Memorial

National WWII Memorial ⑰

17th St, NW, between Constitution Ave & Independence Ave. **Map** 2 E5. **Tel** 426-6841. M Smithsonian or Federal Triangle. ◯ 24 hours daily. ● Dec 25. & **www**.nps.gov/ nwwm The online Registry of Remembrances: **www**.wwiimemorial.com

Sixteen million Americans served in World War II and of them 400,000 died. The 4,000 gold stars, the "Field of Stars," on the Freedom Wall commemorate these war dead, and in front of the wall is the inscription: "Here We Mark the Price of Freedom." Millions more ordinary citizens contributed in some way to the war effort. The National World War II Memorial on the National Mall honors their service and sacrifice.

The establishment of the memorial, however, was not without controversy as to both location and scale. After a bill was first introduced in 1987 it took a further six years before the legislation made its way through Congress. President Clinton signed the bill into law on May 25, 1993 and then there followed a great debate over where it should be located. The Rainbow Pool site was chosen in October 1995 with the condition that the east-west vista from the Washington Monument to the Lincoln Memorial be preserved. Further delays followed because the Commission of Fine Arts criticized the mass and scale of the initial plans and asked that further consideration be given to preserving the vista. Work finally began in September 2001.

Design and construction was awarded to the firm of

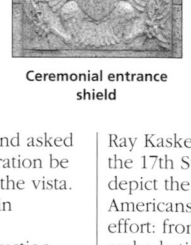

Ceremonial entrance shield

Leo A. Daly, and the design architect was Friedrich St. Florian (former dean of Rhode Island School of Design). Two 43-ft (13-m) pavilions stand on either side of the Rainbow Pool, marking the north and south entrances, and represent the Atlantic and Pacific theaters of war. Fifty-six granite pillars, one for each of the country's states and territories during that time, are adorned with bronze wreaths of oak leaves and wheat, which symbolize the nation's agricultural and industrial strength. Bas-relief panels created by sculptor Ray Kaskey line both sides of the 17th St entrance. They depict the many contributions Americans made to the war effort: from enlistment and embarkation to the Normandy landings, from Rosie the Riveter to medics in the field.

Words spoken by presidents and generals are inscribed throughout the memorial, including these by General Douglas MacArthur marking the war's end: "Today the guns are silent...The skies no longer rain death – the seas bear only commerce – men everywhere walk upright in the sunlight. The entire world is quietly at peace."

The memorial was officially opened to the public in April 2004 and on May 29 some 150,000 people, many of them veterans, joined in the dedication ceremony.

The Freedom Wall lined with 4,000 stars commemorating the US war dead

Vietnam Veterans Memorial ⓘ

21st St & Constitution Ave, NW. **Map** 2 E4. **Tel** 426-6841. **M** Smithsonian. ☐ 24 hours daily. ♿ **www**.nps. gov/vive

Maya Lin, a 21-year-old student at Yale University, submitted a design for the proposed Vietnam Veterans Memorial as part of her architecture course. One of 1,421 entries, Maya Lin's design was simple – two triangular black walls sinking into the earth at an angle of 125 degrees, one end pointing to the Lincoln Memorial, the other to the Washington Monument. On the walls would be inscribed the names of more than 58,000 Americans who died in the Vietnam war, in chronological order, from the first casualty in 1959 to the last in 1975.

Lin received only a B grade on the course, but she won the competition. Her design, called by some a scar on the earth, has become one of the most moving monuments on the Mall. Veterans and their families leave tokens of remembrance –

Touching names on the wall at the Vietnam Veterans Memorial

soft toys, poems, pictures, and flowers – at the site of the fallen soldier's name.

To mollify those opposed to the abstract memorial, a statue of three soldiers, sculpted by Frederick Hart, was added in 1984. Further lobbying led to the Vietnam Women's Memori-al, erected close by in 1993.

Korean War Veterans Memorial ⓘ

21st St & Independence Ave, SW. **Map** 2 E5. **Tel** 426-6841. **M** Smithsonian, Foggy Bottom. ☐ 24 hours daily. ♿ **www**.nps.gov/kwvm

The Korean War Veterans Memorial is a contro-versial tribute to a controversial war. Although 1.5 million Americans served in the conflict, war was never officially declared. It is often known as "The Forgotten War." Intense debate preceded the selection of the memorial's design. On July 27, 1995, the 42nd anniversary of the armistice that ended the war, the memorial was dedicated.

The Vietnam Women's Memorial

Nineteen larger-than-life stainless steel statues, a squad on patrol, are depicted moving towards the American flag as their symbolic objective. The soldiers are wearing ponchos because the Korean War was notorious for being fought in miserable weather conditions. On the south side is a polished black granite wall etched with the images of more than 2,400 veterans. An inscription above the Pool of Remembrance reads: "Our nation honors her sons and daughters who answered the call to defend a country they never knew and a people they never met."

The poignant statues of the Korean War Veterans Memorial

Franklin D. Roosevelt Memorial ⓴

Franklin Roosevelt once told Supreme Court Justice Felix Frankfurter, "If they are to put up any memorial to me, I should like it to be placed in the center of that green plot in front of the Archives Building. I should like it to consist of a block about the size of this," pointing to his desk. It took more than 50 years for a fitting monument to be erected, but Roosevelt's request for modesty was not heeded. Opened in 1997, this memorial is a mammoth park of four granite open-air rooms, one for each of Roosevelt's terms, with statuary and waterfalls. The president, a polio victim, is portrayed in a chair, with his dog Fala by his side.

The statue of Roosevelt, *by Neil Estern, is one of the memorial's most controversial elements as it shows the disabled president sitting in a wheelchair hidden by his Navy cape.*

Third room

The fourth room honors Roosevelt's life and legacy. A statue of his wife, Eleanor, stands in this room.

A relief of Roosevelt's funeral cortège *was carved into the granite wall by artist Leonard Baskin. It depicts the coffin on a horse-drawn cart, followed by the crowds of mourners walking behind.*

Dramatic waterfalls *cascade into a series of pools in the fourth room. The water reflects the peace that Roosevelt was so keen to achieve before his death.*

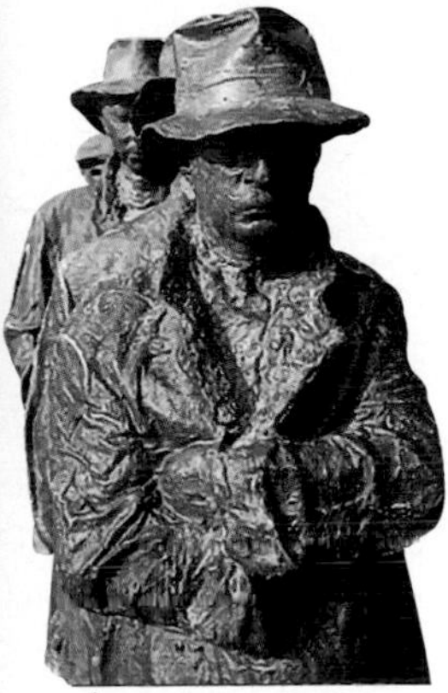

Hunger, a sculpture of figures in the breadline, *by George Segal, recalls the hard times of the Great Depression, during which Roosevelt was elected and reelected three times.*

VISITORS' CHECKLIST

West Basin Drive, SW. **Map** 3 A5. ***Tel*** *426-6841.* *Smithsonian.* *13.* *24 hours daily.* *Dec 25.* ***Interpretive programs and talks.*** **www**.nps.gov/fdrm

Second room

The first room commemorates FDR's first term and includes a bas-relief of his inaugural parade.

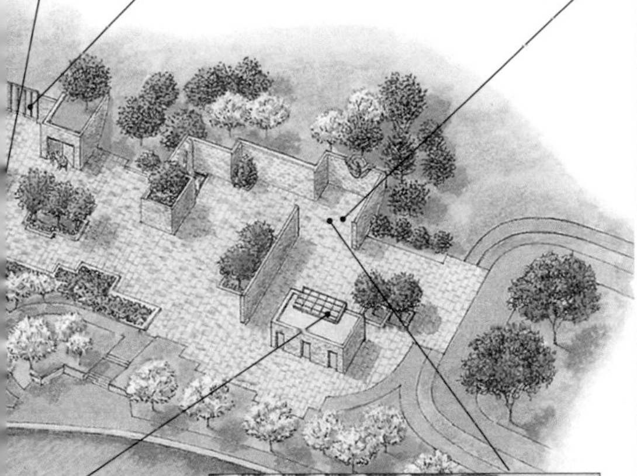

/isitor Center
:les an information
ınd a bookstore.
vheelchair that
used after he had
is also on display.

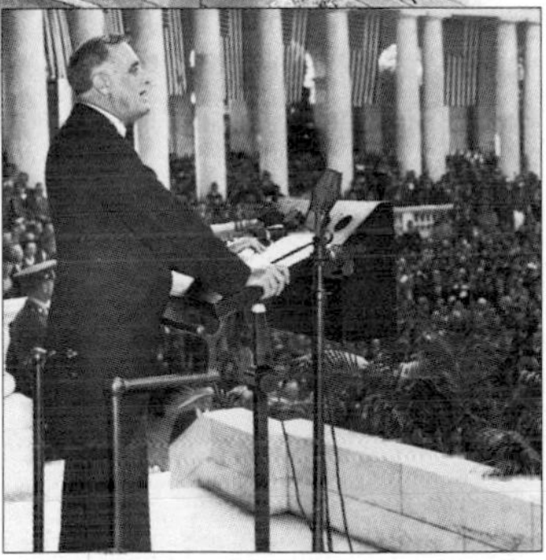

President Roosevelt *initiated the New Deal in the 1930s to create jobs and provide immediate relief during the Great Depression: "...treating the task as we would treat the emergency of war."*

Lincoln Memorial 21

Constitution Ave, between French & Bacon Drives. **Map** 2 E5. ***Tel*** *426-6841.* *Smithsonian, Foggy Bottom.* *24 hours daily.* **www**.nps.gov/linc

Many proposals were made for a memorial to President Abraham Lincoln. One of the least promising was for a monument on a swampy piece of land to the west of the Washington Monument. Yet this was to become one of the most awe inspiring sights in Washington. Looming over the Reflecting Pool is the seated figure of Lincoln in his Neo-classical "temple" with 36 Doric columns, one for each state at the time of Lincoln's death.

Before the monument could be built in 1914, the site had to be drained. Solid concrete piers were poured for the foundation so that the building could be anchored in bedrock. Architect Henry Bacon realized that the original 10-ft (3-m) statue by Daniel Chester French would be dwarfed inside the building, so it was nearly doubled in size. As a result, it had to be carved from 28 blocks of white marble.

Engraved on the south wall is Lincoln's Gettysburg Address *(see p163)*. Above it is a mural painted by Jules Guerin depicting the angel of truth freeing a slave. Dr. Martin Luther King, Jr.'s famous address, "I Have a Dream" *(see p97)*, was given from the steps of the memorial.

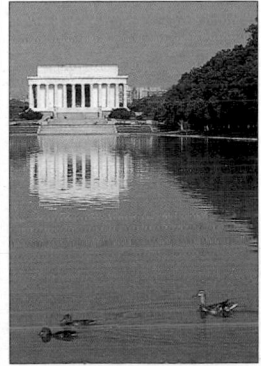

Lincoln Memorial, reflected in the still waters of the pool

PENN QUARTER

Bordered by the Capitol to the east and the White House to the west, Washington's Penn Quarter was the heart of the city one hundred years ago. F Street, the city's first paved road, bustled with shops, newspaper offices, bars, and churches, as well as horses and carriages. Penn Quarter was also an important residential neighborhood. The upper classes maintained elegant homes, while middle-class merchants lived above their shops. But by the 1950s suburbia had lured people away from the area, and in the 1980s Penn Quarter had become a mixture of boarded-up buildings and discount shops. The 1990s saw a dramatic change and the beginnings of regeneration, as the Verizon Center attracted new restaurants and stores.

Sculpture outside the Smithsonian American Art Museum

SIGHTS AT A GLANCE

Museums and Galleries
Carnegie Library Building ⓴
International Spy Museum ⓳
National Building Museum ⓲
National Museum of Women in the Arts ⓭
Newseum ❺
Smithsonian American Art Museum and the National Portrait Gallery pp98–101 ⓲

Statues and Fountains
Benjamin Franklin Statue ❽
Mellon Fountain ❶

Aquarium
National Aquarium ❿

Historic and Official Buildings
Ford's Theatre ⓯
Martin Luther King Memorial Library ⓰
National Archives ❷
National Theatre ⓬
Old Post Office ❼
Ronald Reagan Building ❻
Verizon Center ⓴
Willard Hotel ⓫

Districts, Streets, and Squares
Chinatown ⓱
Freedom Plaza ❾
Pennsylvania Avenue ❹

Memorials
National Law Enforcement Officers' Memorial ㉑
US Navy Memorial ❸

0 meters   500
0 yards   500

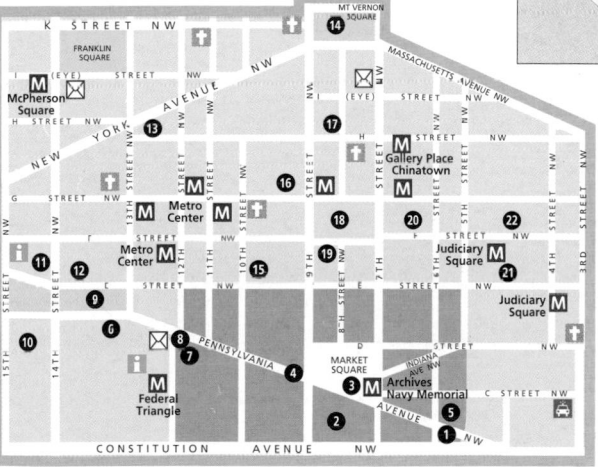

GETTING THERE
Penn Quarter is well served by several Metrorail stops: McPherson Square, Gallery Place-Chinatown, Metro Center, Judiciary Square, Archives-Navy Memorial/Penn Quarter, and Federal Triangle. The 32, 34, and 36 bus lines run along Pennsylvania Avenue.

KEY
▨ Street-by-street map pp88–9
Ⓜ Metro station
ℹ Tourist information
🚓 Police station
▨ Post office
✝ Church

◁ Statue of Benjamin Franklin outside the flag-festooned Old Post Office

Street-by-Street: Penn Quarter

In the mid-20th century, Pennsylvania Avenue, the main route for presidential inaugural parades, was tawdry and run down. It is now a grand boulevard worthy of L'Enfant's original vision. Pennsylvania Avenue links the White House to the US Capitol and is home to some of the city's main sights. Opposite the US Navy Memorial is the US National Archives, housing original copies of the Constitution and the Declaration of Independence. To the east are the Mellon Fountain and the National Gallery of Art. The Ronald Reagan Building was the site of the 1999 NATO summit, and the Old Post Office has an impressive clock tower.

★ Pennsylvania Avenue
Part of L'Enfant's original plan for the city, Pennsylvania Avenue was the first main street to be laid out in Washington. The thoroughfare reflects the architect's grandiose plans ④

Benjamin Franklin Statue
This inventor, statesman, writer, publisher, and man of genius is remembered as "printer, philosopher, philanthopist, patriot" ⑧

FBI Building

11TH STREET NW

PENNSYLVANIA AVENUE NW

12TH STREET NW

10TH STREET NW

Ronald Reagan Building
Built in 1997, this impressive edifice echoes the Classical Revival architecture of other buildings in the Federal Triangle. It houses a visitor information center ⑥

CONSTITUTION AVENUE NW

Interstate Commerce Commission

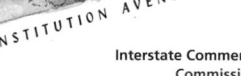

★ Old Post Office
This majestic granite building was completed in 1899. It now houses shops, offices, and a food court. The elegant clock tower measures 315 ft (96 m) in height ⑦

US Navy Memorial

The memorial at Market Square contains a huge etching of the world surrounded by low granite walls ❸

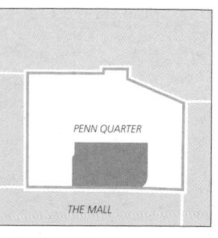

LOCATOR MAP
See Street Finder Maps 3 & 4

PENN QUARTER

THE MALL

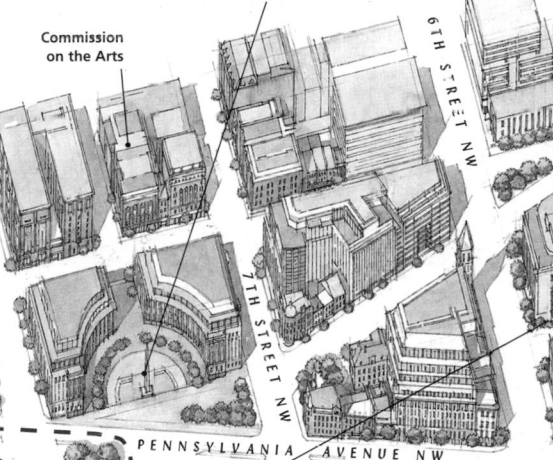

Commission on the Arts

6TH STREET NW

7TH STREET NW

9TH STREET NW

PENNSYLVANIA AVENUE NW

CONSTITUTION AVENUE NW

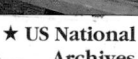

★ US National Archives

The Rotunda houses the National Archives' most precious documents, known as the "Charters of Freedom," including the Bill of Rights. A copy of England's Magna Carta is also on display ❷

Federal Trade Commission

Justice Department

Mellon Fountain

Located by the National Gallery of Art's West Building, this fountain is named after Andrew Mellon, an industrialist and art collector who founded the gallery in the 1930s ❶

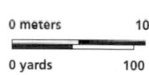

0 meters	100
0 yards	100

KEY

– – – Suggested route

STAR SIGHTS

★ Pennsylvania Avenue

★ Old Post Office

★ US National Archives

The cascading water of the Classical-style Mellon Fountain

Mellon Fountain ❶

Constitution Ave & Pennsylvania Ave, NW. **Map** 4 D4.
Ⓜ *Archives-Navy Memorial.*

Situated opposite the National Gallery of Art *(see pp58–61)*, this fountain commemorates the man who endowed the gallery with its collection. Andrew Mellon was Secretary of the Treasury and a financier and industrialist. At his death, his friends donated $300,000 to build the fountain, which was dedicated on May 9, 1952.

The three bronze basins with their cascades of water were inspired by a fountain seen in a public square in Genoa, Italy. On the bottom of the largest basin, the signs of the Zodiac are engraved in bas-relief. The Classical lines of the fountain echo the architectural style of the National Gallery of Art West Building.

National Archives ❷

7000 Constitution Ave, between 7th St & 9th St, NW. **Map** 3 D3. *Tel* 357-5000. Ⓜ *Archives-Navy Memorial/Penn Quarter.* ◯ *Mar 15–Labor Day: 10am–7pm daily; Sep–Mar: 10am–5:30pm daily.* ● *Sun, Thanksgiving, Dec 25.* 🖼 🎞 ♿
www.archives.gov

In the 1930s, Congress recognized the need to preserve the country's paper records before they deteriorated, were lost or were destroyed. The National Archives building, created for this purpose, was designed by John Russell Pope, architect of the National Gallery of Art and the Jefferson Memorial; it opened in 1934. This impressive library houses the most important historical and legal documents in the United States.

On display are all four pages of the *Constitution of the United States*, as well as the *Declaration of Independence*, the *Bill of Rights*, and a 1297 copy of the *Magna Carta*, which is on indefinite loan from Ross Perot.

Also in the National Archives are millions of documents, photographs, motion picture film, and sound recordings going back over two centuries. There is enough material, in fact, to fill around 250,000 filing cabinets. The National Archives and Records Administration (NARA) is the body responsible for cataloging, managing, and conserving all this material. Much of the Archives' information is now stored on computer. A permanent exhibition, "Public Vaults," offers people an interactive opportunity to explore a representative sample of the Archives' vast collection. The National Archives is of great importance as a research center. The Central Research Room is reserved for scholars, who can order copies of rare documents for study purposes. Copies of military records, immigration papers, slave transit documents, death certificates, and tax information are also available.

Statue outside the US National Archives

The impressive Neoclassical façade of the National Archives Building

The Constitution of the United States

In 1787, delegates from the 13 original American states convened in the city of Philadelphia to redraft the Articles of Confederation *(see p18)*. It soon became clear that an entirely new document was required, rather than a revised one. Weeks of debate grew into months, as delegates drafted the framework for a new country. Cooperation and compromise finally led to the creation of the Constitution, a document that outlines the powers of the central

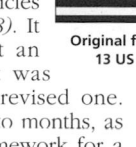
Original flag of the 13 US states

government and the makeup of Congress. One of the main issues, how to elect the representatives, was finally determined to be by direct voting by the people. Once signed, the new Constitution was sent to the states for review. Federalists and anti-Federalists debated fervently over its content in pamphlets, speeches, and articles. In the end, the majority of states ratified the Constitution, giving up some of their power in "order to form a more perfect union."

The Preamble of the Constitution of the United States

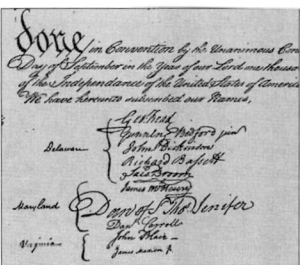
Signatures on the US Constitution

SIGNING OF THE CONSTITUTION
After many months of debate by the delegates to the Federal Convention, the Constitution was completed and signed by 39 of the 55 state delegates on September 17, 1787, at Assembly Hall in Philadelphia. The oldest delegate was 81-year-old Benjamin Franklin. James Madison, another signatory, played a major role in achieving the ratification of the new Constitution during the two years after it was signed.

James Madison

THE CONSTITUTION TODAY
The seven articles of the Constitution (of which the first three lay out the principles of government; *see pp28–9)* still determine the laws of the United States today. In addition there are Amendments. The first ten form the Bill of Rights, which includes such famous issues as the right to bear arms and the freedom of religion and of speech.

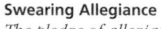

Swearing Allegiance
The pledge of allegiance to the flag was written in 1892 to mark the 400th anniversary of Columbus's discovery of America. Today it is recited daily by schoolchildren and by immigrants taking up American citizenship.

Public Demonstration
Citizens demonstrate their right to free speech by protesting against the Persian Gulf War.

A view down tree-lined Pennsylvania Avenue toward the US Capitol

US Navy Memorial ❸

Market Square, Pennsylvania Ave between 7th St & 9th St, NW. **Map** 3 C3. Ⓜ *Archives-Navy Memorial/Penn Quarter.* 🅱 **Naval Heritage Center** 701 Pennsylvania Ave, NW. **Tel** 737-2300. ◯ *9:30am–5pm daily.* ⬤ *Jan 1, Thanksgiving, Dec 25.* 📄 www.navymemorial.org

The memorial to the US Navy centers on the statue of a single sailor. Sculpted in bronze by Stanley Bleifeld in 1990, the figure provides a poignant tribute to the men and women who have served the US Navy.

The sculpture stands on a vast map of the world – the outlines of the countries are laid into the ground and protected by low walls. Four waterfalls and a group of flagpoles complete the memorial. There are free summer concerts by military bands in the square. Behind the memorial is the **Naval Heritage Center**, with historical exhibits and portraits of famous naval personnel, including John F. Kennedy. A free film "At Sea," is shown daily at noon.

The lone sailor of the US Navy Memorial

Pennsylvania Avenue ❹

Pennsylvania Ave. **Map** 3 A2 to 4 D4. Ⓜ *Federal Triangle, Archives-Navy Memorial.*

When architect and urban designer Pierre L'Enfant drew up his plans in 1789 for the capital city of the new United States, he imagined a grand boulevard running through the center of the city, from the presidential palace to the legislative building. For the first 200 years of its history, however, Pennsylvania Avenue fell sadly short of L'Enfant's dreams. In the early 19th century it was simply a muddy footpath through the woods. Paved in 1833, it became part of a neighborhood of boarding houses, shops, and hotels.

During the Civil War, the area deteriorated quickly into "saloons, gambling dens, lodging houses, quick-lunch rooms, cheap-jack shops, and catch penny amusement places" according to the *Works Progress Administration Guide to Washington.* When President John F. Kennedy's inaugural parade processed down Pennsylvania Avenue in 1961, Kennedy took one look at "America's Main Street" with its shambles of peep shows, pawn shops, and liquor stores and said, "It's a disgrace – fix it." This command by Kennedy provided the impetus to re-evaluate the future of Pennsylvania Avenue.

Almost 15 years later, Congress established the Pennsylvania Avenue Development Corporation – a public and private partnership that developed a comprehensive plan

PRESIDENTIAL INAUGURAL PARADES

The tradition of inaugural parades to mark a new president's coming-to-office started in 1809, when the military accompanied President James Madison from his Virginia home to Washington, DC. The first parade to include floats was held in 1841 for President William Henry Harrison. In 1985, freezing weather forced Ronald Reagan's inaugural ceremony indoors to the Capitol Rotunda. A record crowd of approximately 1.8 million attended the 2009 parade for Barack Obama. The Army Band traditionally leads the procession down Pennsylvania Avenue from the US Capitol to the White House.

President Franklin D. Roosevelt's third inaugural parade in 1941

The multistory building housing the Newseum

of revitalization. Today, Pennsylvania Avenue is a clean, tree-lined street. Parks, memorials, shops, theaters, hotels, museums, and assorted government buildings border the street on either side, providing a suitably grand and formal setting for all future presidential inaugural parades.

Newseum ❺

555 Pennsylvania Ave, NW. **Map** 4 F4. **Tel** 639-7386. Ⓜ *Archives-Navy Memorial.* ◯ *9am–5pm daily.* ◐ *Jan 1, Thanksgiving, Dec 25.*   🏛 🚻 www.newseum.org

This award-winning interactive news and media museum is housed in a beautiful building with a balcony that affords splendid views of the city. The Newseum features seven levels, 14 galleries, and 15 theaters that explore how and why news is made. The galleries span five centuries of news history and include up-to-the-second technology and hands-on exhibits. The gallery of Pulitzer Prize winning photographs is one of the highlights. Among the iconic images on display are the 1945 photograph documenting the raising of the US flag after the Battle of Iwo Jima and a 1969 photograph portraying the execution of a prisoner in Saigon, Vietnam. Other galleries deal with the history of the Berlin Wall and the events of 9/11. There is also an interactive newsroom where visitors can play the role of a reporter or broadcaster, and a moving memorial to journalists who have lost their lives in the line of duty. On the front of the building is an inscription of the First Amendment listing the five freedoms – religion, speech, press, assembly, and petition.

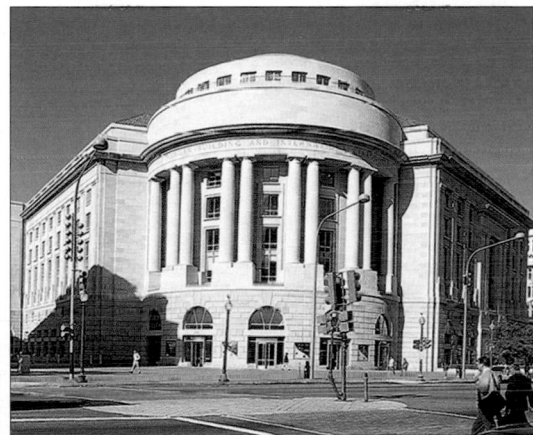

Sculpture from the Oscar Straus Memorial Fountain

Ronald Reagan Building ❻

1300 Pennsylvania Ave, NW. **Map** 3 B3. **Tel** 312-1300. Ⓜ *Federal Triangle.* ◯ *7am–7am Mon–Fri, 11am–6pm Sat; Mar 31–Aug 31: noon–6pm Sun.* ◐ *Federal hols.* 📷 *call 312-1647.* **Visitor Center Tel** 289-8317. 🚻 🏛   www. itcdc.com

The Ronald Reagan Building is a modern 3.1 million sq ft limestone structure that is Classical in appearance on the outside and modern on the inside. Completed in 1997, it was the most expensive federal building project ever undertaken. Designed by Pei Cobb Freed & Partners, architects of the US Holocaust Memorial Museum (*see pp80–81*) and the National Gallery of Art's East Wing, the building houses a mix of federal, trade, and public spaces. It is named after President Ronald Reagan, who authorized the construction in the late 1980s.

On the east end of the atrium is the largest neon sculpture North America – "Route Zenith," a creation of Keith Sonnier. Outside the building is the Oscar Straus Memorial Fountain, with sculpture by Adolph Alexander Weinman.

In summer the four-acre Woodrow Wilson Plaza, graced by sculptures by such artists as Martin Puryear and Stephen Rodin, is the venue for free concerts from noon to 1:30pm every weekday.

The building is the home of the Washington DC Visitor Information Center due to its location in the heart of the capital. The Center provides tour information and tickets to shows and events.

Mock-Classical entrance to the immense Ronald Reagan Building

Food court in the spectacular galleried hall of the Old Post Office

Postmaster general, writer, and scientist, Benjamin Franklin was also a key member of the committee that drafted the 1776 Declaration of Independence. As a diplomat to the court of Louis XVI of France, he went to Versailles in 1777 to gain support for the American cause of independence from Britain. Franklin returned to France in 1783 to negotiate the Treaty of Paris that ended the American Revolution *(see p18)*.

Stately ↑ of Benj, Frank

Old Post Office ❼

1100 Pennsylvania Ave, NW. **Map** 3 C3. *Tel* 289-4224. **M** *Federal Triangle.* ☐ Mar–Aug: 10am–8pm Mon–Sat, noon–7pm Sun; Sep–Feb: 10am–7pm Mon–Sat, noon–6pm Sun. ● *Jan 1, Thanksgiving, Dec 25.* ☑ *tower only (call 606-8691).* ☐ ☐ **www.**oldpostofficedc.com

Built in 1899, the Old Post Office was Washington's first skyscraper. Soaring 12 stories above the city, it was a fireproof model of modern engineering with a steel frame covered in granite. The huge interior had 3,900 electric lights and its own generator, the first one to be used in the city. Its fanciful Romanesque architecture was fashionable at the time it was built, and the breathtaking hall, with its glass roof and balconies, remains a spectacular mixture of light, color, and gleaming metal.

In the 15 years following its construction, the Post Office became an object of controversy. Its turrets and arches, once praised by critics, were derided. The *New York Times* newspaper said the building looked like "a cross between a cathedral and a cotton mill." Government planners thought the Post Office building clashed with the Neoclassical architecture that dominated the rest of Washington. When the postal system moved its offices in 1934, there seemed

to be no reason to keep the architectural relic. Only a lack of funds during the Great Depression of the 1930s *(see p23)* prevented the Old Post Office from being torn down.

The building was occupied intermittently by various government agencies until the mid-1960s, when its decrepit condition again drew a chorus in favor of demolition. A Washington preservation group, Don't Tear It Down, promoted the historical significance of the Old Post Office, and it was spared once more.

The renovated building, commonly known as the Pavilion, is now home to a broad range of shops and restaurants. The Post Office clock tower has an observation deck rising 270 ft (82 m), above the city, giving one of the best views of Washington.

Benjamin Franklin Statue ❽

Pennsylvania Ave & 10th St, NW. **Map** 3 C3. **M** *Federal Triangle.*

Donated by publisher Stilson Hutchins (1839–1912), it was unveiled by Benjamin Franklin's great-granddaughter in 1889. The words "Printer, Philosopher, Patriot, Philanthropist" are inscribed on the four sides of the statue's pedestal in tribute to this man of diverse talents.

Freedom Plaza ❾

Pennsylvania Ave between 13th St & 14th St, NW. **Map** 3 B3. **M** *Federal Triangle, Metro Center.*

Freedom Plaza was conceived as part of a Pennsylvania Avenue redevelopment plan in the mid-1970s. Designed by Robert Venturi and Denise Scott Brown, and completed in 1980, the plaza displays Pierre L'Enfant's original plan for Washington in black and white stone embedded in the ground. Around the edge are engraved quotations about the new city from Walt Whitman and President Wilson, among others.

Freedom Plaza provides a dramatic entry to Pennsylvania Avenue *(see pp92–3).* On the

The large-scale reproduction of L'Enfant's city plans, Freedom Plaza

north side of the plaza, where Pennsylvania Avenue leads into E Street, are the **Warner Theatre** and the **National Theatre**. South of the plaza is the Beaux Arts **District Building** (housing government employees). The Freedom Plaza is a popular site for festivals and political protests.

National Aquarium ⑩

Commerce Building, 14th St & Constitution Ave, NW. **Map** 3 B3. **Tel** 482-2825. Ⓜ Federal Triangle. 🕙 9am–5pm daily. 🌑 Thanksgiving, Dec 25. ⌨ 📷 ♿ www.nationalaquarium.org

Originally located in 1873 at Woods Hole, Massachusetts (a major center for marine biology), the National Aquarium was moved to Washington in 1888 in order to make it more accessible. Since 1931 it has been located in the US Department of Commerce Building, and today the aquarium is home to around 1,200 specimens and 200 different species.

Green Turtle at the National Aquarium

The Aquarium has a wide range of freshwater and saltwater fish on display, such as nurse sharks, piranhas, and moray eels, and also a number of reptiles and various species of amphibians, all displayed in simulated "natural environments."

There are daily public feedings of the sharks and piranhas, as well as talks.

Willard Hotel ⑪

1401 Pennsylvania Ave, NW. **Map** 3 B3. **Tel** 628-9100, (800) 327-1747. Ⓜ Metro Center. ♿ www.washington.interconti.com

There has been a hotel on this site since 1816. Originally called Tennison's, the hotel was housed in six adjacent two-story buildings. Refurbished in 1847, it was managed by hotel keeper

Henry Willard, who gave his name to the hotel in 1850. Many famous people stayed here during the Civil War (1861–65), including the writer Nathaniel Hawthorne, who was covering the conflict for a magazine, and Julia Ward Howe who wrote the popular Civil War standard *The Battle Hymn of the Republic*. The word "lobbyist" is said to have been coined because it was known by those seeking favors that President Ulysses S. Grant went to the hotel's lobby to smoke his after-dinner cigar.

The present 330-room building, designed by the architect of New York's Plaza Hotel, Henry Hardenbergh, was completed in 1904. It was the most fashionable place to stay in the city until the end of World War II, when the surrounding neighborhood fell into decline. For 20 years it was boarded up and faced demolition. A coalition, formed of preservationists and the Pennsylvania Avenue Development Corporation, worked to restore the Beaux Arts building, and it finally reopened in renewed splendor in 1986.

No other hotel can rival the Willard's grand lobby, with its 35 different kinds of marble, polished wood, and petal-shaped concierge station. There is a style café, a bar, and a restaurant called The Willard Room.

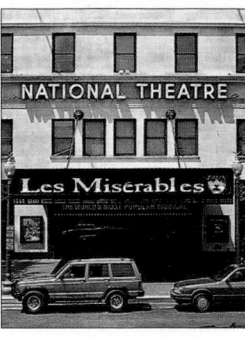

Façade of the National Theatre on E Street

National Theatre ⑫

1321 Pennsylvania Ave, NW. **Map** 3 B3. **Tel** 628-6161, 800-447-7400. Ⓜ Metro Center, Federal Triangle. ♿ www.nationaltheatre.org

The present National Theatre is the sixth theater to occupy this Pennsylvania Avenue site and the oldest cultural institution in the city. The first four theaters burned down, and the fifth one was replaced by the current building in 1922. The National Theatre hosts Broadway-bound productions and touring groups. The National is known as an "actor's theater" because of its excellent acoustics (even a whisper on stage can be heard in the top balcony). It is haunted by the ghost of 19th-century actor John McCullough, murdered by a fellow actor and buried under the stage. There are free performances for children every Monday morning.

Peacock Alley, one of the Willard Hotel's luxuriously decorated corridors

National Museum of Women in the Arts

1250 New York Ave, NW. **Map** 3 C3.
Tel 783-5000, 800-222-7270.
Ⓜ *Metro Center.* ◯ *10am–5pm
Mon–Sat, noon–5pm Sun.*
◉ *Jan 1, Thanksgiving, Dec 25.*
◉ *for groups (call 783-7996).*
◉◉ ◉ ◉ ◉ **www**.nmwa.org

This museum of women's art houses works that span five centuries, from the Renaissance to the present day. The collection was started in the 1960s by Wilhelmina Holladay and her husband, who gathered paintings, sculpture, and photography from all over the world.

The museum operated out of the Holladays' private residence for several years, until it acquired a more permanent home in this Renaissance Revival landmark building, formerly a Masonic Temple. The collection has as its highlights masterpieces by female American artists. Some of the outstanding works on display from the 19th century include *The Bath* (1891) by Mary Cassatt and *The Cage* (1885) by Berthe Morisot. Among the works by 20th-century artists are *Bacchus 3* (1978) by Elaine de Kooning and *Self-Portrait Between the Curtains, Dedication to Trotsky* (1937) by Mexican artist Frida Kahlo. The museum shop sells a range of gifts, also created by women.

Impressive exterior of the National Museum of Women in the Arts

Carnegie Library Building ⓭

801 K St (Mount Vernon Sq), NW.
Map 3 C2. *Tel* 383-1850. Ⓜ *Gallery
Place–Chinatown, Mt Vernon Sq.*
Kiplinger Research Library *Tel*
383-1829. ◯ *10am–5pm Tue–Sat.*
◉ *Jan 1, Jul 4, Thanksgiving, Dec
25.* ◉ ◉ ◉ **www**.historydc.org

The Carnegie Library Building was once Washington's central library. It hosts various events and exhibitions, and in 2003 the Washington Historical Society moved its headquarters to the building and the City

Museum of Washington, DC was created. The state-of-the-art Kiplinger Research Library and Reading Room houses extensive collections of historic materials, including rare publications, prints, maps, photographs, manuscripts, and memorabilia. There are also lectures, workshops, and videos. Washington Perspectives, an overview exhibit, features a giant map of the city set into the floor.

Painting of John Wilkes Booth poised to shoot Abraham Lincoln

Ford's Theatre ⓯

511 10th St between E St & F St, NW.
Map 3 C3. *Tel* 426-6924. Ⓜ *Gallery
Place–Chinatown, Metro Center.*
◯ *9am–5pm daily (except matinee
or rehearsal days – call ahead).* ◉
◉ *Dec 25.* **Petersen House**
◯ *9:30am–5:30pm daily with free
timed ticket.* ◉ *Dec 25.* ◉ **www**.
nps.gov/foth

John T. Ford, a theatrical producer, built this small jewel of a theater in 1863. Washington was a Civil War boomtown, and the theater, located in the thriving business district,

enjoyed great popularity. The fate of the theater was sealed, however, on April 14, 1865, when President Abraham Lincoln was shot here by John Wilkes Booth while watching a performance. Across the road from the theater, **Petersen House**, where the wounded president died the next morning, has been preserved as a museum.

After the tragedy, people stopped patronizing the theater and Ford was forced to sell the building to the federal government a year later. It was left to spiral into decay for nearly a century until the government decided to restore it to its original splendor.

The theater now stages small productions. The Presidential Box is permanently decorated in Lincoln's honor.

Exterior of Ford's Theatre, site of the shooting of President Lincoln

Martin Luther King Memorial Library ⑯

01 G St at 9th St, NW. **Map** 3 C3.
el 727-0321. Ⓜ Gallery Place–
Chinatown, Metro Center. ◯ noon–
pm Mon–Tue, 9:30am–5:30pm
Wed–Sat, 1–5pm Sun. ◯ Federal
ols. ♿ www.dclibrary.org/mlk

Washington's Martin Luther
King Memorial Library is the
only example of the architec-
ure of Ludwig Mies van der
Rohe in the city. A prominent
igure in 20th-century design,
van der Rohe finalized his
plans for the library shortly
before his death in 1969. It was
named in honor of Dr. Martin
Luther King Jr. at the request
of the library's trustees when
t opened in 1972, replacing
he small and out-dated
Carnegie Library as the city's
central public library.

Architecturally, the building
s a classic example of van der
Rohe's theory of "less is more."
t is an austere, simple box
shape with a recessed entrance
obby. Inside, there is a mural
depicting the life of Dr. Martin
Luther King Jr., the leader
of the Civil Rights Movement,
painted by artist Don Miller.

The library sponsors concerts
and readings, as well as a program of children's events.

The "Friendship Archway" spanning H Street in the heart of Chinatown

Chinatown ⑰

6th St to 8th St & G St to H St, NW.
Map 3 C3 & 4 D3. Ⓜ Gallery Place-
Chinatown.

The small area in Washington
known as Chinatown covers
just six square blocks. Formed
around 1930, it has never been
very large and today houses
about 500 Chinese residents.
The area was reinvigorated
with the arrival of the adjacent
Verizon Center (see p102) in
1997. H Street is particularly
lively, with many shops and a
selection of good restaurants.

The "Friendship Archway,"
a dramatic gateway over H
Street at the junction with 7th
Street, marks the center of the
Chinatown area. Built in 1986,
it was paid for by Washington's
sister city, Beijing, as a token
of esteem, and is based on
the architecture of the Qing
Dynasty (1649–1911). Its seven
roofs, topped by 300 painted
dragons, are balanced on a
steel and concrete base,
making it the largest single-
span Chinese arch in the
world. It is lit up at night.

During the Chinese New
Year celebrations in late
January or early Febuary, the
area comes alive with parades,
dragon dances, and live musical
performances (see p59).

DR. MARTIN LUTHER KING, JR.

A charismatic speaker and proponent of
Mahatma Gandhi's theories of non-violence,
Dr. Martin Luther King, Jr. was a black
Baptist minister and leader of the the civil
rights movement in the United States.

Born in Atlanta, Georgia in 1929, King's
career in civil rights began with the 1955
Montgomery, Alabama bus boycott – a protest
of the city's segregated transit system. The
movement escalated to protests at schools,
restaurants, and hotels that did not admit
blacks. King's methods of non-violence were
often met with police dogs and brutal tactics.

The culmination of the movement was the
March on Washington on August 28, 1963,
when 200,000 people gathered at the Lincoln
Memorial in support of civil rights. The highlight of this event was King's "I Have a
Dream" speech, calling for support of the
movement. A direct result was the passing by
Congress of the civil rights legislation in 1964,
and King was awarded the Nobel Peace Prize
the same year. In 1968 he was assassinated
in Memphis, Tennessee, triggering riots in
100 American cities, including Washington.

Dr. King speaking at the Lincoln Memorial

Smithsonian American Art Museum and the National Portrait Gallery ⑱

Nowhere in Washington is the city's penchant to copy Greek and Roman architecture more obvious than in the former US Patent Office Building, now the home of the Smithsonian American Art Museum and the National Portrait Gallery (NPG). The wonderfully ornate 1836 building was converted into the twin museums in 1968. The American Art Museum contains a permanent collection of works by more than 7,000 American artists. The NPG is America's family album, featuring paintings, photographs, and sculptures of thousands of famous Americans.

Façade of the building, housing the main entrance to both galleries

★ ACHELOUS AND HERCULES

This painting (1947) by Thomas Hart Benton (1889–1975) is a mythological analogy of early American life. Interpreted in many ways, it is widely accepted that Hercules is man taming the wild, then enjoying the results of his labors.

Hercules tries to capture the bull.

Achelous, the rive god, appears as a bull being wrestled by Hercules, representing the struggle of the American people

An African-American is depicted climbing over a fence to the idealized equality of America.

★ **Among the Sierra Nevada, California**
Albert Bierstadt painted this Western landscape in 1867–8. He was later criticized by some for not offering a topographically correct view of the West.

Old Bear, a Medicine Man
This vibrant painting by George Caitlin dates from 1832. Native Americans were a popular choice of subject matter for this artist.

Mary Cassatt
This portrait by Edgar Degas, painted c.1882, depicts his fellow artist Mary Cassatt playing cards.

"Casey" Stengel
This bronze sculpture of the baseball great was created by Rhoda Sherbell in 1981 from a 1965 cast.

John Singleton Copley
This self-portrait of the artist, who was largely known for his depictions of others, was painted c.1780.

The man working in the field represents the people of America, enjoying the fruits of the land after laboring.

Hercules is about to break off the bull's horn.

The horn is transformed into a cornucopia, or horn of plenty, symbolizing America as a land of abundance and opportunity.

★ Manhattan
This 1932 oil painting by Georgia O'Keeffe was created for an exhibition at New York's Museum of Modern Art. It portrays her vision of the city's architectural landscape.

In the Garden
This charming depiction of the poet Celia Thaxter is by the artist Childe Hassam and was painted in 1892.

STAR SIGHTS

★ Achelous and Hercules

★ Manhattan

★ Among the Sierra Nevada, California

Exploring the Smithsonian American Art Museum

The Smithsonian American Art Museum was established in 1829 and is the first federal art collection. It began with gifts from private collections and art organizations that existed in Washington, DC before the founding of the Smithsonian in 1846. The museum is a center for America's cultural heritage, with more than 42,000 artworks spanning 300 years. The Renwick Gallery, the museum's branch of decorative arts and craft, is nearby *(see p113)*.

A bottlecap giraffe

19TH- AND EARLY 20TH-CENTURY ART

Some of the highlights in this collection from the last two centuries are the Thomas Moran Western landscapes and those of Albert Bierstadt. This subject matter can be seen in *Among the Sierra Nevada, California* (1867–8), Bierstadt's evocative depiction of the landscape.

Many of the American artists such as Albert Pinkham Ryder, Winslow Homer, and John Singer Sargent, were contemporaries to the Impressionists. Homer's *High Cliffs, Coast of Maine* (1894) is a dramatic meeting of land and sea. Seascapes were also a popular subject for Ryder. *Jonah*, painted c.1885, illustrates the Bible story of Jonah and the whale, depicting Jonah floundering in the sea during a storm, overlooked by God.

The museum holds hundreds of paintings of Native Americans, many of them works by George Caitlin. This was also a popular subject for

Charles Bird King and John Mix Stanley. American Impressionists are also well represented in the museum, including Mary Cassatt, William Merritt Chase, John Henry Twachtman, and Childe Hassam. Hassam's paintings, inspired by the French Impressionists, are refreshing yet tranquil. The calm seascape of *The South Ledges, Appledore* (1913) is typical of his style.

AMERICAN MODERNISTS

The enormous canvases of the Modernists provide a dramatic contrast to the landscapes and portraits of the 19th and 20th centuries. Franz Kline's black slashes on a white canvas in *Merce C* (1961), which was inspired by his involvement with dancer Merce Cunningham, are the antithesis of the delicacy of the Impressionists. Kenneth Noland's geometrical compositions resemble firing targets. Other Modernists here include Georgia O'Keefe, Robert Rauschenberg, and David Hockney.

AMERICAN FOLK ART

The collection of American folk art includes some truly amazing pieces of work, created from a wide range of materials. James Hampton's *Throne of the Third Heaven of the Nations' Millennium General Assembly* (c. 1950–1964) is one of the star pieces in the collection.

Robert Rauschenberg's *Reservoir* (1961), mixed media on canvas

CONTEMPORARY ART

Roy Lichtenstein's 6.5-ton (5,900-kg) sculpture *Modern Head* (1989) greets visitors at the main entrance to the museum, and reflects the Smithsonian's dedication to the acquisition of modern and contemporary works. Inside are works by Jenny Holzer, Nam June Paik, and Edward Kienholz, among others. Karen LaMonte's *Reclining Dress Impression with Drapery* (2009) is a glorious, almost luminous, life-size sculpture in rippling cast glass.

LUCE FOUNDATION CENTER

The three-story Luce Foundation Center for American Art holds about 3,300 artworks from the museum's collection. The items on display include paintings and sculptures, contemporary craft objects, folk art, and jewelry.

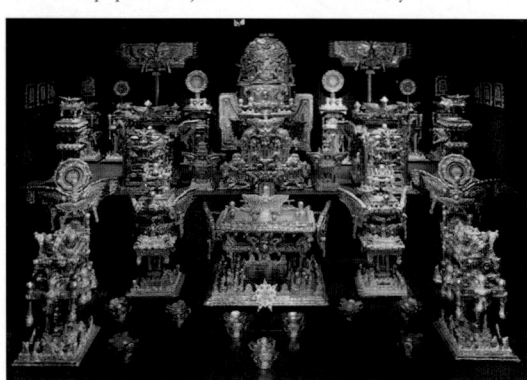

Throne of the Third Heaven of the Nations' Millennium General Assembly

Exploring the National Portrait Gallery

The National Portrait Gallery keeps generations of remarkable Americans in the company of their fellow citizens. The gallery's mission is to collect and display images of "men and women who have made significant contributions to the history, development and culture of the people of the United States." Through the visual and performing arts, the lives of leaders such as George Washington and Martin Luther King Jr., artists such as George Gershwin and Mary Cassatt, and activists such as Rosa Parks and Sequoyah are celebrated.

Ronald Reagan, an oil on canvas by Henry C. Casselli, Jr. painted in 1989

OVERVIEW OF THE COLLECTION

The National Portrait Gallery illuminates America's family album, magnificently combining history, biography, and art in its collections. The portraits are fascinating not only because they reveal their subjects but also because they illustrate the times in which they were produced. There are more than 20,000 images in the permanent collection, which includes paintings, photographs, sculptures, etchings, and drawings. Both heroes and villains are represented. Portraits taken from life sittings are favored by the gallery.

THE GREAT HALL

The third-floor Great Hall is a crazy quilt of tiles and ceiling medallions. A frieze showing the evolution of technology in America also runs around the room. Once a display area for new inventions, it is a reminder of the building's past as the Patent Office.

20TH-CENTURY AMERICANS

The National Portrait Gallery's collection is not limited to the political history of the country. There is also a large collection of portraits of American people notable for their achievements in the arts, sports, or in the

country's religious or cultural history. Athletes include the famous baseball player Babe Ruth and baseball manager Casey Stengel. Among figures from the world of entertainment are portraits of actresses Judy Garland, Tallulah Bankhead, and Mary Pickford. John Wayne also features among the Hollywood stars, as do Buster Keaton, Clark Gable, and James Cagney. There are also bronze busts of the poet T.S. Eliot and the humorist Will Rogers. Religious leaders, business magnates, pioneers in women's rights and civil rights (such as Dr. Martin Luther King Jr.), explorers, and scientists are portrayed in a whole range of media, including oils, clay, and bronze. There are also many photographic portraits, including some of Marilyn Monroe, which were taken during a morale-boosting visit the actress made to soldiers during the Korean War.

Portrait of Pocahontas by an unidentified artist

THE HALL OF PRESIDENTS

In 1857, Congress commissioned George Peter Alexander Healy to paint portraits of the presidents. The chronologically ordered portrayal of all of the country's leaders remains the heart of the National Portrait Gallery's exhibitions.

Two portraits of George and Martha Washington are featured prominently in the Portrait Gallery. The most famous portrait of George Washington is Gilbert Stuart's "Landsdowne", painted from life in 1796. Abraham Lincoln posed for photographer Alexander Gardener several months before he was assassinated (see p96).

The exhibition also features modern-day presidents, such as Bill Clinton and George W. Bush. Shepard Fairey's iconic portrait of Barack Obama, an image seen throughout the latter's presidential campaign, is also here.

Diana Ross and The Supremes, photographed by Bruce Davidson in 1965

The unique and innovative International Spy Museum

International Spy Museum ⑲

800 F St, NW. **Map** 3 C3. **Tel** 393-7798, EYE-SPY-U. Ⓜ *Gallery Place-Chinatown.* ◯ *Apr–Oct: 9am–7pm; Nov–Mar: 10am–6pm.* ⬤ *Jan 1, Thanksgiving, Dec 25.* 📷🔒⬛📱 *group tours by reservation.* **www**.spymuseum.org

The Spy Museum is the first museum in the world devoted to international espionage. Its huge collection includes the German Enigma cipher machine from World War II, a Soviet shoe transmitter, a wristwatch camera, and a lipstick pistol, displayed in a variety of themed exhibits. A visit to the museum begins with a film on the real life of a spy, revealing what motivates people to enter this clandestine world. The "School for Spies" exhibit displays over 200 artifacts used by spies to disguise and protect themselves during operations. "The Secret History of Histories" traces the art of spying from

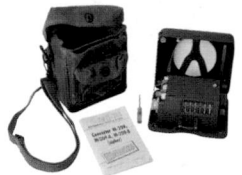

World War II cipher machine, essential for breaking enemy codes

biblical times to the early 20th century. "Spies Among Us" examines the making and breaking of codes during World War II, and highlights famous spies such as Marlene Dietrich, John Ford, and Josephine Baker. Other permanent exhibits explore espionage from the Cold War to the present day, featuring spy planes, listening and tracking devices, and the lives of spies, such as Aldrich Ames and Robert Hanssen.

Verizon Center ⑳

601 F St, NW. **Map** 4 D3. **Tel** 628-3200. Ⓜ *Gallery Place-Chinatown.* **Team Store** ◯ *10am–5:30pm daily (later on event days).* 📷 *for National Sports Gallery.* 🔒🍴📱 **www**. verizoncenter.com

Opened in 1997, the Verizon Center is a sports and entertainment complex that houses many shops and restaurants.

The 20,000-seat Verizon stadium is the home of Washington's basketball teams, the Wizards (men's team), Georgetown Hoyas, and the Mystics (women's), as well as the ice hockey team, the Capitals. The presence of the complex has revived the surrounding area beyond recognition. Half of the arena's seats are below ground level, in a vast but harmonious structure. It hosts rock concerts as well as sports events and exhibitions.

PENN QUARTER RENAISSANCE

During the 1990s, Washington's Penn Quarter was transformed from a derelict historic area to prime real estate. The construction of the Verizon Center and renewed appreciation for the restoration of dilapidated Victorian buildings helped to accelerate this process. As a result of losing its shabby image, Penn Quarter also lost many of the artists who carved studios out of the high-ceilinged, low-rent spaces, but their influence can still be seen in the large number of art galleries and exhibitions in the area. Some of the non-profit organizations and small businesses that leased offices in the big, aging buildings were forced to relocate due to an increase in rent. Soaring prices also closed a number of traditional Chinese restaurants around the Verizon Center, which have been replaced by upscale eateries. Today Penn Quarter is a safer area for those on foot, with a buzzing selection of nightly activities available, including sports events, theater shows, concerts, and lively restaurants.

A contemporary office building linking two Victorian façades on 7th Street

IN VALOR
THERE IS HOPE

Majestic lion statue alongside a marble wall at the police memorial

National Law Enforcement Officers Memorial ㉑

E St, NW, between 4th St & 5th St, NW. **Map** 4 D3. **Tel** 737-3213. **M** *Judiciary Square*. **Visitor Center** 605 E St, NW. ⬜ *9am–5pm Mon–Fri, 10am–5pm Sat, noon–5pm Sun*. ● *Jan 1, Thanksgiving, Dec 25*. 🔒 ♿ 🔲 www.nleomf.org

Dedicated by President George Bush in 1991, the National Law Enforcement Officers Memorial honors the 18,600 police officers who have been killed since the first known death in 1792. Spread over three acres in the center of Judiciary Square, the memorial's flower lined pathways are spectacular in springtime. The names of the fallen officers are inscribed on marble walls. Each path is guarded by a statue of an adult lion shielding its cubs, symbolic of the US police force's protective role.

National Building Museum ㉒

401 F St at 4th St, NW. **Map** 4 D3. **Tel** 272-2448. **M** *Judiciary Square, Gallery Place-Chinatown*. ⬜ *10am–5pm Mon–Sat, 11am–5pm Sun*. ● *Jan 1, Thanksgiving, Dec 25*. 🔲 ♿ 🖥 🔲 www.nbm.org

It is fitting that the National Building Museum, dedicated to the building trade, should be housed in the architecturally audacious former Pension Bureau building. Civil War General Montgomery C. Meigs saw Michelangelo's Palazzo Farnese on a trip to Rome and decided to duplicate it as a Washington office building, albeit twice as big and in red brick as opposed to the stone masonry of the Rome original.

Completed in 1887, the building is topped by a dramatic terracotta frieze of the Civil War measuring 3 ft (1 m) in height. The daring exterior of the building is matched by its flamboyant interior. The vast concourse, measuring 316 ft by 116 ft (96 m by 35 m), is lined with balconies containing exhibitions. The roof is supported by huge columns, constructed of brick, plastered, and faux-painted to give the appearance of marble. The Great Hall has been the impressive venue for many presidential balls.

In 1926 the Pension Bureau relocated to different offices, and there was a move to demolish Meigs' building.

Ornamental plinth in the grounds of the museum

Instead it was occupied by various government agencies for a time and was even used as a courthouse for a while.

The building was eventually restored, and in 1985 opened in renewed splendor as the National Building Museum. A privately owned collection, the museum has a display on the architectural history of the city – "Washington: Symbol and City." It includes an excellent illustration of Pierre L'Enfant's original plans for the capital, as well as other photographs, models, and interactive exhibits demonstrating how the city grew and changed. The temporary exhibits in the museum often highlight controversial issues in the field of design and architecture. There is a small café in the courtyard, and a gift shop. For children under six, the "Building Zone" offers some hands-on fun including giant lego blocks, bulldozers, and a playhouse.

The splendid, colonnaded Great Hall in the National Building Museum

THE WHITE HOUSE AND FOGGY BOTTOM

The official residence of the President, the White House is one of the most distinguished buildings in DC and was first inhabited in 1800. Although burned by the British during the War of 1812, most of today's building remains as it was planned. Other buildings surrounding the White House are worth a visit, such as the Daughters of the American Revolution building and the Corcoran Gallery. East of the White House is the Foggy Bottom area, which was built on swampland. Notable edifices here include the Kennedy Center, the State Department building, and the notorious Watergate Complex, focus of the 1970s Nixon scandal.

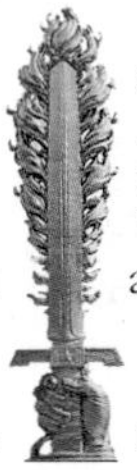

Second Division Memorial

SIGHTS AT A GLANCE

Galleries
Corcoran Gallery of Art 7
Renwick Gallery 5

Squares
Lafayette Square 3
Washington Circle 17

Historic Buildings
Daughters of the American Revolution 9
Eisenhower Old Executive Office Building 6
George Washington University 15
Hay-Adams Hotel 4
Octagon Museum 8
Watergate Complex 18

Official Buildings
Department of the Interior 11
Federal Reserve Building 12
National Academy of Sciences 13
Organization of the American States 10
State Department 14
Treasury Building 2
The White House pp108–11 1

Performing Arts Center
Kennedy Center pp118–19 19

Church
St. Mary's Episcopal Church 16

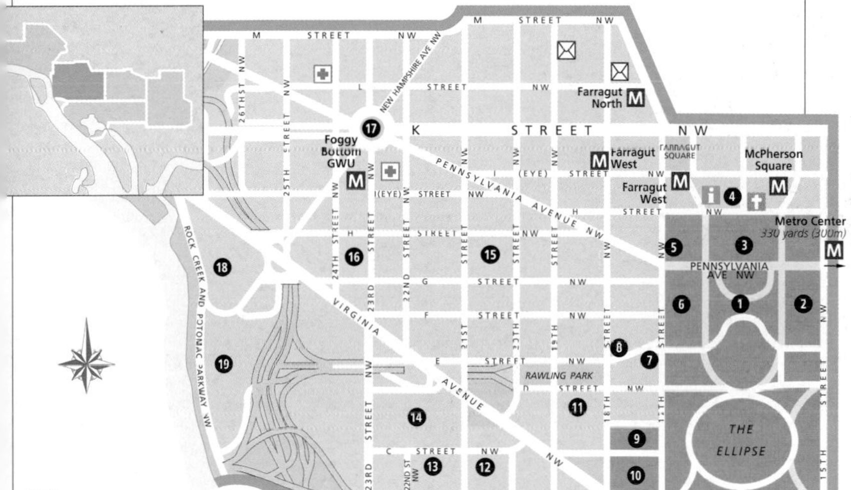

KEY

- Street-by-street map *pp106–7*
- Metro station
- Tourist information
- Hospital emergency room
- Post office
- Church

GETTING THERE

The closest Metrorail stations to the White House and Foggy Bottom area are Metro Center, McPherson Square, Farragut West and Foggy Bottom-GWU station. Also, Metrobuses 32, 34, and 36 travel east to west and will take you to most of the major sights within the area.

◁ **The First Division Monument in front of Eisenhower Old Executive Office Building**

Street-by-Street: Around The White House

The area surrounding the White House is filled with grand architecture and political history, and the vistas from the Ellipse lawn are breathtaking. It is worth spending a day exploring the area and seeing some of its buildings, such as the Treasury Building with its statue of Alexander Hamilton (the first Secretary of the Treasury) and the Eisenhower Old Executive Office Building. The buildings of the Daughters of the American Revolution and the OAS both offer the visitor an insight into the pride the nation takes in its past.

Eisenhower Old Execu Office Buil
Although it was poorly rece on its completion in 1888, attractive building now ho staff of the Executive branc

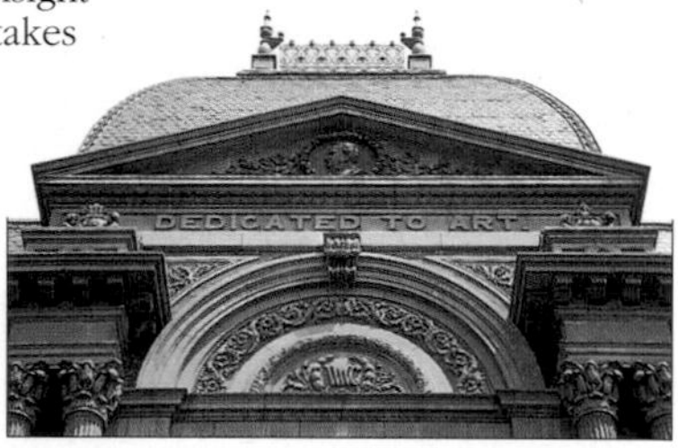

Renwick Gallery
The gallery is part of the Smithsonian American Art Museum. The inscription above the entrance of the building reads "Dedicated to Art" 5

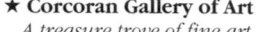

Octagon Museum
At one time James Madison's home, this building has had a varied history functioning as a hospital and a school, among other things 8

★ Corcoran Gallery of Art
A treasure trove of fine art, the Corcoran Gallery counts works by Rembrandt, Monet, Picasso, and de Kooning among its many exhibits 7

0 meters 100
0 yards 100

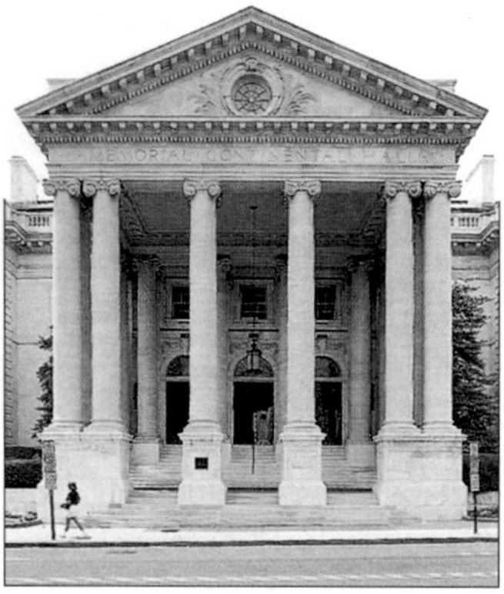

DAR Building
This beautiful Neoclassical building is one of three founded by the historical organization, the Daughters of the American Revolution 9

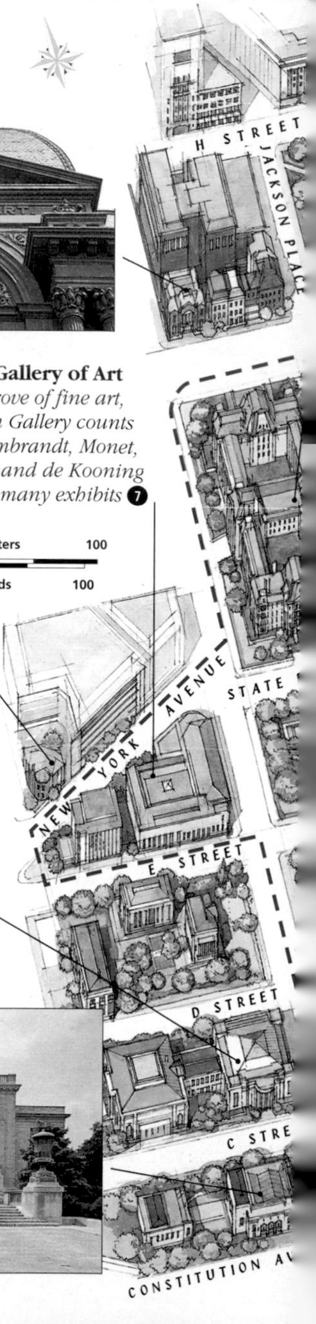

KEY

— — — Suggested route

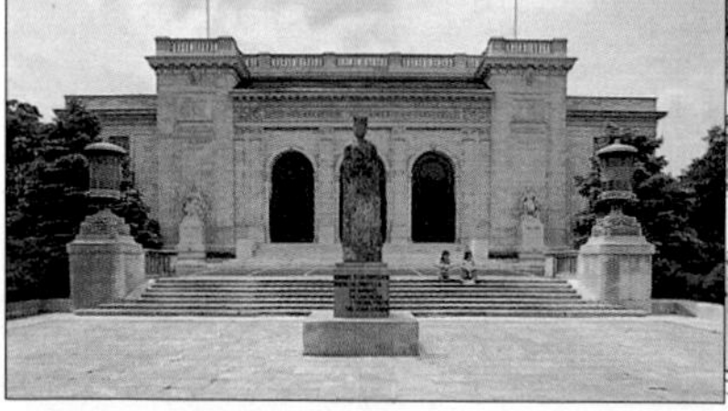

OAS Building
The central statue of Queen Isabella of Spain stands in front of this Spanish Colonial-style mansion. Built in 1910, it houses the Organization of American States 10

Hay-Adams Hotel
Formed by the joining of two town houses, this luxurious hotel has been the scene of political activity since it opened in the 1920s ❹

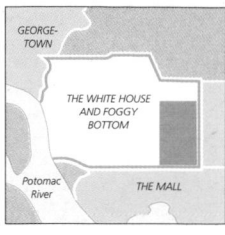

GEORGE-
TOWN

THE WHITE HOUSE
AND FOGGY
BOTTOM

Potomac
River

THE MALL

LOCATOR MAP
See Street Finder map 3

H STREET

MADISON PLACE

PENNSYLVANIA AVENUE

A. HAMILTON PLACE

EXECUTIVE AVENUE

E STREET

15TH STREET

THE ELLIPSE

Lafayette Square
Named after the Marquis de Lafayette, a Revolutionary War hero, this leafy square has at its center this statue of Andrew Jackson, the seventh president, sculpted by Clark Mills ❸

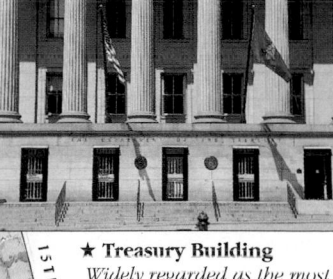

★ Treasury Building
Widely regarded as the most impressive Neoclassical structure in the city, this building took over 60 years to complete ❷

★ The White House
One of the most famous sights in Washington, DC, this has been the President's official residence since the 1800s ❶

STAR SIGHTS

★ Corcoran Gallery of Art

★ Treasury Building

★ The White House

The White House ❶

In 1791 George Washington chose this site as the location for the new President's House. Irish-born architect James Hoban was selected to design the building, known as the Executive Mansion. In 1800, President and Mrs. John Adams became the first occupants, even though the building was not yet completed. Burned by the British in 1814, the restored edifice was occupied again in 1817, by James Monroe. In 1901, President Theodore Roosevelt changed the official name of the building to the White House and in 1902 ordered the West Wing to be built. The East Wing was added in 1942 on the instruction of President Franklin D. Roosevelt, completing the building as it is today.

The White House
The official residence of the US president for over 200 years, the White House façade is familiar to millions of people around the world.

★ State Dining Room
Able to seat as many as 140 people, the State Dining Room was enlarged in 1902. A portrait of President Abraham Lincoln, by George P.A. Healy, hangs above the mantel.

The West Terrace leads to the West Wing and the Oval Office, the President's official office.

The stonework has been painted over and over to maintain the building's white façade.

STAR ROOMS

★ Red Room

★ State Dining Room

★ Vermeil Room

★ Red Room
One of three reception rooms on the state floor, the Red Room is furnished in red in the Empire Style (1810–30).

Lincoln Bedroom
President Lincoln used this room as his Cabinet Room. Today it is used as a guest bedroom furnished in Lincoln-era decor.

VISITORS' CHECKLIST

1600 Pennsylvania Ave, NW.
Map 3 B3. ☐ 7:30–10am Tue–Sat only for groups with congressional or embassy appointments. Contact Visitor Center for information. ● federal hols and official functions. ✓ obligatory; call 456-7041 for more information. www.nps.gov
White House Visitor Center
1450 Pennsylvania Ave, NW. **Tel** 208-1631. Ⓜ Federal Triangle. ☐ 7:30am–4pm daily. ● Jan 1, Thanksgiving, Dec 25. ☐ ♿
✓ www.nps.gov/whho

The East Terrace leads to the East Wing.

The East Room is used for large gatherings, such as concerts and press conferences.

Treaty Room

The Green Room was first used by Thomas Jefferson as a dining room.

Blue Room

★ **The Vermeil Room**
This yellow room houses six paintings of first ladies, including this portrait of Eleanor Roosevelt by Douglas Chandor.

Diplomatic Reception
This room is used to welcome friends and ambassadors. It is elegantly furnished in the Federal Period style (1790–1820).

WHITE HOUSE ARCHITECTS

After selecting the site, George Washington held a design competition to find an architect to build the residence where the US president would live. In 1792 James Hoban, an Irish-born architect, was chosen for the task. It is from Hoban's original drawings that the White House was initially built and all subsequent changes grew. In 1902 President Teddy Roosevelt hired the New York architectural firm of McKim, Mead, and White to check the structural condition of the building and refurbish areas as necessary. The White House underwent further renovations and refurbishments during the administrations of Truman and Kennedy.

James Hoban, architect of the White House

Exploring the White House

The rooms in the White House are beautifully decorated in period styles and filled with valuable antique furniture, china, and silverware. Hanging on their walls are some of America's most treasured paintings, including portraits of past presidents and first ladies. Those not lucky enough to be granted permission to tour the White House can experience a virtual tour at the White House Visitor Center.

THE LIBRARY

Originally used as a laundry area, this room was turned into a "gentleman's ante-room" at the request of President Theodore Roosevelt in 1902. In 1935 it was remodeled into a library. Furnished in 1962 in the style of the late Federal period (1800–1820), the library was redecorated in 1962, and then again in 1976. It had its latest update in 2006 when it was painted in classic cream and red tones. Today, it is often used for media tapings.

Portraits of four native-American chiefs, painted by Charles Bird King, are displayed in the library. The chandelier was crafted in the early 1800s and was originally owned by the family of James Fenimore Cooper, author of *The Last of the Mohicans*.

THE VERMEIL ROOM

Refurbished in 2006, the Vermeil Room is named after the collection of vermeil, or gilded silver, that is on display in the cabinets. On show are 18th-, 19th-, and 20th-century tableware, including pieces

crafted by English Regency silversmith Paul Storr (1771–1836) and French Empire silversmith Jean-Baptist Claude Odiot (1763–1850). The collection was bequeathed to the White House in 1958 by Margaret Thompson Biddle.

Six portraits of first ladies hang on the walls: Elizabeth Shoumatoff's painting of Claudia (Lady Bird) Johnson, Aaron Shikler's portrait of Jacqueline Kennedy in her New York apartment, and an unusual portrait of Eleanor Roosevelt, caught in various moods, by Douglas Chandor. Also on display are portraits of Lou Hoover, Mamie Eisenhower, and Pat Nixon.

THE CHINA ROOM

Edith Wilson created this room in 1917 to display examples of tableware used in the White House. Today it is used as a reception room. The rich red color scheme is suggested by the stunning portrait of Grace Coolidge, painted in 1924 by Howard Chandler Christy. The Indo-Isfahan rug dates from the early 20th century.

The red and cream color scheme of the China Room

THE BLUE ROOM

President James Monroe chose the French Empire-style decor for this magnificent, oval-shaped room in 1817. The Classically inspired furniture and accompanying motifs, such as urns, acanthus leaves, and imperial eagles, typify the style. The settee and seven chairs were created by Parisian cabinetmaker, Pierre-Antoine Bellangé.

A portrait of Thomas Jefferson by Rembrandt Peale, dating from 1800, hangs in this elegant room, along with a portrait of President John Adams, painted in 1793 by artist John Trumball. The Blue Room has always been used as a reception room, except for a brief period during the John Adams administration.

THE RED ROOM

This room was decorated in the Empire style by Jacqueline Kennedy in 1962 and was refurbished in 1971 and again in 2000. Much of the wooden furniture in the room, including the beautiful inlaid round table, was created by cabinetmaker Charles-Honoré Lannuier in his New York workshop. Above the mantel hangs a portrait of Angelica Singleton Van Buren, the daughter-in-law of President Martin Van Buren, which was painted by Henry Inman in 1842. The room is used as a parlor or sitting room; in recent times it has been used for small dinner parties.

THE STATE DINING ROOM

As a result of the growing nation and its international standing, the size of official dinners in the White House increased. Finally in 1902 the architects McKim, Mead, and White were called in to enlarge the State Dining Room. The plaster and paneling was modeled on the style of 18th-century Neoclassical English houses. The mahogany dining table was created in 1997. The pieces of French giltware on

the table were bought by
President Monroe in 1817.

The dining room was
redecorated in 1998, when
the Queen Anne-style chairs,
which date from 1902, were
reupholstered.

THE LINCOLN BEDROOM

Used today as the guest room
for the friends and family of
the President, the Lincoln
Bedroom is decorated in the
American Victorian style,
dating from around 1860.
Used by Lincoln as an office
and cabinet room, this room
became the Lincoln Bedroom
when President Truman
decided to fill it with furniture
from Lincoln's era. In the
center is a 6 ft- (1.8 m-) wide
rosewood bed with an 8 ft-
(2.5 m-) high headboard. The
portrait of General Andrew
Jackson next to the bed is
said to have been one of
President Lincoln's favorites.

THE TREATY ROOM

Beginning with Andrew
Johnson's presidency in 1865,
the Treaty Room served as
the Cabinet Room for 10
presidential Administrations.
The room contains many
Victorian pieces bought by
President Ulysses S. Grant,
including the original table
used by the Cabinet. The
cut-glass chandelier that
hangs here was made in
Birmingham, England around

THE WHITE HOUSE VISITOR CENTER

The White House Visitor Center has interesting exhibits
about the history of the White House and its décor, as well
as royal gifts on display. There are also seasonal lectures

by renowned speakers on
aspects of history in and out
of the White House. The
Center has a monthly Living
History program with actors
portraying historic figures.
The gift shop carries an
extensive range, including the
annual White House
Christmas ornament. Tours of
the state rooms of the White
House are extremely limited
at this time. Guided tours can
only be booked by special
arrangement through a member
of Congress or, if a non-US
citizen, through an embassy.
Requests need to be made at
least 30 days in advance.

Façade of the White House Visitor Center

1850. The chandelier has 20
arms, each one fitted with a
frosted-glass globe.

THE EAST WING

The East Wing houses offices
rather than ceremonial rooms.
The walls of the Lobby are
adorned with portraits of
presidents. Both the East
Landing and the East Colon-
nade, which fronts the East
Terrace, look out onto the
Jacqueline Kennedy Garden.
The Terrace, which links the
East Wing to the Residence,
houses the White House movie
theater. It was once Theodore
Roosevelt's coatroom.

The interior of the Oval Office, located in the West Wing

THE WEST WING

In 1902, the West Wing was
built by the architectural firm
McKim, Mead, and White for
a total cost of $65,196. In this
wing, the former Fish Room
was renamed the Roosevelt
Room by President Nixon, in
honor of presidents Theodore
and Franklin Roosevelt who
created this wing. Their
portraits still hang in the room.

Also in the West Wing are
the Cabinet Room, where
government officials meet
with the president, and the
Oval Office, added in 1909,
where the president meets
with visiting heads of state.
Over the years, many
presidents have personalized
this room in some way.

The Victorian-era interior of the Treaty Room

The colonnaded portico of the Neoclassical Treasury Building

Treasury Building ❷

15th St & Pennsylvania Ave, NW.
Map 3 B3. *Tel* 622-2000.
Ⓜ *McPherson Square.*
🏛 *Tours for US citizens only, by appointment through congressman.*
♿ **www**.ustreas.gov

The site of this massive, four-story Greek Revival building, home to the Department of the Treasury, was chosen by President Andrew Jackson. The grand, sandstone-and-granite edifice was designed by architect Robert Mills, who also designed the Washington Monument *(see p78)*.
A statue of Alexander Hamilton, the first Secretary of the Treasury, stands in front of the southern entrance to the building.

The official guided tour, shows visitors the restored historic rooms, including the 1864 burglar-proof vault, the Andrew Johnson suite (Johnson's temporary office after the assassination of President Lincoln in 1865), and the marble Cash Room.

Between 1863 and 1880, US currency was printed in the basement, and during the Civil War it was used as storage space for food and arms. Today, the building is home to the Department of the Treasury, which manages the government's finances and protects US financial systems.

Lafayette Square ❸

Map 2 F3 & 3 B3. Ⓜ *Farragut West, McPherson Square.*

Set behind the White House is Lafayette Square, named after the Marquis de Lafayette (1757–1834), a hero of the American Revolutionary War *(see p19)*. Due to its proximity to the White House, this public park is often the scene of peaceful demonstrations. It is home to 19th-century former mansions and the historic church of St. John's (the "Church of the Presidents"), built in 1816 by Benjamin Latrobe, who designed

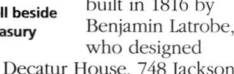

Liberty Bell beside the Treasury

Decatur House, 748 Jackson Place, which was home to famous figures such as Henry Clay and Martin Van Buren,

Federal-style 19th-century houses overlooking tranquil Lafayette Square

and is open to the public.
In the center of the Square is a huge statue of President Andrew Jackson (1767–1845) seated on a horse. Cast in bronze by Clark Mills, it was the first equestrian statue of its size to be built in the US and was dedicated in 1853.

At each of the square's four corners stand statues of men who took part in America's struggle for liberty. The southeast corner has the bronze figure of French compatriot Lafayette. In the southwest corner is a statue of another Frenchman, Jean-Baptiste Donatien de Vimeur, Comte de Rochambeau (1725–1807). This was a gift from France to the American people and accepted by Theodore Roosevelt in 1902. A statue of Polish general, Thaddeus Kosciuszko (1746–1817), who fought with the American colonists in the Revolutionary War, stands in the northeast corner. Baron von Steuben (1730–94), a German officer and George Washington's aide at the Battle of Valley Forge, is honored at the northwest end.

Hay-Adams Hotel ❹

1 Lafayette Square, NW. **Map** 2 F3 & 3 B3. *Tel* 638-6600, 1-800-424-5054. Ⓜ *Farragut North, Farragut West.* **www**.hayadams.com

Situated close to the White House, the historic Hay-Adams Hotel is an Italian Renaissance landmark in Washington. Its plush interior is adorned with European and Oriental antiques.

It was originally two adjacent houses, built by Henry Hobson Richardson in 1885, belonging to statesman and author John Hay and diplomat and historian Henry Adams. A popular hotel since its conversion in 1927 by developer Harry Wardman, the exclusive Hay-Adams remains one of Washington's top establishments *(see p175)*, well situated for all the major sights. Afternoon tea and drinks are available in the Lafayette Restaurant.

Renwick Gallery ❺

Pennsylvania Ave at 17th St, NW.
Map 2 F3 & 3 A3. **Tel** 633-1000.
Ⓜ *Farragut West.* ◯ *10am–5:30pm daily.* ⬤ *Dec 25.* 🎫 & 📷
www.americanart.si.edu

Forming part of the Smithsonian American Art Museum *(see p100)*, this red-brick building was designed and constructed by James Renwick Jr. in 1858. It originally housed the art collection of William Wilson Corcoran until this was moved to the current Corcoran Gallery of Art in 1897.

The building was later bought by the Smithsonian. Refurbished and renamed, the Renwick Gallery opened in 1972. It is dedicated primarily to 20th-century American arts, crafts, and design, and houses some impressive exhibits in every medium including metal, clay, and glass. *Game Fish* (1988) by Larry Fuente is a stunning example of mixed media art. The museum shop sells craft gifts and contemporary art pieces.

Eisenhower Old Executive Office Building ❻

17th St at Pennsylvania Ave, NW.
Map 2 F4 & 3 A3. Ⓜ *Farragut West.*
⬤ *to the public.* & **www**.
whitehouse.gov/about/eeob

Formerly known simply as the Old Executive Office Building, this structure stands on the West side of the White House.

Imposing façade of Eisenhower Old Executive Office Building

The magnificent Renwick Gallery, a fine example of French Empire style

It was once the home of the War, Navy, and State Departments. Built over 17 years between 1871 and 1888 by Alfred B. Mullett, its exuberant French Second Empire design, which was inspired by the 1852 expansion of the Louvre in Paris, generated much criticism at the time.

The building has long been the site of historic events, such as the meeting between Secretary of State Cordell Hull and the Japanese after the bombing of Pearl Harbor.

Lion statue guarding the Corcoran Gallery

Today the building houses government agencies, including the White House Office, the Office of the Vice President, and the National Security Council.

Corcoran Gallery of Art ❼

500 17th St, NW. **Map** 2 F4 & 3 A3.
Tel 639-1700. Ⓜ *Farragut West, Farragut North.* ◯ *10am–5pm Wed–Sun (to 9pm Thu, except Thanksgiving).* ⬤ *Jan 1, Dec 25.*
📷 🎫 & 🖥 & 🔪 📷
www.corcoran.org

One of the first fine art museums in the country, the Corcoran Gallery of Art opened in 1874. It outgrew its original home (what is now the Renwick Gallery building) and moved to this massive

edifice designed in 1897 by Ernest Flagg. A privately funded art collection, the Corcoran was founded by William Wilson Corcoran – a banker whose main interest was American art. Many of the European works in the collection were added in 1925 by art collector and US senator William A. Clark.

The Corcoran Gallery of Art is filled with works by European and American masters that span the centuries. These include 16th- and 17th-century French works, 19th-century French Impressionist paintings by Monet and Renoir, and other 19th-century works by Eakins, Homer, and Hassam. The gallery also contains the largest collection of paintings by Jean-Baptiste Camille Corot outside France. There is a fine collection of modern and African American art, which includes sculpture, paintings, textiles, and photographs. Paintings from the 20th century include a selection by Picasso and Singer Sargent.

Within the building is the only accredited art school in Washington. A brunch takes place every Sunday in the beautiful atrium, with seatings at 11am, 12:30, and 2pm. The Corcoran also has a shop selling an excellent selection of books, postcards, and other items.

Octagon Museum ⑧

1799 New York Ave, NW.
Map 2 F4 & 3 A3. *Tel 626-7312.*
Ⓜ *Farragut West and Farragut North.* ☐ *by appointment.*
● *Jan 1, Thanksgiving, Dec 25.*
▨ ☐ ⓱ *(first floor only).*
www.theoctagon.org

Actually hexagonal in shape, the Octagon is a three-story red-brick building, designed in the late-Federal style by Dr. William Thornton (1759–1828), first architect of the US Capitol. The Octagon was completed in 1801 for Colonel John Tayloe III, a rich plantation owner from Richmond County, Virginia, and a friend of George Washington.

When the White House was burned in the War of 1812 against Britain *(see p19)*, President James Madison and his wife, Dolley, lived here from 1814 to 1815. The Treaty of Ghent that ended the war was signed by Madison on the second floor of the house on February 17, 1815.

In the early 1900s, the building was taken over by the American Institute of Architects. The American Architectural Foundation, established in 1970, set up a museum of architecture in the Octagon. The building has been restored to its historically accurate 1815 appearance, and has some original furnishings and fine architectural features, such as a circular entrance hall. Ongoing restoration work causes occasional suspension of tours (check website).

The circular main entrance to the attractive Octagon Museum

South portico of the DAR Memorial Continental Hall

Daughters of the American Revolution ⑨

1776 D St, NW. **Map** 2 F4 & 3 A3.
Tel 628-1776. Ⓜ *Farragut West.*
☐ *9:30am–4pm Mon–Fri, 9am–5pm Sat.* ● *1 week in Jul, Federal hols.*
▨ *9am–3pm Sat (book in advance for groups of 5 or more).* ⓱ ⓱
www.dar.org/museum

Founded in 1890 as a non-profit organization, the Daughters of the American Revolution (DAR) is dedicated to historic preservation and promoting education and patriotism. In order to become a member, you must be a woman with blood relations to any person, male or female, who fought in or aided the Revolution. There are currently over 160,000 members in 3,000 regional branches throughout the USA and in nine other countries.

The DAR museum is located in the Memorial Continental Hall, designed for the organization by Edward Pearce Casey and completed in 1910. The 13 columns in the south portico symbolize the 13 original states of the Union. Entrance to the museum is through the gallery, which displays an eclectic range of pieces from quilts to glassware and china.

The 33 period rooms that form the State Rooms in the museum house a collection of over 50,000 items, from silver to porcelain, ceramics, stoneware, and furniture. Each room is decorated in a unique style particular to an American state from different periods during the 18th and 19th centuries. An attic room filled with 18th- and 19th-century toys will delight children. Also, there is a huge genealogical library, consisting of approximately 125,000 publications.

DAR Museum banners proclaiming Preservation, Patriotism, Education

Fountain in the courtyard of the OAS building

Organization of American States ⑩

17th St & Constitution Ave, NW. **Map** 2 F4 & 3 A4. **Tel** 458-3000. ☐ 9am–5:30pm Mon–Fri. ☐ Sat–Sun, Federal hols. **Art Museum of the Americas** 201 18th St, NW. **Tel** 458-6016. ☐ 10am–5pm Tue–Sun. ☐ Good Friday, Federal hols. M Farragut West. ☑ call 458-6016. **www**.oas.org

Dating back to the First International Conference of the American States, held from October 1889 to April 1890 in Washington, the Organization of American States (OAS) is the oldest alliance of nations dedicated to reinforcing the peace and security of the continent, and maintaining democracy. The Charter of the OAS was signed in Bogotá, Colombia, in 1948 by the United States and 20 Latin American republics. Today there are 35 members. The building dates from 1910 and houses the Columbus Memorial Library and the **Art Museum of the Americas**, which exhibits 20th-century Latin American and Caribbean art.

Department of the Interior Building ⑪

19th St, between C St & E St, NW. **Map** 2 F4 & 3 A3. **Tel** 208-4743. M Farragut West. ☐ to the public for restoration until late 2011. ☑ ☐ **www**.doi.gov/interiormuseum

Designed by architect Waddy Butler Wood and built in 1935, this huge limestone building is the headquarters of the Department of the Interior. The building has a long central section, with six wings that extend off each side. In total it covers more than 16 acres of floor space, and has 2 miles (3 km) of corridors.

The Department of the Interior was originally formed of only the Departments of Agriculture, Labor, Education, and Energy, but it expanded to oversee all federally owned land across the United States. Visible inside, but only when taking the official guided tour, are 36 murals painted by Native American artists in the 1930s, including one of the singer Marian Anderson performing at the Lincoln Memorial in 1939 (see pp84–5).

The small **Department of the Interior Museum**, located on the first floor, opened in 1938. The displays include an overview of the Department's history, and some intricate dioramas of American wildlife and important historical events, such as the 1929 Kinloch Mine explosion. Also on display are paintings by 19th-century surveyors, and crafts by Native Americans, including a great collection of basketry.

The south façade of the immense Department of the Interior Building

---

THE TAYLOE FAMILY

Portrait, in crayon, by Saint Memin of Colonel John Tayloe III

John Tayloe III (1771–1828), a colonel in the War of 1812, was responsible for the construction of the unusual Octagon building. He and his wife Ann, the daughter of Benjamin Ogle (the governor of Maryland), had their primary residence at Mount Airy, an estate and tobacco plantation in Richmond County, Virginia. The Tayloes decided they wanted to build a second house where they could spend the inclement winter seasons. President George Washington, a close friend of Tayloe and his father, was at the time overseeing the building of the US Capitol and was eager for people to move into the new city. The president encouraged Tayloe and his family to choose a plot in Washington rather than in the more popular Philadelphia. The family heeded his advice and the triangular-shaped corner plot for the Octagon was chosen. Tayloe's vast wealth enabled him to employ the services of William Thornton, the original designer of the US Capitol building, and spend a total of $35,000 on the construction of the house.

Federal Reserve Building ⑫

Constitution Ave & 20th St NW.
Map 2 E4 & 3 A4. **Tel** 452-3778, for
art exhibitions. Ⓜ Foggy Bottom.
◯ by appointment. ◉ Federal hols.
♿ www.federalreserve.gov

Known to most people as
"the Fed," this building is
home to the Federal Reserve
System. This is the US banking system under which 12
Federal Reserve banks in 12
districts across the country
regulate and hold reserves
for member banks in their
districts. Dollar bills are
not printed here,
however, but at
the Bureau of
Engraving and
Printing (see p79).

The four-story,
white marble edifice
was designed by
Paul Philippe Cret,
architect for the
OAS building
(see p115) and the
Folger Shakespeare Library
(see p48). The building
opened in 1937.

Small art exhibitions are
held throughout the year.

The gleaming, white marble exterior of the Federal Reserve Building

National Academy of Sciences ⑬

2101 Constitution Ave, NW.
Map 2 E4. **Tel** 334-2000.
Ⓜ Foggy Bottom. ◉ Federal hols.
♿ www.nationalacademies.org

Established in 1863, the
National Academy of Sciences
is a non-profit organization
that conducts over 200
studies a year on
subjects such as
health, science,
and technology,
and educates
the nation by
providing
news of

Marble eagle above the
entrance to "the Fed"

scientific discoveries. Among
the past and present Members
of the Academy are nearly
200 Nobel Prize winners,
most notably Albert
Einstein. To be
elected as a
member is
considered a great
honor for a scientist.

The three-story
white marble
building, designed
by Bertram
Grosvenor
Goodhue, was completed in
1924. Inside is a gold dome
adorned with portraits of
Greek philosophers and
panels illustrating various
scientists. A 700-seat auditorium hosts a series of free
chamber recitals throughout
the year. On the building's
upper floors are the offices of
the National Research Council,
the National Academy of
Sciences, and the National
Academy of Engineering.

Nestled among the trees in
front of the Academy is the
much-admired bronze statue
of Albert Einstein, sculpted
by Robert Berks. The same
artist created the bust of
President John F.
Kennedy, which can be
seen in the Grand Foyer
of the Kennedy Center
(see pp118–9). The
huge statue of
Albert Ein-
stein reaches

12 ft (4 m) in height and
weighs 7,000 pounds (4 tons).
It was erected in 1979.

State Department ⑭

23rd St & C St, NW. **Map** 2 E4 & 3
A3. **Tel** 647-3241. Ⓜ Foggy
Bottom-GWU. 🎟 daily by
appointment; must show photo ID;
reserve up to 3 months in advance.
◉ Federal hols. ♿ www.
receptiontours.state.gov

As the oldest executive
department of the United
States government, established
in 1781, the State Department
handles all foreign policy.

Covering an expanse of
2.5 million sq ft (232,250 sq
m) over four city blocks, the
State Department building
rises eight stories high.
Workplace of the Secretary of
State, the State Department,
and the United States
Diplomatic Corps, the building
is host to 80,000 guests and
60,000 visitors every year.
The State Department's
Diplomatic Reception Rooms
were lavishly refurbished
in the late 1960s, and now
contain antiques worth
over $90 million.

George Washington University ⑮

2121 I (Eye) St, NW. **Map** 2 E3. **Tel**
994-1000. Ⓜ Foggy Bottom-GWU.
Lisner and Betts Auditoriums
Tel 994-6800. www.gwu.edu

Founded in 1821, George
Washington University,
known as "GW" to many
people, is named after the
first president of the United

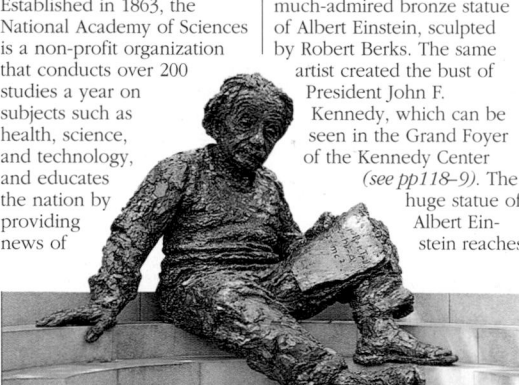
Sculpture of Albert Einstein outside the National Academy of Sciences

States. George Washington is the largest university in Washington, DC. There are nine schools offering both undergraduate and graduate studies. Strong subjects on offer include International Affairs, Business Administration, Medicine, Law, and Political Science.

As a result of its location, the university has many famous alumni, including Colin Powell (US Secretary of State in George W. Bush's administration) and Jacqueline Bouvier (who married John Kennedy) as well as a number of children of past presidents, including Lynda Johnson, Margaret Truman, and D. Jeffrey Carter.

The on-campus Lisner, Morton and Betts auditoriums host a series of plays, dances, lectures, and concerts.

St. Mary's Episcopal Church, built for freed slaves

St. Mary's Episcopal Church ⓰

728 23rd St, NW. **Map** 2 E3.
Tel 333-3985. Ⓜ *Foggy Bottom-GWU.* ◯ *9:30am–3pm Mon–Thu.*
✝ *9:30am Sun, noon Wed.* &
www.stmarysfoggybottom.org

Opened on January 20, 1887, the red-brick, Gothic St. Mary's Episcopal Church was the first church in Washington to be built specifically for freed slaves.

St Mary's was designed by James Renwick, the architect of the Renwick Gallery *(see p113)*, the Smithsonian Castle *(see p72)*, and St. Patrick's

The distinctive curved walls of the infamous Watergate Complex

Cathedral in New York City. The church was placed on the city's register of protected historic buildings in 1972.

Washington Circle ⓱

Map 2 E3. Ⓜ *Foggy Bottom-GWU.*

One of several circles and squares created by Pierre L'Enfant's original design of the city *(see p19)*, Washington Circle lies at the northern edge of Foggy Bottom. It forms the point where Pennsylvania Avenue and New Hampshire Avenue meet K Street and 23rd Street. The circle boasts an imposing bronze statue of George Washington astride his horse, designed by artist Clark Mills and unveiled in 1860. The statue faces east, looking toward the White House and the US Capitol.

Watergate Complex ⓲

Virginia Ave between Rock Creek Parkway and New Hampshire Ave, NW. **Map** 2 D3. Ⓜ *Foggy Bottom-GWU.* &

Located next to the Kennedy Center *(see pp118–19)*, on the bank of the Potomac River, the impressive, Italian-designed Watergate Complex was completed in 1971. The four rounded buildings that make up the complex were designed to contain shops, offices, apartments, hotels, and diplomatic missions.

In the summer of 1972 the complex found itself at the center of international news. Burglars, linked to President Nixon, broke into the offices of the Democratic National Committee, sparking off the Watergate scandal that led to the president's resignation.

THE WATERGATE SCANDAL

On June 17, 1972, during the US presidential campaign, five men were arrested for breaking into the Democratic Party headquarters in the Watergate Complex. The burglars were employed by the re-election organization of President

President Nixon addressing the nation while still in office

Richard Nixon, a Republican. Found guilty of burglary and attempting to bug telephones, the men were not initially linked to the White House. However, further investigation, led by *Washington Post* reporters Woodward and Bernstein, uncovered the extent of the president's involvement, including the possession of incriminating tapes and proven bribery. This led to an impeachment hearing, but before Nixon could be impeached, he resigned. Vice-President Gerald Ford succeeded him.

The Kennedy Center ⑲

In 1958, President Dwight D. Eisenhower signed an act to begin fund-raising for a national cultural center that would attract the world's best orchestras, opera, and dance companies to the US capital. President John F. Kennedy was an ardent supporter of the arts, taking the lead in fund-raising for it. He never saw the completion of the center, which was named in his honor. Designed by Edward Durrell Stone, it was opened on September 8, 1971. This vast complex houses several huge theaters; the Opera House, the Concert Hall, the Eisenhower Theater, and the Family Theater; on the roof are the Jazz Club, the Terrace Theater, and the Theater Lab.

Don Quixote Statue
This bronze and stone statue by Aurelio Teno was a gift to the center from Spain.

African sculpture

The Eisenhower Theater
This is one of the three main theaters. A bronze bust of President Eisenhower by Felix de Weldon hangs in the lobby.

East Roof Terrace

Millennium Stage
The Millennium Stage provides free performances put on in the Grand Foyer every evening at 6pm.

STAR FEATURES
★ Bust of JFK
★ The Grand Foyer
★ The Opera House

The Hall of States
The flags of each of the 50 American states, the five US territories, and the District of Columbia hang here.

The Hall of Nations houses the flag of every country with which the US has diplomatic relations.

★ **The Opera House**
The Opera House seats over 2,300 people. The vast chandelier is made of Lobmeyr crystal and was a gift from Austria.

VISITORS' CHECKLIST

New Hampshire Ave & Rock Creek Parkway, NW. **Map** 2 D4. **Tel** 467-4600. Ⓜ Foggy Bottom. 🚌 80. ⬜ 10am–9pm daily; 10am–9pm Mon–Sat, noon–9pm Sun and hols (box office). 🎭 10am–5pm Mon–Fri, 10am–1pm Sat–Sun (call 416-8340). ♿ 🚻 🍴 ⬇
www.kennedy-center.org

The Concert Hall is the largest auditorium, seating more than 2,400 people. It is the home of the National Symphony Orchestra.

★ **Bust of JFK**
Created by sculptor Robert Berks, this bronze bust stands in the Grand Foyer.

★ **The Grand Foyer**
This enormous room stretches 630 ft (192 m) and provides an impressive entrance into the Opera House, the Concert Hall, and the Eisenhower Theater.

The JFK Terrace
This stretches the length of the Center and overlooks the Potomac and has glorious views up and down the river. Quotes by John F. Kennedy are engraved into the marble walls.

GEORGETOWN

Georgetown developed well before Washington, DC. Native Americans had a settlement here, and in 1703 a land grant was given to Ninian Beall, who named the area the Rock of Dumbarton. By the mid-18th century immigrants from Scotland had swelled the population, and in 1751 the town was renamed George Town. It grew rapidly into a wealthy tobacco and flour port and finally, in 1789, the city of Georgetown was formed. The harbor and the Chesapeake and Ohio Canal were built in 1828, and the streets were lined with townhouses. The birth of the railroad undercut Georgetown's economy, which by the mid-1800s was in decline. But by the 1950s the cobblestone streets and charming houses were attracting wealthy young couples, and restaurants and shops sprang up on Wisconsin Avenue and M Street. Today Georgetown retains its quiet distinction from the rest of the city, and is a pleasant area in which to stroll for a few hours *(see pp148–9)*.

John Carroll, University founder

SIGHTS AT A GLANCE

Historic Buildings
- Dumbarton Oaks 13
- Georgetown University 9
- Old Stone House 5
- Tudor Place 10
- Washington Post Office 7

Churches and Cemeteries
- Grace Church 3
- Mt. Zion Church 11
- Oak Hill Cemetery 12

Streets, Canals, and Harbors
- Chesapeake and Ohio Canal 4
- M Street 6
- N Street 8
- Washington Harbor 1
- Wisconsin Avenue 2

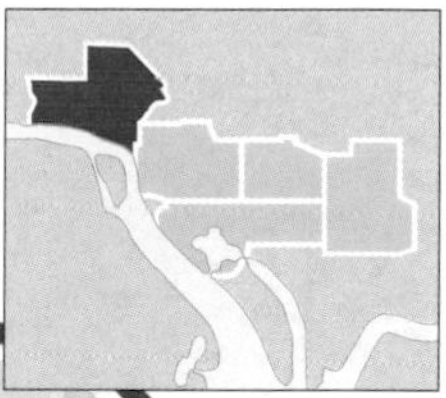

WHITEHAVEN ST NW
DUMBARTON OAKS PARK
MONTROSE PARK
OAK HILL CEMETERY
LOVERS LANE WALKWAY NW
MASSACHUSETTS AVENUE NW
SHERIDAN CIRCLE
Rock Creek
RESERVOIR ROAD NW
S STREET NW
DENT PLACE NW
Q STREET NW
VOLTA PLACE NW
P STREET NW
O STREET NW
N STREET NW
PROSPECT STREET NW
M STREET NW
WISCONSIN AVENUE NW
DUMBARTON STREET NW
OLIVE STREET NW
EAST PL NW
CANAL ROAD NW
Chesapeake and Ohio Canal
WHITEHURST FREEWAY NW
FRANCIS SCOTT KEY MEMORIAL BRIDGE
Foggy Bottom GWU
880 yards (800m)
0 meters 500
0 yards 500

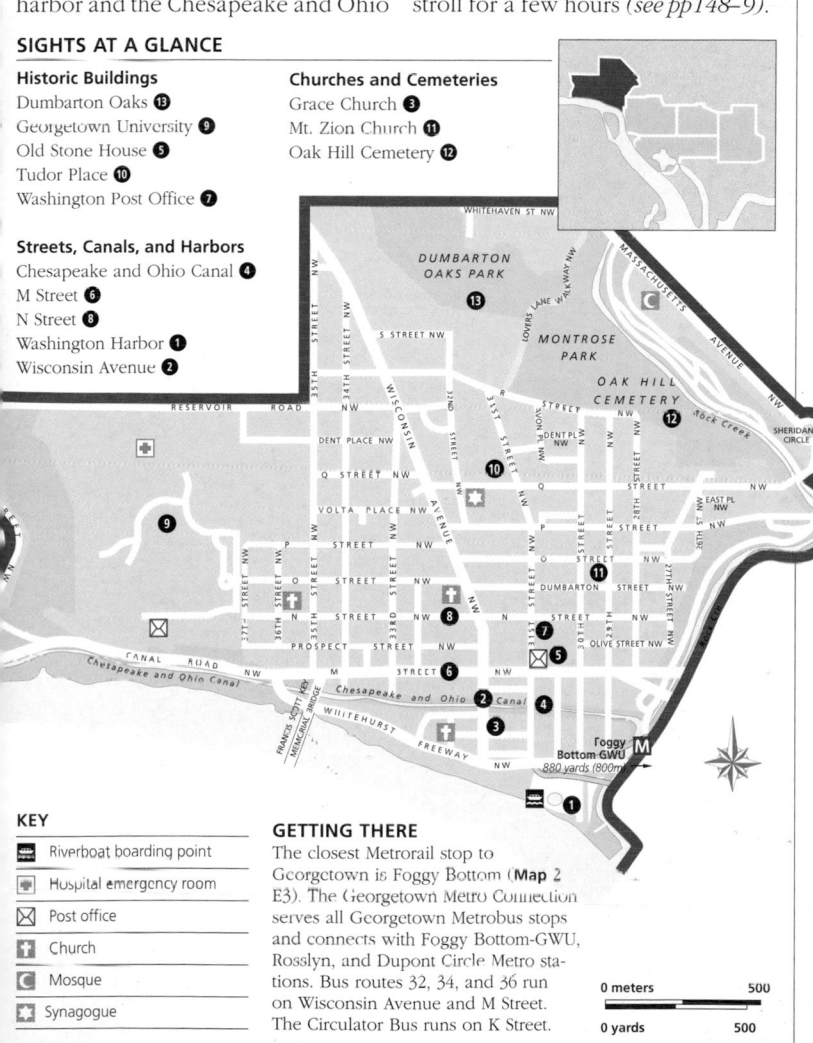

KEY
- Riverboat boarding point
- Hospital emergency room
- Post office
- Church
- Mosque
- Synagogue

GETTING THERE

The closest Metrorail stop to Georgetown is Foggy Bottom (**Map** 2 E3). The Georgetown Metro Connection serves all Georgetown Metrobus stops and connects with Foggy Bottom-GWU, Rosslyn, and Dupont Circle Metro stations. Bus routes 32, 34, and 36 run on Wisconsin Avenue and M Street. The Circulator Bus runs on K Street.

◁ **Typical colorful house in Georgetown**

Fountain at Washington Harbor

Washington Harbor **❶**

3000-3020 K Street, NW. **Map** 2 D3.

Washington is a city where few architectural risks have been taken. However, the approach used by architect Arthur Cotton Moore for Washington Harbor, which is a combination residential and commercial building on the Potomac River, is unusually audacious.

Built on a site that was once filled with factories and warehouses, Moore's creation is a structure that hugs the waterfront and surrounds a semi-circular pedestrian plaza. The architect borrowed motifs from almost every type of design, such as turrets, columns, and even flying buttresses. The harbor has a pleasant boardwalk, a huge fountain, and tall, columned lamp-posts. Under the ground are steel gates that can be raised to protect the building from floods. The top floors of the harbor are apartments. On the bottom floors are office complexes, restaurants, and shops. Sightseeing boats dock at the river's edge for trips to the Mall and back.

Wisconsin Avenue **❷**

Wisconsin Ave. **Map** 1 C2.
Ⓜ *Tenleytown.*

Wisconsin Avenue is one of two main business streets in Georgetown and is home to a wide variety of shops and restaurants. It is also one of the few streets in Washington that pre-dates L'Enfant's grid plan *(see p67)*. Once called High Street and then 32nd Street, it starts at the bank of the Potomac River and runs north through Georgetown right up to the city line, where it

---

The Chesapeake and Ohio Canal **❹**

When it was constructed in 1828, the C&O Canal featured an ingenious and revolutionary transportation system of locks, aqueducts, and tunnels that ran along its 184 miles (296 km) from Georgetown to Cumberland, Maryland. With the arrival of the railroad in the late 19th century, the canal fell out of use. It was only as a result of the efforts of Supreme Court Justice William Douglas that the Chesapeake and Ohio Canal was finally declared a protected national park in 1971. Today visitors come to enjoy its recreational facilities and also to study its fascinating transportation system.

Georgetown
The attractive federal houses of Georgetown line the banks of the canal for about 1.5 miles (2 km).

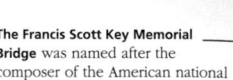

The Francis Scott Key Memorial Bridge was named after the composer of the American national anthem, *The Star-Spangled Banner.*

Canal Trips
Rides in mule-drawn canal clippers guided by park rangers dressed in period costumes are popular with visitors to the canal.

continues as Rockville Pike. On the junction of Wisconsin Ave and M Street is the landmark gold dome of Riggs National Bank (now the PNC bank).

During the French and Indian Wars, George Washington marched his troops up the avenue on his way to Pittsburgh to engage the British.

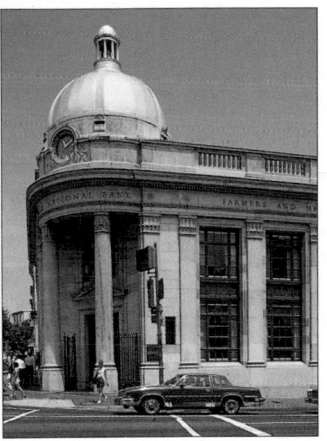

NATIONAL BANK
FARMERS AND
The gold dome of Riggs National Bank

Grace Church ❸

1041 Wisconsin Avenue, NW. **Map** 1 C3. ***Tel*** *333-7100.* *call office in advance (office open 10am–6pm Mon, Tue, Fri).* **www**.gracedc.org

Built in 1866, Grace Church was designed to serve the religious needs of the boatmen who worked on the Chesapeake and Ohio Canal and the sailors of the port of Georgetown. Set on a tree-filled plot south of the canal and M Street, the Gothic Revival church, with its quaint exterior, is an oasis in Georgetown.

The building has undergone few extensive alterations over the years and has a certain timeless quality. The church's multi-ethnic congregation makes great efforts to reach out to the larger DC community and works with soup kitchens and shelters for the homeless. The church also sponsors the "Thank God It's Friday" lunchtime discussion group, and holds a poetry coffee house on the third Tuesday of the month. Classical concerts, including chamber pieces, organ, and piano works, are held here regularly. There is also a popular annual festival devoted to the music of the German composer J.S. Bach.

THE
PISCOPAL CHURCH
WELCOMES YOU
ACE CHURCH
Sign for Grace Church

Rowing on the Canal
Boating is popular on the C&O and is best between Georgetown and Violette's Lock – the first 22 miles (35 km) of the canal.

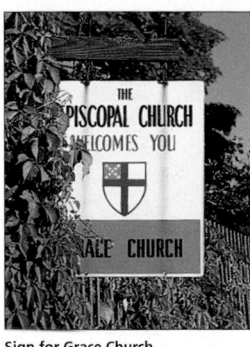

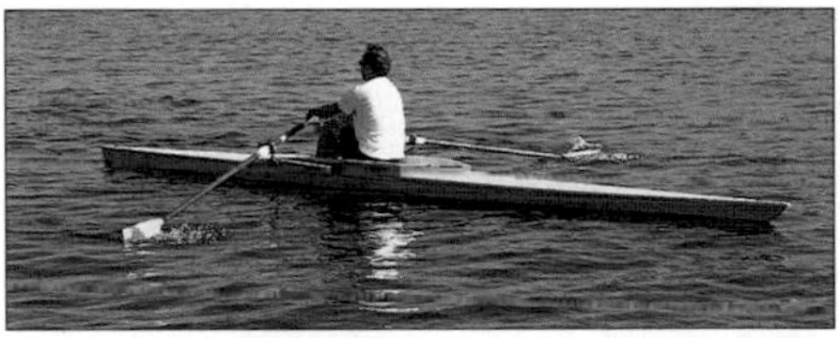

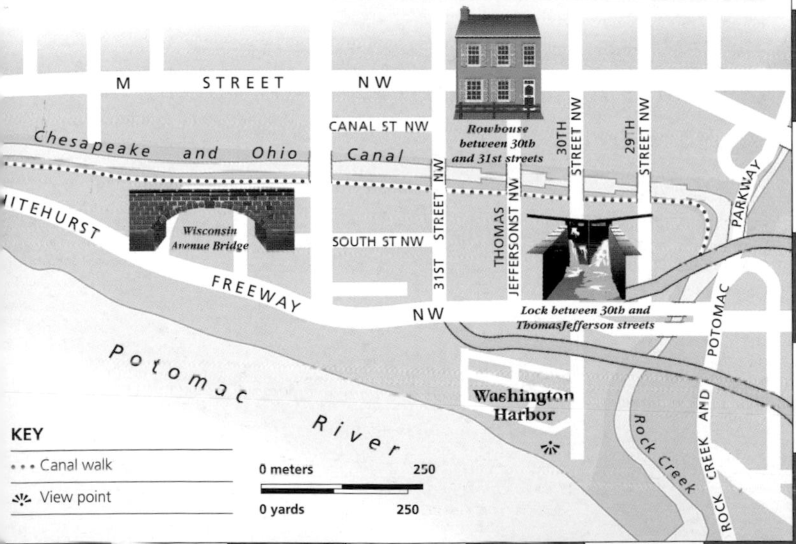

M STREET NW
CANAL ST NW
Rowhouse between 30th and 31st streets
30TH STREET NW
29TH STREET NW
Chesapeake and Ohio Canal
31ST STREET NW
THOMAS JEFFERSONST NW
PARKWAY
ITEHURST FREEWAY NW
Wisconsin Avenue Bridge
SOUTH ST NW
Lock between 30th and ThomasJefferson streets
POTOMAC
Potomac River
Washington Harbor
Rock Creek
ROCK CREEK AND
KEY
Canal walk
View point
0 meters 250
0 yards 250

Old Stone House [5]

3051 M St, NW. **Map** 2 D2. ***Tel*** *426-6851.* ⏰ *noon–5pm daily.* 🚌 *30, 32, 34, 36, 38.* 🚶 *call 895-6070.* ♿ *limited.* **www**.nps.gov/olst

The Old Stone House may be the only building in Washington that pre-dates the American Revolution. It was built in 1765 by Christopher Layman, and the tiny two-story cottage has a large garden, which is a welcome respite from the shops of busy M Street.

There is a legend that still persists about the Old Stone House – that it was the Suter's Tavern where Washington and Pierre L'Enfant made their plans for the city. However, most historians today now believe that they met in a tavern located elsewhere in Georgetown.

Over the years, the building has housed a series of artisans, and in the 1950s it even served as offices for a used-car dealership. In 1960 the National Park Service restored it to its pre-Revolutionary War appearance. Today park rangers give talks about what Georgetown would have been like during the Colonial days. The Old Stone House is technically the oldest house in DC, although The Lindens, which is now in Kalorama, was built in Massachusetts in the mid-1750s and later moved to Washington.

The picturesque Old Stone House

M Street [6]

M St, NW. **Map** 1 C2.
🚌 *30, 32, 34, 36, 38.*

One of two main shopping streets in Georgetown, M Street is also home to some of the most historic spots in the city. On the northeast corner of 30th and M Streets, on the current site of a bank, stood Union Tavern. Built in 1796, the tavern played host to, among others, Presidents George Washington and John Adams, Napoleon's younger brother Jerome Bonaparte, author Washington Irving, and Francis Scott Key, the composer of the "Star Spangled Banner." During the Civil War, the inn was turned into a temporary hospital where Louisa May Alcott, the author of *Little Women,* nursed wounded soldiers. In the 1930s the tavern was torn down and replaced by a gas station. Dr. William Thornton, architect of the US Capitol and Tudor Place *(see p126)* lived at 3219 M Street.

On the south side of M Street is Market House, which has been the location of Georgetown's market since 1751. In 1796 a wood frame market house was constructed and later replaced by the

Only the two end houses *in this group of fine Federal homes (numbers 3327–3339) are still in their original state.*

N Street [8]

N St, NW. **Map** 1 C2.
🚌 *30, 32, 34, 36.*

N Street is a sampler of 18th-century American Federal architecture – a style favored by leaders of the new nation as being of a lighter and more refined design than the earlier Georgian houses.

At the corner of 30th and N Streets is the Laird-Dunlop House. Today it is owned by Benjamin Bradlee, the former editor of the *Washington Post.*

An excellent example of a Federal house is the Riggs-Riley House at 3038 N Street, most recently owned by Averill and Pamela Harriman. At 3041–3045 N Street is Wheatley Row. These houses were designed to provide not only maximum light from large windows but also maximum privacy as they were placed above street level.

Known as Wheatley Row, these three well-designed Victorian town homes were built in 1859.

current brick market in 1865. In the 1930s the market became an auto supply store, and in the 1990s the New York gourmet food store Dean and Deluca opened a branch here.

Today M Street is home to a collection of fashionable stores and restaurants. Young buyers shop for alternative music at Smash and alternative clothing at Urban Outfitters. National chainstores such as Barnes and Noble, Pottery Barn, and Starbucks have branches along M Street.

Clyde's restaurant at number 3236 is a Georgetown institution, famous for its "happy hour." Bill Danoff, of the Starland Vocal Band, wrote his song "Afternoon Delight" about Clyde's; his gold disc hangs in the bar.

The elegant façade of the Post Office in Georgetown

Attractive houses lining the bustling M Street

Washington Post Office, Georgetown Branch ❼

1215 31st St, NW. **Map** 2 D2.
🚌 30, 32, 34, 36.

Built in 1857 as a custom-house, the still-functioning Georgetown Branch of the Washington Post Office is interesting both historically and architecturally. A custom-house was a money-producing venture for the Federal government, and the US government's investment in such an expensive building provides evidence of Georgetown's importance

as a viable port for many years. Architect Ammi B. Young, who was also responsible for the design of the Vermont State Capitol building in 1832 and the Boston Custom House in 1837, was called to Washington in 1852. He designed several other Italianate buildings in the capital, but this post office is his finest work. The granite custom-house was converted to a post office when Georgetown's fortunes declined.

The building underwent a renovation in 1997 that increased its efficiency and accessibility but retained the integrity of Young's simple, functional design.

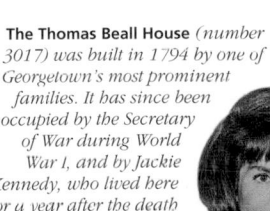

The Thomas Beall House *(number 3017) was built in 1794 by one of Georgetown's most prominent families. It has since been occupied by the Secretary of War during World War I, and by Jackie Kennedy, who lived here for a year after the death of JFK.*

Number 3025–3027, with its raised mansard roof, shows the influence of the French during this period.

The Laird-Dunlop House *(number 3014) was built by John Laird who owned many of Georgetown's tobacco warehouses. Laird modeled his home on those in his native Edinburgh. It was subsequently owned by President Lincoln's son, Robert.*

Unusual flat roof

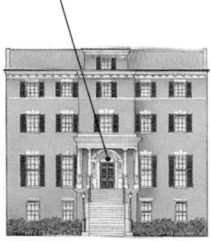

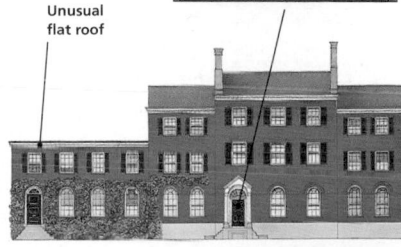

Georgetown University ➒

37th St & O St, NW. **Map** 1 B2.
Tel 687-0100. ◯ varies,
depending on university schedule.
◪ & www.georgetown.edu

Georgetown University was the first Catholic college to be established in America. Founded in 1789 by John Carroll, and affiliated with the Jesuit Order, the university now attracts students of all faiths from over 100 countries around the world.

The oldest building on the campus is the Old North Building, completed in 1872, but the most recognizable structure is the Healy Building, a Germanic design topped by a fanciful spiral. The university's most famous graduate is President Bill Clinton.

The Gothic-inspired Healy Building, Georgetown University

Tudor Place ➓

1644 31st St, NW. **Map** 1 C2.
Tel 965-0400. ◯ 10am–4pm
Tue–Sat, noon–4pm Sun. ● Jan,
Easter Sunday, Memorial Day, Jul 4,
Labor Day, Thanksgiving, Dec 24, 25.
◪ ◪ ◻ www.tudorplace.org

The manor house and large gardens of this Georgetown estate, designed by William Thornton, offer a unique glimpse into a bygone era.

Martha Washington, the First Lady, gave $8,000 to her grand-daughter, Martha Custis Peter, and her granddaughter's husband. With the money, they purchased eight acres and commissioned Thornton, the

Stone dog in the garden of Tudor Place

architect of the Capitol (see pp50–51), to design a house. Generations of the Peters family lived here from 1805 to 1984. It is a mystery as to why this stuccoed, two-story Georgian structure with a "temple" porch is called Tudor Place, but it was perhaps illustrative of the family's English sympathies at the time.

The furniture, silver, china, and portraits provide a glimpse into American social and cultural history; some of the pieces on display come from Mount Vernon (see pp160–61).

Mt. Zion Church ⓫

1334 29th St, NW. **Map** 2 D2.
Tel 234-0148. ✝ 11am Sun. ◪ &

This church is thought to have had the first black congregation in DC. The first church, at 27th and P Streets, was a "station" on the city's original Underground Railroad.

Altar in Mt. Zion church

It provided shelter for runaway slaves on their journey north to freedom. The present redbrick building was completed in 1884 after the first church burned down.

Mt. Zion Cemetery, the oldest black burial ground in Washington, is located a short distance away, in the middle of the 2500 block of Q Street.

Oak Hill Cemetery ⓬

3001 R St, NW. **Map** 2 D1.
Tel 337-2835. ◯ 9am–4:30pm
Mon–Fri, 1–4pm Sun (weather
permitting). ● Federal hols.
www.oakhillcemeterydc.org

William Wilson Corcoran (see p113) bought the land and Congress then established Oak Hill Cemetery in 1849. Today, about 18,000 graves cover the 25-acre site, which is planted with huge oak trees.

Members of some of the city's most prominent families are buried here, their names featuring throughout Washington's history, including Magruder, Thomas, Beall, and Marbury.

At the entrance to the cemetery is an Italianate gatehouse that is still used as the superintendent's lodge and office. Northeast of the gatehouse is the Spencer family monument, designed by Louis Comfort Tiffany. The granite low-relief of an angel is signed by Tiffany.

THE FOUNDING OF THE UNITED NATIONS

In 1944, a conference held at the Dumbarton Oaks estate laid the groundwork for establishing the United Nations. President Franklin Roosevelt and the British Prime Minister, Winston Churchill, wanted to create a "world government" that would supervise the peace at the end of World War II. Roosevelt proposed that a conference be held in Washington, but at the time the State Department did not have a room big enough to accommodate all the delegates. As a solution, Robert Woods Bliss offered the use of the music room in his former home, Dumbarton Oaks, for the event.

The structure of the United Nations was settled at the Dumbarton Oaks Conference and then refined at the San Francisco Conference a year later when the United Nations' charter was ratified. The UN Headquarters building, the permanent home of the organization, was built in New York on the East River site after John D. Rockefeller donated $8.5 million toward its construction.

The conference members in the music room of Dumbarton Oaks

Also notable is the Gothic chapel designed by James Renwick. Nearby is the grave of John Howard Payne, composer of "Home, Sweet Home," who died in 1852. The bust that tops Payne's monument was originally sculpted with a full beard, but Corcoran requested a stonemason to "shave the statue" and so now it is clean shaven.

Dumbarton Oaks ❸

1703 32nd St, NW. **Map** 2 D2. **Tel** 339-6401 *(call ahead to check times).* 🏠 **House** 2–5pm Tue–Sun. **Gardens** 2–6pm Tue–Sun (to 5pm Nov–Feb). Federal hols. for groups call 339-6409. house only. **www**.doaks.org

In 1703, a Scottish colonist named Ninian Beall was granted around 800 acres of land in this area. In later years the land was sold off and in 1801, 22 acres were bought by Senator William Dorsey of Maryland, who proceeded to build a Federal-style brick home here. A year later, financial difficulties caused him to sell it, and over the next century the property changed hands many times.

By the time pharmaceutical heirs Robert and Mildred Woods Bliss bought the run-down estate in 1920, it was overgrown and neglected. The Blisses altered and expanded the house, with the architectural advice of the prestigious firm McKim, Mead and White *(see p109),* to meet 20th-century family needs. They engaged their friend, Beatrix Jones Farrand, one of the few female landscape architects at the time, to lay out the grounds. Farrand designed a series of terraces that progress from the formal gardens near the house to the more informal landscapes farther away from it.

Fountain in Dumbarton Oaks

In 1940 the Blisses moved to California and donated the whole estate to Harvard University. It was then converted into a library, research institution, and museum. Many of the 1,400 pieces of Byzantine Art on display were collected by the Blisses themselves. Examples of Greco-Roman coins, late Roman and early Byzantine bas-reliefs, Egyptian fabrics, and Roman glass and bronzeware are just some of the highlights. In 1962 Robert Woods Bliss donated his collection of pre-Columbian art. In order to house it, architect Philip Johnson designed a new wing, consisting of eight domes surrounding a circular garden. Although markedly different from the original house, a separate wing is well suited to the dramatic art collection it houses, which includes masks, stunning gold jewelry from Central America, and Aztec carvings.

Swimming pool in the grounds of Dumbarton Oaks

FARTHER AFIELD

North of the White House is Dupont Circle, a neighborhood of museums, galleries, and restaurants. The Embassy Row, Kalorama, Adams-Morgan, and Cleveland Park neighborhoods are a walker's paradise, especially for visitors interested in architecture.

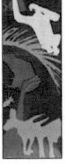

Zoo sign

Arlington, Virginia, across the Potomac River, was one of DC's first suburbs. Arlington National Cemetery was founded in 1864 to honor those who died for the Union. The Pentagon was built 80 years later by Franklin D. Roosevelt and is the area's most famous landmark.

SIGHTS AT A GLANCE

Museums and Galleries
African American Civil War Memorial and Museum 7
Anacostia Museum 28
Hillwood Estate Museum 18
Mary McLeod Bethune Council House 17
National Geographic Museum 10
The Phillips Collection 11
Textile Museum 12

Historic Districts, Streets, and Buildings
Adams-Morgan 16
Dupont Circle 9
Embassy Row 14
Frederick Douglass House 27
Heurich Mansion 6
Howard University 26
Kalorama 15
Lincoln Theatre 19
Washington National Cathedral pp142–3 21
The Pentagon 2
Southwest Waterfront 4
Woodrow Wilson House 13

Monuments
Air Force Memorial 3
Basilica of the National Shrine of the Immaculate Conception 24
Iwo Jima Statue 8

Parks and Gardens
Cleveland Park 22
National Arboretum 25
National Zoological Park pp138–9 20
Rock Creek Park 23
Theodore Roosevelt Island 5

Cemetery
Arlington National Cemetery pp130–31 1

KEY
Central Washington
District of Columbia
Greater Washington
Domestic airport
Metro line
Freeway (motorway)
Major road
Minor road

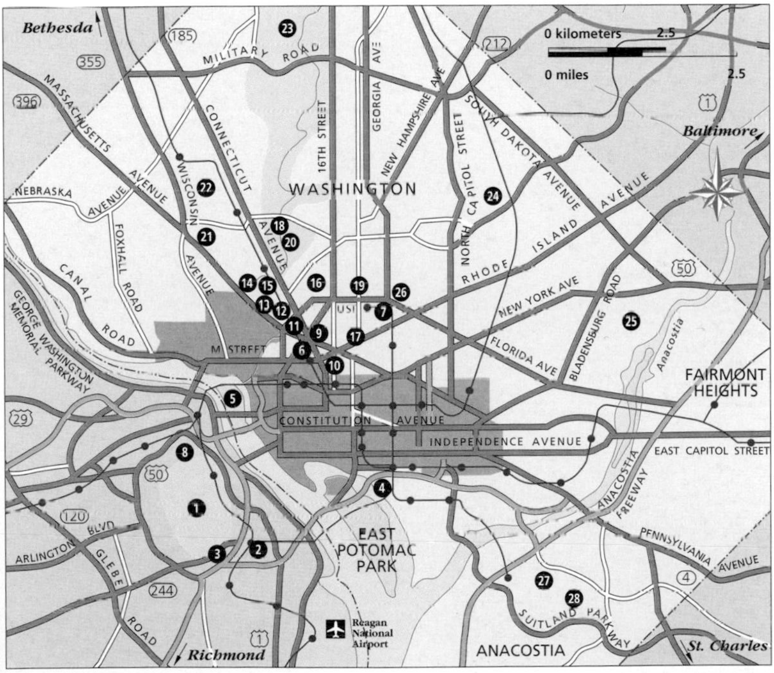

◁ Chinese-style pagoda in the Asian collection at the National Arboretum

Arlington National Cemetery ❶

For 30 years, Confederate General Robert E. Lee (1807–70) lived at Arlington House. In 1861 he left his home to lead Virginia's armed forces, and the Union confiscated the estate for a military cemetery. By the end of the Civil War in 1865, 16,000 soldiers were interred in the consecrated Arlington National Cemetery. Since then, around another 300,000 veterans have joined them. Simple headstones mark the graves of soldiers who died in every major conflict from the Revolution to the present.

Soldier on guard

The focus of the cemetery is the Tomb of the Unknowns, which honors the thousands of unidentified soldiers who have died in battle.

Confederate Memorial
This bronze and granite monument honors the Confederate soldiers who died in the Civil War. It was dedicated in 191

Sea of Graves
More than 330,000 service members and their families are buried on the 624 acres of Arlington Cemetery.

★ Tomb of the Unknowns
This tomb contains four vaults – for World War I and II, Vietnam, and Korea. Each vault held one unidentified soldier until recently when the Vietnam soldier was identified by DNA analysis and reburied in his home town.

```
0 meters        200
0 yards         200
```

STAR FEATURES

★ Arlington House

★ Grave of John F. Kennedy

★ Tomb of the Unknowns

Memorial Amphitheater
This marble amphitheater is the setting of the annual services on Memorial Day (see p36) when the nation's leaders pay tribute to the dead who served their country. It has also hosted many military ceremonies.

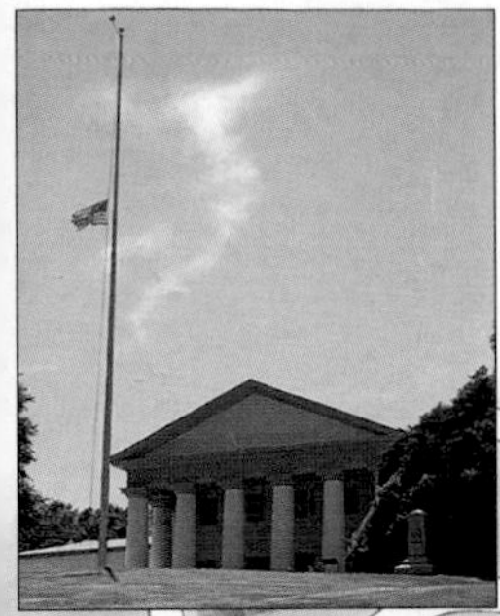

★ Arlington House
Once home to Robert E. Lee, this Georgian-Revival house is now a memorial to the general and his family. It is possible to tour the house during cemetery visiting hours.

VISITORS' CHECKLIST

Arlington, VA. **Tel** *(703) 607-8000.* [M] *Arlington National Cemetery.* ◯ *Oct–Mar: 8am–5pm daily; Apr–Sep: 8am–6:30pm daily.* ● *Dec 25.* 🚌 *Tourmobile leaves the Visitor Center and stops at the John F. Kennedy grave, Arlington House, and Tomb of the Unknowns every 15–30 mins.* ◯ *8:30am–4:30pm.* **Tel** *554-5100.* ♿ 🛍 **www**.arlingtoncemetery.org; **www**.tourmobile.com

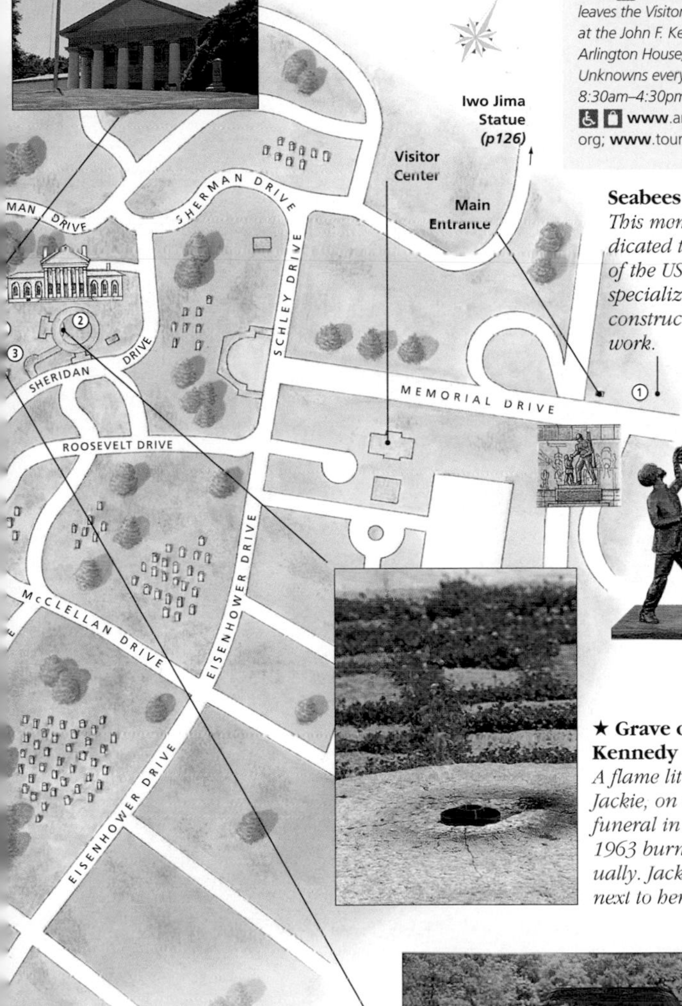

Iwo Jima Statue (p126)
Visitor Center
Main Entrance
SHERMAN DRIVE
SCHLEY DRIVE
MEMORIAL DRIVE
SHERIDAN DRIVE
ROOSEVELT DRIVE
EISENHOWER DRIVE
McCLELLAN DRIVE
1
2
3

Seabees Memorial
This memorial is dedicated to the section of the US Navy that specializes in construction work.

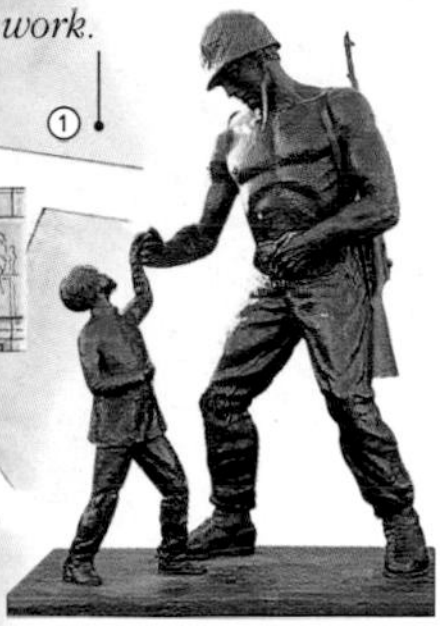

★ Grave of John F. Kennedy
A flame lit by his wife, Jackie, on the day of his funeral in December 1963 burns here continually. Jackie is buried next to her husband.

KEY TO TOMBS AND SITES

- Arlington House 5
- Challenger and Columbia Shuttle Memorials 9
- Confederate Memorial 7
- Grave of John F. Kennedy 2
- Grave of Robert F. Kennedy 3
- Lockerbie Memorial 6
- Memorial Amphitheater 10
- Rough Riders Memorial 8
- Seabees Memorial 1
- Tomb of Pierre L'Enfant 4
- Tomb of the Unknowns 11

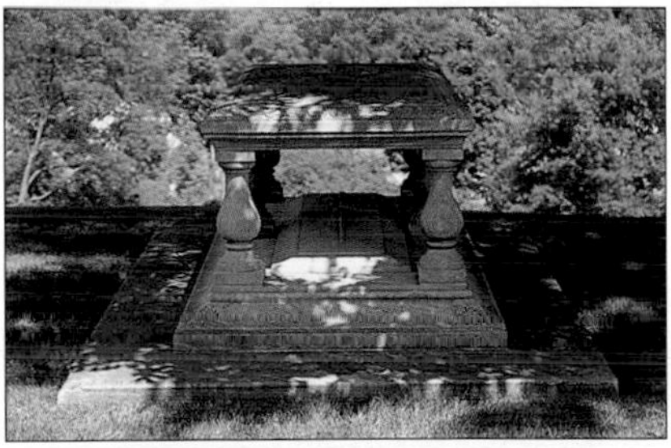

Tomb of Pierre L'Enfant
The architect responsible for planning the city of Washington has a suitably grand burial site in the cemetery (see p67).

View of the Pentagon building's formidable concrete façade from the Potomac River

The Pentagon ❷

1000 Defense Pentagon, Hwy 1-395, Arlington, VA. **Tel** *(703) 697-1776.* M *Pentagon. Tours by appointment for US citizens only. For information call the above number.* www.*pentagon.afis.osd.mil*

President Franklin Roosevelt decided in the early 1940s to consolidate the 17 buildings that comprised the Department of War (the original name for the Department of Defense) into one building. Designed by army engineers, and built of gravel dredged from the Potomac River and molded into concrete, the Pentagon was started on September 11, 1941 and completed on January 15, 1943, at a cost of $83 million. As the world's largest office building, it is almost a city in itself. Yet despite its size, the Pentagon's unique five-sided design is very efficient, and it takes only seven minutes to walk between any two points.

The Pentagon is the head-quarters of the Department of Defense, a Cabinet-level organization consisting of three military departments, the Army, Navy, and Air Force, as well as 14 defense agencies. Leading personnel are the Secretary of Defense and the Chairman of the Joint Chiefs of Staff.

On September 11, 2001, the building was damaged in a terrorist attack. A memorial to the 184 people who died in the Pentagon and on Flight 77 was dedicated on September 11, 2008.

Air Force Memorial ❸

Off Columbia Pike. **Tel** *(703) 979-0674.* M *Pentagon City & Pentagon.* ◯ *Apr–Oct: 8am–11pm daily; Nov–Mar: 8am–9pm daily.* ✆ *by appt.* www.*airforcememorial.org*

Located on a promontory overlooking the Pentagon, this memorial honors the service and sacrifices of the men and women of the United States Air Force and its predecessor organizations. Central to the bold, graceful design, intended to evoke flight, are three stainless steel spires which soar skyward, the highest reaching 270 ft (82 m). President George W. Bush accepted the Memorial on behalf of the American people in October 2006.

The elegant Air Force Memorial

Southwest Waterfront ❹

M *Waterfront.* **Fish Market** ◯ *7:30am–8pm daily.* www.*swdcwaterfront.com*

In the 1960s, urban planners tested their new architectural theories on Washington's southwest waterfront along the Potomac River. Old neighborhoods were torn down, and apartment high-rises put up in their place. Eventually new restaurants developed along

A stall at the water-front's fish market

the waterfront, and Arena Stage, a popular regional theater company, built an experimental theater here. The area enjoyed a regeneration, and today it is a relaxed place to eat or just take a stroll.

The fish market, a remnant of the old waterfront culture, is located off Maine Avenue. Today it is still a thriving business, drawing customers from all over Washington and enjoying its reputation as one of the most vibrant spots in the area. Customers can buy lobster, crabs, oysters, and all kinds of fresh fish from the vendors selling from their barges on the river. There are also several good restaurants along the waterfront that specialize in freshly caught local fish and seafood. Arrive early during the summer months as this is a popular place to dine.

SEPTEMBER 11

On September 11, 2001, one of four airplanes hijacked by terrorists was flown into the Pentagon, resulting in huge loss of life and causing the side of the building to collapse.

Crews at the Pentagon worked tirelessly to rebuild the damaged 10 percent of the building (400,000 to 500,000 square feet). It was estimated that repairs would take three years to finish but they were completed in less than a year. The west wall has a dedication capsule and a single charred capstone. A memorial has been erected.

The damaged Pentagon after the September 11 attack

Theodore Roosevelt Island ❺

GW Memorial Pkwy, McLean, VA. **Map** 1 C4. *Tel (703) 289-2500.* Ⓜ *Rosslyn.* ☐ *6am–10pm daily.* ☐ *by appt only.* **www**.nps.gov/this

A haven for naturalists, Theodore Roosevelt Island's 91 acres of marshlands and two and a half miles (4 km) of nature trails are home to a variety of wildlife including red-tailed hawks, great owls, groundhogs, and wood ducks, as well as many species of trees and plants. President Theodore Roosevelt (1858–1919), a great naturalist himself, is honored with a 17-ft (5-m) tall memorial in bronze, and four granite tablets, each inscribed with quotes by the president.

The island is just one of several sites that form part of the George Washington Memorial Parkway. Enjoy a quiet stroll or visit one of the parkway's other historical sites. Remember to carry drinking water, especially during the summer months.

There is a carpark on the George Washington Memorial Parkway (northbound) from where you can access the footbridge leading to the island. Bicycles are not permitted on the island.

Heurich Mansion ❻

1307 New Hampshire Ave, NW. *Tel 429-1894.* Ⓜ *Dupont Circle.* ☐ *11:30am & 1pm Thu & Fri; (2:30pm Sat). Wed by appt.* ● *Federal hols.* ✎ *donation.* ♿ **www**.brewmasterscastle.com

Brewer Christian Heurich built this wonderful Bavarian fantasy for his family just south of Dupont Circle in 1894. The turreted mansion built in the Romanesque Revival architectural style was home to the Historical Society of Washington, DC until 2003, when it relocated to the City Museum in the Carnegie Library Building *(see p96).* The Heurich Mansion is a fine example of an upper-middle-class family house in Washington in the late 1800s.

The ornate carving in Heurich's Beer Hall

African American Civil War Memorial and Museum ❼

Museum 1200 U St, NW. **Memorial** 10th St, NW and Vermont Ave, NW. *Tel 667-2667.* Ⓜ *U Street.* ☐ *10am–5pm Mon–Fri, 10am–2pm Sat (call for tours).* **www**.afroamcivilwar.org

Opened in January 1999, the African American Museum uses photographs, documents and audiovisual equipment to explain the still largely unknown story of African Americans' long struggle for freedom. The Museum's permanent exhibition is entitled "Slavery to Freedom; Civil War to Civil Rights." Interactive kiosks bring together historic documents, photographs, and music in a powerful and evocative way. There is also a service for anyone interested in tracing relatives who may have served with United States Colored Troops during the Civil War. At the center of a paved plaza is situated the "Spirit of Freedom," a sculpture by Ed Hamilton, which was unveiled on July 18, 1998. It is the first major art piece by a black sculptor on federal land in the District of Columbia. It stands 10ft tall and features uniformed black soldiers and a sailor poised to leave home.

Statue of President Roosevelt and granite tablets on Theodore Roosevelt Island

The elaborate fountain at the heart of the Dupont Circle intersection

Iwo Jima Statue (US Marine Corps Memorial) **8**

Meade St, between Arlington National Cemetery & Arlington Blvd. **Map** 1 B5. Ⓜ *Rosslyn*. ♿

The horrific battle of Iwo Jima that took place during World War II was captured by photographer Joe Rosenthal. His Pulitzer Prize-winning picture of five Marines and a Navy Corpsman raising the American flag on the tiny Pacific island came to symbolize in the American psyche the heroic struggle of the American forces in the war against Japan.

This image was magnificently translated into bronze by sculptor Felix DeWeldon and paid for by private donations. The three surviving soldiers from Rosenthal's photograph actually posed for DeWeldon; the other three men, however, were killed in further fighting on the islands. The Iwo Jima Memorial is dedicated to all members of the Marine Corps who have died defending their country.

A poignant memorial to the men who died in the battle of Iwo Jima

Dupont Circle **9**

Map 2 F2 & 3 A1. Ⓜ *Dupont Circle*.

This area to the north of the White House gets its name from the fountain and is at the intersection of Massachusetts, Connecticut, and New Hampshire Avenues, and 19th Street, NW. At the heart of this traffic island is the Francis Dupont Memorial Fountain, named for the first naval hero of the Civil War, Admiral Samuel Francis Dupont. Built by his family, the original memorial was a bronze statue that was moved eventually to Wilmington, Delaware. The present marble fountain, which was constructed in 1921, has four figures (which represent the sea, the wind, the stars, and the

Playing chess in Dupont Circle

navigational arts) supporting a marble basin.

The park area around the fountain draws a cross section of the community – chess players engrossed in their games, cyclists pausing at the fountain, picnickers, and tourists taking a break from sightseeing. Do not stray into the Circle after dark as it may not be safe at night.

In the early 20th century the Dupont Circle area was a place of grand mansions. Its fortunes then declined until the 1970s, when Washingtonians began to buy the decaying mansions. The district is now filled with art galleries, bars, restaurants, and bookstores. The old Victorian buildings have been divided into apartments, restored as single family homes, or converted into small office buildings. Dupont Circle is also the center of Washington's gay community. The bars and clubs on the section of P Street between Dupont Circle and Rock Creek Park are the most popular area for gay men and women to meet.

National Geographic Museum **10**

1145 17th St at M St, NW. **Map** 3 B2. **Tel** 857-7588. Ⓜ *Farragut North, Farragut West*. ◷ 9am–5pm Mon–Sat & Federal hols, 10am–5pm Sun. ⬤ Dec 25. ♿ 📷 **www.** nationalgeographic.com/museum

This small museum is located in the National Geographic Society's headquarters, designed by Edward Durrell Stone, the architect behind the Kennedy Center. A series of permanent and temporary exhibitions documents the richness of nature and the diversity of human culture all over the world. Past exhibitions include the Terra-Cotta Warriors and an exploration of the Golden Age of the pharaohs.

Auguste Renoir's masterpiece, *The Luncheon of the Boating Party* (1881)

The Phillips Collection ⑪

1600 21st St at Q St, NW.
Map 2 E2 & 3 A1. **Tel** 387-2151.
Ⓜ Dupont Circle. ◯ 10am–5pm
Tue–Sat (to 8:30pm Thu), 11am–6pm
Sun. ◯ Jan 1, Jul 4, Thanksgiving,
Dec 25, Federal hols. 🎨 🎫 11am
Fri & Sat ♿ ▢ ▢
www.phillipscollection.org

This is one of the finest collections of Impressionist works in the world and the first museum devoted to modern art in the United States. Duncan and Marjorie Phillips, who founded the collection, lived in the older of the museum's two adjacent buildings. Following the death of his father and brother in 1917, Duncan Phillips decided to open two of the mansion's rooms as The Phillips Memorial Gallery.

The couple spent their time traveling and adding to their already extensive collection. During the 1920s they acquired some of the most important modern European paintings, including *The Luncheon of the Boating Party* (1881) by Renoir, for which they paid $125,000 (one of the highest prices ever paid at the time).

In 1930 the Phillips family moved to a new home on Foxhall Road in northwest Washington and converted the rest of their former 1897 Georgian Revival residence into a private gallery. The Phillips Gallery was then reopened to the public in 1960 and renamed The Phillips Collection. The museum currently has over 3,000 pieces of 19th-, 20th-, and 21st-century American and European art.

The elegant Georgian Revival building that was the Phillips' home makes for a more intimate and personal gallery than the big Smithsonian art museums.

The Phillips Collection is best known for its wonderful selection of Impressionist and Post-Impressionist paintings; *Dancers at the Barre* by Degas, *Self-Portrait* by Cézanne and *Entrance to the Public Gardens in Arles* by Van Gogh are just three examples. The museum also has one of the largest collections in the world of pieces by French artist Pierre Bonnard, including *The Open Window* (1921).

Other great paintings to be seen in the collection include El Greco's *The Repentant Saint Peter* (1600), *The Blue Room* (1901) by Pablo Picasso, and the huge *Ochre and Red on Red* (1954) by Mark Rothko.

Collector Duncan Phillips (1886–1966)

In addition to the permanent exhibits, the museum supports traveling exhibitions, which start at The Phillips Collection before appearing in galleries around the country. The exhibitions often feature one artist (such as Georgia O'Keeffe) or one particular topic or period (such as the *Twentieth-Century Still-Life Paintings* exhibition).

The Phillips Collection encourages enthusiasts of modern art to visit the museum for a number of special events. On the first Thursday of each month the museum hosts "Phillips after 5." These evenings include gallery talks, live music, and light refreshments, and give people the opportunity to discuss the issues of the art world in a relaxed, social atmosphere. On Sunday afternoons from September through May, a series of concerts are staged in the gallery's Music Room. Running since 1941, these popular concerts are free to anyone who has purchased a ticket to the museum on that day. They range from piano recitals and string quartets to performances by established singers of world renown, such as the famous operatic soprano Jessye Norman.

The museum shop sells merchandise linked to permanent and temporary exhibitions. Books, posters, and prints can be found as well as ceramics, glassware, and other creations by contemporary artists. There are also hand-painted silks and artworks based on the major paintings in the collection.

***Entrance to the Public Gardens in Arles* (1888), by Vincent Van Gogh**

18th-century Turkish embroidery on silk in the Textile Museum

Textile Museum ⑫

421 7th St, NW. **Map** 2 E1.
Tel 667-0441. Ⓜ *Dupont Circle.*
◯ *10am–5pm Tue–Sat, 1–5pm Sun.*
◐ *Dec 24 & 25, Federal hols.*
🈺 *donation.* ✔ *"Highlights" tours 1:30pm Sat & Sun.* **Library**
◯ *10am–2pm Wed–Fri, 10am–4pm Sat.* 🔒 ♿ *call in advance.*
www.textilemuseum.org

George Hewitt Myers, the founder of the Textile Museum, began collecting oriental rugs while he was at college. In 1925 he opened a museum in his home to display his collection of 275 rugs and 60 textiles. It was a private museum, open only by appointment, until Myers' death in 1957.

Today the museum is still housed in Myers' home, which was designed by John Russell Pope, architect of the Jefferson Memorial *(see p79)*. The collection is also now in an adjacent building by Waddy B. Wood, architect of Woodrow Wilson's house.

There are around 17,000 objects in the collection from all over the world, including textiles from Peru, India, Indonesia, and Central America. Some pieces date from 3000 BC. The museum also hosts traveling exhibitions from other collections. During museum hours, the public can access the large formal gardens at the back of the building.

Woodrow Wilson House ⑬

2340 S St, NW. **Map** 2 E1.
Tel 387-4062. Ⓜ *Dupont Circle.*
◯ *10am–4pm Tue–Sun.*
◐ *Federal hols.* 🈺 ✔ ♿
www.woodrowwilsonhouse.org

Located in the Kalorama neighborhood, the former home of Woodrow Wilson (1856–1924), who served as president from 1913 to 1921, is the only presidential museum within the District of Columbia.

Wilson led the US through World War I and advocated the formation of the League of Nations, the precursor to the United Nations. Although exhausted by the war effort, Wilson campaigned tirelessly for the League.

In 1919 he collapsed from a stroke and became an invalid for the rest of his life. Many believe that Wilson's second wife, Edith Galt, assumed many of the presidential duties herself (she guided his hand when he signed documents). Unable to leave his sickbed, Wilson saw his dream, the League of Nations, defeated in the Senate. In 1920 he was awarded the Nobel Peace Prize – small consolation for the failure of the League.

Wilson and his wife moved to this townhouse, designed by Waddy B. Wood, at the end of his second term in 1921.

Statue of Churchill, British Embassy

Edith Galt Wilson arranged for the home to be bequeathed to the nation. Since then the building has been maintained as it was during the President's lifetime, containing artifacts from his life, such as his Rolls-Royce, and reflecting the style of an upper-middle-class home of the 1920s. The house today belongs to the National Trust for Historic Preservation.

Embassy Row ⑭

Massachusetts Avenue. **Map** 2 E1.
Ⓜ *Dupont Circle. See also pp146–7.*

Embassy Row stretches along Massachusetts Avenue from Scott Circle toward Observatory Circle. It developed during the Depression when many of Washington's wealthy families were forced to sell their mansions to diplomats, who bought them for foreign missions. Since then, many new embassies have been built, often in the vernacular style of their native country, making Embassy Row architecturally fascinating.

At No. 2315 Massachusetts Avenue, the Embassy of Pakistan is an opulent mansion built in 1908, with a mansard roof (four steep sloping sides) and a rounded wall that hugs the corner.

Farther down the road, at No. 2349, is the Embassy of the Republic of Cameroon, one of the Avenue's great

An elaborately decorated room in the Georgian Revival Woodrow Wilson House

early 20th-century Beaux Arts masterpieces. This romantic, Norwegian chateau-style building was commissioned in 1905 to be the home of Christian Hauge, first Norwegian ambassador to the United States, before passing to Cameroon.

Situated opposite the Irish Embassy stands a bronze statue of the hanged Irish revolutionary Robert Emmet (1778–1803). The statue was commissioned by Irish Americans to commemorate Irish independence.

At No. 2536 is the India Supply Mission. Two carved elephants stand outside as symbols of Indian culture and mythology. In the park in front of the Indian Embassy is an impressive bronze sculpture of Mahatma Gandhi.

The British Embassy, at No. 3100, was designed by Sir Edwin Lutyens in 1928. The English-style gardens were planted by the American wife of the then British ambassador, Sir Ronald Lindsay. Outside the embassy is an arresting statue of Sir Winston Churchill by William M. McVey.

Façade of the Croatian Embassy on Massachusetts Avenue

Kalorama 🟒

Map 2 D1 & 2 E1.
Ⓜ *Woodley Park or Dupont Circle.*

The neighborhood of Kalorama, situated north of Dupont Circle, is an area of stately private homes and elegant apartment buildings. From its development at the turn of the 20th century as a suburb close to the city center, Kalorama (Greek for "beautiful view") has been home to the wealthy and upwardly mobile.

The apartments at 2311 Connecticut Avenue, Kalorama

Five presidents had homes here: Herbert Hoover, Franklin D. Roosevelt, Warren Harding, William Taft, and Woodrow Wilson. Only Wilson's home served as his permanent post-presidential residence.

Some of the most striking and ornate apartment buildings in Washington are found on Connecticut Avenue, south of the Taft Bridge that crosses Rock Creek Park. Most notable are the Georgian Revival-style Dresden apartments at No. 2126, the Beaux Arts-inspired Highlands building at number 1914, and the Spanish Colonial-style Woodward apartments at No. 2311 Connecticut Avenue. Also worth viewing is the Tudor-style building at No. 2221 Kalorama Road.

The best views of nearby Rock Creek Park *(see p141)* are from Kalorama Circle at the northern end of 24th Street.

Adams-Morgan 🟏

North of Dupont Circle, east of Rock Creek Park, and south of Mt. Pleasant. **Map** 2 E1 & 2 F1.
Ⓜ *Dupont Circle or Woodley Park.*

Adams-Morgan is the only racially and ethnically diverse neighborhood in the city. It was given its name in the 1950s when the Supreme Court ruled that Washington must desegregate its educational system, and forced the combination of two schools in the area – Adams (for white children) and Morgan (an all-black school).

Packed with cafés, bookstores, clubs, and galleries, the district is a vibrant and eclectic mix of African, Hispanic, and Caribbean immigrants, as well as white urban pioneers, both gay and straight. People are attracted by the neighborhood's lively streets and its beautiful, and relatively affordable, early 20th-century houses and apartments.

The area has a thriving music scene and, on any night, rap, reggae, salsa, and Washington's indigenous go-go can be heard in the clubs and bars. The cosmopolitan feel of Adams-Morgan is reflected in its wide variety of restaurants *(see p190)*. Cajun, New Orleans, Ethiopian, French, Italian, Caribbean, Mexican, and Lebanese food can all be found along 18th Street and Columbia Road, the two main streets.

Although the area is becoming increasingly modern and trendy, its 1950s Hispanic roots are still evident. They are loudly celebrated in the Hispanic-Latino Festival that takes place every July and spreads from the Mall up to Adams-Morgan *(see p37)*.

It should be noted that this area can be dangerous after dark, so be wary if you are walking around at night. The area is not served by Metrorail and parking, especially on weekends, can be difficult.

Colorful mural on the wall of a parking lot in Adams-Morgan

National Zoological Park 20

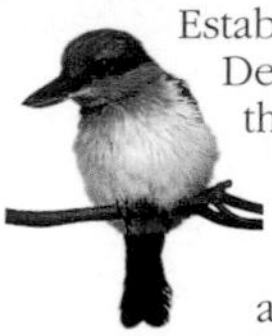

Micronesian Kingfisher

Established in 1889 as the Smithsonian's Department of Living Animals and sited on the Mall, Washington's National Zoo moved to its present location in 1891. The park, which covers 163 acres, was designed by Frederick Law Olmsted, the landscape architect responsible for New York's Central Park. Today, the zoo is home to more than 2,000 animals, many of which are endangered. The zoo also runs a number of breeding programs, one of the most successful of which is the Sumatran tiger program.

Giant Panda Habitat
The National Zoo was the first zoo in the US to house pandas. Since 1972 these beloved bears have been the zoo's top attraction.

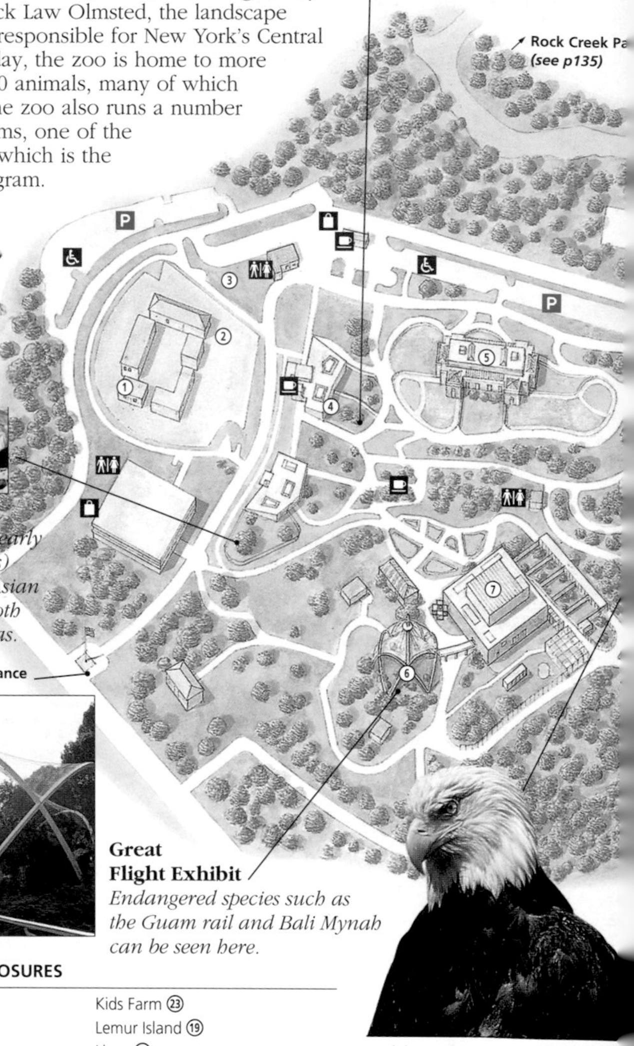

Rock Creek Pa
(see p135)
Main Entrance

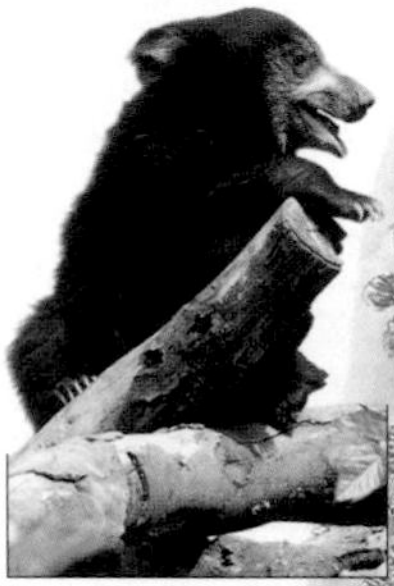

★ Asia Trail
This exhibit covers nearly 6 acres (2.4 hectares) and features seven Asian species, including sloth bears and red pandas.

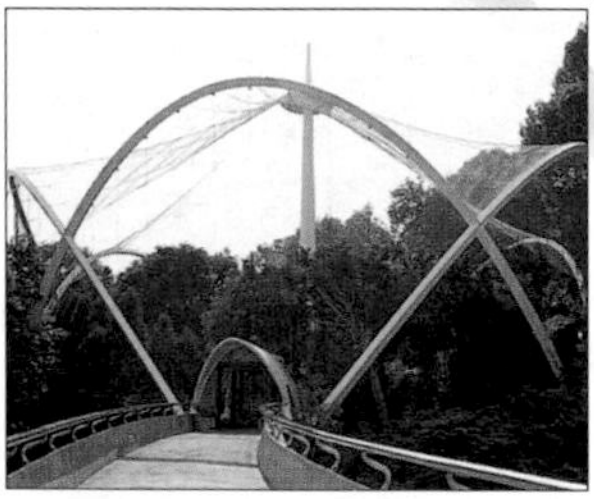

Great Flight Exhibit
Endangered species such as the Guam rail and Bali Mynah can be seen here.

Bald Eagle
The only eagle unique to North America, the bald eagle is named for its white head, which appears to be "bald" against its dark body.

KEY TO ANIMAL ENCLOSURES

Amazonia 13
Andean Bears 12
Bald Eagles 12
Bird House 7
Cheetah Conservation Station 1
Elephants 5
Giant Panda Habitat 4
Gibbon Ridge 14
Golden Lion Tamarins 8
Great Ape House 15
Great Flight Exhibit 6
Invertebrates 17
Kids Farm 23
Lemur Island 19
Lions 22
Otters 9
Reptile Discovery Center 18
Seals and Sea Lions 11
Small Mammal House 16
Sumatran Tigers 21
Think Tank 20
Wallabies 3
Zebras 2

0 meters 100
0 yards 100

Golden Lion Tamarins
These endangered mammals are protected by an international conservation program, which includes breeding and conservation education.

★ Great Ape House
Western Lowland Gorillas – males can weigh over 400 pounds (180 kg) – can be seen in the Great Ape House. Other occupants include tree-dwelling orangutans.

★ Komodo Dragons
These rare lizards can grow up to 10 ft (3 m) in length, and weigh up to 200 lbs (90 kg). They are the first to be born in captivity outside Indonesia.

Sumatran Tigers
Native to the Indonesian island of Sumatra, these are the smallest of all surviving tiger subspecies and are excellent swimmers.

Amazonia
This exhibit re-creates the Amazonian habitat. Visitors can see many creatures from poison-dart frogs to giant catfish.

STAR EXHIBITS

★ Asia Trail

★ Great Ape House

★ Komodo Dragons

Mary McLeod Bethune Council House National Historic Site 🔟

1318 Vermont Ave, NW. **Map** 3 B1. **Tel** 673-2402. Ⓜ McPherson Square/U Street. ☐ 9am–5pm Mon–Sat. ● Jan 1, Thanksgiving, Dec 25. ✎ plus interactive tour for children. 🏠 www.nps.gov/mamc

Born in 1875 to two former-slaves, Mary McLeod Bethune was an educator and civil and women's rights activist. In 1904 she founded a college for impoverished black women in Florida, the Daytona Educational and Industrial School for Negro Girls. Renamed the Bethune-Cookman College, it is still going strong.

In the 1930s, President Franklin D. Roosevelt asked her to be his special advisor on racial affairs, and she later became director of the Division of Negro Affairs in the National Youth Administration. As part of Roosevelt's cabinet, Bethune enjoyed the highest position ever held by a black woman in the US government.

Bethune went on to found the National Council of Negro Women, which gives voice to the concerns of black women. The Council grew to have a membership of 10,000, and

Mary McLeod Bethune

Entrance to the Mary McLeod Bethune Council House

The stunning interior of the restored Lincoln Theatre

this house on Vermont Avenue was bought by Bethune and the Council as its headquarters.

It was not until November 1979, 24 years after Bethune's death, that the original Council House was opened to the public, with photographs, manuscripts, and other artifacts from her life on display. In 1982 the house was declared a National Historic Site and was bought by the National Park Service.

Hillwood Estate Museum and Gardens 🔟

4155 Linnean Avenue, NW. **Tel** 686-5807. Ⓜ Van Ness/ UDC. ☐ 10am–5pm Tue–Sat. ● Jan, Federal hols. ✎ ✎ 🏠 🖼 www.hillwoodmuseum.org

Hillwood was owned by Marjorie Merriweather Post, and it was opened to the public in 1977. The Museum contains the most comprehensive collection of 18th- and 19th-century Russian imperial art to be found outside of Russia, including Fabergé eggs and Russian Orthodox icons. It also has some renowned pieces of 18th-century French decorative art. The Gardens are set within a 25-acre estate, surrounded by woodlands in the heart of Washington, and have important collections of azaleas and orchids.

Lincoln Theatre 🔟

1215 U St, NW. **Map** 2 F1. **Tel** 328-6000 (box office). Ⓜ U Street-Cardozo. ☐ 10am–6pm Mon–Fri. ● Federal hols. ✎ groups by appt. ♿ www.thelincolntheatre.org

Built in 1922, the Lincoln Theatre was once the centerpiece of cultural life for Washington's downtown African American community. Like the Apollo Theater in New York, the Lincoln presented big-name entertainment, such as jazz singer and native Washingtonian Duke Ellington, Ella Fitzgerald, and Billie Holiday.

By the 1960s the area around the theater began to deteriorate; the 1968 riots turned U Street into a corridor of abandoned and burned-out buildings, and attendance at the theater dropped dramatically. By the 1970s the theater had closed down. Then, in the early 1980s fundraising began for the $10 million renovation. Even the original, highly elaborate plasterwork was carefully cleaned and repaired, and the theater reopened in 1994.

Today the Lincoln Theatre is a center for the performing arts, and one of the linchpins of U Street's renaissance. The magnificent auditorium hosts a program of concerts, stage shows, and events including the DC Film Festival (see p202).

National Zoological Park 🔟

See pp138–9.

Washington National Cathedral ㉑

See pp142–3.

Cleveland Park ㉒

Ⓜ *Cleveland Park.*

Cleveland Park is a beautiful residential neighborhood that resembles the picture on a postcard of small-town America. It was originally a summer community for those wanting to escape the less bucolic parts of the city. In 1885, President Grover Cleveland (1885–9) bought a stone farmhouse here as a summer home for his bride.

The town's Victorian summer houses are now much sought after by people wanting to be close to the city but live in a small-town environment. There are interesting shops and good restaurants, as well as a grand old Art Deco movie theater, called the Uptown.

Rock Creek Park ㉓

Ⓜ *Cleveland Park.* **Rock Creek Park Nature Center** *5200 Glover Rd, NW.* **Map** *2 D1–D3.* *Tel 895-6070.* Ⓜ *Friendship Heights.* 🚌 *E2, E3, E4.* ⏰ *9am–5pm Wed–Sun.* ⬤ *Federal hols.* 📷 *by appt.* **www**.nps.gov/rocr

Named for the creek that flows through it, Rock Creek Park bisects the city of Washington. This 1,800-acre stretch

Pierce Mill, the 19th-century gristmill in Rock Creek Park

THE SHAW NEIGHBORHOOD

This neighborhood is named for Union Colonel Robert Gould Shaw, the white commander of an all-black regiment from Massachusetts. He supported his men in their struggle to attain the same rights as white soldiers. Until the 1960s, U Street was the focus of black-dominated businesses and organizations. Thriving theaters, such as the Howard and the Lincoln, attracted top-name performers, and Howard University was the center of intellectual life for black students. The 1968 riots, sparked by the assassination of Dr. Martin Luther King Jr., wiped out much of Shaw's business district, and many thought the area could never be revived. However, the restoration of the Lincoln Theatre, the renewal of the U Street business district, and an influx of homebuyers renovating historic houses, have all contributed to the rejuvenation. In the part of U Street closest to the U Street Cardoza metro stop, many fashionable bars and clubs have opened.

Mural in the Shaw neighborhood depicting Duke Ellington

of land runs from the Maryland border south to the Potomac River and constitutes nearly five percent of the city. Unlike the crowded lawns of Central Park, Rock Creek Park has a feeling of the wilderness. Although the elk, bison, and bears that used to roam the park have vanished, raccoons, foxes, and deer can still be found here in abundance.

The park was endowed in 1890 and is now run by the National Park Service. In addition to hiking and picnicking, the park has a riding stable and horse trails, tennis courts, and an 18-hole golf course. On Sundays, a portion of Beach Drive – one of the main roads running through the park – is closed to cars to allow cyclists and in-line skaters freedom of the road. The creek itself is

inviting, with little eddies and waterfalls, but visitors are advised not to go into the water because it is polluted.

The **Rock Creek Park Nature Center** is a good place to begin an exploration of the park. It includes a small planetarium, and a 1-mile (1.6-km) nature trail, which is very manageable for children.

Pierce Mill near Tilden Street was an active gristmill, which was restored by the National Park Service in 1936. It was kept working as a visitor exhibit until 1993 when it was deemed unsafe to work any more. There is a barn next to the mill where works by local artists can be bought. The Carter Barron Amphitheater, near 16th Street and Colorado Avenue, stages free performances of Shakespeare's plays and summer jazz concerts.

Washington National Cathedral ㉑

The building of the Cathedral Church of Saint Peter and Saint Paul (its official name) began in 1907 and was completed in 1990. The world's sixth-largest cathedral, it dominates the city's skyline and measures 301 ft (94.8 m) from grade to the top of the central tower and 518 ft (158 m) in length – almost the length of two soccer fields. Built with Indiana limestone, the Washington National Cathedral boasts elements typical of Gothic religious architecture, such as soaring vaulting, stained glass windows, and intricate carvings. The exterior features fanciful gargoyles and dramatic sculpture. Although an Episcopal church, the cathedral welcomes people of all faiths. It has also been the location of funeral and memorial services for several US presidents.

Exterior
A masterpiece of Gothic style architecture, the towers of the cathedral dominate the skyline.

Pilgrim Observation Gallery

★ **Ex Nihilo**
Above the center portal is Ex Nihilo by artist Frederick Hart. It depicts figures of men and women emerging from the swirling background.

Main Entrance
Three huge Gothic arches dominate the west façade, with pierced bronze gates depicting stories from the book of Genesis.

George Washington Bay

Space Window
Mankind's achievements in science and technology are commemorated in this window with the flight of Apollo 11 and a piece of moon rock.

The pinnacles on the cathedral towers are decorated with leaf-shaped ornaments and topped by elaborately carved finials.

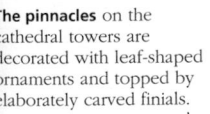

High Altar
Carved on the high altar are 110 figures, surrounding the central statue of Christ. Encased in the floor in front of the altar is stone from Mt. Sinai.

VISITORS' CHECKLIST

3101 Wisconsin Ave and Massachusetts Ave, NW.
Tel 537-6200. 🏢 364-6616.
Ⓜ Tenleytown/AU, Red Line.
🚌 32, 34, 36. ⏰ 10am–5:30pm Mon–Fri, 10am–4:30pm Sat, 8am–5pm Sun. ⛪ 10–11:30am, 12:45–4pm Mon–Sat, 1–2:30pm Sun. 📷 Group reservations call 537-6207.
🎧 ♿ 💻 📷 ⛪ daily.
www.nationalcathedral.org

Children's Chapel
A statue of Jesus as a boy stands by this chapel built to the scale of a six-year-old. There are also motifs of baby and mythical animals.

★ **South Rose Window**
The theme of this window by Joseph Reynolds and Wilbur Burnham is "The Church Triumphant."

Nave
From the West Portal to the High Altar, the iconography tells the story of humanity to redemption.

STAR FEATURES

★ South Rose Window

★ Ex Nihilo

Basilica of the National Shrine of the Immaculate Conception ㉔

400 Michigan at 4th St, NE.
Tel 526-8300. M *Brookland-CUA.*
◯ *Apr 1–Oct 31: 7am–7pm daily;*
Nov 1–Mar 31: 7am–6pm daily.
🚻 ♿ 🖥 🏠 ⚹
www.nationalshrine.com

Completed in 1959, this enormous Catholic Church is dedicated to the Virgin Mary. The church was designed in the shape of a crucifix and has many stained-glass windows. The building can seat a congregation of 2,500 people or more.

In the early 1900s, Bishop Thomas Shahan, rector of the Catholic University of America, proposed building a national shrine in Washington. Shahan gained the Pope's support in 1913, and in 1920 the cornerstone was laid. The Great Upper Church was dedicated on November 20, 1959. An unusual and striking combination of Romanesque and Byzantine styles, the shrine boasts classical towers as well as minarets in its design. The basilica's large interior includes a number of chapels, each with a distinctive design of its own.

Visitors can also enjoy the peaceful and extensive Prayer Garden, which covers almost an acre (4,050 sq m).

Entrance to the Chinese Pavilion at the National Arboretum

View down the nave to the Basilica's altar

National Arboretum ㉕

3501 New York Ave or 24th St & R St off Bladensburg Rd, NE.
Tel 245-2726. M *Stadium Armory.*
◯ *8am– 5pm daily. Museum 10am–4pm daily.* ◯ *Federal hols.* 🎟 *by appt only.* 🏠 ♿ *limited.* **www**.usna.usda.gov

Tucked away in a corner of northeast Washington is the 446-acre National Arboretum – a center for research, education, and the preservation of trees, shrubs, flowers, and other plants. The many different collections here mean that the Arboretum is an ever-changing, Year round spectacle.

The Japanese Garden, which encompasses the National Bonsai and Penjing Museum, has bonsai that are from 20 to 380 Years old. The 2-acre herb garden has ten specialty gardens, where herbs are grouped according to use and historical significance. At the entrance to the garden is an elaborate 16th-century European-style "knot garden," with about 200 varieties of old roses. The Perennial Collection includes peonies, daylilies, and irises, which bloom in late spring and summer. The National Grove of State Trees has trees representing every state.

Bonsai tree in the Arboretum

Howard University ㉖

2400 Sixth St, NW. *Tel* 806-6100. M *Shaw-Howard.* **www**.howard.edu

In 1866 the first Congregational Society of Washington considered establishing a seminary for the education of African-Americans – a school intended for "teachers and preachers." The concept expanded to include a multi-purpose university, and within two years the Colleges of Liberal Arts and Medicine of Howard University were founded. Named for General Oliver O. Howard (1830–1909), an abolitionist and Civil War hero who later became a commissioner of the Freedman's Bureau. The impetus for establishing such a university was the arrival of newly-freed men from the South who were coming to the North seeking education to improve their lives. The university's charter was enacted by Congress and approved by President Andrew Jackson.

Famous graduates include Thurgood Marshall, who championed desegregation of public schools and was the first African-American Supreme Court Justice, Carter Woodson, Toni Morrison, Ralph Bunche, Stokely Carmichael, and Ossie Davis.

FREDERICK DOUGLASS (1817–95)

Born a slave around 1818, Frederick Douglass became the leading voice in the abolitionist movement that fought to end slavery in the United States. Douglass was taught to read and write by his white owners. At the age of 20 he fled to Europe. British friends in the anti-slavery movement purchased him from his former masters, and he was at last a free man. For most of his career he lived in New York, where he worked as a spokesman for the abolitionist movement. A brilliant speaker, he was sent by the American Anti-Slavery Society on a lecture tour and won added fame with the publication of his autobiography in 1845. In 1847 he became editor of the anti-slavery newspaper *The North Star*, named after the constellation point followed by escaping slaves on their way to freedom. During the Civil War *(see p21)*, Douglass was an advisor to President Lincoln and fought for the constitutional amendments that guaranteed equal rights to freed blacks.

Frederick Douglass

Frederick Douglass House ㉗

1411 W St, SE. **Tel** 426-5961.
Ⓜ *Anacostia.* ◯ *mid-Oct–mid-Apr: 9am–4:30pm daily; mid-Apr–mid-Oct: 9am–5pm daily.* ● *Jan 1, Thanksgiving, Dec 25.* 🎟️ 📷 ♿ *call ahead.* **www**.nps.gov/frdo

The abolitionist leader Frederick Douglass lived in Washington only toward the end of his illustrious career. After the Civil War he moved first to a townhouse on Capitol Hill, and then to Anacostia. In 1877 he bought this white framed house, named it Cedar Hill, and lived here, with his family, until his death in 1895.

Douglass's widow opened Cedar Hill for public tours in 1903, and in 1962 the house was donated to the National Park Service. Most of the furnishings are original to the Douglass family and include

"The Growlery" in the garden of the Frederick Douglass House

gifts to Douglass from President Lincoln and the writer Harriet Beecher Stowe, author of *Uncle Tom's Cabin* (1852).

In the garden is a small stone building that Douglass used as an alternative study, and which he nicknamed "The Growlery." From the front steps of the house there is a magnificent view across the Anacostia River.

Anacostia Museum ㉘

1901 Fort Place, SE. **Tel** 633-4820.
Ⓜ *Anacostia* ◯ *10am–5pm daily for tours.* ● *Dec 25.* 📷 *by appointment only; call 287-3369 or book online.* ♿ **www**.anacostia.si.edu

The full name of this museum is the Anacostia Museum and Center for African-American History and Culture. It is part of the Smithsonian Institution *(see p72)*, and is dedicated to increasing public understanding and awareness of the history and culture of people of African descent and heritage living in the Americas.

Basic needs such as housing, transportation, healthcare, and employment were long denied to members of the African-American community, and the Anacostia Museum sponsors exhibits addressing these concerns. Two of its major initiatives have been *Black Mosaic*, a research project on Washington's diverse Afro-Caribbean culture, and *Speak to MY Heart: African American Communities of Faith and Contemporary Life*.

The museum is as much a resource center as it is a space for art and history exhibitions; it has an extensive library and computers for visitors. Its collections include historical objects, documents, videos, and works of art. A nationally traveling exhibit, *Reflections in Black*, traces the history of African-American photography from 1840 to the present.

Façade of Cedar Hill, the Frederick Douglass House

THREE GUIDED WALKS

The best way to discover Washington's historic neighborhoods, diverse architecture, parks and gardens is on foot. The first walk takes you up and down Massachusetts Avenue, past many of the city's larger embassies and grand, imposing mansions into Kalorama, a pretty area that's home to many of the smaller embassies. Afterwards, you may wish to spend more time exploring. You'll find at least one hidden gem; the Embassy area also houses the Phillips Collection (see p135) and several art galleries. On the walks through Georgetown and Old Town Alexandria you'll notice that many of the historic buildings you pass are open to the public.

Fountain at Dumbarton Oaks

A CLOSER LOOK

In Georgetown you could tour Dumbarton Oaks, Tudor Place, or Georgetown University (see pp120–27). In Alexandria you might look inside the churches, the Lyceum (the local history museum), the Lee-Fendall House, Gadsby's Tavern Museum, or the Carlyle House (see pp158–9).

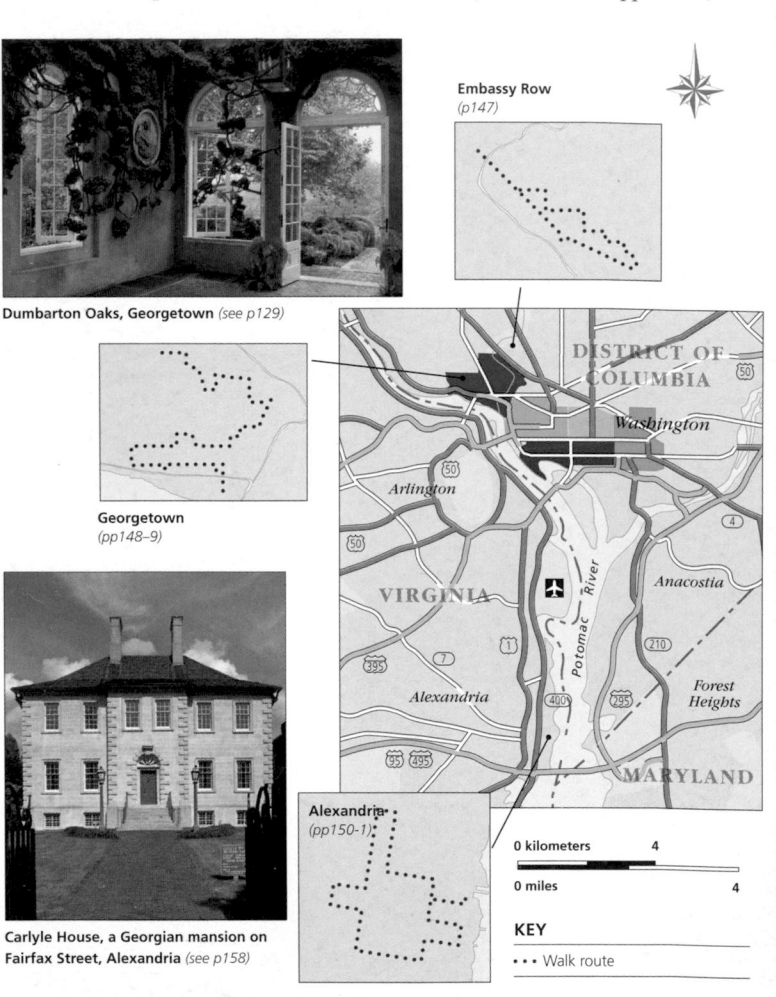

Dumbarton Oaks, Georgetown (see p129)

Embassy Row (p147)

Georgetown (pp148–9)

Carlyle House, a Georgian mansion on Fairfax Street, Alexandria (see p158)

Alexandria (pp150-1)

DISTRICT OF COLUMBIA

Washington

Arlington

VIRGINIA

Potomac River

Anacostia

Alexandria

Forest Heights

MARYLAND

0 kilometers   4

0 miles   4

KEY

••• Walk route

A Walk Around Embassy Row

For those fans of eclectic architecture this walk is a fascinating experience. Starting from Dupont Circle west it takes you along Massachusetts Avenue, past many of the larger embassies to the Italian Embassy and then back along Massachusetts Avenue to Kalorama, a quiet residential area where smaller embassies and museums are tucked away in its tree-lined streets.

Ornate Embassy of Indonesia ①

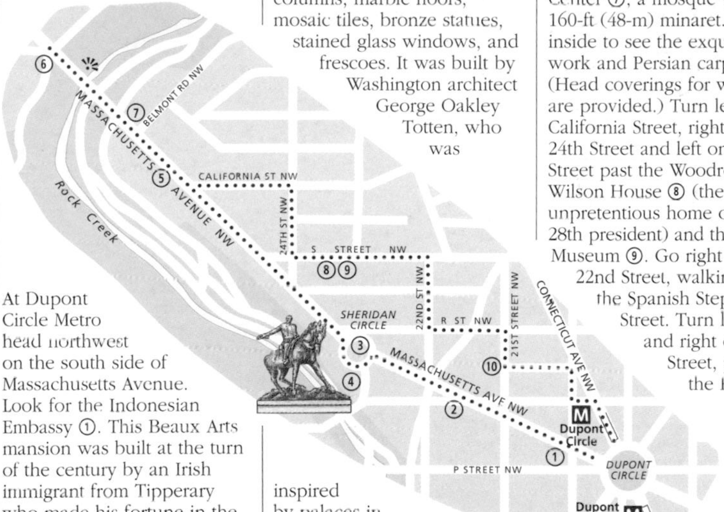

At Dupont Circle Metro head northwest on the south side of Massachusetts Avenue. Look for the Indonesian Embassy ①. This Beaux Arts mansion was built at the turn of the century by an Irish immigrant from Tipperary who made his fortune in the gold mines. The house later became the property of Evalyn Walsh McLean (his daughter), who also owned the 44-carat Hope Diamond, which is at the Natural History Museum. Farther on, there's an Italianate palace, now home to the Society of Cincinnati ②, a charitable organization set up by George Washington. A statue of Civil War General Philip T. Sheridan on his horse greets You at Sheridan Circle ③. Walk around the circle to the left, passing the Irish and Romanian embassies. You'll see the Turkish Embassy ④, an ornate mansion that boasts a mixture of Romanesque and Turkish styles on the exterior, while inside there are Doric columns, marble floors, mosaic tiles, bronze statues, stained glass windows, and frescoes. It was built by Washington architect George Oakley Totten, who was inspired by palaces in Istanbul, for wealthy industrialist Edward Hamlin Everett. Known as the "bottle top king" (he obtained the patent for corrugated bottle tops), Everett staged elaborate musical evenings here. As you stroll along Massachusetts Avenue, take a look at the garden behind the gate of the Japanese Embassy ⑤, a simple and graceful Georgian Revival building. After crossing the bridge over Rock Creek Park, you reach the Italian Embassy ⑥, a stunning contemporary structure that was designed by Piero Sartogo Architetti in Rome and Leo A. Daly in Washington. Its cantilevered copper eaves are reminiscent of a Renaissance palazzo. Cross Massachusetts Avenue and turn back toward Dupont Circle. Keep walking until you come to the the Islamic Center ⑦, a mosque with a 160-ft (48-m) minaret. Wander inside to see the exquisite tile work and Persian carpets. (Head coverings for women are provided.) Turn left on California Street, right onto 24th Street and left onto S Street past the Woodrow Wilson House ⑧ (the unpretentious home of the 28th president) and the Textile Museum ⑨. Go right onto 22nd Street, walking down the Spanish Steps to R Street. Turn left on R and right on 21st Street, passing the Phillips Collection ⑩, one of the country's most delightful modern art museums. Turn left on Q Street to make your way back to your start at the Dupont Circle Metro.

TIPS FOR WALKERS

Starting point: *Dupont Circle Metro.*
Length: *2.5 miles (4 km).*
Stopping off points: *Choose from one of several good restaurants near the Dupont Circle Metro stop.*

Islamic Center's striking minaret ⑦

0 meters 400

0 yards 400

KEY

• • • Walk route

Good viewing point

[M] Metro station

A 90-Minute Walk in Georgetown

Renowned for its beautiful and historic architecture, eclectic shops, and delightful restaurants, Georgetown has it all. Starting in upper Georgetown, this walk takes you along residential streets past grand homes and Federal-style rowhouses, past early churches and cemeteries, parks and river vistas, quiet lanes and crowded streets. The walk ends on M Street in the commercial heart of Georgetown at the oldest house built in the district. Details of many sights mentioned are in the section on Georgetown *(see pp120–27)*.

Dumbarton House, beautifully designed inside and out ⑥

Start at Wisconsin Avenue and S Street where you head east and then right on to 32nd Street. Dumbarton Oaks ① at 1703, a Federal-style mansion owned by Harvard University, contains a huge collection of pre-Columbian and Byzantine art, and may be worth returning to explore at length one afternoon *(see p127)*.

Turn left on R Street and right onto 31st Street. Admire Tudor Place ②, designed by the Capitol architect William Thornton on the right *(see p126)*. Turn left onto Avon Lane and left again on Avon Place. Walk across R Street to Montrose Park ③, which has a maze where you might like to meander for a bit, and then return to R Street. Head east and go into Oak Hill Cemetery ④. James Renwick, architect of New York's St. Patrick's Cathedral, designed the chapel inside *(see p126)*.

Back on R Street, head east to 28th Street. Turn right past Evermay ⑤, a Georgian manor, built by Scotsman Samuel Davidson in 1792. Turn left on Q Street. On your left, the Federal-style Dumbarton House ⑥, is noted for its beautiful 18th- and 19th-century furnishings. Make a left at the corner on 27th Street. Facing you is the Mt. Zion cemetery ⑦ where African Americans were buried before the Civil War.

Turning around, walk back on 27th Street until you come to O Street. Turn right on O Street and then left on 29th Street. Mt. Zion Church ⑧, on your right at 1334, was Washington's first African-American church, and has a tin ceiling that shows a West African influence *(see p126)*.

At the corner, turn right on Dumbarton Street, left on 30th Street, and right on N Street, which is full of elegant

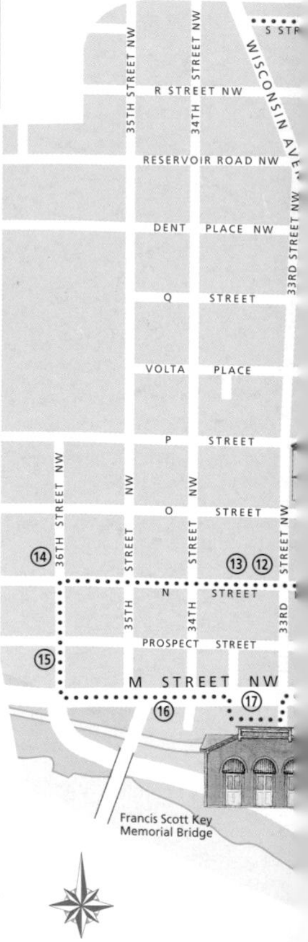

TIPS FOR WALKERS

Starting point: *Wisconsin Ave & S Street.* ***Length:*** *3 miles (5 km).* ***Getting there:*** *Metro Connection express bus from Foggy Bottom metro stop to Wisconsin Ave & R St, or Circulator bus from Union Station and points along K St NW.*

Smith Row, American Federal-style architecture on N Street ⑪

Montrose Park, a tranquil space for city relaxation ③

18th-century architecture. On your right you pass 3017 N Street, the house where Jackie Kennedy once lived ⑨. At Wisconsin Avenue you can take a break at Martin's Tavern (est. 1933) or one of many cafés here. Turn right on Wisconsin and then left on O Street. Note the old streetcar tracks and St. John's Episcopal Church ⑩ at 3240, once attended by Thomas Jefferson. Turn left on Potomac Street then right and

walk along N Street for several blocks. You'll pass Smith Row ⑪ with its brick Federal-style houses at 3255-63, John and Jackie Kennedy's home ⑫ from 1957 to 1961 at 3307, and Cox's Row ⑬ at 3327-39, built by Colonel Cox, a former merchant and mayor. Farther along N Street

Georgetown University ⑭

is Georgetown University ⑭ (see p126). Turn left on 36th Street to find The Tombs bar, a favorite haunt of students. On Prospect Street ⑮ next to the Car Barn (once used to house trolleys and now part of the university), go down three flights of steep steps (where a scene from The Exorcist was filmed) to M Street (the city's busiest and most colorful street) and the Potomac River.

Cross M Street and turn left, passing the Key Bridge and the Francis Scott Key Park ⑯, named for the author of "The Star-Spangled Banner". Still on M Street, look for the sign to Cady's Alley at 3316, make a right, and go down the steps. Turn left on Cady's Alley ⑰, browse in the high-end home furnishing shops, left again on 33rd Street to return to M Street. Turn right and you may want to stop at Dean & DeLuca ⑱, a lively café and gourmet market built in 1866. Stroll past the Victorian-style Georgetown Park ⑲, a former tobacco warehouse that now houses over 100 shops. Cross Wisconsin Avenue and go along M Street to 31st Street. Turn right then left onto the towpath by the C & O Canal ⑳ for a block, turning right on Thomas Jefferson Street and head toward Washington Harbor ㉑ (see pp122–3). Walk through this large complex of shops to the waterfront. After admiring the magnificent river view, retrace your steps to M Street and visit the Old Stone House ㉒, which dates from pre-Revolutionary days.

KEY

• • • Walk route

⚛ Good viewing point

Ⓜ Metro station

0 meters 300
0 yards 300

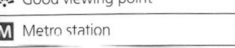

Passenger barge on the C & O Canal, a reminder of 19th-century shippers ⑳

A 90-Minute Walk in Alexandria

Stroll along cobblestone streets to see historic Alexandria, settled in the 18th century. This walk through the Old Town will take you by many historic homes, two of the oldest churches (George Washington attended both of them at one time or another), Gadsby's Tavern, and an old firehouse. The walk ends at the Torpedo Factory, now a thriving art center where over 200 artists exhibit their work. Afterward, go around to the back of the Torpedo Factory for a view of the Potomac River.

Historic Farmer's Market in Market Square ②

Start at the Ramsay House Visitor Center ①, once the home of a Scottish merchant and city founder, William Ramsay. Built in 1724, it is the oldest house in Alexandria. Outside Ramsay House, you'll see Market Square ② where farmers have sold their produce for over 250 Years. At the corner of Fairfax and King Streets turn left onto South Fairfax Street. Walk past the Stabler-Leadbeater Apothecary Shop ③ *(see p158)*, built in 1792. This was formerly run by Edward Stabler who worked with the "Society for the Relief of People Illegally Held in Bondage" to free enslaved African Americans. Turn left on Prince Street to find 211, which was the former home of Dr. Elisha Cullen Dick, the doctor who attended George Washington on his deathbed. At the corner is the Athenaeum ④, a Greek Revival building dating from 1851, once the Bank of the Old Dominion. Cross Lee Street and continue walking on Prince Street. This block, dubbed Captain's Row ⑤, is still paved with cobblestones and was once home to sea captains and shipbuilders. Turn right on Union Street. You'll pass several art galleries and catch a glimpse of the river on your left. Turn right on Duke Street to see the Federal-style homes and pretty gardens. Turn left on South Fairfax Street. The Old Presbyterian Meeting House ⑥ *(see p158)*, a brick church built by Scottish settlers in 1775 and rebuilt in 1837 after a fire, is on your right. On George Washington's death the bell of the Old Presbyterian tolled for four days. You'll find the Tomb of the Unknown Soldier of the American Revolution in the churchyard.

Go to the corner of South Fairfax Street and turn right onto Wolfe Street. This cuts through what was once a neighborhood called Hayti, home to many prominent African-American leaders in the early 1800s. Continue until you reach Royal Street. The house at 404 South Royal Street ⑦ is the home of George Seaton, a black master carpenter whose

TIPS FOR WALKERS

Starting point: *The Ramsay House Visitor's Center.*
Length: *2.5 m (4 km).*
Getting there: *Take the Dash bus from the King Street Metro stop to the Ramsay House Visitor's Center.*
Stopping Off Points: *The Friendship Firehouse is open Fri–Sun. For lunch try Gadsby's Tavern or one of the restaurants on King Street.*

Ramsay House, the oldest building in Alexandria ①

mother was freed by Martha Washington. Continue for three blocks. At 604 Wolfe Street is the Alexandria Academy ⑧, built with the support of George Washington and others. This free school was attended by white children before it became a school for African Americans in the first half of the 19th century.

Cross South Washington Street and turn right. After two blocks you'll come to the Lyceum ⑨, a building inspired by a Doric temple, which was originally a library, then a hospital for Union troops during the Civil War, and now a local history museum. A statue of a Confederate soldier, "Appomattox," stands in the center of the Prince and Washington Streets intersection, marking the spot where troops left Alexandria to join

Gadsby's Tavern, where President Jefferson's inaugural banquet was held ⑯

the Confederate army on May 24, 1861. Turn left on Prince Street and walk two blocks to South Alfred Street. Turn right to see the Friendship Firehouse ⑩ at 107. Turn right on King Street where you'll find colorful shops and restaurants. Turn left on Washington Street. Christ Church ⑪ will be on your left. Wander through the historic cemetery and into the church – this is where every year presidents have come to honor George Washington on his birthday. Continue on Washington Street past Lloyd House ⑫, a Georgian home built in 1796, once a station on the underground railroad. After two blocks turn right on Oronoco Street at the Lee-Fendall House ⑬ (see p159). The house, now a museum, was built by Philip Fendall who then married the sister of "Light Horse" Harry Lee (Robert E. Lee's father and a Revolutionary hero). Across the road at 607 Oronoco Street is Robert E. Lee's boyhood home ⑭ (see p158), which is now closed to the public.

Portrait of Robert E. Lee ⑭

Alexandria loves its dogs and they are all welcome at the Olde Towne School of Dogs on the corner of Oronoco and St. Asaph Streets. Turn right on St. Asaph and cross Princess Street with its cobblestones that were laid in the 1790s. Cross Cameron Street and turn left. A replica of the small house built by George Washington in 1769 is at 508 Cameron Steet ⑮.

Turning right on Royal Street, you'll find Gadsby's Tavern ⑯ (see p158), where Jefferson's inaugural banquet was held. Across the street is the City Hall ⑰. Continue on Cameron Street and cross Fairfax Street. The Bank of Alexandria, the city's oldest bank, established in 1792, stands on the corner. Next door is Carlyle House ⑱ (see p158), a Georgian mansion modeled after the Scottish estate Craigiehall. Go around to the rear to see the gardens. Back on Fairfax Street, continue on King Street and turn left. Enjoy the shop windows for two blocks to The Torpedo Factory on Union Street ⑲ (see p159), a dynamic arts center.

FOUNDERS PARK

WATERFRONT PARK

Potomac River

NORTH FAIRFAX ST

NORTH LEE STREET

NORTH UNION ST

SOUTH FAIRFAX ST

SOUTH LEE STREET

SOUTH UNION ST

STREET

STREET

MARKET SQUARE

⑰

⑱

②

①

③

④

⑤

⑲

0 meters   300
0 yards   300

KEY

• • • Walk route

🔆 Good viewing point

Ⓜ Metro station

ℹ Tourist information

The Torpedo Factory, with riverview studios, art galleries, and archaeology museum ⑲

Autumn in Shenandoah National Park ▷

EXCURSIONS BEYOND WASHINGTON, DC

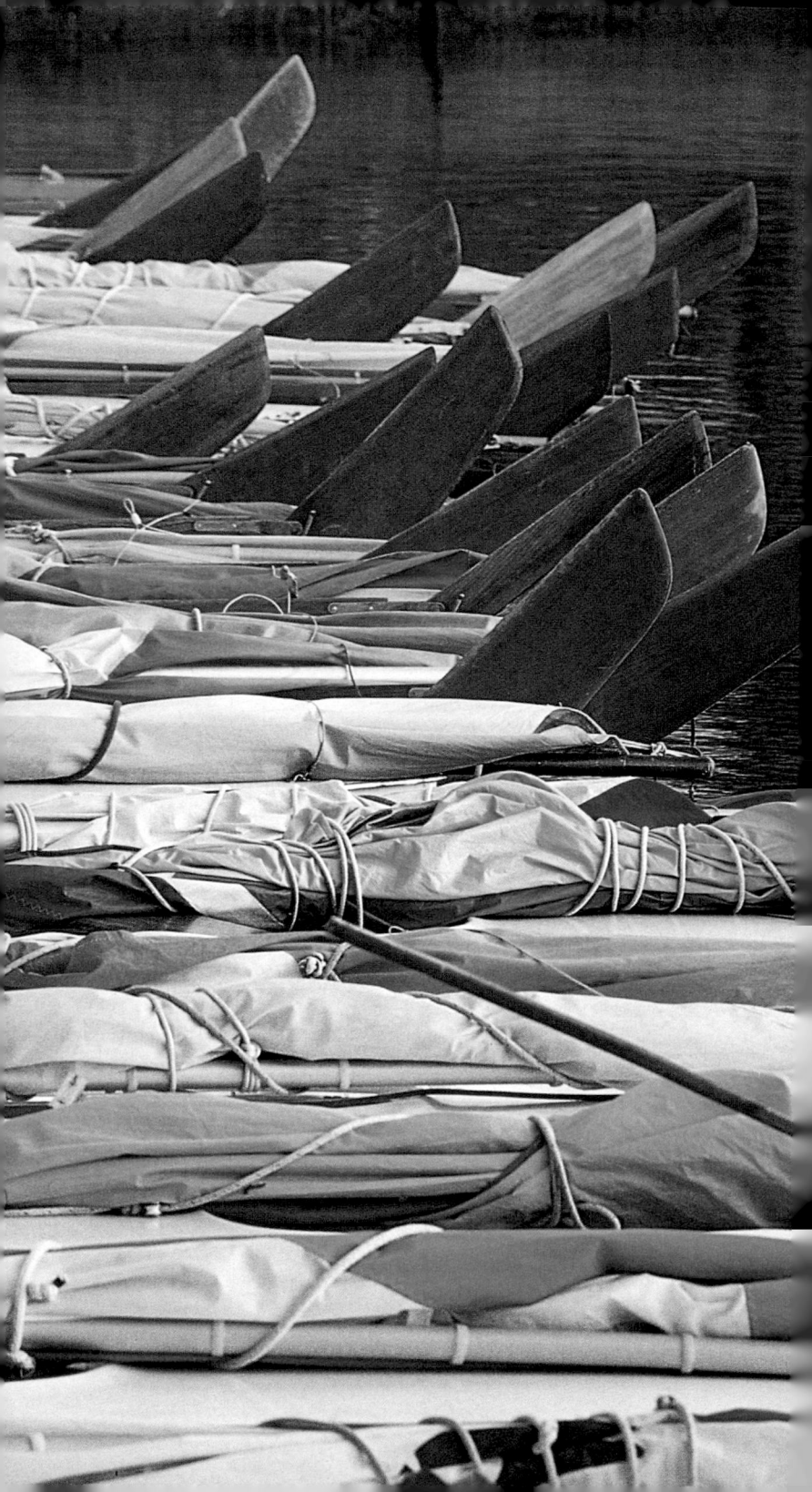

BEYOND WASHINGTON, DC

Within a half-day's drive of Washington lies enough history and natural beauty to satisfy the most insatiable sightseer. Alexandria and Williamsburg are a must for history buffs, while Chesapeake Bay and the islands of Chincoteague and Assateague offer a wealth of natural beauty. This area of Virginia and Maryland, along with parts of West Virginia and Pennsylvania, has been at the center of 400 years of turbulent American history.

Founded in 1623, Jamestown was the first permanent English settlement in America. In the 18th century, Williamsburg became the capital of Virginia and the first colony to declare independence from England. Today, Williamsburg is a living museum of the Colonial era.

A Civil War Howitzer cannon

The cultural influence of Europe is clearly seen in the architecture of this region. The two presidents largely responsible for crafting the character of the early republic lived in Virginia – George Washington at Mount Vernon, and Thomas Jefferson at Monticello. These homes reveal the lives their occupants led, at once imaginative, agrarian, inventive, comfortable – and, like many wealthy landowners, relying on slavery.

Cities and towns throughout the area have attractive historic districts that are a welcome contrast to the modern commercial strips on their outskirts.

Annapolis, for example, is a pleasant Colonial and naval port city. Baltimore also has a diverse charm, combining working-class neighborhoods and Old World character, and the town of Richmond blends the Old South's Victorian gentility with the luxuries of modern life.

Civil War battlefields are spread over the map as far as Gettysburg and tell the war's painful story with monuments, museums, cemeteries, and the very contours of the land itself.

The 105-mile (170-km) Skyline Drive through Shenandoah National Park, situated west of DC, makes the beautiful Blue Ridge Mountains accessible to hikers, cyclists, and drivers alike. To the east of the city, the Chesapeake Bay region attracts sailors and fishermen, as well as seafood lovers who can indulge in the delicious local specialty – blue crabs.

Farm fields in front of the treading barn at Mount Vernon

◁ Colorful furled sails at the Dangerfield Island marina

Exploring Beyond Washington, DC

Just minutes outside the bustling center of Washington is a striking and varied area of mountains, plains, and historic towns. To the west are Virginia's Blue Ridge Mountains, the setting for Shenandoah National Park. To the south is the Piedmont, an area of gently rolling hills that supports the vineyards of Virginia's burgeoning wine industry. To the east, the Chesapeake Bay divides Maryland almost in two, and to the south it travels the length of the Virginia coastline. To the north is the big port city of Baltimore, with its pleasant waterfront promenade, shops, museums, and stunning National Aquarium.

The Philadelphia Brigade Monument at Gettysburg

A re-created fort in Jamestown

SIGHTS AT A GLANCE

The dramatic Bearfence Mountain, part of Shenandoah National Park

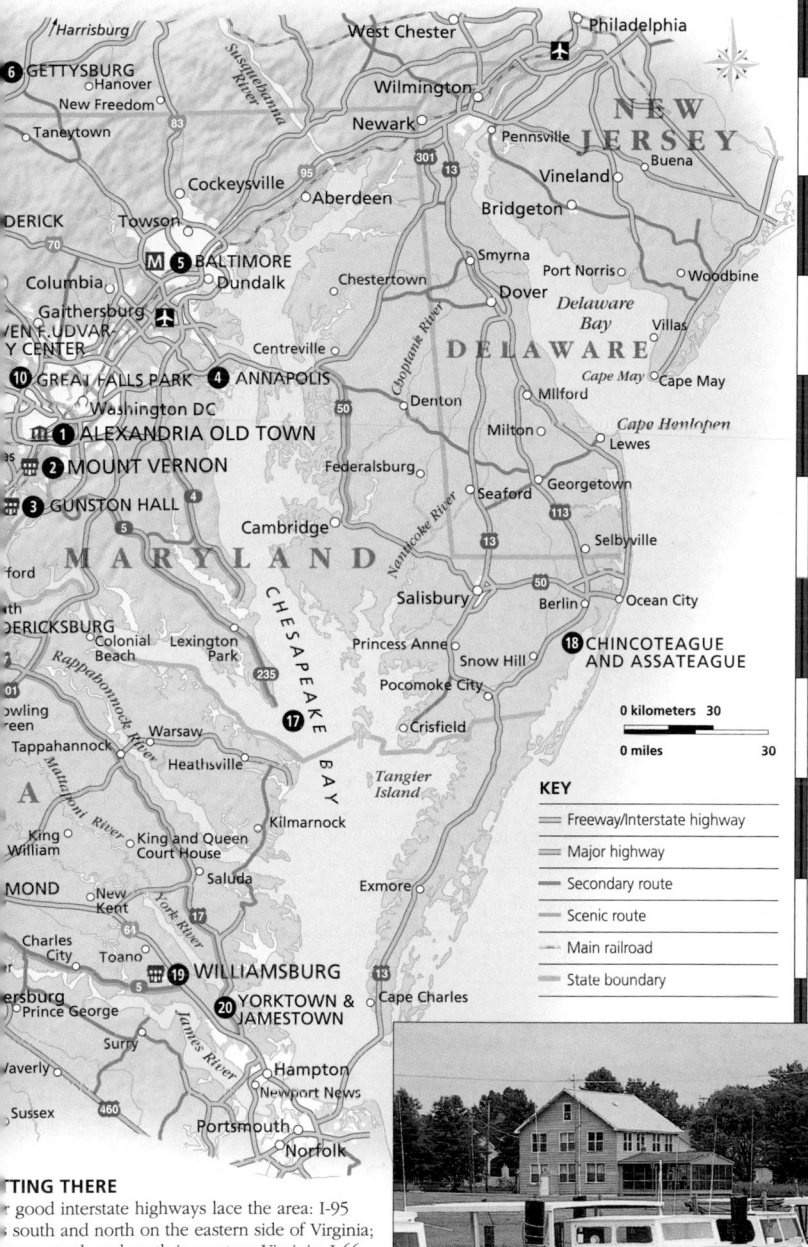

6 GETTYSBURG
Harrisburg
Hanover
New Freedom
Taneytown
West Chester
Wilmington
Newark
Philadelphia
NEW JERSEY
Pennsville
Buena
Vineland
Bridgeton
DERICK
Towson
Cockeysville
Aberdeen
Smyrna
Port Norris
Woodbine
Columbia
M 5 BALTIMORE
Dundalk
Chestertown
Dover
Delaware Bay
Villas
Gaithersburg
Centreville
DELAWARE
Cape May
Cape May
EN F. UDVAR-Y CENTER
10 GREAT FALLS PARK
4 ANNAPOLIS
Milford
Milton
Cape Henlopen
Lewes
Washington DC
Denton
1 ALEXANDRIA OLD TOWN
2 MOUNT VERNON
Federalsburg
Seaford
Georgetown
3 GUNSTON HALL
Cambridge
Selbyville
MARYLAND
Salisbury
Berlin
Ocean City
ford
DERICKSBURG
Colonial Beach
Lexington Park
Princess Anne
Snow Hill
18 CHINCOTEAGUE AND ASSATEAGUE
Rappahannock
Pocomoke City
owling green
Tappahannock
Warsaw
Heathsville
Crisfield
17
Tangier Island

0 kilometers 30
0 miles 30

A
King William
King and Queen Court House
Saluda
Kilmarnock
Exmore
KEY

= Freeway/Interstate highway
= Major highway
— Secondary route
— Scenic route
-- Main railroad
= State boundary

MOND
New Kent
Toano
Charles City
19 WILLIAMSBURG
20 YORKTOWN & JAMESTOWN
Cape Charles
ersburg
Prince George
Surry
Hampton
Newport News
averly
Sussex
Portsmouth
Norfolk

TING THERE

r good interstate highways lace the area: I-95
s south and north on the eastern side of Virginia;
runs south and north in western Virginia; I-66
ds west from Washington; and I-270 goes toward
lerick. Trains depart from Union Station to most
he main towns, such as Baltimore, Alexandria,
mond, Williamsburg, and Harpers Ferry, which
so served by the MARC *(see pp218–19)*. Virginia
way Express goes from Union Station to Alex-
ria and Fredericksburg. Greyhound buses also
el to most towns.

Boats moored in the Chesapeake Bay area

Old Town Alexandria ❶

Detail from the Apothecary Museum

Old Town Alexandria has kept a special historical flavor, dating back to its incorporation in 1749. It is still a busy seaport and offers many historic sights, as well as shops selling everything from antique hat racks to banana splits. Restaurants are abundant, art thrives here, and the socializing goes on day and night, in and around Market Square.

Exploring Alexandria

Alexandria's tree-lined streets are filled with elegant, historic buildings and make for a pleasant stroll (*see pp150–51*). Alternatively, a boat tour offers an attractive prospect as does a leisurely lunch on the patio overlooking the waterfront. Nearby Founder's Park is the perfect place to bask on the grass by the river.

Façade of the elegant Carlyle House

⊞ Carlyle House

121 N Fairfax St. *Tel (703) 549-2997.*
◯ 10am–4pm Tue–Sat, noon–4pm Sun; Last tour at 4pm. ◐ Jan 1, Thanksgiving, Dec 25. 🖼 🔳 🔆 (call in advance.) 🔳
www.carlylehouse.org
This elegant Georgian Palladian mansion was built by wealthy Scottish merchant John Carlyle in 1753. The house fell into disrepair in the 19th century but was bought in 1970 by the Northern Virginia Regional Park Authority; it has since been beautifully restored. A guided tour provides fascinating details about 18th-century daily life. One room, known as the "architecture room," has been deliberately left unfinished to show the original construction of the house. The back garden is planted with 18th-century plant species.

⊞ Stabler-Leadbeater Apothecary Museum

105 S Fairfax St. *Tel (703) 746-3852.*
◯ Apr–Oct: 10am–5pm Tue–Sat, 1–5pm Mon, Sun; Nov–Mar: 11am–4pm Wed–Sat, 1–4pm Sun. ◐ Jan 1, Thanksgiving, Dec 25. 🖼 🔳 🔳
www.apothecarymuseum.org
Established in 1792, this family apothecary was in business for 141 years, until 1933. It is now a museum, and the shop's mahogany drawers still contain the potions noted on their labels. Jars containing herbal remedies line the shelves. Huge mortars and pestles and a collection of glass baby bottles are among 8,000 original objects. George Washington was a patron, as was Robert E. Lee, who bought the paint for his Arlington house here.

🏛 Gadsby's Tavern Museum

134 N Royal St. *Tel (703) 838-4242.*
◯ Apr–Oct: 10am–5pm Tue–Sat, 1–5pm Sun, Mon; Nov–Mar: 11am–4pm Wed–Sat, 1–4pm Sun.
◐ Federal hols. 🖼 🔳 🔳 🔳
www.gadsbystavern.org
Dating from 1770, this tavern and the adjoining hotel, owned by John Gadsby, were the Waldorf-Astoria of their day. Now completely restored, they evoke the atmosphere of a hostelry in this busy port.
You can see the dining room with buffet and gaming tables, the bedrooms where travelers reserved not the room but a space in a bed, and the private dining room for the wealthy. The hotel's ballroom, where George and Martha Washington were fêted on his last birthday in 1799, can be rented out. This is also a working restaurant.

Interior of the Old Presbyterian Meeting House

⊞ Old Presbyterian Meeting House

323 S Fairfax St. *Tel (703) 549-6670.*
◯ 9am–4pm Mon–Fri. 🔳 🔆
www.opmh.org
Memorial services for George Washington were held in this meeting house, founded in 1772. In the churchyard are buried Dr. John Craig, a close friend of Washington, merchant John Carlyle, the Reverend Muir, who officiated at Washington's funeral, and the American Revolution's unknown soldier.

⊞ Boyhood Home of Robert E. Lee

607 Oronoco St.
Unfortunately, the boyhood home of Robert E. Lee is currently a private residence and not open to the public. General Lee lived in this 1795 Federal townhouse from the age of 11 until he went to West Point Military Academy. The drawing room was the setting for the marriage of Mary Lee Fitzhugh to Martha Washington's grandson, George Washington Parke Custis.

Bedroom of Robert E. Lee

🏛 Lee-Fendall House Museum

614 Oronoco St. **Tel** *(703) 548-1789.* 🕐 *10am–4pm Wed–Sat, 1–4pm Sun.* ⛔ *Dec 25–Jan 31 (except 3rd Sun, Lee's birthday celebration).* 📷 🎧 ♿ **www**.leefendallhouse.org

Philip Fendall built this stylish house in 1785, then married the sister of Revolutionary War hero "Light Horse" Harry Lee. Lee descendants lived here until 1904. Restored to its early Victorian motif, the house is rich with artifacts from the Revolution to the 1930s Labor Movement.

Lee-Fendall House Museum

🏛 Torpedo Factory Art Center

105 N Union St. **Tel** *(703) 838-4565.* 🕐 *10am–6pm daily (to 9pm Thu).* ⛔ *Jan 1, Easter, July 4, Thanksgiving, Dec 25.* ♿ **www**.torpedofactory.org

Originally a real torpedo factory during World War II, it was converted into an arts center by a partnership between the town and a group of local artists in 1974. Today there is gallery and studio space for over 150 artists to create and exhibit their work. Visitors can watch a potter at his wheel, sculptors, print-makers, and jewelry-makers.

⛪ Christ Church

Cameron & N Washington Sts. **Tel** *(703) 549-1450.* 🕐 *9am–4pm Mon–Sat, 2–4:30pm Sun.* ⛔ *Jan 1, Thanksgiving, Dec 25.* ♿ **www**.historicchristchurch.org

The oldest church in continuous use in the town, this Georgian edifice was completed in 1773. George Washington's square pew is still preserved with his nameplate, as is that of Robert E. Lee.

On the other side of this Episcopalian church, a label reads "William E. Cazenove. Free pew for strangers." In the churchyard 18th-century gravestones wear away under the weather of the centuries.

VISITORS' CHECKLIST

Alexandria. 👥 *143,000.* 🚉 *Union Station, 110 Callahan St.* [M] *King Street.* ℹ *Ramsay House Visitor Center, 221 King St (703-746-3300.)* **www**.visitalexandriava.com

🛍 Farmers Market

Market Square, King & Fairfax Sts. **Tel** *(703) 746-3200.* 🕐 *5:30am–10:30am Sat.*

This market dates back to the city's incorporation in 1749. George Washington, a trustee of the market, regularly sent produce to be sold at the market from his farm at Mount Vernon *(see pp160–61)*. A very pleasant aspect of the market square today is its central fountain. Shoppers can find fresh fruits and vegetables, cut flowers, herbs, baked goods, meats, and crafts.

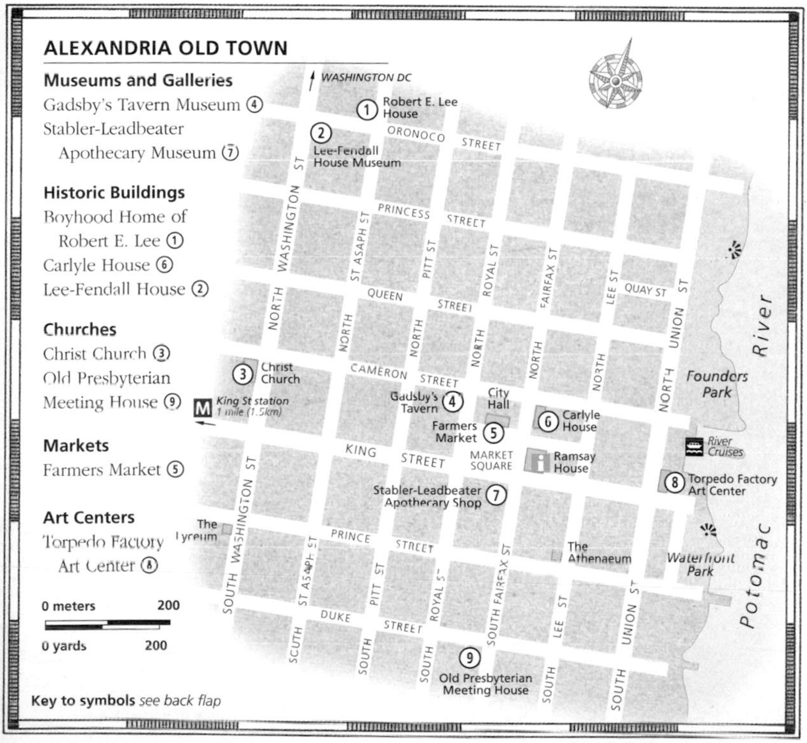
ALEXANDRIA OLD TOWN
Museums and Galleries
Gadsby's Tavern Museum 4
Stabler-Leadbeater Apothecary Museum 7
Historic Buildings
Boyhood Home of Robert E. Lee 1
Carlyle House 6
Lee-Fendall House 2
Churches
Christ Church 3
Old Presbyterian Meeting House 9
Markets
Farmers Market 5
Art Centers
Torpedo Factory Art Center 8
0 meters 200
0 yards 200
Key to symbols see back flap
WASHINGTON DC
1 Robert E. Lee House
2 Lee-Fendall House Museum
3 Christ Church
4 Gadsby's Tavern
5 Farmers Market
6 Carlyle House
7 Stabler-Leadbeater Apothecary Shop
8 Torpedo Factory Art Center
9 Old Presbyterian Meeting House
City Hall
Ramsay House
MARKET SQUARE
The Lyceum
The Athenaeum
King St station 1 mile (1.5km)
River Cruises
Founders Park
Waterfront Park
Potomac River
ORONOCO STREET
PRINCESS STREET
QUEEN STREET
CAMERON STREET
KING STREET
PRINCE STREET
DUKE STREET
QUAY ST
NORTH WASHINGTON ST
NORTH ST ASAPH ST
NORTH PITT ST
NORTH ROYAL ST
NORTH FAIRFAX ST
NORTH LEE ST
NORTH UNION ST
SOUTH WASHINGTON ST
SOUTH ST ASAPH ST
SOUTH PITT ST
SOUTH ROYAL ST
SOUTH FAIRFAX ST
SOUTH LEE ST
SOUTH UNION ST

Mount Vernon ❷

This country estate on the Potomac River was George Washington's home for 45 years. Built as a farmhouse by his father, Augustine, Washington made many changes, including adding the cupola and curving colonnades. The house is furnished as it would have been during Washington's presidency (1789–97), and the 500-acre grounds still retain aspects of Washington's farm. The Ford Orientation Center and Donald W. Reynolds Museum offer exhibitions, films, and artifacts about the life of the first US president, including his military and presidential career. Three miles (4.8 km) from the estate is the George Washington Whiskey Distillery and Gristmill.

Cameo of Washington

Kitchen
Set slightly apart from the main house, the kitchen has been completely restored.

★ Mansion Tour
Visitors can see the study and the large dining room, as well as Washington's bedroom and the bed in which he died.

Overseer's House

Slave Quarters
Washington freed all his slaves in his will. Reconstructed quarters show their living conditions.

★ Upper Garden
The plants in this colorful flower garden are known to have grown here in Washington's time.

Wharf
Daytrip boats from central DC bring visitors to this wharf. Potomac cruise boats also stop off here.

VISITORS' CHECKLIST

South end of George Washington Memorial Parkway, Fairfax County, VA. **Tel** (703) 780-2000. Ⓜ Yellow line to Huntington Station. 🚌 Fairfax Connector bus 101 to Mount Vernon: call (703) 780-2000. **Boat cruises available.** ⬜ Apr–Aug: 8am–5pm; Mar, Sep, Oct: 9am–5pm; Nov–Feb: 9am–4pm. first floor http://visitmount vernon. org **Distillery** State Route 235 South. ⬜ Apr–Oct: daily.

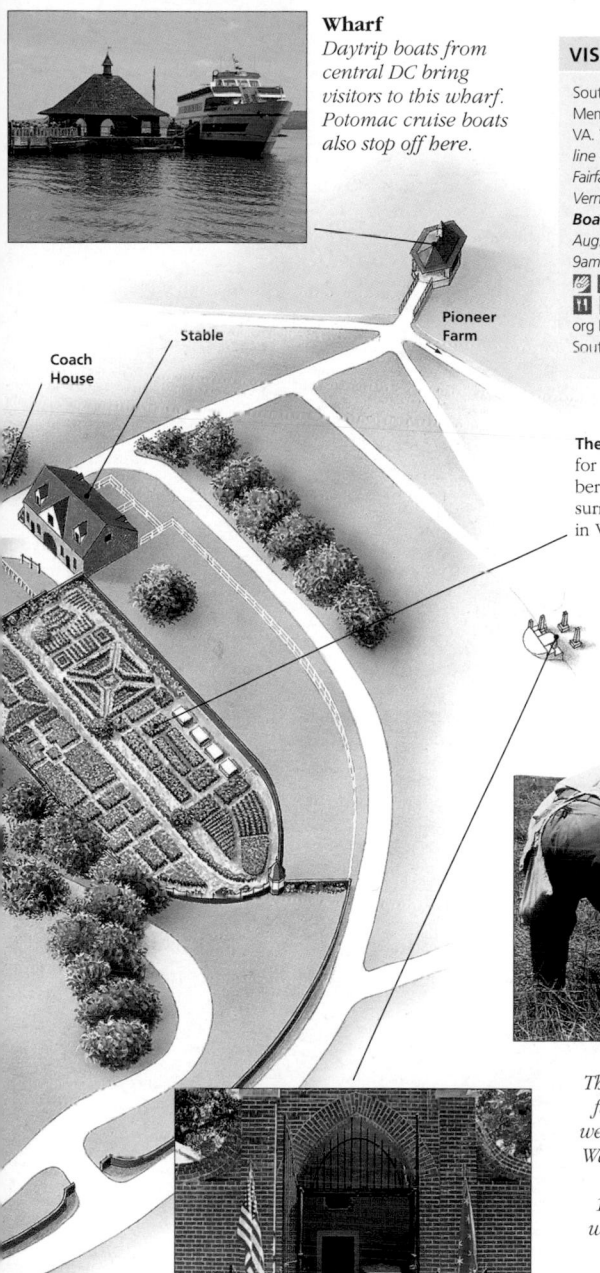

Pioneer Farm

Stable

Coach House

The Lower Garden was used for growing vegetables and berries. The boxwood bushes surrounding it were planted in Washington's time.

★ Pioneer Farm
This exhibit demonstrates farming techniques that were pioneered by George Washington. There is also a replica of his unique 16-sided treading barn, which was created using authentic tools.

he Bowling Green /as added to the state by George /ashington.

Washington's Tomb
In his will, Washington requested that a new brick tomb be built for his family at Mount Vernon. Washington died in 1799 but the tomb was not completed until 1831.

STAR SIGHTS

★ Mansion Tour

★ Pioneer Farm

★ Upper Garden

Gunston Hall 🟡

10709 Gunston Road, Mason
Neck, VA. *Tel (703) 550-9220.*
⬛ *9:30am–5pm daily.* ⬛ *Jan 1,
Thanksgiving, Dec 25.* 🖼️ 🗝️ ♿ 🏠
www.gunstonhall.org

This Georgian house, built
in 1755, was the home of
George Mason, author of the
1776 Virginia Declaration
of Rights. Situated 20 miles
(32 km) south of Washington,
DC, it is an exquisite example
of careful historic restoration.

Of particular interest is the
finely carved woodwork in
the entrance hall, the chinoi-
serie mantel and fireplace in
the formal dining room, and
the servants' staircase which
was used by the slaves so that
they wouldn't be seen by
guests. Outside are the beautiful boxwood gardens.

Annapolis 🟡

Anne Arundel County, MD.
🚶 *36,000.* ℹ️ *Annapolis and Anne
Arundel County Conference and
Visitors Bureau, 26 West St.
(410) 280-0445.* ⬛ *9am–5pm.*
www.visitannapolis.org

The capital of Maryland,
Annapolis is the jewel of
Chesapeake Bay. It is defined
by the nautical character that
comes with 17 miles
(27 km) of shoreline
and the longtime
presence of the US
Naval Academy.

A walk down
Main Street takes
you past the 200-
year-old Maryland
Inn, and the shops
and restaurants, to
the City Dock lined
with boats. It is
then a short walk
to the 150-year-
old **US Naval
Academy**. Inside
the visitor center
is the Freedom 7
space capsule
that carried the
first American, Alan Shepard,
into space. The US Naval
Academy Museum in Preble
Hall is also worth visiting,
especially to see the gallery
of detailed ship models. The

The beautiful formal gardens of the William Paca House, in Annapolis

**Tiffany window in the
Naval Academy, Annapolis**

Maryland State House is the
oldest state capitol in continuous use. Its Old Senate Chamber is where the Continental
Congress (delegates from
each of the American colonies) met when Annapolis
was briefly the capital of the
United States in 1783–4.

Annapolis teems with
Colonial-era buildings, most
still in everyday use. The
William Paca House, home of
Governor Paca, who signed
the Declaration of Independence, is a fine Georgian
house with an enchanting
garden, both of which
have been lovingly
restored. The
**Hammond Harwood
House** has also been
restored. This mas-
terpiece of Geor-
gian design was
named after the
Hammond and Har-
wood families, both
prominent in the
area. Cornhill and
Duke of Gloucester
streets are beautiful
examples of the
city's historic
residential streets.

Many tours
are offered in
Annapolis,
including walking, bus, and
boat tours. It is particularly
enjoyable to view the city
from the water, be it by sightseeing boat, chartered
schooner, or even by kayak.

🏛️ **US Naval Academy**
52 King George St. *Tel (410)
293-8687.* ⬛ *9am–4pm daily.
Photo ID needed.* ⬛ *Jan 1,
Thanksgiving, Dec 25.* 🖼️
www.navyonline.com

🏫 **Maryland State House**
State Circle. *Tel (410) 974-3400.*
⬛ *8:30am–5pm (call ahead).
Photo ID needed.* ⬛ *Dec 25.*
🖼️ *11am & 3pm.* ♿

🏫 **William Paca House**
186 Prince George St. *Tel (410)
990-4543.* ⬛ *10am–5pm daily
(weekends only in winter).* ⬛ *Jan,
Thanksgiving, Dec 24, Dec 25.* 🖼️ 🏠

🏫 **Hammond Harwood House**
19 Maryland Ave at King George St.
Tel (410) 263-4683 (ext. 16).
⬛ *Apr–Oct: noon–5pm Tue–Sun.*
⬛ *Winter.* 🖼️ **www**.hammond
harwoodhouse.org

Baltimore 🟡

Chesapeake Bay, MD. 🚶 *785,500.*
ℹ️ *Inner Harbor West Wall
(410) 837-4636. Visitor services
(877) BALTIMORE.* 🚍 🚌
www.baltimore.org

There is much to do and
see in this pleasant city.
A good place to start is the
Inner Harbor, the city's
redeveloped waterfront, with
the harborside complex of
shops and restaurants. The
centerpiece is the **National
Aquarium**, which has many
exhibits, including a seal pool
and dolphin show. The Harbor
is home to the **Maryland**

People walking along Baltimore's pleasant Inner Harbor promenade

Science Center, where "do touch" is the rule. The planetarium and an IMAX® theater thrill visitors with images of earth and space.

The **American Visionary Art Museum** houses a collection of extraordinary works by self-taught artists whose materials range from matchsticks to faux pearls.

Uptown is the **Baltimore Museum of Art**, with its world-renowned collection of modern art, including works by Matisse, Picasso, Degas, and Van Gogh. There is also a large collection of Warhol pieces and two sculpture gardens featuring work by Rodin and Calder.

The diversity of art at the **Walters Art Museum**, on Mount Vernon Square, includes pieces by Fabergé and Monet, among others; it is reknown for its ancient Egyptian art.

The Little Italy area is worth a visit for its knock-out Italian restaurants and also for the games of bocce ball (Italian lawn bowling) played around Pratt or Stiles Streets on warm evenings.

✈ National Aquarium
501 E Pratt St, Pier 3, N side of Inner Harbor. *Tel (410) 576-3800.*
⏱ *Hours vary. Call ahead or check website for details.* ● *Thanksgiving, Dec 25.* 🅿 ♿ 🎫 **www.aqua.org**

🏛 Maryland Science Center
601 Light St. *Tel (410) 685-5225.*
⏱ *Hours vary. Call ahead or check website for details.* ● *Thanksgiving, Dec 25.* 🅿 ♿ 🎫 **www.mdsci.org**

🏛 American Visionary Art Museum
800 Key Highway at Inner Harbor.
Tel (410) 244-1900. ⏱ *10am–6pm Tue–Sun.* ● *Mon, Thanksgiving, Dec 25.* 🅿 ♿ 🍴 🎫 **www.avam.org**

🏛 Baltimore Museum of Art
N Charles St & 31st St *Tel (443) 573-1700.* ⏱ *11am–5pm Wed–Sun (to 6pm Sat, Sun).* ● *Jan 1, Memorial Day, Jul 4, Thanksgiving, Dec 25.* 🎫 ♿ 🍴 🎫

🏛 Walters Art Museum
600 N Charles St. *Tel (410) 547-9000.* ⏱ *10am–5pm Wed–Sun (8pm 1st Fri of month).* ● *Jan 1, Memorial Day, Jul 4, Thanksgiving, Dec 24, 25.* 🅿 *weekends.* ♿ 🎫 **www.thewalters.org**

Gettysburg National Military Park ⑥

1195 Baltimore Pike, Gettysburg, Adams County, PA. *Tel (717) 334-1124.* **Park** ⏱ *6am–7pm daily (to 10pm Apr–Oct).* **Visitor Center** ⏱ *8am–5pm daily (to 6pm Apr–Oct).* ● *Jan 1, Thanksgiving, Dec 25.* 🅿 ♿ 🎫 **www.nps.gov/gett**

This 6,000-acre park, south of the town of Gettysburg, Pennsylvania, marks the site of the three-day Civil War battle on July 1–3, 1863. It was the bloodiest event ever to take place on American soil,

THE GETTYSBURG ADDRESS

The main speaker at the dedication of the National Cemetery in Gettysburg on November 19, 1863 was the orator Edward Everett. President Lincoln had been asked to follow with "a few appropriate remarks." His two-minute, 272-word speech paid tribute to the fallen soldiers, restated his goals for the Civil War, and re-phrased the meaning of democracy: "government of the people, by the people, for the people." The speech was inaudible to many, and Lincoln declared it a failure. However, once published, his speech revitalized the North's resolve to preserve the Union. Today it is known to every school-child in America.

Abraham Lincoln

with 51,000 fatalities. A two- or three-hour driving tour begins at the visitor center. The National Cemetery, where Abraham Lincoln gave his Gettysburg Address, is opposite. Other sights include the Eternal Light Peace Memorial.

Frederick ⑦

Frederick County, MD. 👥 59,000.
ℹ *19 E Church St (800) 999 3613, (301) 600-2888.* ⏱ *9am–5pm daily.* ● *Jan 1, Easter, Thanksgiving, Dec 25.* **www.fredericktourism.org**

Dating back to the mid-18th century, Frederick's historic center was renovated in the 1970s.

This charming town is a major antique center and home to hundreds of antique dealers. Its shops, galleries, and eateries are all in 18th- and 19th-century settings. Francis Scott Key, author of "The Star Spangled Banner," is buried in Mt. Olivet Cemetery.

The eye-catching architecture of the National Aquarium, Baltimore

Antietam National Battlefield **8**

Route 65, 10 miles (16 km) S of Hagerstown, Washington County, MD. *Tel (301) 432-5124.*
◯ *Jun–Aug: 8:30am–7pm daily; Sep–May: 8:30am–5pm.* ⬤ *Jan 1, Thanksgiving, Dec 25.* 📷 🅿 ♿ www.nps.gov/anti

One of the worst battles of the Civil War was waged here on September 17, 1862. There were 23,000 casualties but no decisive victory.

An observation tower offers a panoramic view of the battlefield. Antietam Creek runs peacefully under the costly Burnside Bridge. General Lee's defeat at Antietam inspired President Lincoln to issue the Emancipation Proclamation. The Visitors' Center movie recreating the battle is excellent.

John Brown's Fort in Harpers Ferry National Historic Park

Harpers Ferry **9**

171 Shoreline Dr, off Rte 340, Harpers Ferry, Jefferson County, WV. *Tel (304) 535-6029.* ◯ *8am–5pm daily.* ⬤ *Jan 1, Thanksgiving, Dec 25.* 📷 🎞 *Spring–Fall.* www.nps.gov/hafe

Nestled at the confluence of the Shenandoah and Potomac rivers in the Blue Ridge

Mountains is Harpers Ferry National Historical Park. The town was named for Robert Harper, a builder from Philadelphia who established a ferry across the Potomac here in 1761. There are stunning views from Maryland Heights to the foot of Shenandoah Street, near abolitionist John Brown's fort. Brown's ill-fated raid in 1859 on the Federal arsenal, established by George Washington, became tinder in igniting the Civil War.

The great importance of the town led to the area being designated a national park in 1944. It has been restored by the National Park Service.

Great Falls Park **10**

Georgetown Pike, Great Falls, Fairfax County, VA. *Tel (703) 285-2965.* ◯ *daily (closes at dusk).* 📷 🅿 ♿ www.nps.gov/gwmp/grfa

The first view of the falls, near the visitor center, is breathtaking. The waters of the Potomac roar through a gorge of jagged rock over a 76-ft (23-m) drop at the point that divides Virginia's undulating Piedmont from the coastal plain. Only experienced kayakers are permitted to take to the tubulent whitewater below, which varies with rainfall upstream.

The park is crisscrossed by 15 miles of hiking trails, some showing evidence of commerce from the early 19th-century Patowmack, America's first canal. Guided history and nature walks are offered.

Situated just across the river, in Maryland, is the C&O Canal National Historical Park, entry to which is free for visitors to Great Falls Park.

The Red Fox Inn in Middleburg

Middleburg **11**

Route 50, Loudoun County, VA. 🏇 *600.* ℹ *Visitors' Center, 12 N Madison St. Tel (540) 687-8888.* ◯ *11am–3pm Mon–Fri, 11am–4pm Sat–Sun.* www.middleburgonline.com

Horse and fox are king in this little piece of England in the Virginia countryside. Middleburg's history began in 1728, with Joseph Chinn's fieldstone tavern on the Ashby's Gap Road, still operating today as the Red Fox Inn. Colonel John S. Mosby and General Jeb Stuart met here to plan Confederate strategy during the Civil War.

The exquisite countryside has thoroughbred horse farms, some opening during the Hunt Country Stable Tour in May.

Foxcroft Road, north of the town, winds past immaculate horse farms. East of Route 50 is **Chrysalis Vineyard and Winery**. On the Plains Road at the west end of town is **Piedmont Vineyards**, and a mile east of Middleburg is **Swedenburg Winery**. All three have tours and tastings.

🍷 **Chrysalis Vineyard**
23876 Champe Ford Rd (off Route 50). *Tel (540) 687-8222, 800-235-8804.* ◯ *10am–5pm daily.* ⬤ *Jan 1, Thanksgiving, Dec 25.* www.chrysaliswine.com

🍷 **Piedmont Vineyards**
Off Route 626. *Tel (540) 687-5528.* ◯ *by appt Mon–Fri, 11am–5pm Sat, Sun.* ⬤ *Jan 1, Thanksgiving, Dec 24, 25, 31.* www.piedmontwines.com

🍷 **Swedenburg Winery**
23595 Winery Lane. *Tel (540) 687-5219.* ◯ *by appt Mon–Fri, 11am–5pm Sat, Sun.* ⬤ *Jan 1, Thanksgiving, Dec 25.* www.swedenburgwines.com

The roaring waterfalls in Great Falls Park

Steven F. Udvar-Hazy Center ⓬

Near Dulles International Airport, intersection of Rtes 28 and 50, Chantilly, VA. ***Tel*** *(202) 633-1000.* 🚌 *Bus from Dulles International Airport.* 🕐 *10am–5:30pm daily.* ⛔ *Dec 25.* 🍴 **www**.nasm.si.edu/udvarhazycenter

This is a must for anyone who would like to view the Space Shuttle "Enterprise," or who wants to find out about rockets and satellites, or see a rare Boeing B-29 Stratoliner. Opened in December 2003 to coincide with the 100th anniversary of the Wright brothers' first powered flight, and named in honor of its major donor, this museum was built to display and also preserve historic aviation and space artifacts. The vast building of over 760,000 sq ft (7,000 sq m) houses exhibit hangars with more than 300 aircraft and spacecraft. Visitors can walk among exhibits, view hanging aircraft from elevated walkways, and go up an observation tower to watch air traffic at Dulles Airport. As well as an education center and Imax® theater, a Wall of Honor offers a permanent memorial to those men and women who contributed to America's space exploration and aviation heritage.

Skyline Drive ⓭

Skyline Drive runs along the backbone of the Shenandoah National Park's Blue Ridge Mountains. Originally farmland, the government designated the area a national park in 1926. Deer, wild turkey, bears, and bobcats inhabit the park, and wildflowers, azaleas, and mountain laurel are abundant. The park's many hiking trails and its 75 viewpoints offer stunning natural scenery.

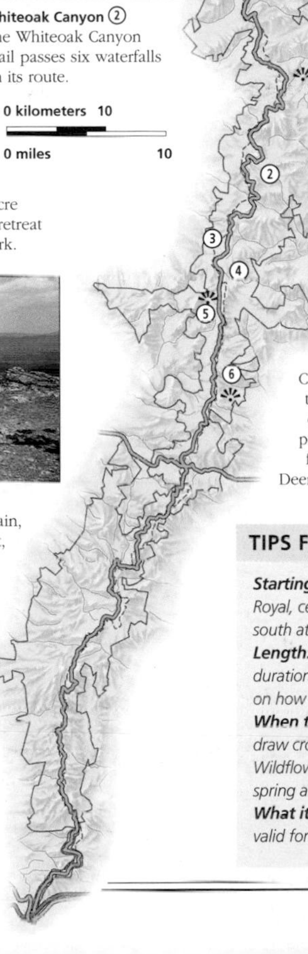
North entrance station
① ② ③ ④ ⑤ ⑥
0 kilometers 10
0 miles 10

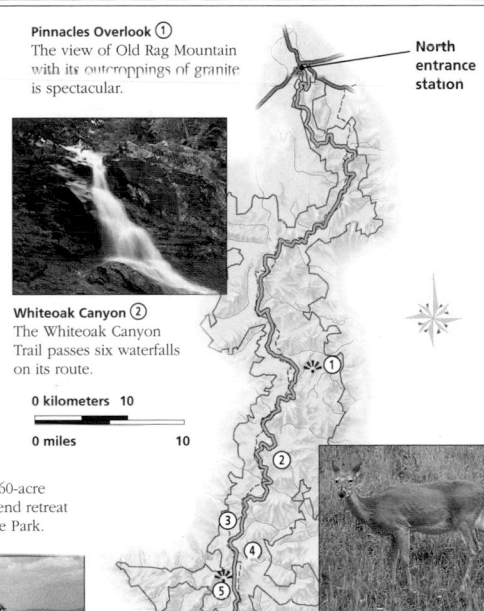

Pinnacles Overlook ①
The view of Old Rag Mountain with its outcroppings of granite is spectacular.

Whiteoak Canyon ②
The Whiteoak Canyon Trail passes six waterfalls on its route.

Big Meadows ③
Close to the Visitor Center, this meadow is kept in its centuries-old state. It was probably kept clear by fire from lightning or Indians. Deer can easily be seen here.

Camp Hoover ④
At the end of Mill Prong Trail, this 160-acre resort was President Hoover's weekend retreat until 1933, when he donated it to the Park.

Bearfence Mountain ⑤
Although it is a bit of a climb up this mountain, partly on rock scramble, it is not too difficult, and the reward is a breathtaking 360-degree view of the surrounding landscape.

Lewis Mountain ⑥
This awe-inspiring view from Lewis Mountain shows Shenandoah Valley in spring, when the lush scenery is interspersed with beautiful wildflowers.

KEY

- - - Walk route
Lookout point
Road

TIPS FOR DRIVERS

Starting points: *north at Front Royal, central at Thornton Gap, south at Rockfish Gap.*
Length: *105 miles (168 km), duration of 3–8 hrs depending on how many stops are taken.*
When to go: *Fall leaf colors draw crowds in mid-October. Wildflowers bloom through spring and summer.*
What it costs: *$15 per car, valid for 7 days ($10 Nov–Feb).*

Charlottesville ⑭

Virginia. 👥 *41,000.* 🚉 🚌 ℹ️ *Visitors Bureau, 610 E Main St; Monticello Visitors Center, Route 20 South.* **Tel** *(434) 293-6789, (877) 386-1103 (toll free).* **www.** *pursuecharlottesville.com*

Charlottesville was Thomas Jefferson's hometown. It is dominated by the University of Virginia, which he founded and designed, and also by his home, **Monticello**.

Jefferson was a Renaissance man: author of the Declaration of Independence, US president, farmer, architect, inventor, and vintner. It took him 40 years to complete Monticello, beginning in 1769. It is now one of the most celebrated houses in the country. The entrance hall doubled as a private museum, and the library held a collection of around 6,700 books.

The grounds include a large terraced vegetable garden where Jefferson grew and experimented with varieties.

The obelisk over Jefferson's grave in the family cemetery lauds him as "Father of the University of Virginia." Tours of the house are available year round.

Vineyards and wineries surround Charlottesville. Michie Tavern, joined to the Virginia Wine Museum, has been restored to its 18th-century appearance, and serves a buffet of typical Southern food.

Montpelier, on a 2,500 acre site 25 miles (40 km) to the north, was the home of former US president James Madison.

🏛️ Monticello

Route 53, 3 miles (5 km) SE of Charlottesville. **Tel** *(434) 984-9822.* ⏰ *Mar–Nov: 9am–5pm; Dec–Feb: 10am–4pm.* ⬤ *Dec 25.* 📷 ♿ 🛍️ 🏠 **www.**monticello.org

Fredericksburg ⑮

Virginia. 👥 *22,600.* 🚉 🚌 ℹ️ *Fredericksburg Visitor Center, 706 Caroline St.* **Tel** *(800) 678-4748.* ⏰ *9am–5pm daily (to 7pm May–Aug).* ⬤ *Jan 1, Dec 25.* **www.**visitfred.com

Fredericksburg's attractions are its historic downtown district, and four Civil War battlefields,

The elegant dining room at Kenmore House

including The Wilderness. The Rising Sun Tavern and Hugh Mercer Apothecary Shop offer living history accounts of life in a town that began as a port on the Rappahannock River. **Kenmore Plantation**, home of George Washington's sister, is famous for its beautiful rooms.

The visitor center offers useful maps as well as horse-and-carriage or trolley tours.

🏛️ Kenmore Plantation

1201 Washington Ave. **Tel** *(540) 373-3381.* ⏰ *Mar–Oct: 10am–5pm daily; Nov, Dec: 10am–4pm daily.* ⬤ *Jan, Feb, Thanksgiving, Dec 24, 25, 31.* **www.**kenmore.org **George Washington's Ferry Farm** 268 Kings Hwy. **Tel** *(540) 370-0732.* ⏰ *as above.*

MONTICELLO, CHARLOTTESVILLE

Situated in the leafy foothills of the Blue Ridge Mountains, this Palladian masterpiece was built between 1769 and 1809 by Thomas Jefferson.

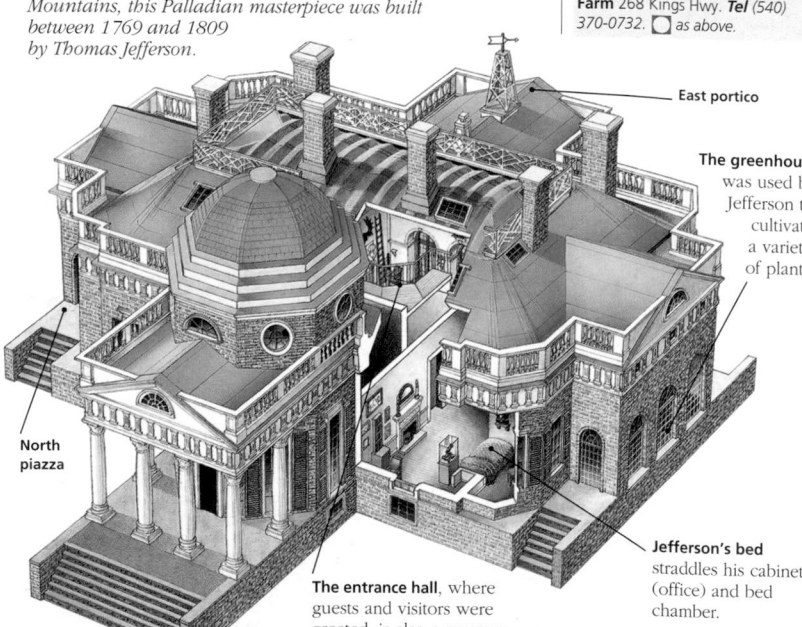

East portico

The greenhouse was used by Jefferson to cultivate a variety of plants.

North piazza

The entrance hall, where guests and visitors were greeted, is also a museum.

Jefferson's bed straddles his cabinet (office) and bed chamber.

Richmond 🔢

Virginia. 👥 202,000. 🚇 🚌 ℹ️
Richmond Metropolitan Convention and Visitors Bureau, 405 N. Third St.
Tel (804) 783-7450. Toll free 888-RICHMOND. ⏰ *9am–5pm Mon–Fri.*
www.visitrichmondva.com

Richmond, the old capital of the Confederacy *(see p19)*, still retains an Old South aura. Bronze images of Civil War generals punctuate Monument Avenue. Brownstones and Victorian houses testify to this area's postwar prosperity.

The Museum of the Confederacy contains Civil War artifacts, including Robert E. Lee's coat and sword. The restored White House of the Confederacy is next door. Another popular museum is the fascinating **Science Museum of Virginia**.

The Neoclassical State Capitol, inside which is the life-sized Houdon sculpture of George Washington, was designed by Charles-Louis-Clérisseau. Hollywood Cemetery is the resting place of presidents John Tyler and James Monroe, and also 18,000 Confederate soldiers.

Statue of Robert E. Lee in Richmond

🏛 **Museum of the Confederacy**
1201 E Clay St.
Tel (804) 649-1861. ⏰ *10am–5pm Mon–Sat, noon–5pm Sun.* ● *Jan 1, Thanksgiving, Dec 25.* 📷 ℹ️ **www**.moc.org

🏛 **Science Museum of Virginia**
2500 W Broad St.
Tel (804) 864-1400. ⏰ *9:30am–5pm Tue–Sat, 11:30am–5pm Sun.* ● *Thanksgiving, Dec 24 & 25.* 📷 ♿ 🚻 ℹ️ **www**.smv.org

Chesapeake Bay 🔢

www.baydreaming.com

Known as "the land of pleasant living," Chesapeake Bay offers historic towns, fishing villages, bed-and-breakfasts, seafood restaurants, beaches, wildlife, and farmland. Much of its Colonial history is preserved in towns such as Cambridge and Easton. The Chesapeake Bay Maritime Museum, in the town of St. Michael's, depicts life on the bay, both past and present. Watermen unload the catch in Crisfield, where cruises depart for Smith Island. The place really feels like a step back in time, particularly with the local Elizabethan dialect.

Chincoteague and Assateague 🔢

Chincoteague, Accomack County, VA. 👥 4,000 Assateague, Accomack County, VA and MD *(unpopulated).* **www**.nps.gov/asis ℹ️ *Chincoteague Chamber of Commerce, 6733 Maddox Blvd. (757) 336-6161.* **www**.chincoteaguechamber.com

These sister islands offer a wealth of natural beauty. Chincoteague is a town situated on the Delmarva (Delaware, Maryland and Virginia) Peninsula. Assateague is an unspoiled strip of nature with an ocean beach and hiking trails that wind through woods and marshes. It is famously populated by wild ponies, thought to be descended from animals grazed on the island by 17th-century farmers. The woodlands and salt marshes of Assateague attract over 300 species of birds, and in fall peregrine falcons and snow geese fly in. Monarch butterflies migrate here in October. There are several campgrounds in the area, and the ocean beach is ideal for swimming and surf fishing. **Toms Cove Visitor Center** and **Chincoteague Wildlife Refuge Center** can provide extra information.

ℹ️ **Toms Cove Visitor Center**
Tel (757) 336-6577.

ℹ️ **Chincoteague Wildlife Refuge Center**
Tel (757) 336-6122.

Yorktown and Jamestowne 🔢

York County, VA, and James City County, VA. ℹ️ *York County Public Information Office (757) 890-3300.*

Established in 1607, Jamestowne was the first permanent English settlement in America. It has 1,500 acres of marshland and forest, threaded with tour routes. There are ruins of the original English settlement and a museum. There is a re-creation of James Fort, full-scale reproductions of the ships that brought the first colonists to America and a traditional Indian village.

Yorktown was the site of the decisive battle of the American Revolution in 1781. **Colonial National Historical Park**'s battlefield tours and exhibits explain the siege at Yorktown.

🏛 **Historic Jamestowne**
Tel (757) 229-1733. ⏰ *8:30am–4:30pm daily.* ● *Jan 1, Dec 25.* 📷 ♿ 🚻 **www**.historicjamestowne.org

🌿 **Colonial National Historical Park**
Tel (757) 898-2410 ⏰ *9am–5pm daily.* ● *Jan 1, Thanksgiving, Dec 25.* 📷 ♿ **www**.nps.gov/colo

Historic Jamestowne, a re-creation of Colonial James Fort

Colonial Williamsburg ⑲

As Virginia's capital from 1699 to 1780, Williamsburg was the hub of the loyal British colony. After 1780 the town went into decline. Then in 1926, John D. Rockefeller embarked on a massive restoration project. Today, in the midst of the modern-day city, the 18th-century city has been re-created. People in colonial dress re-enact the lifestyle

Colonial couple

of the original townspeople; blacksmiths, silversmiths, and cabinet makers show off their skills while horsedrawn carriages pass through the streets, providing visitors with a fascinating insight into America's past.

Courthouse
Built in 1770–71 this was the home of the county court for more than 150 years.

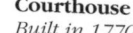

★ Governor's Palace
Originally built in 1720 by Governor Alexander Spotswood, the palace has been reconstructed in its full pre-Revolution glory.

Nursery
Costumed living-history interpreters work the land in Colonial Williamsburg using replica tools and the same techniques as the original settlers.

| 0 meters | 200 |
| 0 yards | 200 |

STAR SIGHTS

★ Governor's Palace

★ Capitol

Fifes and Drums Display
Revolutionary field music is recreated in these colorful parades. Local school children begin learning these instruments aged ten.

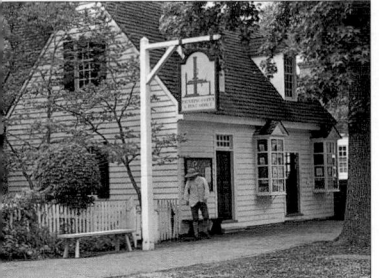

Print Office
This store stocks authentic 18th-century foods, including wine, Virginia ham, and peanuts.

VISITORS' CHECKLIST

Virginia.
101a Visitor Center Drive.
Colonial Williamsburg: 1-800 447-8679.
www.colonialwilliamsburg.com

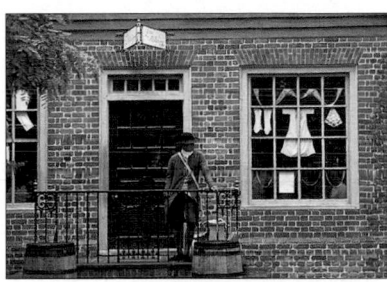

Milliner
Owned by Margaret Hunter, the milliner shop stocked a wide range of items. Imported clothes for women and children, jewelry, and toys could all be bought here.

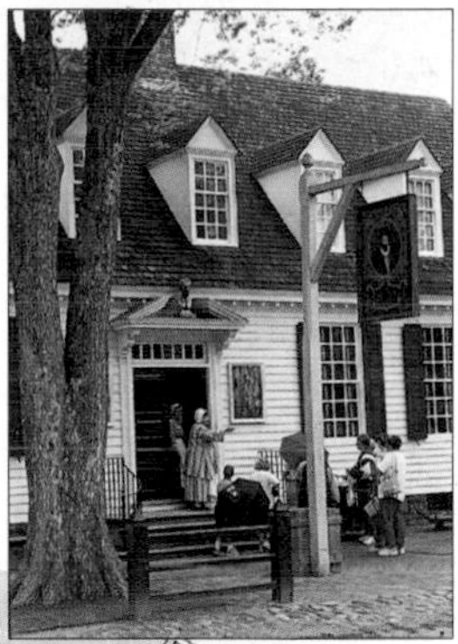

Raleigh Tavern
The Raleigh was once an important center for social, political and commercial gatherings. The original burned in 1859, but this reproduction has its genuine flavor.

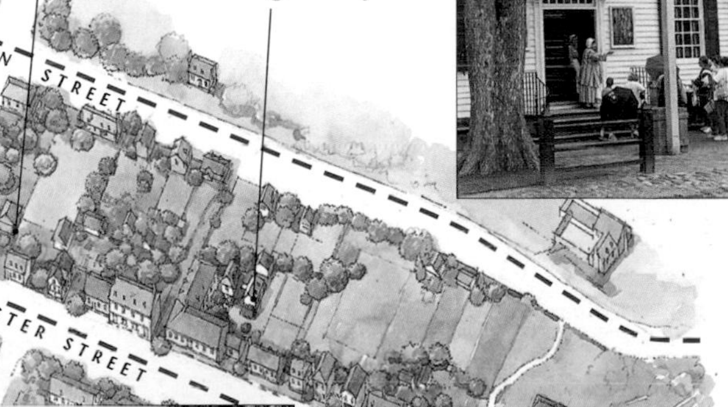
NICHOLSON STREET
BOTETOURT ST
DUKE OF GLOUCESTER STREET

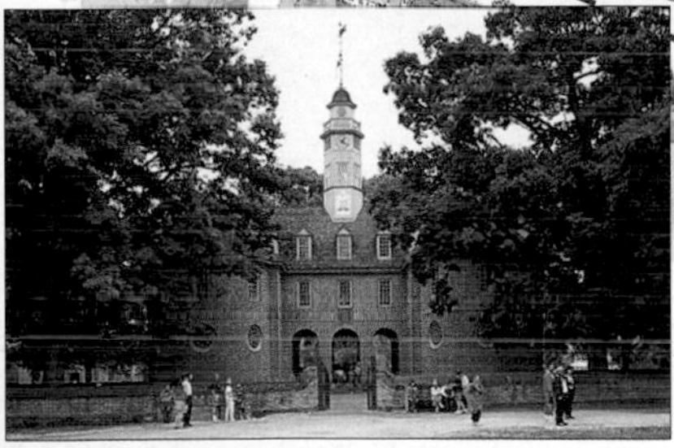

★ Capitol
The capitol is a 1945 reconstruction of the original 1705 building. The government resided in the West Wing, while the General Court was in the East Wing.

KEY

— — — Suggested route

TRAVELERS' NEEDS

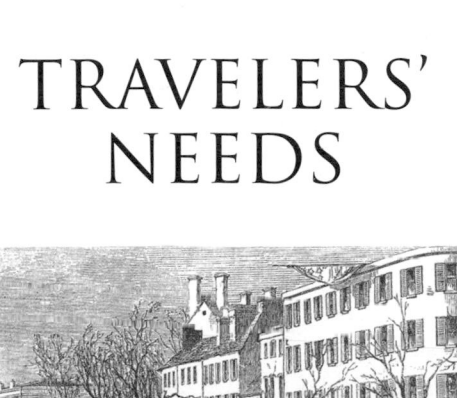

WHERE TO STAY

If you plan to be doing the sights in Washington from dawn until midnight, you may simply need a roof over your head and a bed for your weary body. If you intend to take your time and relax, you may want to have a hotel with all the amenities: pool, health club, deluxe restaurant, room service. Washington can offer a wide range of accommodations. Generally, hotels that are closer to downtown and the Mall are more expensive, and those in the city suburbs are more affordable. Being a tourist destination as well as a business center, Washington's room rates are the second highest in the United States next to New York City. However, there are bargains to be had, especially during the off season and on weekends. Package deals are advertised regularly in the Sunday travel sections of *The New York Times* and the *Washington Post*.

Hotel doorman

Lobby of the plush Hilton Hotel

HOW TO RESERVE

Many hotels have toll-free numbers for making reservations. It is also often possible to preview the accommodations on the hotel's website. If you want to stay at a bed-and-breakfast, either reserve one through an agent or pick one from the phone book. Many hotels sell unreserved rooms at a discount, just as airlines sell unsold tickets. Some companies specialize in offering hotel discounts, including **Capitol Reservations/ Discounter** and **Washington DC Accommodations**.

HOTEL GRADING AND FACILITIES

A five-star hotel will offer everything the visitor could wish for. Room service, health facilities, bathrooms with a jacuzzi, valet parking, and 24-hour maid and butler service are just some of the luxury services provided, but at a price. At the opposite end of the spectrum, a one-star hotel will have a television and a telephone in the bedroom but may have shared bathrooms. Hotels of all price ranges are available in the city.

DISCOUNTS

Washington has different "seasons" from other cities. When the cherry blossoms around the Tidal Basin bloom in April, it is impossible to find a reasonably priced room in the city. Then in June the city is full of school groups taking end-of-the-year trips. Despite often broiling temperatures, families are lured to the capital in the summer. Labor Day in September is very big for tourists as is, of course, the Fourth of July.

However, you can find bargains during the winter months from November through March. Washington is a Monday-through-Friday convention town, so the best prices are on the weekend, often at a fraction of the vacation season, midweek rate.

HIDDEN EXTRAS

Beware the hefty 14.5% tax levied on hotels in Washington. Also note that most hotels will invariably charge you extra for parking in the hotel's parking lot. There is no way to escape the tax, but you can shop around for a hotel with free parking. If you have to park your car in a garage, you can expect to have another $10 to $20 added to each night's tab.

CHAINS AND BOUTIQUE HOTELS

Staying at a **Hilton**, **Holiday Inn**, or **Marriott** hotel will guarantee a level of service and cleanliness mandated by the chain. An alternative to the large chain hotels are the increasingly popular boutique hotels. These small, unique places all have their own character. The Hotel George on Capitol Hill, for instance, is sleek and modern. It also houses Bis, one of the city's most talked-about restaurants. The Henley Park has the decor of a British aristocratic home and serves afternoon tea. The Morrison Clark Inn on Massachusetts

The George, a boutique hotel

◁ Dining at the Old Post Office Pavilion, Pennsylvania Avenue

Avenue is a restored mansion filled with Victorian antiques. The Phoenix Park Hotel on Capitol Hill has an Irish theme and staff – and a pub popular with Irish nationals and Irish-American politicians.

BUSINESS TRAVELERS

Washington hotels increasingly accommodate the sophisticated communications needs of the business traveler. Fax machines and wireless internet access are usually available in rooms, and secretarial services can be arranged through the (often multilingual) concierge. **Meeting Solutions** (a division of Washington DC Accommodations) can help arrange block bookings for a business convention.

Entrance to the Hay-Adams hotel

BED-AND-BREAKFASTS

Although bed-and-breakfast accommodations are not as popular or as plentiful in the United States as they are in Europe, both American and foreign travelers are starting to seek them out as an alternative to the more sterile and expensive hotels. **Bed-and-Breakfast Accommodations Ltd.** tries to match visitors with the perfect room in a bed-and-breakfast, an apartment or small hotel, or even a private home. They have 85 properties in the city and suburbs, and charge a one-time booking fee of $10. Suburban hotels near a Metro stop are a good alternative.

BUDGET OPTIONS

The best value accommodation option for young travelers in Washington is through Hosteling International. It is located in the center of the city, in an area that is close to all major amenities. Young travelers are advised to be cautious when returning after dark. The rate is around $40 per night for a bunk bed in a single-sex dormitory room.

Camping is another inexpensive alternative. There are no campgrounds in the city itself, but camping facilities are available in the outer suburbs. The closest facility approved by Kampgrounds of America is in Millersville, Maryland, 17 miles (27 km) from central DC.

DISABLED TRAVELERS

Nearly all the large, modern hotels are wheelchair accessible, but the independent hotels and bed-and-breakfasts may not be. Call in advance to ask about stairs, elevators, and door widths if you have special needs.

CHILDREN

Traveling with children may dictate your hotel reservations. There are many hotels, such as Embassy Suites *(see p176)* and Georgetown Suites *(see p177)*, that have kitchens or kitchenettes and living rooms with sofabeds that provide space and privacy for parents. The Courtyard by Marriott NW *(see p178)* has a safe outdoor pool and free cookies every afternoon. After walking around the Mall, children may crave a hotel with a pool or a game room. Consider a more expensive room in town rather than a less expensive room in the suburbs. The suburban rates may look appealing until you face a long drive back to your hotel during Washington's unpleasant rush hour.

Some hotels may ban children completely, but these are few and far between. More often than not hotels will be very accommodating toward young guests.

Doormen at the Willard Hotel

DIRECTORY

DISCOUNT COMPANIES

Capitol Reservations/ Discounter
Tel (800) 847-4832.
www.visitdc.com

Washington DC Accommodations; Meeting Solutions
Tel (800) 554-2220.
www.wdcahotels.com

CHAIN HOTELS

Hilton
Tel (800) HILTONS.
www.hilton.com

Holiday Inn
Tel (800) HOLIDAY.
www.holidayinn.com

Howard Johnson
Tel (800) 446-4656.
www.hojo.com

Marriott
Tel (888) 236-2427.
www.marriott.com

BED-AND-BREAKFAST

Bed-and-Breakfast Accommodations Ltd.
Tel (877) 893-3233 (toll free).
www.bedandbreakfastdc.com

CHILDREN

Embassy Suites
1250 22nd St, NW
Tel (202) 857-3388.
www.washingtondc.embassy suites.com

Choosing a Hotel

These hotels have been selected across a wide price range for facilities, good value, and location. They are listed by area and within these by price, both for central Washington, DC and the surrounding areas. All rooms have air conditioning and private bathrooms, unless stated otherwise. The best hotel rates can be found online.

PRICE CATEGORIES
For a standard double room per night, inclusive of breakfast, service charges and any additional taxes such as VAT:

$ Under $125
$$ $125–$175
$$$ $175–$275
$$$$ $275–$375
$$$$$ over $375

CAPITOL HILL

The Capitol Hill Suites
P M H & $$
200 C St, SE (at 2nd St), 20003 **Tel** *543-6000* **Fax** *547-2608* **Rooms** *152*   **Map** *4 F5*

Located two blocks from the Capitol, this boutique-style all-suites hotel was recreated from an apartment building. It has a large, but cozy lobby. It offers free Continental breakfast. Each room comes with a spacious kitchen or kitchenette. Rooms have complimentary high-speed Internet. **www.capitolhillsuites.com**

Carriage House on Capitol Hill
P $$
3rd St at South Carolina Av SE, 20003 **Tel** *877-893-3233* **Rooms** *2*   **Map** *4 F4*

This bed and breakfast comprises a main house and a historic turn-of-the-century carriage house. Rooms are furnished with a mix of new furniture and hand-picked antiques. Continental breakfast is included and there is a lovely central patio with a beautiful walled garden. **www.bbonline.com/dc/coach**

Maison Orleans Bed 'n Breakfast
P $$
414 5th St, SE, 20003 **Tel** *544-3694* **Rooms** *3*   **Map** *4 F5*

This beautiful old Federal front-row house, built in 1902, is furnished with lovely family pieces from the 1930s and 40s. There is a lovely deck overlooking fountains and a fish pond. Wi-Fi is available throughout the house. Located in a quiet neighborhood, close to Eastern Market. **www.bbonline.com/dc/maisonorleans**

Hyatt Regency Washington Capitol Hill
P H ≋ M H & $$$
400 New Jersey Ave, NW (at D St), 20001 **Tel** *737-1234* **Fax** *737-5773* **Rooms** *834*   **Map** *4 E3*

Entrance to the Hyatt is through a five-story atrium. Rooms have wireless Internet and flatscreen TVs, while many suites offer views of the Capitol. You'll also find here the Article One American Grill Restaurant and Lounge. Children under 18 stay for free. Two and a half blocks from Union Station. **www.hyattregencywashington.com**

Liaison Capitol Hill
P H ≋ M H & $$$
415 New Jersey Ave, NW, 20001 **Tel** *638-1616* **Fax** *638-0707* **Rooms** *343*   **Map** *4 E3*

Close to the Smithsonian, this hotel offers a welcome respite from the busy streets around the Capitol. A great choice for families, it also appeals to business travelers. All rooms have Internet access. There is a rooftop pool, and the fitness center is open 24 hours. **www.affinia.com/liaison**

Phoenix Park Hotel
P H M H & $$$$
520 N Capitol St, NW (at F St & N Capitol), 20001 **Tel** *638-6900* **Fax** *393-3236* **Rooms** *149*   **Map** *4 E3*

Located one block from Union Station, this historic hotel features rooms furnished in an 18th-century European manor style. Three of the suites have spiral staircases and three have balconies. Irish entertainers perform nightly at The Dubliner, a pub with good Irish and American food. **www.phoenixparkhotel.com**

The Hotel George
P H M H & $$$$
15 E St, NW, 20001 **Tel** *347-4200* **Fax** *347-4213* **Rooms** *139*   **Map** *4 E3*

This modern boutique hotel, located one and a half blocks away from Union Station, is one of the most fashionable in the city. The large, airy rooms with wide desks will appeal to business travelers. There is a trendy French restaurant called Bistro Bis *(see p186)*. Pet-friendly establishment. **www.hotelgeorge.com**

THE MALL

Holiday Inn Capitol
P H ≋ M H & $
550 C St, SW, 20024 **Tel** *479-4000* **Fax** *479-4353* **Rooms** *532*   **Map** *4 D5*

This hotel is near L'Enfant Plaza Metro and one block from the National Air and Space Museum. There is an outdoor pool on the roof. American food is served at the Capitol Bistro restaurant, where children under 12 eat free when accompanied by an adult. Broadband and wireless Internet available. **www.hicapitoldc.com**

Key to Symbols *see back cover flap*

L'Enfant Plaza Hotel

P **⬛** **⬛** **⬛** **⬛** **⬛** **⬛**   **$$$**

480 L'Enfant Plaza, SW, 20024 **Tel** *484-1000* **Fax** *646-4456* **Rooms** *370*   **Map** *3 C4*

Many of the rooms in this 3-star luxury hotel have spectacular views. Conveniently located near the Smithsonian with easy access to the metro station. The American Grill features steaks and seafood. A good choice for families, the hotel has an indoor pool and is pet friendly. **www.lenfantplazahotel.com**

Mandarin Oriental, Washington, DC

P **⬛** **⬛** **⬛** **⬛** **⬛** **⬛**   **$$$$$**

1330 Maryland Ave, SW, 20024 **Tel** *554-8588* **Fax** *554-8999* **Rooms** *400*   **Map** *3 C5*

This luxury hotel has exotic decor and impeccable service. Enjoy live music and cocktails in the Empress Lounge. Cityzen, Washington's only AAA Five Diamond restaurant, serves Asian-inspired fusion dishes. It is located three blocks from the Smithsonian museums. Rated one of the world's top ten hotels. **www.mandarinoriental.com**

PENN QUARTER

Hostelling International, Washington, DC

⬛   **$**

1009 11th St, NW (at K St), 20001 **Tel** *737-2333* **Fax** *737-1508* **Beds** *250*   **Map** *3 C2*

Attracting an international clientele, this hostel is located three blocks away from Metro Center. The rooms are clean, spacious, and air-conditioned. Amenities include a community kitchen, laundry, TV lounge, and luggage storage. Continental breakfast included. Dormitory and private rooms are available. **www.hiwashingtondc.org**

Henley Park Hotel

P **⬛** **⬛** **⬛**   **$$**

926 Massachusetts Ave, NW, 20001 **Tel** *638-5200* **Fax** *638-6740* **Rooms** *96*   **Map** *3 C2*

The hotel, built in 1918 as an upscale apartment building, was once home to senators and Congressmen. The bar here features live jazz on weekends, and the Coeur de Lion restaurant is top-notch. Room service is available 24-hours. Four blocks from Metro Center. **www.henleypark.com**

J. W. Marriott on Pennsylvania Avenue

P **⬛** **⬛** **⬛** **⬛** **⬛**   **$$$**

1331 Pennsylvania Ave, NW (at 14th St), 20004 **Tel** *393-2000* **Fax** *626-6991* **Rooms** *738*   **Map** *3 B3*

The columned lobby has several cozy sitting areas. The rooms are plush with wireless Internet access. Many rooms offer a beautiful view of the city and the Washington Monument. Close to the White House, National Theater, shops, and Metro Center. **www.marriott.com/wasjw**

Morrison-Clark Inn

P **⬛** **⬛** **⬛**   **$$$**

1015 L St, NW (at Massachusetts Ave), 20001 **Tel** *898-1200* **Fax** *289-8576* **Rooms** *54*   **Map** *3 C2*

This historic 1864 inn was originally two separate townhouses. The Victorian style rooms are beautifully appointed, some with marble fireplaces. The hotel also houses an award-winning restaurant. One and a half blocks from the Convention Center and the metro. **www.morrisonclark.com**

Grand Hyatt Washington

P **⬛** **⬛** **⬛** **⬛** **⬛**   **$$$$**

1000 H St, NW (at 11th St), 20001 **Tel** *582-1234* **Fax** *637-4781* **Rooms** *888*   **Map** *3 C3*

The Grand Hyatt's fanciful interior includes a waterfall-fed lagoon, surrounding an island where a pianist plays. Facilities include a sports bar, atrium café, martini lounge, and a restaurant. Wireless access in every room. Underground entrance to Metro Center. **www.grandhyattwashington.com**

The Madison

P **⬛** **⬛** **⬛** **⬛**   **$$$$**

1177 15th & M Sts, NW, 20005 **Tel** *862-1600* **Fax** *785-1255* **Rooms** *353*   **Map** *3 B2*

The Georgian Federal-style rooms of this elegant hotel are comfortable and luxurious, with oversized desks. The Palette restaurant doubles as an art gallery, with seasonally changing exhibitions. Four blocks north of the White House. **www.loewshotels.com**

The Westin Washington, DC City Center

P **⬛** **⬛** **⬛** **⬛** **⬛**   **$$$$**

1400 M St, NW (at Thomas Circle), 20005 **Tel** *429-1700* **Fax** *785-0786* **Rooms** *406*   **Map** *3 B2*

Four blocks from the McPherson Metro, the Westin has a large central atrium and all the amenities one would expect for a largely business clientele. The restaurant here offers American cuisine. The hotel also provides a 24-hour fitness center. Pet friendly. **www.westin.com**

Willard InterContinental Hotel

P **⬛** **⬛** **⬛** **⬛** **⬛**   **$$$$**

1401 Pennsylvania Ave, NW (at 14th St), 20004 **Tel** *628-9100* **Fax** *637-7326* **Rooms** *332*   **Map** *3 B2*

A grand historic hotel (see p95) offers luxury rooms with marble bathrooms and high speed Internet. Mark Twain, Abraham Lincoln, and Walt Whitman were once guests, and it was here that Martin Luther King wrote his "I Have a Dream" speech. Located two blocks from the White House. **www.washington.intercontinental.com**

Hotel Monaco Washington DC

P **⬛** **⬛** **⬛** **⬛** **⬛**   **$$$$$**

700 F St, NW, 20004 **Tel** *628-7177* **Fax** *628-7277* **Rooms** *183*   **Map** *3 C3*

This magnificent hotel is housed in the Old General Post Office, built in 1836. The architect was Robert Mills who also designed the Washington Monument. Conveniently located near the National Portrait Gallery and the MCI Center. Pet friendly. The restaurant, Poste, is delightful. **www.monaco-dc.com**

THE WHITE HOUSE AND FOGGY BOTTOM

George Washington University Inn
824 New Hampshire Ave, NW, 20037 **Tel** *337-6620* **Fax** *298-7499* **Rooms** *95*
Map *2 E3*

This boutique-style hotel has a marble lobby. All rooms, with a Williamsburg-inspired decor, come with a refrigerator, microwave, and coffee-maker, while some of them have complete kitchens. Free high-speed Internet available. Conveniently located, near the university, Kennedy Center, and metro. **www.gwuinn.com**

Embassy Suites Washington, DC
1250 22nd St, NW, 20037 **Tel** *857-3388* **Fax** *293-3173* **Rooms** *318*
Map *2 E2*

With suites that accommodate up to five people, this hotel is very suitable for families. The modern atrium has a waterfall, columns, and palm trees. A full buffet breakfast is included in the tariff. Close to Dupont Circle shops and restaurants. Swimming pool and fitness center. **www.washingtondc.embassysuites.com**

The Quincy
1823 L St, NW, 20036 **Tel** *223-4320* **Fax** *293-4977* **Rooms** *99*
Map *3 A2*

A modern boutique suite hotel offering a range of kitchen amenities in the apartments. Guests can enjoy free passes to Bally Fitness with gym and pool. Room service from Mackey's Pub, an Irish bar and restaurant; breakfast not included. Pet friendly. Complimentary high-speed Internet access. **www.thequincy.com**

State Plaza Hotel
2117 E St, NW **Tel** *861-8200* **Rooms** *230*
Map *2 E4*

This all-suites hotel, located between White House and Kennedy Center, features a café with outdoor seating and a rooftop sun deck. Suites have equipped kitchens and high speed Internet. Special features are complimentary shoe-shine and *Washington Post*. **www.stateplaza.com**

Beacon Hotel and Corporate Quarters
1615 Rhode Island Ave, NW (at 17th St), 20036 **Tel** *296-2100* **Fax** *331-0227* **Rooms** *199*
Map *3 B2*

The comfortable rooms are decorated with cosmopolitan flair. Eight deluxe turret suites and 60 corporate suites come with fully equipped kitchens, high-speed Internet and web TV. The Beacon Bar & Grill restaurant serves food throughout the day, from breakfast to dinner. **www.beaconhotelwdc.com**

Hotel Lombardy
2019 Pennsylvania Ave, NW (at I St), 20002 **Tel** *828-2600* **Fax** *872-0503* **Rooms** *160*
Map *2 E3*

This European-style boutique hotel has an accommodating multilingual staff. Café Lombardy serves gourmet European food, and a limited menu is available in the Venetian Room lounge. Two blocks from the Farragut West Metro and three blocks from the White House. **www.hotellombardy.com**

One Washington Circle
1 Washington Circle, NW, 20037 **Tel** *872-1680* **Fax** *887-4989* **Rooms** *151*
Map *2 E3*

Frequented by business and leisure travelers, this all-suite hotel has rooms with private balconies. There is an outdoor pool. The Circle Bistro serves Mediterranean food. Convenient for George Washington University and Hospital. **www.thecirclehotel.com**

Renaissance Mayflower Hotel
1127 Connecticut Ave, NW, 20036 **Tel** *347-3000* **Fax** *776-9128* **Rooms** *657*
Map *2 F3*

The elegant and stately Mayflower, built in 1925, is on the National Register of Historic Places. Elegant dining is accompanied by live piano music between 6 and 8pm. Located near Farragut North Metro and the White House. **www.marriott.com**

Capital Hilton
1001 16th St, NW (at K St), 20036 **Tel** *393-1000* **Fax** *639-5784* **Rooms** *544*
Map *3 B2*

A large, bustling hotel. The inviting lobby has several seating areas. The nicest rooms are on the top floors. The Twigs Grill restaurant serves American cuisine. The hotel's City Club & Spa is one of Washington's premier health and fitness centers. Two blocks from the White House and near several metro stops. **www.hilton.com**

The Fairmont Washington, DC
2401 M St, NW (at 24th St), 20037 **Tel** *429-2400* **Fax** *457-5089* **Rooms** *415*
Map *2 E2*

Guests will enjoy the plant-filled atrium and luxurious rooms, some overlooking the central courtyard and gardens. The service is impeccable. The Juniper restaurant serves top-quality American cuisine. Located within walking distance of Georgetown. **www.fairmont.com**

The Westin Grand
2350 M St, NW, 20037 **Tel** *429-0100* **Fax** *857-0127* **Rooms** *267*
Map *2 E2*

CD players, coffee makers, minibars, and luxurious marble bathrooms with extra-deep bathtubs are just a few of the amenities in the rooms of this well-appointed hotel. The Westin Café serves American food. There is an outdoor pool. Pets allowed by appointment. **www.westin.com/washington.dc**

Key to Price Guide *see p174* **Key to Symbols** *see back cover flap*

Hay-Adams Hotel [P] 🍴 🏋 ♿ $$$$$

800 16th St, NW (at H St), 20006 ***Tel*** *638-6600* ***Fax*** *638-2716* ***Rooms*** *144* ***Map*** *3 B2*

This historic Italian Renaissance-style hotel overlooking Lafayette Square and the White House combines the two homes of John Hay and Henry Adams, both renowned authors and diplomats. Beautiful rooms feature antiques and ornamental ceilings. **www.hayadams.com**

The Jefferson [P] 🍴 🍸 ♿ $$$$$

1200 16th St, NW (at M St), 20036 ***Tel*** *448-2300* ***Fax*** *448-2301* ***Rooms*** *100* ***Map*** *2F2*

Erected in 1923, this hotel – part of the luxury Relais & Châteaux group – is housed within a historic building of the city. The impeccable service and well-appointed fine dining restaurant show a superb mix of sophisticated polish and upscale conveniences. There is an onsite spa. **www.jeffersondc.com**

St. Regis Washington [P] 🍴 🍸 🏋 ♿ $$$$$

923 16th St, NW (at K St), 20006 ***Tel*** *638-2626* ***Fax*** *638-4231* ***Rooms*** *175* ***Map*** *3 B2*

A historic, luxury hotel with a warm, European ambience. Elegantly furnished with antiques, chandeliers, and exquisite tapestries, reminiscent of a Renaissance palace. Guests will enjoy the romantic setting and cuisine in the elegant restaurant. Personal butler service available. **www.stregis.com/washington**

W Hotel [P] 🍴 🍸 🏋 ♿ $$$$$

514 15th St, NW, 20004 ***Tel*** *661-2400* ***Fax*** *661-2405* ***Rooms*** *317* ***Map*** *3 B3*

A registered historic landmark and one of the oldest hotels in the city, the former Hotel Washington is now part of the Starwood Resorts and Hotels empire. Conveniently located one block from the White House and three blocks from Metro Center. Amenities include an onsite spa and a rooftop bar. **www.whotels.com/washingtondc**

GEORGETOWN

The Georgetown Inn [P] 🍴 🏊 🍸 🏋 ♿ $

1310 Wisconsin Ave, NW, 20007 ***Tel*** *333-8900* ***Fax*** *965-3378* ***Rooms*** *90* ***Map*** *1 C2*

A small, boutique hotel built in the style of historic Georgetown. The large rooms have Colonial-style decor and luxurious bathrooms. The Daily Grill restaurant displays scenes of old Washington on the walls. Located in the heart of Georgetown. **www.georgetowninn.com**

The Georgetown Latham Hotel [P] 🍴 🏊 🏋 ♿ $$

3000 M St, NW (at 30th St), 20007 ***Tel*** *726-5000* ***Fax*** *337-4250* ***Rooms*** *133* ***Map*** *2 D2*

This is an upscale, European-style boutique hotel with a luxurious lobby. There is a rooftop pool and quaint two-story carriage suites. Guests have access to a free fitness center. The service is top-notch. The Latham's excellent five-star restaurant, Citronelle, serves French cuisine. **www.thelatham.com**

Hotel Monticello [P] 🍸 🏋 ♿ $$

1075 Thomas Jefferson St, NW, 20007 ***Tel*** *337-0900* ***Fax*** *333-6526* ***Rooms*** *47* ***Map*** *2 D3*

Located below M Street, near the C&O Canal, this Georgian-style all-suite boutique hotel has a lobby furnished with 18th-century antiques. It has spacious rooms, one-bedroom suites, and two-story penthouses. Continental breakfast is included in the tariff. Parking is limited to small and midsize cars. **www.monticellohotel.com**

Georgetown Suites [P] 🍸 🏋 ♿ $$$

1111 30th St NW (at K St) & 1000 29th St NW, 20007 ***Tel*** *298-7800* ***Fax*** *333-5792* ***Rooms*** *222* ***Map*** *2 D2*

This establishment provides one- and two-bedroom suites, studios, two-story townhomes, and penthouses. Each suite has fully-equipped kitchens with microwave, dishwasher, and ice-maker. The tariff includes a complimentary Continental breakfast. Free local calls and wireless Internet access. **www.georgetownsuites.com**

Holiday Inn Georgetown [P] 🍴 🏊 🍸 🏋 ♿ $$$

2101 Wisconsin Ave, NW, 20007 ***Tel*** *338-3120* ***Fax*** *338-4458* ***Rooms*** *285* ***Map*** *1 C1*

Conveniently located just north of Georgetown, this seven-story hotel features a rich traditional decor and has an outdoor pool. John F's Café features American fare and Italian dishes. Close to many specialty shops and restaurants. **www.higeorgetown.com**

Four Seasons Hotel [P] 🍴 🏊 🍸 🏋 ♿ $$$$$

2800 Pennsylvania Ave, NW, 20007 ***Tel*** *342-0444* ***Fax*** *944-2076* ***Rooms*** *222* ***Map*** *2 D3*

With a contemporary elegance, the Four Seasons prides itself on its excellent service. Rooms are spacious and well-appointed. There is an onsite spa, and the Bourbon Steak restaurant is the place for a leisurely Sunday brunch. Near shops, restaurants, and the Washington Harbor. **www.fourseasons.com**

Ritz-Carlton Hotel [P] 🍴 🍸 🏋 ♿ $$$$$

3100 South St, NW, 20007 ***Tel*** *912-4100* ***Fax*** *912-4199* ***Rooms*** *86* ***Map*** *1 C3*

Located close to Washington Harbor and the C&O Canal, as well as Georgetown's shops, bars, and restaurants, this historic building offers understated, contemporary accommodation. Some rooms overlook the waterfront, and pets are welcome for a nightly fee. The boutique spa continues the theme of simple luxury. **www.ritzcarlton.com**

FARTHER AFIELD

ADAMS MORGAN Adam's Inn [P] $

1746 Lanier Pl, NW, 20009 ***Tel*** *745-3600* ***Fax*** *319-7958* ***Rooms*** *26*

This European-style inn with guest kitchen and laundry facilities is located in three 100-year-old brick townhouses on a quiet residential street. Some of the rooms have an "urban country" look; others are Victorian. Sixteen rooms have private baths. Continental breakfast and high-speed Internet access. **www.adamsinn.com**

ADAMS MORGAN Kalorama Guest House [P] $

1854 Mintwood Pl, NW (near Columbia Rd & 19th St), 20009 ***Tel*** *667-6369* ***Fax*** *319-1262* ***Rooms*** *29* ***Map*** *2 E1*

A Victorian townhouse in a charming residential neighborhood. The rooms are tastefully decorated in period decor. Children under six are not allowed. A sister establishment is located at 2700 Cathedral Avenue, at Woodley Park (Tel: 328-0860). Continental breakfast and wireless Internet access. **www.kaloramaguesthouse.com**

DUPONT CIRCLE District Hotel $

1440 Rhode Island Ave, NW, 20005 ***Tel*** *232-7800* ***Fax*** *265-3725* ***Rooms*** *58* ***Map*** *3 B1*

This small hotel is located close to Logan Circle and within walking distance of Dupont Circle and U Street. Rooms come with cable TV and some have refrigerators. Continental breakfast is included in the tariff. All major credit cards are accepted. **www.districthotel.com**

DUPONT CIRCLE Hotel Madera [P] 🍴 🏋 ♿ $

1310 New Hampshire Ave, NW (at 13th St), 20036 ***Tel*** *296-7600* ***Fax*** *293-2476* ***Rooms*** *82* ***Map*** *2 E2*

This small but exquisitly decorated boutique hotel, is a stylish gem in the heart of the fashionable Dupont Circle district. The hotel restaurant, The Firefly Bistro, offers modern American cuisine. Daily passes to a gym can be arranged, and the hotel offers in-room massages and spa treatments. Pet friendly. **www.hotelmadera.com**

DUPONT CIRCLE Tabard Inn 🍴 🏋 $

1739 N St, NW, 20036 ***Tel*** *785-1277* ***Fax*** *785-6173* ***Rooms*** *40* ***Map*** *2 F2*

This boutique hotel, named for the inn in Chaucer's *The Canterbury Tales*, is converted from three townhouses. The rooms are charming and eclectic; some are Victorian. Several of the rooms have a shared bath. The restaurant serves superb American-Continental cuisine. Free access to a gym is available. **www.tabardinn.com**

DUPONT CIRCLE Topaz Hotel [P] 🍴 🏋 ♿ $

1733 N St, NW, 20036 ***Tel*** *393-3000* ***Fax*** *785-9581* ***Rooms*** *99* ***Map*** *2 F2*

This European-style inn provides stylish accommodation with modern facilities in an atmosphere of Eastern-inspired calm. A yoga program is available. The Topaz bar and restaurant serve Asian-inspired cocktails and food. Pet friendly. High-speed Internet access is available. **www.topazhotel.com**

DUPONT CIRCLE The Dupont at the Circle Bed & Breakfast [P] $$

1604 19th St, NW (at Dupont Circle), 20009 ***Tel*** *332-5251* ***Fax*** *332-3244* ***Rooms*** *9* ***Map*** *2 F2*

This comfortable bed-and-breakfast is located in two Victorian townhouses just off Dupont Circle. Rooms have period antiques and high-speed Internet. The Continental breakfast includes homemade granola. Daily passes to a nearby gym are available. Parking is limited. **www.dupontatthecircle.com**

DUPONT CIRCLE The Churchill Hotel [P] 🍴 🍸 🏋 ♿ $$$

1914 Connecticut Ave, NW, 20009 ***Tel*** *797-2000* ***Fax*** *462-0944* ***Rooms*** *173* ***Map*** *2 E1*

A luxury hotel with a predominantly European clientele, the Churchill Hotel was opened as an apartment building in 1906. Its rooms are huge and tastefully furnished. The Chartwell Grill restaurant features American cuisine. High-speed Internet access available. **www.thechurchillhotel.com**

DUPONT CIRCLE Courtyard by Marriott NW [P] 🍴 🏊 🍸 🏋 ♿ $$$

1900 Connecticut Ave, NW, 20009 ***Tel*** *332-9300* ***Fax*** *328-7039* ***Rooms*** *147* ***Map*** *2 E1*

This hotel features a dark wood-paneled lobby, standard rooms, and an outdoor pool. The rooms are designed with the business traveler in mind. Free cookies and coffee are available in the afternoon. The Clarets restaurant serves American cuisine. **www.marriott.com**

DUPONT CIRCLE Dupont Hotel [P] 🍴 🍸 🏋 ♿ $$$$

1500 New Hampshire Ave, NW, 20036 ***Tel*** *483-6000* ***Fax*** *328-3265* ***Rooms*** *324* ***Map*** *2 F2*

Boasting an interior that cost $52 million to decorate, the Dupont Hotel – part of the exclusive Doyles Collection of hotels – offers the last word in elegance and comfort. For the VIP guest, level nine's hotel-within-a-hotel features designer furnishings, a private elevator, and personal concierge. **www.doylecollection.com**

DUPONT CIRCLE Mansion on O Street [P] 🍴 🏋 ♿ $$$$

2020 O Street, NW (at 20th St), 20036 ***Tel*** *496-2000* ***Fax*** *659-0547* ***Rooms*** *23* ***Map*** *2 E2*

The decor is eclectic and charming – part Victorian, part avant-garde. Suites come with wireless Internet connections, and they are decorated with fine art. Breakfast is included in the tariff. Passes to a sports club are available. Pet friendly. **www.omansion.com**

Key to Price Guide *see p174* **Key to Symbols** *see back cover flap*

DUPONT CIRCLE Swann House   P ≋ ⓣ $$$$

1808 New Hampshire Ave, NW, 20009 **Tel** *265-4414* **Fax** *265-6755* **Rooms** *9*   **Map** *2 F1*

This B&B in a Romanesque-style house built in 1883 is filled with beautiful antiques, as well as "modern treasures" such as whirlpool bathtubs. There is an outdoor pool in the courtyard, and afternoon refreshments are available to guests. There is complimentary high-speed Wi-Fi and Internet access. **www.swannhouse.com**

DUPONT CIRCLE The Fairfax at Embassy Row   P ⑪ ⓜ ⓣ � $$$$

2100 Massachusetts Ave, NW, 20008 **Tel** *293-2100* **Fax** *293-0641* **Rooms** *259*   **Map** *2 E2*

A posh hotel with an elegant decor. Its prime location on Embassy Row attracts diplomats. It is located close to the Phillips Gallery and Dupont Circle. The Jockey Club and the Fairfax Lounge restaurants both serve classic American cuisine. **www.luxurycollection.com**

WISCONSIN AVE Embassy Suites Hotel at the Chevy Chase Pavilion   P ≋ ⓜ ⓖ $$$

4300 Military Rd, NW (at Wisconsin & Western Aves), 20015 **Tel** *362-9300* **Fax** *686-3405* **Rooms** *198*

Situated in the popular Chevy Chase shopping district, the all-suite hotel accesses a wide range of shops, restaurants, as well as the Friendship Heights Metro, all within the Pavilion. Breakfast is included in the tariff. There are complimentary drinks and appetizers served during the daily "Manager's Reception." **www.embassysuitesdc.com**

WISCONSIN AVE Savoy Suites   P ⑪ ⓖ $$$

2505 Wisconsin Ave, NW, 20007 **Tel** *337-9700* **Fax** *337-3644* **Rooms** *150*

Rooms are fresh and smart, with a luxurious feel that is even more appealing when you realize that the hotel is totally powered by wind energy. There is access to the Washington Sports Club facility nearby, and live jazz in the restaurant on Thursday evenings. Complimentary shuttle service to the DC metro. **www.savoysuites.com**

WOODLEY PARK/CLEVELAND PARK Days Inn Connecticut Avenue   P ⑪ ⓣ ⓖ $

4400 Connecticut Ave, NW, 20008 **Tel** *244-5600* **Fax** *244-6794* **Rooms** *155*

A convenient, affordable place, north of Cleveland Park near the Van Ness Metro, with clean rooms. Several restaurants are located nearby, including the Tesoro next door, which serves authentic Italian cuisine. **www.dcdaysinn.com**

WOODLEY PARK/CLEVELAND PARK Omni Shoreham Hotel   P ⑪ ≋ ⓜ ⓣ ⓖ $$$

2500 Calvert St, NW, 20008 **Tel** *234-0700* **Fax** *765-5145* **Rooms** *834*

This four-diamond hotel features a grand Art Deco-style lobby, spacious rooms, and marble-floored bathrooms. Set in 11 acres of beautifully landscaped grounds overlooking Rock Creek Park. The outdoor pool has splendid views and poolside service. **www.omnihotels.com**

WOODLEY PARK/CLEVELAND PARK Marriott Wardman Park Hotel   P ⑪ ≋ ⓜ ⓣ ⓖ $$$$

2660 Woodley Rd, NW, 20008 **Tel** *328-2000* **Fax** *234-0015* **Rooms** *1334*

Surrounded by 16 acres of parkland, the original apartment building has been extended to include a modern glass complex. This large convention hotel has two pools, several restaurants, and spacious, comfortable rooms. The grounds are well maintained. The Woodley Park Metro is adjacent. **www.marriott.com**

BEYOND WASHINGTON, DC

ALEXANDRIA, VA Morrison House   P ⑪ ⓣ ⓖ $$$

116 S Alfred St, 22314 **Tel** *703-838-8000* **Fax** *703-684-6283* **Rooms** *45*

Modeled after a Federal manor home, this four-star hotel has attractive rooms with four-poster beds, armoires, and Italian marble bathrooms. The Grille restaurant offers fine dining and a varied menu in elegant surroundings. Pet friendly. **www.morrisonhouse.com**

ALEXANDRIA, VA Hotel Monaco Alexandria   P ≋ ⓜ ⓣ ⓖ $$$$$

480 King St (at S Pitt St), 22314 **Tel** *703-549-6080* **Fax** *703-684-6508* **Rooms** *241*   **Map** *3 C3*

This four-star luxury hotel is conveniently located in the heart of the historic Old Town. It features stylish guestrooms and suites, and a destination restaurant, Jackson 20. The hotel provides transportation to and from Reagan National Airport. Pet friendly. **www.monaco-alexandria.com**

ANNAPOLIS, MD Maryland Inn   P ⑪ ⓜ ⓖ $$$

16 Church Circle, 21401 **Tel** *410-263-2641* **Fax** *410-268-3613* **Rooms** *44*

This lovely, award-winning brick inn near the water was built in the 1760s. The Victorian-style rooms are comfortable and The Treaty of Paris is a warm, inviting restaurant. Reservations are made through the Historic Inns of Annapolis, which also runs the Governor Calvert House and the Robert Johnson House. **www.historicinnsofannapolis.com**

ARLINGTON, VA Crystal City Marriott   P ⑪ ≋ ⓜ ⓣ ⓖ $$$

1999 Jefferson Davis Hwy (at S 20th St), 22202 **Tel** *703-413-5500* **Fax** *703-413-0192* **Rooms** *333*

The lobby has a marble floor and Art Deco fixtures and the rooms are quite elegant. The hotel, minutes from Reagan National Airport, provides a complimentary airport shuttle service. The CC Bistro features American and Italian dishes. High-speed Internet access available. **www.crystalcitymarriott.com**

ARLINGTON, VA Hyatt
1325 Wilson Blvd, 22209 **Tel** *703-525-1234* **Fax** *703-908-4790* **Rooms** *317*

Located a short walk across Key Bridge to Georgetown, the Hyatt is just a 15-minute metro ride from the Mall. Ask for a room on a high floor for a partial view of the Potomac River. This comfortable, stylish, and modern hotel has a good restaurant, but there are also many eateries nearby. Wi-Fi and iPod docking. **www.arlington.hyatt.com**

ARLINGTON, VA Ritz-Carlton Pentagon City
1250 S Hayes St, 22202 **Tel** *703-415-5000* **Fax** *703-415-5061* **Rooms** *366*

The hotel's look incorporates contemporary lines and shades with classic elegance. Afternoon tea is served between 2 and 4:30pm daily. The four-star hotel is conveniently located next to the metro and Pentagon City Mall, one mile from Reagan National Airport. High-speed and wireless Internet service. **www.ritzcarlton.com**

BALTIMORE, MD Pier 5
711 Eastern Ave, 21202 **Tel** *410-539-2000* **Fax** *410-783-1787* **Rooms** *66*

This hotel is decorated in vibrant oranges and purples. It's whimsical and fun. Well located on the waterfront, next to the National Aquarium. Small pets are welcome for an extra charge. Internet access and Wi-Fi are available in every room. Access to nearby fitness center and pool for a small fee. **www.harbormagic.com**

BALTIMORE, MD Renaissance Harborplace Hotel
202 E Pratt St, 21202 **Tel** *410-547-1200* **Fax** *410-539-5780* **Rooms** *622*

The rooms in this four-star hotel have a view either of the harbor or of the indoor courtyard. The staff are attentive and cordial. Watertable, the fine hotel restaurant, has a beautiful view of the water and specializes in excellent seafood from Chesapeake Bay. **www.renaissancehotels.com**

BALTIMORE, MD Peabody Court, a Clarion Hotel
612 Cathedral St, 21201 **Tel** *410-727-7101* **Fax** *410-789-3312* **Rooms** *104*

A boutique-style hotel, with a Renaissance Revival façade and a well-appointed lobby, provides excellent service. Located close to the Walters Art Museum in a charming neighborhood. The George's restaurant offers casual fine dining. **www.peabodycourthotel.com**

BERKELEY SPRINGS, WV Cacapon Resort State Park
818 Cacapon Lodge Dr, 25411 **Tel** *304-258-1022* **Fax** *304-258-5323* **Rooms** *48*

Choose from modern rooms or rustic cabins in the lodge with hiking, fishing, horseback riding, and golf facilities. The Park is located two hours from Washington and 10 miles (16 km) from Berkeley Springs, a historic town known for its spa that dates back to Colonial times. **www.cacaponresort.com**

BERLIN, MD Merry Sherwood Plantation
8909 Worcester Highway, 21811 **Tel** *410-641-2112* **Rooms** *8*

This bed-and-breakfast is a restored 1850s Italianate Revival-style pre-Civil War mansion, set on 21 acres. The rooms have Victorian-style furniture and working fireplaces. The gourmet breakfast includes homemade muffins. TV and phone are not provided. Two and a half hours from DC. **www.merrysherwood.com**

BETHESDA, MD Hyatt Regency Bethesda
1 Bethesda Metro Center, 20814 **Tel** *301-657-1234* **Fax** *657-6453* **Rooms** *390*

This luxurious hotel is in a nearby suburb, directly above a Metrorail stop on the Red Line for easy access into central Washington. Movie theaters, a wide variety of restaurants, bookstores, and shops are all within walking distance. **www.hyattregency.com**

CHARLOTTESVILLE, VA The Boar's Head Inn
200 Ednam Dr, 22903 **Tel** *434-296-2181* **Fax** *434-972-6024* **Rooms** *171*

A romantic and charming inn in a beautiful country setting near the foothills of the Blue Ridge Mountains with two lakes on the grounds. Facilities include an 18-hole golf course, tennis, fishing, biking, four pools, and a spa. The Old Mill Room, built from the timbers of an old gristmill, offers fine dining. **www.boarsheadinn.com**

CHINCOTEAGUE, VA Refuge Inn
7058 Maddox Blvd, 23336 **Tel** *757-336-5511* **Fax** *757-336-6134* **Rooms** *72*

This inn is only half a mile away from the National Wildlife Refuge and close to the National Seashore. The convenient location, inexpensive rooms, and friendly atmosphere make it a good choice for families. Two of the suites are equipped with kitchens. Continental breakfast available. **www.refugeinn.com**

FREDERICKSBURG, VA Kenmore Inn
1200 Princess Anne St, 22401 **Tel** *540-371-7622* **Fax** *540-371-5480* **Rooms** *9*

Built in 1793, this inn has Colonial furnishings and is two blocks from downtown Fredericksburg. Many of the rooms have working fireplaces. The candle-lit dining room features Virginia specialties, and the English-style pub provides lighter fare. **www.kenmoreinn.com**

GETTYSBURG, VA Baladerry Inn Bed & Breakfast
40 Hospital Rd, 17325 **Tel** *717-337-1342* **Rooms** *10*

The cozy Baladerry Inn dates back to 1812. It later served as a hospital in the Civil War *(see p21)*. There are four rooms in the original house and five in the carriage houses, some with fireplaces. Serves a three-course country-style gourmet breakfast. **www.baladerryinn.com**

Key to Price Guide *see p174* **Key to Symbols** *see back cover flap*

LURAY, VA Big Meadows and Skyline Lodges [P] 🍴 🚸 ♿ $

PO Box 727 (Skyline Drive), 22835 ***Tel*** *540-999-2221* ***Fax*** *540-999-2011* ***Rooms*** *97*

Located at Milepost 51 and 43.7 respectively on the scenic Skyline Drive in the Shenandoah National Park. The rustic accommodations, which include cabins, suites or guest rooms in the chestnut-paneled lodge, offer attractive views of the forest and the valley. Closed from December to early March. **www.visitshenandoah.com**

MIDDLEBURG, VA The Red Fox Inn [P] 🍴 $$

2 East Washington St, 20117 ***Tel*** *540-687-6301* ***Fax*** *540-687-6053* ***Rooms*** *23*

This inn, on the main street of Middleburg, was built in 1728. The motif is Virginia hunt country. Each guest room is different and decorated with antiques – several with four-poster canopy beds. Continental breakfast included. The dimly lit romantic restaurant is reminiscent of an 18th-century tavern. The food is superb. **www.redfox.com**

MIDDLETOWN, VA The Wayside Inn [P] 🍴 ♿ $

7783 Main St, 22645 ***Tel*** *540-869-1797* ***Fax*** *540-869-6038* ***Rooms*** *22*

This charming inn has been in operation since 1797. Each room is appointed with beautiful antiques. The firelit dining room serves Southern regional dishes. The Wayside Theater, a block away, provides evening entertainment. Located in the Shenandoah Valley, one and a half hours away from DC. **www.alongthewayside.com**

PARIS, VA The Ashby Inn and Restaurant [P] 🍴 🌳 $$$

692 Federal St, 20130 ***Tel*** *540-592-3900* ***Fax*** *540-592-3781* ***Rooms*** *6*

Built in 1829, this attractive inn has rooms with views of the foothills of the Blue Ridge Mountains. The restaurant is excellent. Located in a small village, 12 miles (19 km) from Middleburg and an hour's drive from Washington. AmEx, MasterCard, and Visa are accepted. **www.ashbyinn.com**

RICHMOND, VA The Berkeley Hotel [P] 🍴 🏊 🏋 🌳 ♿ $$

1200 East Cary St, 23219 ***Tel*** *804-780-1300* ***Fax*** *804-648-4728* ***Rooms*** *55*

A warm welcome is given at this gracious four-diamond hotel with lavish, traditional furnishings. The most popular rooms are those with balconies. Situated in the heart of downtown Richmond. Berkeley's restaurant, The Dining Room, specializes in regional cuisine. High-speed Internet access. **www.berkeleyhotel.com**

RICHMOND, VA The Jefferson [P] 🍴 🏊 🏋 🌳 ♿ $$$$

101 W Franklin St, 23220 ***Tel*** *804-788-8000* ***Fax*** *804-225-0334* ***Rooms*** *262*

The oldest hotel in the area, the five-star Mobil Jefferson was built in 1895. It has a European feel and Southern charm. The lobby boasts a magnificent stained-glass ceiling. There are two excellent restaurants. Located in downtown Richmond, close to the historic and business districts. **www.jeffersonhotel.com**

SHEPHERDSTOWN, WV Bavarian Inn [P] 🍴 🏊 🏋 🌳 ♿ $

164 Shepherd Grade Road, 25443 ***Tel*** *304-876-2551* ***Fax*** *304-876-9355* ***Rooms*** *72*

The AAA and four-diamond inn is located in a picturesque town, 15 miles (24 km) from Harper's Ferry. Rooms are individually decorated with Old World elegance – some with fireplaces, canopy beds, and magnificent views of the Potomac. Excellent German cuisine is served here. **www.bavarianinnwv.com**

TILGHMAN ISLAND, MD Chesapeake Wood Duck Inn [P] $$

21490 Gibsontown Rd, at Dogwood Harbor, 21671 ***Tel*** *410-886-2070* ***Fax*** *413-677 7256* ***Rooms*** *7*

Winner of the AAA and three-star Mobil awards, this waterfront bed-and-breakfast, built in 1890, offering great hospitality and innovative cuisine. A three-course gourmet complimentary breakfast and a four-course dinner available Saturday evenings, for inn guests by reservation only. **www.woodduckinn.com**

TREVILIANS, VA Prospect Hill Plantation Inn [P] 🍴 🏊 🌳 ♿ $$$

2887 Poindexter Rd (near Charlottesville), 23093 ***Tel*** *540-967-0844* ***Fax*** *540-967-0102* ***Rooms*** *13*

This inn is situated on a 50-acre former plantation in beautiful countryside, 15 miles (24 km) east of Charlottesville. The house dates back to 1732. All of the rooms have fireplaces. Breakfast and dinner are included in the tariff. Limited rooms have been provided with facilities for the disabled. **www.prospecthill.com**

WASHINGTON, VA Inn at Little Washington [P] 🍴 ♿ $$$$$

Middle & Main Sts, 22747 ***Tel*** *540-675-3800* ***Fax*** *540-675-3100* ***Rooms*** *18*

No two rooms are alike at this imaginatively furnished, lovely five-star inn, set in the beautiful Shenandoah Valley. The world-renowned restaurant on the premises offers an unforgettable culinary experience, with a fixed-price multi-course meal. Weekday rates are less expensive. AmEx, MasterCard, and Visa. **www.theinnatlittlewashington.com**

WILLIAMSBURG, VA Colonial Houses ♿ $$$

305 S England St, 23187 ***Tel*** *757-229-1000* ***Fax*** *757-220-7096* ***Rooms*** *26*

Rent a room or an entire house at this restored 18th-century place with modern amenities, except a kitchen. Facilities of the nearby Williamsburg Inn, including restaurant, room service, parking, and swimming pool, are available to the guests of the Colonial houses. Wheelchair access in only three rooms. **www.colonialwilliamsburg.com**

WILLIAMSBURG, VA The Williamsburg Inn [P] 🍴 🏊 ♿ $$$$

136 East Francis St, 23187 ***Tel*** *757-229-1000* ***Fax*** *757-220-7096* ***Rooms*** *62*

This famed hotel offers all the luxuries of a modern hotel in a Regency-style setting inside the historic district. The formal Regency Room provides fine dining, while afternoon tea is served in the Terrace Room. Golf, croquet, and tennis courts are located on the premises. **www.colonialwilliamsburg.com**

RESTAURANTS, CAFES, AND BARS

Joseph Alsop, a renowned Washington host of the early 1960s, routinely gave lavish dinner parties in his Georgetown home. When asked why he gave so many parties, Alsop replied that it was because Washington had no good restaurants. Today the capital rivals New York, offering restaurants of every cuisine and price range. It is largely due to

Façade of Ben's Chili Bowl

Washington's cosmopolitan population that the city offers such a wide array of cuisines, from Ethiopian to Vietnamese, with many new styles of "fusion food" in between. The seafood is also superb, freshly caught from the nearby waters of Chesapeake Bay. Crab and shellfish feature regularly on menus, especially in coastal areas outside the city.

The elegant Matisse café restaurant

PLACES TO EAT

Washington's restaurants are a reflection of its neighborhoods. Adams-Morgan has a mix of ethnic establishments, especially Salvadoran and Ethiopian, and cutting-edge cuisine. Perry's, Cashion's Eat Place, and Felix Restaurant and Bar offer inventive fusion food with Asian and French influences, and the crowd is young and hip. An easy walk from the Mall, Washington's compact Chinatown has some of the best bargains for families. Meals are inexpensive and often served family style. Next to Chinatown is the Penn Quarter district on Seventh Street. Chic restaurants like Capital Grille, Elephant and Castle, and Old Ebbitt Grill are housed in restored early 19th-century buildings. Georgetown has a mix of expensive and inexpensive places. Good value can be found at its many Indian and Vietnamese restaurants. North of the White House and south of Dupont Circle, Penn Quarter restaurants cater to business travelers and high-powered lobbyists. More reasonable places, again mostly ethnic restaurants, are found closer to the Circle.

With very few exceptions, all restaurants in Washington are air conditioned. This has changed the city from one where most of the population used to escape in the summer to a lively, year-round capital.

RESERVATIONS

Reservations may be necessary for popular restaurants; the most fashionable can get booked up weeks in advance. Call ahead if there is somewhere you really want to go. However, walk-in diners are expected in most places. You may be placed on a waiting list and expected to return at the appointed time or wait in the adjacent bar, but you will usually be guaranteed a table within a fairly short time.

PRICES AND PAYING

Restaurant prices range from the very cheap to the very expensive in Washington. Prices vary according to location, cuisine, and décor. Most restaurants take major credit cards, although street vendors and fast food places may only accept cash. Waiters rely on earnings from tips and a 15–20 percent tip is expected for good service in restaurants. The tip is not automatically added to the bill except in the case of large parties, which may incur an automatic 15 percent gratuity.

Unlike many European cities, the fixed price meal is uncommon in Washington. Items are usually listed à la carte unless specified in the menu. Diners should expect to spend between $20 and $40 for dinner and a drink, including tip, at a moderate restaurant. However Indian, Ethiopian, Chinese, and Vietnamese restaurants are often considerably less expensive. It is also worth knowing that you will generally be charged about 25 percent less for the same meal if you eat at lunchtime rather than in the evening, so visitors on a budget may choose to eat their main meal at lunchtime. Breakfasts are usually under $10 for bacon and eggs with coffee and juice, but many hotels include a free continental breakfast (rolls, coffee, and juice) in the cost of the room.

B. Smith's grand Beaux Arts style dining room at historic Union Station

Mural on the side of Madam's Organ bar in Adams-Morgan

OPENING HOURS

It is unusual for a restaurant to be open 24 hours, except for those in very large hotels. Restaurants also rarely serve food continuously throughout the day; they usually have a break of several hours after lunch. Most restaurants are open all year (except Thanksgiving and Christmas Day) but a few may be closed on Sunday or Monday. It is best to call in advance. Restaurants often open for dinner between 5pm and 6pm, with the busiest period usually between 7pm and 8pm. The last seating is often at 9pm, and the last customers usually leave by 11pm. Bars are open until 2am. Remember that Metrorail trains stop running at 2am on Friday and Saturday, and at midnight the rest of the week.

ALCOHOL

Restaurants are required by law to have a liquor license in order to sell alcohol so you will notice that some do not offer it. Others may serve beer and wine only but not hard liquor or mixed drinks.

Bars rarely serve food other than perhaps some appetizers. Other restaurants may have a separate bar as well as a dining section. Patrons are not permitted to bring their own drinks to a restaurant.

The drinking age in DC, in Maryland, and in Virginia is 21. Restaurateurs can and will ask for proof of age in the form of a driver's license or passport since the penalty for serving alcohol to underage drinkers is severe.

SMOKING

In the District of Columbia smoking is not permitted in restaurants or any public buildings. The Smoke-free Workplace law came into effect in April 2006 and extended to restaurants in January 2007. If caught smoking, you could be fined several hundred dollars.

DRESS CODE

Dress varies from the very casual (shorts, t-shirt, and sneakers) to the very formal. In some restaurants men will not be admitted without a jacket and tie (the maître d' may have spares). But as a general guide, the more expensive the restaurant, the more formal the dress code will be. Some bars also have a very strict dress code, and customers may not be admitted in very casual dress. Respectable but casual attire is acceptable in the majority of establishments.

WHAT TO EAT

Washington offers a vast range of types of food to the visitor, but like most American cities it has a high concentration of fast-food establishments. Chains like McDonalds, Burger King, and Wendy's serve the same food worldwide and can be a reliable and popular source of sustenance for a family on the move. The hot dog vendors along the Mall offer an alternative. Other than fast food, Washington's cuisine is immensely multicultural, and you will find French, Chinese, Ethiopian, and Vietnamese restaurants, among others.

CHILDREN

The best indication as to whether children are welcome in a restaurant is the presence of a children's menu or the availability of high chairs. When dining in more formal places with children, it is best to reserve the earliest seating when the restaurant will not be too busy.

Tony and Joe's bar on the side of Washington harbor

WHEELCHAIR ACCESS

Restaurants are not required to be wheelchair accessible. In general, restaurants in older neighborhoods like Dupont Circle and Adams-Morgan are less likely to accommodate wheelchairs than modern establishments on K Street. The Smithsonian Museum restaurants are all accessible for the disabled.

Street vendor selling hot dogs, pretzels, ice cream, and drinks

What to Eat in Washington, DC

Washington is a place where everyone has an opinion, and culinary preferences are no exception. For some it's a power dining town, where châteaubriand is the dish of choice and "two-martini lunches" are common. Others would point to nearby Chesapeake Bay, and its delectable seafood dishes that appear on many menus. Still others would see the city's vibrant ethnic communities as the key to current food trends. There's no disagreement, however, that DC's dining scene reflects the diversity of the city. As well as drawing on the bountiful harvest of the Atlantic, the city's chefs also make good use of seasonal, local produce from the farms of Maryland and Virginia.

Chef at work in Kinkead's restaurant *(see p189)*

POWER DINING

True to its reputation, the city boasts an impressive collection of "power dining" restaurants, where lobbyists, pundits, and lawyers gather for steaks and cocktails. Slip into a cozy booth at one of these reputed steakhouses and you're likely to spot at least a few members of the United States Congress.

GLOBAL FLAVOURS

As the capital of the United States, Washington has long served as a gathering place for leaders and dignitaries from across the country and around the world, who have brought their own recipes and culinary traditions to the city. Refugees from places such as El Salvador, Ethiopia, and Cambodia have settled in Washington, introducing its well-traveled, globally-minded citizens to unusual flavors and dishes. In such ethnically diverse neighborhoods as Adams Morgan or Mount Pleasant, it's not unusual to find African, Asian, and South American restaurants standing side by side.

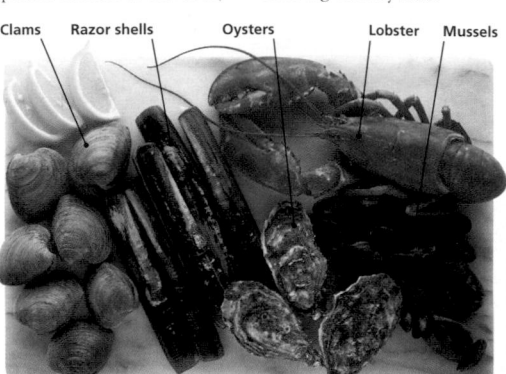

Clams   Razor shells   Oysters   Lobster   Mussels

Mouthwatering selection of Chesapeake Bay seafood

WASHINGTON'S SIGNATURE DISHES

The unique nature of the capital makes it difficult to pin down its specialty dishes. The *Washington Post* has made a case for the "half-smoke," a mildly spicy hybrid of hot dog and smoked sausage, smothered in chili and cheese and often sold in sidewalk kiosks. Ben's Chili Bowl *(see p192)*, is the best known purveyor, and a favorite of comedian Bill Cosby.

Maryland crab cakes

Maryland Blue Crabs are also popular, often appearing as succulent crab cakes or tangy She-Crab Soup. The federal side of the city could be summed up with Senate Navy Bean Soup which has been served every day in the Senate Dining Room for more than 100 years. It's a humble, unassuming dish, and yet it is eaten on a regular basis by the some of Washington's most influential residents.

Senate Navy Bean Soup *uses navy (haricot) beans and ham hock to make a delicious, simple yet hearty soup fit for Senators.*

Choosing a Restaurant

The restaurants have been selected across a range of price categories for their exceptional food, good value, and interesting location. Restaurants are listed by area, and within these by price, both for central Washington, DC and the surrounding areas. Map references refer to the Street Finder, pages 224–229.

PRICE CATEGORIES
For a three-course meal for one, with a glass of wine where available, including cover, service, and tax:

$ Under $20
$$ $20–$30
$$$ $30–$45
$$$$ $45–$60
$$$$$ over $60

CAPITOL HILL

Market Lunch $
Eastern Market, 225 7th St, SE (at C St), 20003 **Tel** *547-8444* — Map 4 F4

The menu features authentic regional food and extensive seafood delicacies, such as crab cakes, crab sandwiches, river fish, and flavorful salads. The cafeteria-style breakfast and lunch is as casual as it is delicious. Expect a long wait on Sunday mornings. Closed on Mondays.

Bullfeathers $$
410 1st St, SE, 20003 **Tel** *488-2701* — Map 4 E5

This Victorian-style pub and outdoor café, popular with Congressional staffers and neighborhood residents, is known for "the best burgers on the Hill." Those curious about the name are told that "Bullfeathers!" was flamboyant President Teddy Roosevelt's favorite exclamation.

Capitol City Brewing Company $$
2 Massachusetts Ave, NE (near 1st St), 20002 **Tel** *842-2337* — Map 4 E3

Situated above the National Postal Museum, this restaurant/bar offers good pub food and a large award-winning selection of beers. Free parking is available in the lot across the street in the evenings. Day parking can be in the Union Station lot or on the street.

Hawk and Dove $$
329 Pennsylvania Ave, SE, 20003 **Tel** *543-3300* — Map 4 F4

The oldest Irish bar in town offers a typically American menu including good burgers and pasta. You'll find an interesting mixture of locals and politicians, as well as 17 TVs with satellite programming. The Hawk and Dove also provides a good children's menu.

Tortilla Coast $$
400 1st St, SE, 20003 **Tel** *546-6768* — Map 4 F5

Great food and a friendly atmosphere are the main draws at Tortilla Coast. The menu is mostly Tex-Mex, but it includes some American dishes as well. Burritos are a big hit, as are the margaritas. Sample frozen Margaritas by the pitcher, a favorite of local politicians. Closed on Sundays.

Tunnicliff's $$
222 7th St, SE (opposite Eastern Market), 20003 **Tel** *544-5680* — Map 4 F4

The restaurant attracts a casual and diverse crowd. The popular Sunday brunch at Tunnicliff's features Eggs Chesapeake (a crab cake with two poached eggs), as well as peanut butter and jelly pizza. Sit outside on the patio and enjoy the sites of Eastern Market.

America $$$
Union Station, 50 Massachusetts Ave, NE, 20002 **Tel** *682-9555* — Map 4 E3

Located inside Union Station, with a great view of the Capitol, America features regional dishes. Death by Chocolate is a favorite dessert on the 200-item menu. An enormous restaurant with an enormous menu, the place is spread over two stories of Union Station.

B. Smith's $$$
Union Station, 50 Massachusetts Ave, NE, 20002 **Tel** *289-6188* — Map 4 E3

The ornate setting of the former Presidential Waiting Room of Union Station is now one of the best places for Southern cooking. The *swamp thang* (shrimp, crawfish and scallops in a cream sauce over a bed of collard greens) is a specialty of the house. A jazz trio plays on Friday and Saturday evening, and at Sunday brunch.

The Monocle $$$
107 D St, NE, 20002 **Tel** *546-4488* — Map 4 E3

A Capitol Hill institution popular with Senators and their staffers, the Monocle has a history of fostering alliances and deals. Steaks and crab cakes are their specialty. Closest restaurant to the Senate side of the Capitol, so call ahead for reservations when Congress is in session. Valet parking is available.

Key to Symbols *see back cover flap*

Sanoma 🚸 ☂ ☰ $$$

223 Pennsylvania Ave, SE, 20003 ***Tel*** *544-8088* **Map** *4 F3*

Sanoma brings together the best of American and Italian food and wine. The menu is built around local produce and is designed to encourage sharing; juicy platters of antipasti and charcuterie feature alongside pizzas and pasta. Choose to eat downstairs in the bistro-style restaurant, upstairs in the contemporary lounge, or outside on the patio.

Belga Café 🚸 ☂ ☰ $$$$

514 8th St, SE, 20003 ***Tel*** *544-0100* **Map** *4 F5*

There's more to this local favorite than the typical *moules-frites* usually associated with Belgian cuisine. House specialties include leg of rabbit cooked in beer and *Waterzooi* (stew) of fish. The open kitchen and exposed-brick wall make for a warm, inviting interior, or you can sit out on the patio. The drinks menu boasts over 130 types of beer.

Bistro Bis [P] 🚸 ♿ ☂ $$$$

15 E St, NW, 20001 ***Tel*** *661-2700* **Map** *4 E3*

French bistro fare with a modern American twist is served in a beautiful, cozy dining area. This chic modern restaurant located near the Senate attracts a fashionable clientele. The duck confit and salmon Provençal come highly recommended.

THE MALL

The Atrium Café 🚸 ♿ $

National Museum of Natural History, Constitution Ave &10th St, NW, 20560 ***Tel*** *633-1000* **Map** *3 C4*

The atrium of Washington's National Museum of Natural History is six stories high. This large food court on the ground level of the museum offers a wide selection of food including, pizza, sandwiches, soups, hot entrées, salads, and mouth-watering desserts. Lunch only.

Cascade Café 🚸 ♿ $

National Gallery of Art, Concourse level, Constitution Ave, NW, 20565 ***Tel*** *712-7458* **Map** *4 D4*

One of the better options for hungry museum-goers, this café offers fast and convenient buffet-style foods. The Cascade's "open-kitchens" allow you the added pleasure of watching food being freshly prepared. There is also a separate Espresso and Gelato Bar next to the café. Lunch only.

Mitsitam Café 🚸 ♿ $

National Museum of the American Indian, Independence Ave & 4th St, SW, 20560 ***Tel*** *633-7038* **Map** *4 D4*

Mitsitam means "let's eat" in the language of the Piscataway. It features an interesting menu inspired by Native Americans from the Northwest Coast, the Great Plains, Northern Woodlands, and Central and South America. The buffet-style café also has a range of prices. Lunch only.

Pavilion Café 🚸 ♿ ☂ $

Sculpture Garden, adjacent to the National Gallery West Building at 7th St, NW, 20565 ***Tel*** *289-3360* **Map** *4 D4*

This indoor/outdoor café offers a splendid view of the Sculpture Garden and of the ice-skating rink in winter. Choices include gourmet pizzas, wraps, and hot chocolate. There is a children's menu. Open Monday to Saturday 10am–4:30pm and Sunday 11am–5pm. Extended hours during the ice-skating season.

CityZen [P] ♿ $$$$$

Mandarin Oriental Hotel, 1330 Maryland Ave, SW, 20024 ***Tel*** *787-6006* **Map** *3 C5*

This 70-seat restaurant in the posh Mandarin Oriental Hotel offers an exquisite dining experience. Each dish is imaginatively prepared and beautifully presented. The talented chef, Eric Ziebold, spent eight years at the world-renowned French Laundry in Napa Valley. Dinner only Tuesday to Saturday.

PENN QUARTER

Courtyard Café 🚸 ♿ ☰ $

8th St and F St, NW ***Tel*** *633-8300* **Map** *3 C3*

Located inside the Smithsonian American Art Museum, this beautiful, light-filled space is designed to make you feel as if you are outside. The café offers a seasonal menu of American-inspired dishes, using local, organic ingredients whenever possible. Soups, salads, sandwiches, panini, and desserts. Open 11:30am–6:30pm.

Full Kee 🍴 🚸 $

509 H St, NW, 20001 ***Tel*** *371-2233* **Map** *4 D3*

The Cantonese noodles, dumplings, and soups are excellent at this rather sparsely decorated Chinatown restaurant. Full Kee is certainly a great place to grab a cheap, as well as quick, meal before a Verizon Center event.This restaurant is popular with locals and tourists.

Key to Price Guide *see p185* **Key to Symbols** *see back cover flap*

Nirvana
1810 K St, NW, 20006 **Tel** *223-5043*

Map 2 F3

The luncheon buffet at Nirvana changes daily to reflect and spotlight different regions of India. Crêpe-like *dosas* (thin, savory pancakes) are filled with vegetables and basmati rice, then flavored with tamarind, nuts, and raisins. Open daily for lunch and dinner.

Fadó Irish Pub
808 7th St, NW, 20001 **Tel** *789-0066*

Map 3 C3

Fadó has the look of an authentic Irish pub, with furnishings shipped over from Ireland. It serves typical Irish fare and fusion dishes. Contemporary Irish rock performances on Thursday nights. Live sporting events are shown regularly, including hurling and Gaelic football. Located near the Verizon Center.

Hard Rock Café
999 E St, NW (at 10th St), 20004 **Tel** *737-7625*

Map 3 C3

All the American classics are available, including burgers, sandwiches and salads. Videos, music, and memorabilia make the two floors of this restaurant an exciting tourist experience, though it can get a little hectic. Stained-glass windows honor rock-and-roll greats in this worldwide chain.

Jaleo
487 7th St, NW, 20004 **Tel** *628-7949*

Map 3 C3

Not far from the monuments, and a stone's throw from the Verizon Center, this Spanish tapas restaurant is a refreshing alternative with its colorful menu and decor. Chef José Andrés has his own TV show and was voted GQ Magazine's Chef of the Year in 2009.

Austin Grill
750 E St, NW, 20004 **Tel** *393-3776*

Map 3 C3

There's a fun atmosphere at Austin Grill, where the music is loud and the walls sport coyotes and cowboys. Considered Washington's most authentic Tex-Mex restaurant – the managers here visit Austin, Texas, several times a year for research purposes. Enjoy $5.50 Margaritas and $4 draft beers during happy hour, 2–7pm Mon–Fri.

District Chophouse and Brewery
509 7th St, NW, 20004 **Tel** *347-3434*

Map 3 C3

This upscale hangout echoes the style and ambience of the 1940s with a cigar bar, pool tables, and swing music. Huge portions of steak, burgers and pizza can be washed down by the beers, which are brewed on the premises. It caters to sports fans from the Verizon Center.

Elephant and Castle
1201 Pennsylvania Ave, NW, 20004 **Tel** *347-7707*

Map 3 C3

Try UK beverages such as Fuller's Porter Draught, Boddington's Cream Ale, and Strongbow cider to accompany traditional British comfort food: roast beef-filled Yorkshire pudding, shepherd's pie, and sausage and mash. Enjoy the typical atmosphere of a British pub lounge with dark-wood booths. The bar area is also very welcoming.

Old Ebbitt Grill
675 15th St, NW, 20005 **Tel** *347-4801*

Map 3 B3

Expect this upbeat American grill to be packed with both locals and tourists. It's a chance to sample the DC scene as well as savor quality seafood, pasta, steaks, an excellent raw bar and wine list. The crab cakes and trout parmesan are house favorites.

Zaytinya's
701 9th St, NW (at G St), 20001 **Tel** *638-0800*

Map 3 C3

This romantic restaurant with a striking modern decor offers a superb variety of authentic Greek, Turkish, and Lebanese mezze with excellent vegetarian selections. The ambience is sophisticated, warm and inviting, making this a favorite choice for Washingtonians.

Ceiba
701 14th St, NW, 20005 **Tel** *393-3983*

Map 3 B3

This Latino-themed eatery is decorated in hacienda chic and has a pan-Latin menu to match. Offerings include traditional black bean soup, skewered shrimp with pineapple salsa, and red snapper Vera Cruz (in a herby tomato sauce). Desserts include fabulous *churros* (sweet dough strips). Closed Sundays.

Proof
775 G St, NW, 20001 **Tel** *737-7663*

Map 3 C3

Graze on a huge choice of cheese and charcuterie as you watch the world go by from this restaurant's pavement patio, opposite the National Portrait Gallery. The "small plates" are great for sharing, or try the four-course tasting menu (with wine pairings). Wine lovers will be spoilt for choice with a 1,400-strong list.

Rasika
633 D Street, NW, 20004 **Tel** *637-1222*

Map 4 D3

One of the top Indian restaurants in Washington, DC. For a selection of dishes that will have your mouth watering, order the chef's four- or six-course fixed-price menu ($52 and $68) or, for a lighter meal, try something from the tandoor oven. The decor oozes understated glamour. No lunch at weekends.

Tenpenh
P 🚶 ♿ $$$$
1001 Pennsylvania Ave, NW (at 10th St), 20004 **Tel** *393-4500*
   Map *3 C3*

Tenpenh has an eclectic fusion-menu featuring Southeast Asian cuisine with American nuances, and sophisticated modern decor. Furnishings come from Vietnam and other Southeast Asian countries. Open for lunch and dinner from Monday to Friday. Dinner only on Saturdays. Closed on Sundays.

Zola
P 🚶 ♿ $$$$
800 F St, NW, 20004 **Tel** *654-0999*
   Map *3 C2*

Upscale American cuisine in a stylish atmosphere, with booths, befitting the Spy Museum to which it is connected. A varied menu includes dishes such as citrus-cured pork belly, smoked ruby trout and local Virginian veal. It boasts a good wine list as well.

Capital Grille
P 🚶 ♿ 📋 $$$$$
601 Pennsylvania Avenue, NW, 20004 **Tel** *737-6200*
   Map *4 D3*

With a menu this fantastic, it's no surprise that the great and the good are lining up to dine here. The lobster and oysters are tempting, but it's the dry-aged steaks that really hit the spot. Rich mahogany paneling and Art Deco chandeliers create a warm ambience. The wine list is outstanding. No lunch on Sundays. Valet parking evenings only.

Fogo de Chao
P 🚶 ♿ 📋 $$$$$
1101 Pennsylvania Avenue, NW, 20004 **Tel** *347-4668*
   Map *3 C3*

Dark wood, natural stone, and murals depicting ranch life in Brazil are offset by dramatic lighting at Fogo de Chao. Dine on sizzling fire-roasted morsels accompanied by unlimited warm cheese bread, fried bananas, crispy hot polenta, and seasoned mashed potatoes. No lunch at weekends. Valet parking evenings only.

Oceanaire
P ♿ 📋 $$$$$
1201 F Street, NW, 20004 **Tel** *347-2277*
   Map *3 C3*

It may seem a little twee to model oneself on a 1930s ocean liner, but Oceanaire is an enduringly popular restaurant, thanks in large part to its comprehensive seafood menu. Oysters are flown in from as far afield as New Zealand, with Australian lobsters to boot. No lunch at weekends. Valet parking available.

Poste Brasserie
P 🚶 ♿ 📻 $$$$$
Hotel Monaco, 555 8th St, NW, 20004 **Tel** *783-6060*
   Map *3 C3*

The Poste Brasserie was once part of the Old General Post Office, the first all-marble building in Washington. The menu has a slight French influence (venison, rabbit, snails), but limited vegetarian choices. There's a friendly bar area, a quiet room in the back, and a patio open in good weather.

The Source
🚶 ♿ 📻 📋 $$$$$
575 Pennsylvania Ave, NW, 20001 **Tel** *637-6100.*
   Map *4 D4*

Wolfgang Puck's restaurant offers an Asian-influenced menu, including crispy suckling pig and tempura soft-shell crab. The seven-course tasting menu is $125–200; the three-course fixed-price lunch a more affordable $28. The casual Izakaya lounge below serves smaller plates, including a range of sushi. Closed Sunday.

THE WHITE HOUSE AND FOGGY BOTTOM

Corcoran Café
🚶 ♿ $
Corcoran Gallery of Art, 500 17th St, NW, 20006 **Tel** *639-1786*
   Map *3 A3*

A pleasant café on the ground floor of the Corcoran Gallery of Art, which serves breakfast, lunch, and snacks through the day (and dinner on Thursdays). The Sunday brunch is served 11am–2pm ($35, including admission to the gallery). Closed on Mondays and Tuesdays.

Teaism
🚶 ♿ 📻 $
800 Connecticut Ave, NW (at H St), 20006 **Tel** *835-2233*
   Map *3 B2*

One can enjoy an exquisite selection of teas, as well as a good choice of Asian-inspired dishes in the restaurant's cozy surroundings. The menu features curries, bento boxes, and salads. Go for a meal or just for tea. Open Monday to Friday 7:30am–5:30pm. Afternoon tea served 2:30–5:30pm.

Aroma
🚶 ♿ $$
1919 I St, NW, 20006 **Tel** *833-4700*
   Map *2 E3*

This North Indian restaurant is one of the best-kept secrets in Washington. It is casual yet elegant, and the food is excellent. Aroma offers an all-you-can-eat lunchtime buffet for a very reasonable price on Saturdays. The restaurant is closed for lunch on Sundays.

Luigi's
🚶 📻 $$
1132 19th St, NW, 20036 **Tel** *331-7574*
   Map *2 E2*

This attractive trattoria with its red and white checkered tablecloths is one of the oldest Italian restaurants in the city. Its extensive menu includes a wide range of pizzas with 40 different kinds of toppings, delicious pasta dishes, and a very good tiramisu.

600 Restaurant at the Watergate

📊♿🏠📋 $$$

600 New Hampshire Ave, NW, 20037 **Tel** *337-5890*

Map 2 D4

The luscious menu here includes succulent steaks and Australian rack of lamb. A three-course fixed-price menu starts at $30 and includes non-alcoholic drinks. The summer garden terrace overlooks the Potomac River. A good choice for pre-concert dinner, being situated close to the Kennedy Center. Closed for lunch on Saturdays and Sundays.

Circle Bistro

📊♿🏠📋 $$$

1 Washington Circle, 20037 **Tel** *872-1680*

Map 2 E3

A great spot for pre-theater drinks and dinner: there's a daily happy hour and a good value three-course fixed-price menu. The cuisine is styled as French-American, so expect dishes such as grilled trout with artichoke hearts, pine nuts, and capers. The menu puts an emphasis on seasonal, local produce. Reservations recommended.

Dish and Drinks

📊♿📋 $$$

924 25th St, NW 20037 **Tel** *1-888-874-0100*

Map 2 D3

Within walking distance of the Kennedy Center, this friendly and intimate neighborhood restaurant serves American classics with a contemporary twist. Typical dishes include crab cakes and oyster po'boys. The fixed-price pre-theatre menu is particularly good value. Reservations recommended.

Firefly

📦📊♿🏠 $$$

1310 New Hampshire Ave (Dupont Circle), NW, 20036 **Tel** *861-1310*

Map 3 A1

Comfort food is served at this cozy restaurant located in a small, golden-lit room with birch branches lining the walls. On the menu diners will find options such as chicken soup with buckwheat noodles; roast chicken with a casserole of tortillas, salsa, and cheese; and home-made pasta dishes. Open daily.

Georgia Brown's

📦📊♿🎵 $$$

950 15th St, NW 20005 **Tel** *393-4499*

Map 3 B3

Anyone who craves Carolina shrimp, grits (fried, coarse grain), gumbo, or fried green tomatoes should come here. Low-country Southern cooking with style is served in an inviting, but hectic atmosphere. A jazz trio performs during the Sunday brunch.

Primi Piatti

♿🏠 $$$

2013 I St, NW, 20006 **Tel** *223-3600*

Map 2 E3

This lively Northern Italian restaurant offers a variety of both pasta and meat dishes. The staff is friendly, the food and wine list are reliably good, and the atmosphere is both fun and sophisticated. Closed for lunch on Saturday and all day Sunday.

Trattoria Nicola's

📦📊♿🏠📋 $$$

1250 22nd St, NW, 20037 **Tel** *449-4011*

Map 2 E2

Try the veal escalopes sautéed with white wine, lemon, and garlic, or choose from a selection of pasta dishes and pizzas. Martini specials are available at the bar. The decor is inviting, with care taken to make each dish a work of art. Romantic high-backed booths give a cozy atmosphere. The weekday lunch buffet offers good value for money.

Bombay Club

📦📊♿🎵🏠 $$$$

815 Connecticut Ave, NW, 20006 **Tel** *659-3727*

Map 2 F3

The attentive service and formal atmosphere provide a glimpse of upper-crust Washington. Specialties include Ajwaini trout and green chili chicken. A classical pianist performs nightly. Open for lunch from Monday to Friday, brunch on Sunday, and for dinner every night.

Kinkead's

📦♿🎵🏠 $$$$

Red Lion Row, 2000 Pennsylvania Ave, NW, 20006 **Tel** *296-7700*

Map 2 E3

You won't be disappointed at this American brasserie with an excellent seafood menu, one of the finest in town. Bob Kinkead's creations, such as the pepita-crusted salmon with cilantro, are wonderfully complemented by the extensive wine list. Live piano is performed on Friday and Saturday nights.

Occidental

📦📊♿🏠 $$$$

1475 Pennsylvania Ave, NW (at 14th St), 20004 **Tel** *783-1475*

Map 3 B3

An elegant setting and a varied menu including an excellent selection of seafood. Only a few blocks from the White House, it's a place to see and be seen. Pictures of the power elite, past and present, line the walls. Closed Sundays.

Renaissance Mayflower, Café Promenade

📦📊♿🎵 $$$$

1127 Connecticut Ave, NW (at DeSales St), 20036 **Tel** *347-2233*

Map 3 A2

The Mediterranean-influenced Café Promenade offers a menu featuring a variety of dishes from Spain, Greece, France, and Italy. Specialties include crab cakes and red snapper. Afternoon tea is served 3–5pm daily. Reservations recommended.

Roof Terrace Restaurant and Bar

📦📊♿🎵 $$$$

Kennedy Center, New Hampshire Ave & Rock Creek Pkwy, 20037 **Tel** *416-8555*

Map 2 D4

Theater-goers can enjoy a contemporary American meal here, coupled with a fabulous view of the Virginia skyline. Dishes include smoked salmon carpaccio, crab cakes, lamb *ossu buco*, and home-made ice creams and sorbets. The Sunday brunch buffet is superb.

Vidalia [P] ♿ [$][$][$][$][$]

1990 M St, NW 20036 ***Tel*** *659-1990* ***Map*** *3 A2*

There's a distinctive cosmopolitan atmosphere to Vidalia's – call it swanky. This four-star restaurant in the Hotel George offers superb American cuisine with a Southern accent. Lunch is served from Monday to Friday, and dinner nightly. Valet parking is available in the evenings.

GEORGETOWN

Patisserie Poupon 👪 ☂ [$]

1645 Wisconsin Ave, NW, 20007 ***Tel*** *342-3248* ***Map*** *1 C2*

A bright and charming café that offers some of the best pastries in town. The soups, quiches, and salads are popular with a neighborhood crowd. There is also a coffee bar in the back. Lunchtimes tend to be very busy. Closed on Mondays.

Bangkok Bistro 👪 ♿ ☂ 📋 [$][$]

3251 Prospect St, NW, 20007 ***Tel*** *337-2424* ***Map*** *1 C2*

This is a contemporary Thai restaurant, with a great cocktail and sushi bar. There are various fixed-price options (the lunchtime sampler platter is particularly good value) and an extensive à la carte menu of Thai and sushi dishes. The Martini menu is also pleasingly wide-ranging. Outdoor seating when the weather permits.

Café Bonaparte 👪 ♿ ☂ [$][$]

1522 Wisconsin Ave, NW, 20007 ***Tel*** *333-8830* ***Map*** *1 C2*

Warm and cozy, with bright yellow walls and black-and-white photographs of Europe, Café Bonaparte looks out on Wisconsin Avenue. Students and locals flock here to enjoy a French meal comprising crêpes, soup, and salad, or to just while away the afternoon with a cappuccino at a table by the window.

Café Divan 👪 ♿ [$][$]

1834 Wisconsin Ave, NW (north of S St), 20007 ***Tel*** *338-1747* ***Map*** *1 C1*

The mezze platter makes a reasonable lunch. Café Divan has a small take-out area as well as a dining room with bay windows for a leisurely meal. Specialties include lamb, chicken, seafood, and *pides* (Turkish pizza with a thin crust and a choice of eight toppings).

Café la Ruche 👪 ♫ ☂ [$][$]

1039 31st St, NW, 20007 ***Tel*** *965-2684* ***Map*** *2 D3*

A typical Parisian bistro with a comfortable atmosphere that is great for chatting with friends. A wide range of dishes includes rainbow trout, mussels Niçoise, pastries, and an excellent brunch. A guitarist performs on Tuesday and Thursday evenings.

Pizzeria Paradiso 👪 ♿ [$][$]

3282 M St, NW (near 33rd St), 20007 ***Tel*** *337-1245* ***Map*** *1 C2*

The lively, friendly atmosphere makes this an excellent choice for a casual meal. Some consider their pizza to be the best in DC – thin crust Neapolitan style, baked in a wood-burning stove. There is a downstairs dining room for private parties. Accepts all major credit cards except American Express. Large selection of draft and bottled beers.

Zed's Ethiopian Cuisine 👪 ☂ [$][$]

1201 28th St, NW, 20007 ***Tel*** *333-4710* ***Map*** *1 C2*

An Ethiopian restaurant, popular with vegetarians, Zed's offers traditional *wats* (red pepper sauces), *alechas* (stews), and *injera* (bread). The atmosphere is quiet and romantic and the decor features Ethiopian textiles, paintings, and woodcarvings.

Bistro Français 👪 ♿ [$][$][$]

3128 M St, NW, 20007 ***Tel*** *338-3830* ***Map*** *1 C2*

This attractive French bistro in the heart of Georgetown, serves traditional-style dishes. The menu includes Coquilles St-Jacques, veal chops, and steak tartare. The *prix fixe* menu ($24.95), served 5–7pm and 10:30pm–1am, includes a glass of house wine.

Café Milano 👪 ♿ ☂ [$][$][$]

3251 Prospect St, NW (off Wisconsin Ave), 20007 ***Tel*** *333-6183* ***Map*** *1 C2*

Café Milano is known for its romantic atmosphere, excellent wine list, great food, and celebrity sightings. The menu includes traditional home-made pasta. There is a main dining room as well as smaller rooms and a wine cellar which can be used for private parties, plus two patios for dining outdoors.

Clyde's of Georgetown [P] 👪 ♿ [$][$][$]

3236 M St, NW, 20007 ***Tel*** *333-9180* ***Map*** *1 C2*

A Washington institution, Clyde's of Georgetown has been highly popular since it first opened 40 years ago. It serves deliciously tasty hamburgers and fresh seafood, and it could also claim to have invented Sunday brunch. The place gets loud and crowded, but the food is always very good.

Key to Price Guide *see p185* **Key to Symbols** *see back cover flap*

Mendocino Grill and Wine Bar

2917 M St, NW, 20007 **Tel** *333-2912*

Map 2 D2

Chef Koslow's background is classical French and here in Mendocino Grill he serves up superb, understated cuisine. Among the choices are black sea bass in mussel broth with saffron and fennel, prosciutto-wrapped trout and grilled local stars. Excellent wine list.

Paolo's

1303 Wisconsin Ave, NW (at N St), 20007 **Tel** *333-7353*

Map 1 C2

This Italian- and Californian-style restaurant is as trendy and international as its Georgetown surroundings. A place to peoplewatch while enjoying a light salad, pasta dish, or a pizza. A Sunday brunch buffet is available 10:30am–3pm. Happy-hour appetizer specials 4–7pm on weekdays.

1789

1226 36th St, NW (at Prospect St), 20007 **Tel** *965-1789*

Map 1 B2

Chef Dan Giusti, one of Washington's premier chefs, makes a creative use of seasonal ingredients. Superb, modern American food is served in four separate dining areas of a Federal town house. The setting is intimate and comfortable, with a cozy country-inn feel. Open for dinner every night. Jacket required for men.

Bistrot Lepic and Wine Bar

1736 Wisconsin Ave, NW, 20007 **Tel** *333-0111*

Map 1 C1

This bistro, two floors of a bright yellow brick townhouse, serves some of the town's best French food. The romantic, intimate setting is quite popular. A wine bar, rated among the top 10 in the US, offers smaller dishes at more reasonable prices. The service is friendly.

Blue Duck Tavern

24 and M Streets, NW, 20037 **Tel** *419-6755*

Map 2 E2

Located in the Park Hyatt hotel, the simple, dark-wood interior creates a warm, inviting ambience. Handcrafted wood furnishings include a 29-ft (8.8-m) long Windsor bench. On the menu is wholesome American fare, featuring traditional roasted, braised, and smoked dishes prepared with local and seasonal ingredients.

Hook

3241 M Street, NW, 20037 **Tel** *625-4488*

Map 2 E2

Hook offers a daily changing fish menu served with vegetable and bean purées, herb-infused oils, and vinaigrettes. There is also one meat dish per day for those who don't like surf offerings. An esoteric wine list and excellent desserts complete the experience. Closed for lunch on Monday. Brunch available on Saturday and Sunday.

Leopold's Kafe

3315 M St, NW, 20007 **Tel** *965-6005*

Map 1 C3

Tucked cozily down Cady's Alley, this wonderful café is renowned for its European-inspired pastries – although it serves a simple breakfast, lunch, and dinner menu too. The Austrian veal schnitzel with potato salad is an excellent choice. Alternatively, just keep ordering from the endless array of meringues and pastries – each is a work of art

Sequoia

Washington Harbor, 3000 K St, NW (at 30th St), 20007 **Tel** *944 4200*

Map 2 D3

A trendy restaurant combining American cuisine with fabulous views of the Potomac and Virginia skyline. The casual, large seating area outside is especially delightful. The menu features lots of seafood, salads, interesting pizzas, pastas, and – of course – steaks. The brunch is excellent. Parking is in the building on the K St side.

Tony & Joe's Seafood Place

Washington Harbor, 3000 K St, NW (at 30th St), 20007 **Tel** *944-4545*

Map 2 D3

The outdoor setting overlooking the Potomac is a wonderful place to spend an afternoon or evening. The seafood is simply prepared, fresh, and delicious. A live jazz combo plays on summer evenings from Wednesday to Sunday, and during Sunday brunch all year round.

Citronelle

Latham Hotel, 3000 M St, NW (at 30th St), 20007 **Tel** *625-2150*

Map 2 D2

This award-winning restaurant serves sophisticated French dishes, such as chateaubriand with pearl vegetables and a Syrah sauce, or Monterey Bay abalone with cream of caviar. Fixed-price for a three-course starts at $105. You can also splurge on a nine-course tasting menu for $190.

FARTHER AFIELD

ADAMS MORGAN Madam's Organ

2461 18th St, NW (near Columbia Rd), 20009 **Tel** *667-5370*

This popular, boisterous nightspot offers a combination of soul food and a blues bar. The venue serves salads, burgers, fried chicken, pulled pork, and chili, as well as dishes such as black-eyed peas and candied yams. Bluegrass, R&B, and blues bands perform nightly. There is a roof deck open in summer.

ADAMS MORGAN Bistro Napoleon   P 🉐 ⚐ 🎵 🖼 ▤ $$$
*1847 Columbia Rd, NW, 20009 **Tel** 299-9630*

Exquisite French fare served in an elegant leather and dark-wood dining room. The red walls and chandeliers create a romantic ambience. Enjoy the varied entrées, sinful array of desserts, and fabulous champagne cocktails. Live music/DJ after 10pm on Thursdays, Fridays, and Saturdays.

ADAMS MORGAN Cashion's Eat Place   P 🉐 ⚐ 🎵 🖼 $$$
*1819 Columbia Rd, NW, 20009 **Tel** 797-1819*

New American cuisine, with European influences, and an award-winning wine list are the main draws of Cashion's Eating Place. The atmosphere is romantic with dim lighting and the staff is friendly. Open for dinner and Sunday brunch. The restaurant is closed on Mondays.

DUPONT CIRCLE Bread and Chocolate   🉐 ⚐ 🖼 $
*2301 M Street, NW, 20037 **Tel** 833-8360*   **Map** 2 E2

This large and spacious neighborhood restaurant offers good French fare, including French onion soup. There's also a selection of quiches and a wide variety of delicious pastries, and freshly baked cakes and breads. A special Sunday brunch is also served. The service is friendly.

DUPONT CIRCLE Iron Gate Inn   🉐 ⚐ 🖼 $$
*1734 N St, NW, 20036 **Tel** 737-1371*   **Map** 3 A2

It's hard to find a more romantic spot with such reasonable prices. The interior is warm and cozy with working fireplaces, and the garden is lovely. Food is imaginatively prepared and nicely presented. Lunch from Monday to Friday and dinner from Monday to Saturday.

DUPONT CIRCLE Hank's Oyster Bar   ⚐ 🖼 $$$
*1624 Q St, NW, 20009 **Tel** 462-4265*   **Map** 3 B1

Serving five oyster varieties nightly as well as comfort food such as molasses-braised short ribs and deep fried Ipswich clams and popcorn shrimp. Other offerings at this intimate restaurant include seared sea scallops and marinated sable fish with soy balsamic glaze, but the main draw is the Hog Island-style barbecue oyster.

DUPONT CIRCLE Pesce   🉐 ⚐ $$$
*2002 P St, NW, 20036 **Tel** 466-3474*   **Map** 2 E2

The Mediterranean menu changes daily, but always includes delicious seafood and a fabulous wine list. The exposed brick walls, fish art, and cozy bar add to Pesce's appeal. Open for lunch from Monday to Friday, and for dinner from Monday to Saturday.

DUPONT CIRCLE Tabard Inn   P 🉐 🎵 🖼 $$$
*1739 N St, NW, 20036 **Tel** 785-1277*

The menu of this historic inn always offers a delicious surprise. The garden is lovely and the funky interior has several inviting nooks and crannies. Valet parking on Friday, Saturday evenings, and Sunday brunch. A jazz duo performs on Sundays 7:30–10pm.

DUPONT CIRCLE Nora's   P 🉐 ⚐ $$$$$
*2132 Florida Ave, NW (corner of R St), 20008 **Tel** 462-5143*   **Map** 2 E1

One of the stalwarts of Washington dining, featuring organic seasonal ingredients and a varied menu of contemporary American cuisine. The decor is warm and cozy with Amish and Mennonite quilts adorning the walls. Open for dinner only and closed on Sundays.

DUPONT CIRCLE Obelisk $$$$$
*2029 P St, NW, 20036 **Tel** 872-1180*   **Map** 2 E2

A five-course fixed-price menu is offered at $75, featuring classic Italian cuisine, but with a contemporary twist. This top-notch, 11-table restaurant has an intimate feel and a menu that changes daily. Reservations are recommended. Dinner only from Tuesday to Saturday. Closed on Sunday and Monday. American Express not accepted.

PALISADES Blacksalt Fishmarket and Restaurant   🉐 ⚐ ▤ $$$$$
*4883 MacArthur Blvd, NW, 20007 **Tel** 342-9101*

Stylish yet cozy, this is a premier spot for seafood. The array of dishes is impressive: from wood-grilled baby octopus and seared scallops to wood-grilled sardines and lip-smackingly good fish stews. The chef's tasting menu is $85. Also a good choice for Sunday brunch. There is a retail fish counter if you fancy re-creating any of the dishes at home.

U STREET/SHAW Ben's Chili Bowl   ▤ 🉐 ⚐ $
*1213 U St, NW, 20009 **Tel** 667-0909*

A Washington institution, Ben's Chili Bowl is popular with anyone who loves a good, high-calorie meal. Bill Cosby is a devoted fan and President Obama has visited. The chili dogs are known nationally and the milk shakes hit the spot. Best loved are its salmon cakes, grits, scrapple, and blueberry pancakes, offered during breakfast hours (6–11am).

U STREET/SHAW Coppi's Organic   ⚐ $$$
*1414 U St, NW, 20009 **Tel** 319-7773*

A small, intimate restaurant, Coppi's Organic serves pizza and pasta made from organic ingredients. Its daily-changing menu also features a selection of antipasti, meat and fish dishes, and desserts. Pictures of bicyclists, the owner's passion, line the walls. Open for dinner only.

Key to Price Guide *see p185* **Key to Symbols** *see back cover flap*

WISCONSIN AVENUE 2 Amy's 👶 ♿ ☂ $

3715 Macomb St, NW (just off Wisconsin Ave), 20016 ***Tel*** *885-5700*

The pizza here has DOC status – it is recognized by the Italian government as authentic Neapolitan pizza. There's an extensive choice of toppings and a good wine selection. Though crowded on weekends, it's worth the wait. Only MasterCard, and Visa accepted.

WISCONSIN AVENUE Cactus Cantina 👶 ♿ ☂ $$

3300 Wisconsin Ave, NW (at Macomb St), 20016 ***Tel*** *686-7222*

Fun, but often crowded, Cacus Cantina is a Mexican restaurant serving great food at reasonable prices. It is popular with families, and the atmosphere is always noisy and festive. Known to use fresh ingredients, its menu also features entrées, such as mesquite chicken, broiled shrimp, succulent pork ribs, and combination platters.

WISCONSIN AVENUE Café Deluxe 👶 ♿ ☂ $$

3228 Wisconsin Ave (near Macomb St), 20016 ***Tel*** *686-2233*

Count on Café Deluxe for a good meal, but you may have to wait. Large windows, wooden booths, and an attractive bar make it one of the more appealing restaurants in the neighborhood. Offers a Sunday brunch. American Express, MasterCard, and Visa accepted.

WISCONSIN AVENUE Krupin's [P] 👶 ♿ $$

4620 Wisconsin Ave, 20016 ***Tel*** *686-1989*

New York deli food served at tables in the bright, well-lit Krupin's just north of the Tenleytown metro. The Reuben sandwich, matzo ball soup, and blintzes are only some of its specialties. The restaurant accepts American Express, MasterCard, and Visa.

WISCONSIN AVENUE Heritage India [P] 👶 $$$

2400 Wisconsin Ave, NW, 20007 ***Tel*** *333-3120*

This elegant Indian restaurant serves special platters with small samplings of a large variety of dishes. Their vegetarian offerings come particularly recommended, but the meat and seafood options are also excellent. Try the *Baigan Mirch Ka Salan*, a dish of eggplants and hot peppers in a sesame-flavoured sauce. Fiery lamb vindaloo is the critics' favorite.

WISCONSIN AVENUE Tabaq Bistro [P] 👶 ☂ ☰ $$$

1336 U St, NW, 20009 ***Tel*** *265-0965*

Enjoy a bird's-eye view of DC from the rooftop dining space of Tabaq Bistro. The retractable glass roof creates an outside dining space in warm weather. Trendsetters come for cocktails and tasty Mediterranean fare: lamb shanks and beef medallions are the highlights. Weekend brunch: 10am–4pm.

WISCONSIN AVENUE Matisse Café Restaurant [P] 👶 ♿ $$$$

4934 Wisconsin Ave, NW (at Fessenden St), 20016 ***Tel*** *244-5222*

Located north of Washington National Cathedral on Wisconsin Avenue, this lovely restaurant is a great place for Sunday brunch. The restaurant's arresting decor was inspired by Matisse and the menu focuses on innovative French dishes. Open for lunch from Tuesday to Friday, dinner nightly.

WOODLEY PARK/CLEVELAND PARK Alero Restaurant 👶 ☂ $$

3500 Connecticut Ave, NW (at Ordway St), 20008 ***Tel*** *966-2530*

You'll find an appealing mix of tasty food, reasonable prices, and friendly staff at this neighborhood Mexican restaurant. The outdoor tables at Alero are pleasant and the interior has charm. All major credit cards, except Discover and Diners Club, are accepted.

WOODLEY PARK/CLEVELAND PARK Lebanese Taverna [P] 👶 ♿ ☂ $$

2641 Connecticut Ave, NW, 20008 ***Tel*** *265-8681*

This lively, often crowded, restaurant has an attractive Middle-Eastern decor and offers an extensive menu. One of the most popular family-dining venues, Lebanese Taverna serves sumptuous platters, both vegetarian and non-vegetarian. It also has an interesting wine list.

WOODLEY PARK/CLEVELAND PARK Nam-Viet 👶 ♿ $$

3419 Connecticut Ave, NW, 20008 ***Tel*** *237-1015*

Nam-Viet is considered one of the best Vietnamese restaurants in the area, offering an overwhelming number of choices including vegetarian dishes. Signature dishes include the specialty, Nam-Viet special seasoned shrimp, and the entrée, Nam-Viet grilled combo.

WOODLEY PARK/CLEVELAND PARK Spice's 👶 ♿ $$

3333a Connecticut Ave, NW, 20008 ***Tel*** *686-3833*

Spice's offers a great selection of Asian dishes from several countries. The sushi bar is very popular, with almost half the menu devoted to sushi dishes. The restaurant attracts a young crowd who are looking for great food at reasonable prices. Spicy ginger chicken and the honey-roasted sea bass are real treats.

WOODLEY PARK/CLEVELAND PARK Indique [P] 👶 ♿ ☂ $$$

3512 Connecticut Ave, NW, 20008 ***Tel*** *244-6600*

Visit Indique to sample a unique selection of excellent southern Indian dishes. This two-story restaurant, has stunning modern decor and a most welcoming atmosphere. The bar area is lively as well as attractive. Valet parking is available from Thursday to Sunday.

WOODLEY PARK/CLEVELAND PARK Lavandou 🚹🔩 $$$

3321 Connecticut Ave, NW, 20008 Tel 966-3003

Walk into this small and charming restaurant and you'll feel transported to southern France. The menu features dishes from Provence, with over 90 wines to complement the fresh grilled seafood and soups. Open for lunch from Monday to Friday, and every night for dinner.

WOODLEY PARK/CLEVELAND PARK Petits Plats 🅿🚹🔩 $$$

2653 Connecticut Ave, NW, 20008 Tel 518-0018

This charming restaurant, located in a Woodley Park townhouse, has several small dining rooms with five working fireplaces. It makes for a comfortable casual lunch or a candlelit dinner. The reasonably priced bistro fare includes shrimp and mussel dishes, prepared in the Provençal style, and delicious crêpes.

WOODLEY PARK/CLEVELAND PARK Ardeo 🅿🚹🔩 $$$$

3311 Connecticut Ave, NW, 20008 Tel 244-6750

This trendy and busy, modern American restaurant features an interesting and innovative menu. Specialties include Black Angus sirloin burger with farm cheddar cheese and French fries. Bardeo, next door, is a wine bar offering small plates with tapas and panini, as well as wine tastings.

BEYOND WASHINGTON, DC

ALEXANDRIA, VA Gadsby's Tavern 🚹🔩🎵🔲 $$

138 N. Royal St, 22314 Tel 703-548-1288

Established in 1792, this historic tavern was frequented by Washington and Jefferson. The waiters are in Colonial costume, and the decor is in the style of the 1700s. The menu includes traditional Virginia fare, such as duck, prime rib, seafood, and meat pies. Live music on Friday and Saturday evenings.

ALEXANDRIA, VA Le Refuge 🚹 $$$$

127 N. Washington St, 22314 Tel 703-548-4661

Across the street from historic Christ Church, this small family-run French restaurant has great charm and wonderful French country food. *Bouillabaisse* and soft shelled crabs (in season) are specialties of the house. Closed on Sundays. All major credit cards, except Discover, are accepted.

ANNAPOLIS, MD Middleton Tavern Oyster Bar & Restaurant 🚹🎵🔲 $$$

2 Market Space, 21401 Tel 410-263-3323

Established in 1750, the historic Middleton Tavern Oyster Bar & Restaurant is located across the street from the harbor. This is an indoor/outdoor spot, perfect to soak up the view. The oyster shooters come with beer. Also on the menu are crab cakes, seafood, and pasta dishes. Live music Friday to Sunday.

ARLINGTON, VA Grand Cru 🚹🔩🔲📋 $$$

4401 Wilson Blvd, 22203 Tel 703-243-7900

This tiny café is attached to a fantastic wine shop. Eat in the pretty courtyard overlooking trees and a fountain or snuggle inside. The menu is small but wonderful; the duck breast and filet mignon are particularly good. Desserts include chocolate fondue and crème brûlée. The wine list, as you might expect, features some outstanding bottles.

ARLINGTON, VA Willow 🅿🔩🔲📋 $$$$

4301 North Fairfax Drive, 22203 Tel 703-465-8800

This stylish restaurant serves modern continental dishes with classic French and Italian influences. The pepper-crusted filet mignon with creamy spinach tart, red-wine mushrooms, and red-onion rings is sensational, as are the soups and desserts. Inviting decor and good service. Pleasant bar area for pre-dinner cocktails.

BALTIMORE, MD Obrycki's Crab House 🅿🚹🔩 $$

1727 East Pratt St, 21231 Tel 410-732-6399

A seasonal restaurant offering superb seafood dining. Obrycki's Crab House is located in Fells Point, the historic district of downtown Baltimore. A favorite of the house is the hard-shell steamed crabs. Closed from early November to mid-March.

BETHESDA, MD Mon Ami Gabi 🅿🚹🔩🎵🔲 $$$

7239 Woodmont Ave (at Bethesda Ave), 20814 Tel 301-654-1234

Located in Bethesda's restaurant row, Mon Ami Gabi is a good choice for traditional French food in a casual atmosphere. While it has the authentic *steak frites, bouillabaisse*, crêpes, and quiches to choose from, the emphasis is on rustic simplicity. Live jazz performance on Tuesday and Thursday evenings. Valet parking is available at night.

BETHESDA, MD Rock Creek 🚹🔩🔲📋 $$$

4917 Elm St, 20814 Tel 301-907-7625

The emphasis at Rock Creek is on sustainability and nutrition, while sacrificing nothing on taste. All produce is local and the majority is organic. Specialties include some award-winning crab cakes, and slow-cooked salmon. And with only 240 calories per serving, don't feel guilty about ordering the molten chocolate cake!

BETHESDA, MD Persimmon

7003 Wisconsin Ave, 20815 **Tel** *301-654-9860*

Considered one of the best restaurants in Bethesda, Persimmon is an American bistro with a cozy, romantic atmosphere. Parking is available on the street and in the municipal lot behind the building. Open for lunch from Monday to Friday and for dinner daily. Sunday brunch: 11am–2pm.

CHARLOTTESVILLE, VA Michie Tavern

683 Thomas Jefferson Parkway, 22902 **Tel** *434-977-1234*

Casual dining (buffet style) with a Colonial touch – the staff dresses in period costume, and the decor is rustic. Take a tour of the 200-year-old inn and outbuildings. The homemade Southern fare, based on 18th-century recipes, is hearty – try the outstanding Southern fried chicken. Open for lunch only.

GETTYSBURG, VA Farnsworth House B & B

401 Baltimore St, 17325 **Tel** *717-334-8838*

The tavern and dining room have a Civil War theme. Waiters dress in period clothes, and the menu features Civil War dishes, including game pie, spoonbread, sweet potato pudding, and pumpkin fritters. The dining room is not wheelchair accessible.

MIDDLEBURG, VA The Coach Stop

9 East Washington Street (Rte 50), 22117 **Tel** *540-687-5515*

Located on the main street of Middleburg, The Coach Stop is a casual restaurant with a relaxed atmosphere. Popular with the locals, its extensive menu includes hamburgers, crab cakes, onion rings, and milk shakes. Open for breakfast, lunch, and dinner.

MIDDLEBURG, VA Red Fox Inn

2 East Washington St, 20117 **Tel** *540-687-6301*

Built in 1728, this inn has tried to retain the look of an 18th-century tavern, with a traditional, cozy atmosphere. As well as an elegant menu featuring blue cheese and onion tart, grilled trout, and filet mignon, diners will be offered a wine list showcasing wines from local vineyards. Serves breakfast, lunch, and dinner daily.

PARIS, VA The Ashby Inn

692 Federal St, 20130 **Tel** *540-592-3900*

Widely considered the region's best restaurant, the inn looks out on the Blue Ridge Mountains. The menu is limited, but each dish is well prepared, locally sourced, and seasonal. Built in 1829, it's located in a small town an hour from Washington. Closed Monday and Tuesday.

POTOMAC, MD Old Angler's Inn

10801 MacArthur Blvd (near Great Falls), 20854 **Tel** *301-365-2425*

This quaint English pub-style resturant is a short trip from the city. Next to the C&O Canal, it is a cozy place to enjoy a meal by the fire. The outdoor seating is equally romantic. The sophisticated kitchen serves new American cuisine with flair. If the weather is pleasant, you could dine on the stone terrace. Closed Mondays.

SHEPHERDSTOWN, WV Yellow Brick Bank

201 E German St, 25443 **Tel** *304-876-2208*

Housed in a former bank, this charming restaurant offers a sophisticated all-American menu, including dishes such as crab cakes, New York stip steak, and pork belly. Bread, pasta, and even mozzarella are home-made. A jazz pianist performs on Saturday evenings. The Yellow Brick Bank is located about an hour and a half away from Washington.

ST. MICHAELS, MD The Crab Claw

304 Mill St at Navy Point (Rte 33 West), 21663 **Tel** *410-745-2900*

A seasonal seafood restaurant, The Crab Claw is located on the harbor, with up-close views of the boats. Maryland blue crabs are a house specialty, as are several other dishes based on shrimps, lobsters, and clams. Closed from December to March.

WASHINGTON, VA Inn at Little Washington

439 Main Street, 22747 **Tel** *540-675-3800*

This five-star and five-diamond restaurant, one of the most celebrated in the world, offers regional, and eclectic American cuisine. The kitchen was inspired by the dairy room at Windsor Castle, no detail has been overlooked. A 90-minute drive from Washington. Reservations must be made several weeks in advance.

WILLIAMSBURG, VA Christiana Campbell's Tavern

101 S Waller St (near the Capitol), 23187 **Tel** *757-229-2141*

Run by Colonial Williamsburg, this historic tavern offers seafood specialties. The menu includes sherried crab stew, crab cakes, and "sea pye" (made with crab, shrimp, lobster, and cream), all served with spoonbread or sweet potato muffins. Reservations required.

WILLIAMSBURG, VA Williamsburg Inn

136 East Francis Street, 23185 **Tel** *757-229-2141*

Located in the beautiful historic district of Colonial Williamsburg, this formal restaurant offers a sophisticated menu, paired with a range of excellent wines. Live music every night, dinner dances on Fridays and Saturdays, and jazz brunch on Sundays. Service is consistently excellent, with great attention to detail.

SHOPPING IN WASHINGTON, DC

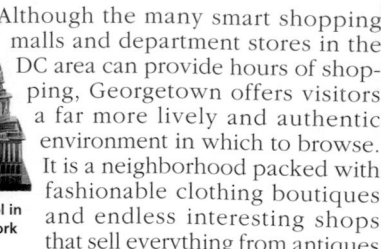

US Capitol in straw-work

Washington's vast selection of stores makes shopping in the capital a pleasurable experience. Souvenirs can be found anywhere from fashion boutiques and specialist food stores to museum and gallery gift shops. The many museums on the Mall and around the city sell a wide variety of unusual gifts, reproduction prints, and replica artifacts selected from all over the world.

Although the many smart shopping malls and department stores in the DC area can provide hours of shopping, Georgetown offers visitors a far more lively and authentic environment in which to browse. It is a neighborhood packed with fashionable clothing boutiques and endless interesting shops that sell everything from antiques to hair dye, from one-dollar bargains to priceless works of art.

East Hall of the Union Station shopping mall

OPENING HOURS

Most department stores, shopping malls, and other centers are open from 10am until 8 or 9pm, Monday through Saturday, and from noon until 6pm on Sunday. Smaller shops and boutiques are generally open from noon until 6pm on Sundays, and from 10 until 6 or 7pm on all other days. Convenience stores such as supermarkets and local grocery stores may open for longer hours. Drugstores (pharmacies) are also often open for extended hours.

HOW TO PAY

Goods may be paid for in cash, in traveler's checks (in US dollars), or by credit card. VISA and MasterCard are the most popular credit cards in the United States, while American Express is often, but not always, accepted. A tax of 5.75% is added to all purchases at the cash register.

SALES

Department stores, such as **Macy's** in the Penn Quarter area and **Nordstrom** farther out in Arlington, often hold sales during holiday weekends, including Memorial Day, the 4th of July, Labor Day, and Columbus Day. Check the newspapers for advertisements to find good prices on electronics, jewelry, kitchenwares, shoes, and clothing. White sales (towels and bedlinen) occur in January.

Stalls selling an eclectic range of goods at Eastern Market

MUSEUM SHOPS

All the museums on the Mall have a wide selection of products on sale in their shops. The **National Gallery of Art** sells artwork reproductions, books, art-related games and children's toys, and the **Museum of African Art** offers a range of African textiles, ceramics, basketry, musical instruments, and books.

The **National Museum of American History** shop carries a range of souvenirs such as American crafts, reproductions, and T-shirts, including merchandise inspired by the Star-Spangled Banner, as well as a range of books on American history. They also sell recordings from the 1940s to the 1970s, including Doo Wop, Motown, and Disco, from the Smithsonian Recordings and Smithsonian Folkways labels. Products can be purchased online too.

Also well worth a visit are two museum shops near the White House. **The Renwick Gallery** museum shop sells contemporary crafts made from glass, wood, fiber, metal, and ceramic, as well as silk scarves and tapestry purses. The shop at the **Decatur House Museum**, home of Stephen Decatur, a naval hero from the War of 1812, has a collection of items for sale related to Washington's history, art, and architecture.

For a selection of interesting books on architecture, contemporary design, and historic preservation, as well as a range of toys, ties, frames, and gifts, pay a visit to the **National Building Museum** shop at Judiciary Square.

Department store entrance
on G Street, NW

MALLS AND
DEPARTMENT STORES

There are a few small-scale
shopping malls in central
Washington, such as
Georgetown Park and Union Station.
Georgetown Park
combines modern
retail shops with a
Victorian-style in-
terior. It is situated
at the intersection of
Wisconsin Avenue
and M Street, right in
the heart of George-
town. **Union Station**, the
beautifully renovated train
station in the Capitol Hill area
(see p55), houses 130 shops
and restaurants on three levels,
in a very pleasant environment.
There are name-brand stores
as well as an extensive collection of specialty shops that
sell clothing, gifts, souvenirs,
crafts, jewelry, and more.

Two small shopping malls –
Mazza Gallerie and **Chevy
Chase Pavilion** – are located on
upper Wisconsin Avenue in the
Friendship Heights neighborhood. The metro is very convenient, but there is also plenty
of parking for cars. Visitors
can shop at Bloomingdale's or
Lord and Taylor department
stores, or the specialty boutiques and name-brand stores.

The larger malls are located
in the Maryland and Virginia
suburbs. The **Fashion Center
at Pentagon City** is easily
reached by metro. Discount-
hunters should head for the
230 outlets at **Potomac Mills**,
situated 30 miles (48 km)
south of the city on I-95.

GALLERIES, ARTS,
AND CRAFTS

Visitors will discover a
cornucopia of art galleries
and crafts shops in three
of Washington's neighbor-
hoods – Georgetown,
Dupont Circle, and Adams-
Morgan. Here visitors can
spend a few hours feasting
their eyes on the delightful
objects on display.

Work by several local artists
is on sale in the **Addison/
Ripley Fine Arts**, located
in Georgetown. Some of the
best pottery can be found
in the **Appalachian Spring**
shops in Georgetown and
at Union Station. **Eastern
Market** in Capitol Hill offers
a vibrant mix of stalls from
antiques to ethnic artifacts,
and is best at weekends.

Torpedo Factory Art
Center logo

Art lovers should
browse along
7th Street, NW,
between D Street
and the Verizon
Center. Among
the highlights
are pieces of
sculpture and
contemporary art
at **Zenith Gallery**
for sale from $50 to $50,000.
Out of town, in Alexandria,
the **Torpedo Factory Art
Center** is excellent for
lovers of all kinds of arts
and crafts.

SOUVENIRS

Collectors' items and
DC memorabilia are
abundant at Political
Americana and Made
in America, two shops
in **Union Station**. The
Old Post Office Pavilion
near Metro Center is
also worth a visit for
DC souvenirs. The gift
shops in the **Kennedy
Center** sell gifts and
books about the per-
forming arts and
Washington in general.
People looking for
religious items or
unusual souvenirs
should try the
**Washington National
Cathedral** museum
and book shop in
the basement of

the cathedral or the Herb
Cottage, a renovated
octagonal baptistry in
the Cathedral grounds.

CLOTHES

Wisconsin Avenue and M
Street in Georgetown are
home to a wide range of
clothing stores. National
highstreet chains include
The Gap, while those seeking
something a little out of the
ordinary should visit **Urban
Outfitters**. **Eddie Bauer** has
relocated to Pentagon City
Mall in Arlington, VA.

Betsey Johnson specializes
in sleek city fashions while
H & M, the international
discount store, has clothing
for men, women, and kids.
There is also a great variety
of clothes shops in the
Friendship Heights
neighborhood.

FOOD AND WINE

For something unusual,
tasty, or exotic in the
culinary field, there are
several delicatessens worth
visiting in Washington.
In particular, try **Dean &
Deluca** in Georgetown,
which stocks an excellent
selection of gourmet foods
and offers a fine range of
American and European
wines. While there, it is
possible to sample the food
and drinks available in the
pleasant on-site café.

The Old Post Office Pavilion

One of many antique centers in Frederick

ANTIQUES

There are some wonderful hidden treasures to be discovered in the many antique stores scattered throughout Washington. Along Wisconsin Avenue, between P and S streets and also along M and O streets, there are around 20 antique shops. Some specialize in expensive antiques, others in prints, lamps, silverware, perfume bottles, or just interesting knick-knacks.

Adams-Morgan and Dupont Circle are also good neighborhoods for antique hunting. **Brass Knob Architectural Antiques**, on 18th Street, is worth visiting for their range of salvaged curiosities, including clawfoot bathtubs and unusual antique light fixtures. Customers are bound to leave with just the perfect relic for their home, which could be anything from a chandelier to an iron gate.

There is also a number of centers for antiques outside central Washington. Kensington in Maryland and Old Town Alexandria in Virginia are areas rich in antiques. **Studio Antiques** in Alexandria sells all kinds of antiques, such as dolls, china, and silver, but specializes in books. In Frederick, Maryland, is the enormous **Emporium Antiques**. This paradise for antiques lovers houses over 100 shops that sell everything from huge pieces of furniture through household wares to jewelry.

BOOKS AND MUSIC

Book lovers are spoiled for choice in Washington and will enjoy spending time browsing in the myriad bookstores that can be found in the city.

In addition to the large chainstores, such as **Barnes and Noble**, there are several excellent independent and second-hand bookstores, especially in the Dupont Circle area. In **Kramerbooks & Afterwords Café**, customers can sit with their new purchase while drinking a coffee. There is also a full-service restaurant. **Second Story Books** is DC's biggest second-hand store.

Farther north, on Connecticut Avenue, is the **Politics & Prose Bookstore**, a favorite among Washingtonians for its combination of books and coffee. Customers can chat with the knowledgeable staff, browse, or attend a reading. (The Sunday book review section of the *Washington Post* lists readings.)

The chainstore **Borders**, like Olsson's, sells both books and compact discs, which are competitively priced. Also located on Connecticut Avenue is the **Melody Record Shop**, which sells a wide variety of music at discount prices.

MISCELLANEOUS

The many department stores in and around Washington, such as **Macy's** and **Neiman-Marcus**, are well-stocked with good quality household wares from linens to cutlery and crockery. They are also prepared to order any out-of-stock items for their customers.

Wake Up Little Suzie sells unusual and unique gifts, such as handmade books, jewelry, and hanging mobiles. Similarly, **Chocolate Moose**, on L Street, is a treasure trove of the unusual and unconventional, including ceramics, chocolates, jewelry, ceramics, and children's toys, among other things. For visitors fascinated by maps and travel, a visit to the **ADC Map and Travel Center** is essential. This shop has over 5,000 maps from around the world, as well as globes, guidebooks, and language books.

Everything in contemporary products for the home, from kitchenware to furniture, can be found at **Crate & Barrel** in Spring Valley and in Georgetown's **Pottery Barn**. Also in Georgetown is **Restoration Hardware**, which offers everything from decorative door knobs through gardening supplies and lamps, to old-fashioned toys and the popular, heavy oak Mission furniture that originated in the Arts and Crafts Movement.

Shoppers browsing in the window of Olsson's bookstore

DIRECTORY

MALLS AND DEPARTMENT STORES

Bloomingdale's
5300 Western Ave, Chevy Chase MD.
Tel 774-3700.

Chevy Chase Pavilion
5335 Wisconsin Ave, NW.
Tel 686-5335.

Fashion Center at Pentagon City
1100 South Hayes St, Arlington, Virginia.
Tel (703) 415-2400.

Georgetown Park
3222 M St, NW.
Map 1 B2. *Tel 298-5577.*

Lord & Taylor
5255 Western Ave, Chevy Chase, MD.
Tel 362-9600.

Macy's Department Store
12th & G St, NW.
Map 3 C3.
Tel 628-6661.

Mazza Gallerie Mall
5300 Wisconsin Ave, NW.
Tel 966-6114.

Neiman-Marcus
Mazza Gallerie. **Map** 1B1.
Tel 966-9700.

Nordstrom
Fashion Center at Pentagon City.
Tel (703) 415-1121.

Potomac Mills
Woodbridge, VA.
Tel (703) 496-9330.

Union Station Shops
40 Massachusetts Ave, NE. **Map** 4 E3.
Tel 371-9441.

GALLERIES, ARTS, AND CRAFTS

Addison/Ripley Fine Arts
1670 Wisconsin Ave, NW.
Map 1 C2.
Tel 338-5180.

Appalachian Spring
1415 Wisconsin Ave, NW.
Map 1C2.
Tel 337-5780.

Eastern Market
225 7th St, SE.
Map 4 F4.

Torpedo Factory Art Center
105 N. Union Street
Alexandria, VA.
Tel (703) 838-4565.

Zenith Gallery
413 7th St, NW.
Map 3 C2.
Tel 783-2963.

ANTIQUES

Brass Knob Architectural Antiques
2311 18th St, NW.
Map 3 A1.
Tel 332-3370.

Emporium Antiques
112 E. Patrick St,
Frederick, MD.
Tel (301) 662-7099.

Georgetown Flea Market
Wisconsin Ave, between S & T Sts, NW.
Map 1 C3.

Studio Antiques
524 N. Washington St,
Alexandria, VA.
Tel (703) 548-5188.

SOUVENIRS

Kennedy Center
New Hampshire Ave & Rock Creek Parkway, NW.
Map 2 D4.
Tel 416-8000.

Old Post Office Pavilion
Pennsylvania Ave & 12th St, NW.
Map 3C3.
Tel 289-4224.

Washington National Cathedral
Massachusetts & Wisconsin Ave, NW.
Tel 537-6200.

BOOKS AND MUSIC

Barnes and Noble
3040 M St, NW.
Map 2 D2.
Tel 965-9880.

Borders
1800 L St, NW. **Map** 2 E3.
Tel 466-4999.

Kramerbooks & Afterwords Café
1517 Connecticut Ave, NW. **Map** 2 E2.
Tel 387-1462.

Melody Record Shop
1623 Connecticut Ave, NW.
Map 2 E2. *Tel 232-4002.*

Politics & Prose Bookstore
5015 Connecticut Ave, NW.
Map 2 E2. *Tel 364-1919.*

Second Story Books
2000 P Street, NW.
Map 1B1.
Tel 659-8884.

MUSEUM SHOPS

Decatur House Museum
1610 H St, NW.
Map 3 A3.
Tel 842-0915.

National Building Museum
401 F St, NW. **Map** 4 D3.
Tel 272-2448.

National Gallery of Art
Constitution Ave at 6th St, NW.
Map 4 D4.
Tel 1-800 697-9350.

National Museum of African Art
950 Independence Ave, SW. **Map** 3 C4.
Tel 786-2147.

National Museum of American History
The Mall between 12th and 14th Sts, NW.
Map 3 B4.
Tel 357-1528.

Renwick Gallery
17th & Pennsylvania Ave, NW. **Map** 3 A3.
Tel 357-1445.

CLOTHES

Betsey Johnson
3029 M Street, NW.
Map 1 C2. *Tel 338-4090.*

Eddie Bauer
Tysons Corner Mall,
McLean, VA.
Tel (703) 893-4483.

The Gap
1120 Connecticut Ave, NW. **Map** 3 A2.
Tel 429-0691.

H & M
Georgetown Park
(Wisconsin Ave and M St, NW). **Map** 1 C2.
Tel 298-6792.

Urban Outfitters
3111 M St, NW.
Map 1 C2.
Tel 342-1012.

FOOD AND WINE

Dean & Deluca
3276 M St, NW.
Map 1 C2.
Tel 342-2500.

MISCELLANEOUS

ADC Map and Travel Center
1636 I (Eye) St, NW.
Map 2 F3.
Tel 628-2608.

Chocolate Moose
1743 L St, NW.
Map 2 F2.
Tel 463-0992.

Crate & Barrel
4820 Massachusetts Ave, NW. *Tel 364-6500.*

Pottery Barn
3077 M St, NW
Map 1 C2.
Tel 337-8900.

Restoration Hardware
1222 Wisconsin Ave, NW.
Map 1 C2. *Tel 625-2771.*

Wake-Up Little Suzie
3409 Connecticut Ave, NW. *Tel 244-0700.*

ENTERTAINMENT IN WASHINGTON, DC

Visitors to Washington will never be at a loss for entertainment, from flying a kite in the grounds of the Washington Monument to attending a concert at the Kennedy Center. The city's diverse, international community offers a rich array of choices. If you are looking for swing dancing you will find it; you will also hear different beats around town, including salsa, jazz, and rhythm and blues. Outdoor enthusiasts can choose from cycling on the Rock Creek bike path to canoeing on the Potomac River. If you are looking for something less active, take in a film at the Smithsonian. Theatergoers have a wide range of choices, from Shakespeare through highly respected repertory companies to Broadway musicals. No matter what your budget is, you will find something to do. There are more free activities in DC than in any other American city.

Baseball player

Façade of the John F. Kennedy Center for the Performing Arts

INFORMATION SOURCES

The best place to find information is in the Weekend section of Friday's edition of the *Washington Post*. This lists concerts, plays, movies, children's activities, outdoor recreation, and fairs and festivals. Internet users can check out *Style Live*, the entertainment guide on the *Washington Post* website.

The "Where & When" section in the monthly *Washingtonian* magazine also lists events.

BOOKING TICKETS

Tickets may be bought in advance at box offices, or by phone and through the Internet. Tickets for all events at the **Kennedy Center** can be obtained by phone through **Instant Charge** or on their website. Tickets for the Verizon Center, the Nissan Pavilion, and the Warner Theater can be bought by phone through **Ticketmaster**. For Arena, Lisner Auditorium, Ford's Theatre, Merriweather Post Pavilion, and Woolly Mammoth tickets, contact **www**.tickets.com.

DISCOUNT TICKETS

Most theaters give group discounts, and several offer student and senior discounts for same-day performances.

Façade of the Shakespeare Theatre on 7th Street

Half-price tickets for seats on the day of the performance may be obtained in person at **Ticketplace**, at 407 7th St, NW, or on their website.

In addition, theaters offer their own special discounts: The Arena sells a limited number of "Hottix," half-price seats, 30 to 90 minutes before the show. The Shakespeare Theatre offers 20 percent off for senior citizens Sunday through Thursday, 50 percent one hour before curtain rise for students, and discounts for all previews. The Kennedy Center has a limited number of half-price tickets available to students, senior citizens, and anyone with permanent disabilities. These go on sale at noon on the day of the performance (some are available before the first performance). Standing-room tickets may be available if a show is sold out.

FREE EVENTS

The daily newspapers provide up-to-date listings of free lectures, concerts, gallery talks, films, book signings, poetry readings, and shows.

Local and international artists offer free performances on the Millennium Stage at the Kennedy Center every evening at 6pm.

The **National Symphony Orchestra** gives a free outdoor concert on the West Lawn of the Capitol on Labor Day and Memorial Day weekends, and on the Fourth of July.

Courtyard concert in the National Gallery of Art

In summer, various military bands such as the **United States Marine Band**, the Navy, Air Force or the **US Army Band** give free concerts (contact them direct for details).

From October to June, the **National Gallery of Art** sponsors free Sunday evening concerts at 7pm in the West Garden Court, and also free summer jazz concerts on Friday evenings in the Sculpture Garden. Free lectures and gallery talks are held at the **Library of Congress** and at the National Gallery of Art.

OPEN-AIR ENTERTAINMENT

During the summer months at **Wolf Trap Farm Park for the Performing Arts** world-famous performers can be seen on any night. Check their calendar of events and find your favorite form of entertainment – opera, jazz, Broadway musical, ballet, folk, or country music. You can bring a picnic to enjoy on the lawn.

On Thursday evenings in summer, the **National Zoo** hosts concerts on Lion Tiger Hill. They start at 6:30pm.

If you are in Washington in June try to catch the **Shakespeare Theatre Free for All** held at Carter Barron Amphitheater in Rock Creek Park.

The *Washington Post* lists the local fairs and festivals, held every weekend in warm weather. On the first weekend in May, the **Washington National Cathedral** sponsors the Flowermart, a festival featuring an old-fashioned carousel, children's games, crafts, and good food. The **Smithsonian Folklife Festival**, a two-week extravaganza held on the Mall at the end of June and early July, brings together folk artists from around the world. For details of other annual events in the city, *see* Washington, DC Through The Year *(pp36–9)*.

FACILITIES FOR THE DISABLED

All the major theaters in Washington are wheelchair accessible. For information on the Kennedy Center's accessibility services, check its website.

Many theaters, including the Kennedy Center, Ford's Theatre, the Shakespeare Theatre, and Arena Stage, have audio enhancement devices, as well as a limited number of signed performances. For the hearing impaired, TTY phone numbers are listed in the Weekend section of the *Washington Post*.

The National Gallery of Art provides assisted listening devices for lectures. Sign-language interpretation is available with three weeks' notice, and a telecommunications device for the deaf (TDD) can be found near the Concourse Sales Shop. For those with limited sight, the theater Arena Stage offers audio description, touch tours of the set, and program books in large print and Braille.

DIRECTORY

INFORMATION SOURCES

Washington Post
www.washingtonpost.com

BOOKING TICKETS

John F. Kennedy Center for the Performing Arts
New Hampshire Ave at Rock Creek Parkway, NW.
Map 2 D4.
Tickets booked via Instant Charge
Tel 467-4600
or (800) 444-1324.
www.kennedy-center.org

Ticketmaster
Tel 397-7328.
www.ticketmaster.com

Tickets.com
Tel (800) 955-5566.
www.tickets.com

DISCOUNT TICKETS

Ticketplace
407 7th St, NW.
Map 3 D3.
www.ticketplace.org

FREE EVENTS

US Army Band
Tel (703) 696-3399.
www.usarmyband.com

Library of Congress
1st St & Independence Ave, SE.
Map 4 F4.
Tel 707-5503.
www.loc.gov

National Gallery of Art
Constitution Ave at 6th St, NW.
Map 4 D4.
Tel 737-4215.
www.nga.gov

National Symphony Orchestra
Tel 467-4600.

US Marine Band
Tel 433-4011.
www.marineband.usmc.mil

OPEN-AIR ENTERTAINMENT

National Zoo
3001 Connecticut Ave, NW.
Tel 633-4800.
www.nationalzoo.si.edu

Shakespeare Theatre Free for All
Carter Barron Amphitheater, 16th St & Colorado Ave, NW.
Tel 547-1122. www.shakespearetheatre.org

Smithsonian Folklife Festival
Tel 633-1000.

Washington National Cathedral
Massachusetts and Wisconsin Aves, NW.
Tel 537-6200.
www.nationalcathedral.org

Wolf Trap Farm Park for the Performing Arts
1551 Trap Rd, Vienna, VA.
Tel (703) 255-1900 (info).
Tel (877) 965-3872 (tickets)
www.wolftrap.org

Cultural Events

For an evening out, Washington has much to offer. A seafood dinner on the waterfront followed by a play at Arena Stage, Washington's oldest repertory company; dancing at one of the new clubs on U Street; jazz in Georgetown; a late-night coffee bar in Dupont Circle; or opening night at the opera at the Kennedy Center and a nightcap in the West End. Or if you are staying downtown and do not want to venture far from your hotel, see a show at the Warner or the National Theater, where the best of Broadway finds a home.

Dancing to live music at the Kennedy Center

Sign on the façade of the Warner Theatre on 13th Street

FILM AND THEATER

Independent and foreign-language films, as well as classic revivals, are screened at the state-of-the-art **Landmark's E Street Cinema**. Film festivals are held at the **Kennedy Center**. Museums such as **The National Gallery of Art** show films relating to current exhibitions. **The Library of Congress** offers a free film series of documentaries and films related to the exhibits in the museum, shown in the Mary Pickford Theater. The DC Film Festival is based at the Lincoln Theatre.

National touring theater companies bring shows to the **John F. Kennedy Center**

for the Performing Arts, the **Warner Theatre**, and the **National Theatre**. For a more intimate setting, try **Ford's Theatre**. **Arena Stage** has a well-established repertory company. **The Studio** and the **Woolly Mammoth Theatre** produce contemporary works.

The Shakespeare Theatre produces works in a modern, elegant setting. For plays performed in Spanish, seek out the **Gala Hispanic Theater**.

OPERA AND CLASSICAL MUSIC

Based at the Kennedy Center, the **Washington National Opera Company** is often considered one of the capital's crown jewels. Although many performances do sell out, standing room tickets are sometimes available. **The National Symphony Orchestra** performs classical and contemporary works.

A rich variety of chamber ensembles and choral groups perform regularly around the city. **The Washington Performing Arts Society** brings internationally renowned performers to DC.

DANCE

The Kennedy Center offers a magnificent ballet and dance season every year, with sell-out productions from the world's finest companies including the Bolshoi, the American Ballet Theater, the Royal Swedish Ballet, and the Dance Theater of Harlem.

Dance Place showcases its own professional modern dance companies, as well as international contemporary dance companies.

If you would prefer to take to the floor yourself, make your way to **Glen Echo Park** where people from ages 7 to 70 enjoy evenings of swing dancing, contra dancing (line dancing), Louisiana Cajun zdeco dancing, and waltzes. The Kennedy Center also occasionally has dancing to live bands.

ROCK, JAZZ, AND BLUES

To see the "biggest names and the hottest newcomers" in jazz, head for the KC Jazz Club at the Kennedy Center. Oscar Brown, Jr., Phil Woods, Ernie Watts, and many more are featured here. You can hear international jazz stars at **Blues Alley** in Georgetown, or visit **Madam's Organ** in Adams-Morgan, home to some of the best R&B in Washington.

If you want to hear big-name rock stars or jazz artists, head to the **Verizon Center** (see p102), the **Merriweather Post Pavilion** in Columbia, Maryland, or the **Nissan Pavilion** in Manassas, Virginia.

Interior of the highly respected Shakespeare Theatre

CLUBS, BARS, AND CAFES

For late night dancing and clubbing, try the U Street neighborhood. Most highly recommended is the **930 Night Club**.

For salsa try the **Rumba Café** in Adams-Morgan. If you fancy a cigar and a martini, then check out **Ozio Martini and Cigar Lounge** downtown. If Irish music is more your thing, head to **Ireland's Four Provinces** in Cleveland Park. **Black Cat** is the place for live music. Billiard parlors are also popular, as are the city's many coffee bars. **Cosi Dupont North** in Dupont Circle serves coffees and cocktails.

GAY CLUBS

Many of the gay bars in DC can be found in the Dupont Circle area. **JR's Bar and Grill** attracts young professionals. **The Fireplace** is popular and stays open late. For a good meal, visit **Annie's Paramount Steak House**.

Interior of Rumba Café

DIRECTORY

FILM AND THEATER

Arena Stage
1800 S. Bell St,
Crystal City, Arlington, VA.
Tel 488-3300.
www.arenastage.org

Ford's Theatre
511 10th St, NW.
Map 3 C3.
Tel 347-4833.
www.fordstheatre.org

Gala Hispanic Theater
3333 14th St, NW.
Tel 234-7174.

Kennedy Center
New Hampshire Ave &
Rock Creek Parkway, NW.
Map 2 D4. *Tel 467-4600*
or (800) 444-1324.
www.kennedy-center.org

Landmark's E Street Cinema
Lincoln Square Building
at 555 11th St, NW.
Map 3 C3.
Tel 452-7672.
www.landmarktheatres.com

Library of Congress
Mary Pickford Theater,
Madison Building,
101 Independence Ave, SE.
Map 4 E4.
Tel 707-5677.
www.loc.gov

National Gallery of Art
Constitution Ave at 6th St,
NW. **Map** 4 D3.
Tel 737-4215.
www.nga.org

National Theatre
1321 Pennsylvania Ave,
NW. **Map** 3 B3.
Tel 628-6161.
www.nationaltheatre.org

Shakespeare Theatre
450 7th St, NW.
Map 3 C3.
Tel 547-1122. www.
shakespearetheatre.org

Signature Theatre
4200 Campbell Ave,
Springfield, VA.
Tel (703) 820-9771.
www.sig-online.com

The Studio Theatre
1501 14th St, NW.
Map 3 B1.
Tel 332-3300.
www.studiotheatre.org

Warner Theatre
13th St (between E and F
Sts), NW. **Map** 3 C3.
Tel 783-4000.
www.warnertheatre.com

Woolly Mammoth Theatre
641 D St, NW.
Map 3 C3.
Tel 393-3939.
www.woollymammoth.net

OPERA AND CLASSICAL MUSIC

National Symphony Orchestra
Tel 467-4600.

Washington Performing Arts Society
Tel 833-9800.
www.wpas.org

DANCE

Dance Place
3225 8th St, NE.
Tel 269-1600.

Glen Echo Park
Spanish Ballroom,
7300 MacArthur Blvd,
Glen Echo, MD.
Tel (301) 320-1400.

ROCK, JAZZ, AND BLUES

Blues Alley
1069 Wisconsin Ave,
NW.
Map 1 C3.
Tel 337-4141.

Madam's Organ
2461 18th St, NW.
Map 2 F1.
Tel 667-5370.

Merriweather Post Pavilion
Columbia, MD.
Tel (410) 715-5550.
www.merriweather
music.com

Nissan Pavilion
7800 Cellar Door Drive,
Bristow, VA.
Tel (703) 754-6400
www.nissanpavilion
online.com

CLUBS, BARS, AND CAFES

Black Cat
1811 14th St, NW.
Map 3 B3.
Tel 667-4490.

Cosi Dupont North
1647 20th St, NW.
Map 3 A1.
Tel 332-6364.

Ireland's Four Provinces
3412 Connecticut Ave,
NW.
Tel 244-0860.

930 Night Club
815 V St, NW.
Tel 265-0930.
www.930.com

Ozio Martini and Cigar Lounge
1813 M St, NW.
Map 3 A1.
Tel 822-6000.

Rumba Café
2443 18th St, NW.
Tel 588-5501.
www.rumbacafe.com

GAY CLUBS

Annie's Paramount Steak House
1609 17th St, NW.
Map 2 F2.
Tel 232-0395.

The Fireplace
2161 P St, NW.
Map 2 E2.
Tel 293-1293.

JR's Bar and Grill
1519 17th St, NW.
Map 2 F2.
Tel 328-0090.

Sports and Outdoor Activities

Washingtonians are known for putting in long hours – whether on the floor of the Senate, the office of a federal agency, or in a newsroom. They compensate, however, by taking their leisure hours very seriously by rooting for their favorite teams or spending as much time as possible outdoors. You can join in the fun at the Nationals Park Stadium or the Verizon Center, both of which attract hordes of fans. You can meet joggers, cyclists, and in-line skaters on the Mall and around the monuments.

Cyclists enjoying the fine weather outdoors in DC

SPECTATOR SPORTS

Fans of the NHL Capitals (National Hockey League), the NBA Wizards (National Basketball Association), and the WNBA Mystics (Women's National Basketball Association) should purchase tickets at the **Verizon Center**, an impressive sports arena that opened in December 1997 and has helped revitalize the downtown area.

Depending on the season, you might also see Disney on Ice, the Harlem Globetrotters, or the Ringling Brothers Circus. Visit the Verizon's National Sports Gallery, which houses sports memorabilia and interactive sports games. There is plenty to eat at the Verizon Center, but you may prefer to slip out to one of the restaurants in Chinatown, which surrounds the center.

If you are not a season-pass holder, it is very difficult to get a ticket to a Washington Redskins' game at the **FedEx Field** stadium, but you can always watch the game from one of Washington's popular sports

bars. The DC United soccer team plays at the **RFK Stadium**. College sports are also very popular in DC – you will find Washingtonians cheering either for the **Georgetown Hoyas** or the **Maryland Terrapins**. Baseball fans lend their support to the Washington Nationals at **Nationals Park Stadium**, which opened in March 2008.

Redskins team member

FISHING AND BOATING

If you want to spend an hour or perhaps an entire day by the Potomac River, head to **Fletcher's Boat House** at Canal and Reservoir Roads. You must obtain a permit if you are between 16 and 64, which lasts for a year but does not cost much. You can fish from the riverbank or rent a rowboat or canoe, which are available by the hour or the day.

In Georgetown there are boats for rent at **Thompson's Boat Center** and **Jack's Boat House**. Fletcher's sells snacks; if you go to Thompson's or Jack's there are cafés and restaurants along the waterfront.

CYCLING

Rock Creek Park is one of Washington's greatest treasures and offers amazing respite from busy city life. Closed to traffic on weekends, it is a great place for cycling. Another popular trail is the Capital Crescent, which starts on the C&O Canal towpath in Georgetown and runs to Maryland.

One of the more beautiful bike trails in the area will take you 16 miles (26 km) to Mount Vernon. Bikes can be rented at Fletcher's Boat House, Thompson's Boat Center, **Bike and Roll**, or **Big Wheels** in Georgetown. For maps or trail information call or write to the **Washington Area Bicyclist Association**, or consult one of the bike rental shops in the city.

TENNIS, GOLF, AND HORSEBACK RIDING

Many neighborhood parks have outdoor tennis courts, available on a first-come, first-served basis. Two public clubs in the city accept reservations: **East Potomac Tennis Center** at Hains Point, and the **Washington Tennis Center**. Each has outdoor and indoor courts.

If you want to take in views of the monuments while walking the golf fairways, go to the **East Potomac Golf Course & Driving Range**. (There is an 18-hole miniature golf course here as well.) Two other courses are open to the public: **Langston Golf Course** on the Anacostia River and

RFK Stadium, a major sports and entertainment venue

Rock Creek Golf Course, tucked into Rock Creek Park. You will also find **Rock Creek Park Horse Center**, where you can make reservations for a guided trail ride.

EXPLORING NATURE

For an amazing array of trees and plants, visit the **National Arboretum** *(see p144)*, which covers 444 acres in northeast Washington. There is something interesting to see all year round in the arboretum. Special displays, such as the National Bonsai Collection of miniature plants, can be enjoyed at any time of year. To catch the best of the flowering shrubs, the beautiful camellias and magnolias flower in late March through early April, and the stunning, rich colors of the azaleas, rhododendron, and dogwood appear from late April through early May. There is a 1,600-ft (490-m) long "touch and see trail" at the garden for visually impaired visitors.

The beautiful and tranquil grounds of the National Arboretum

An alternative to the arboretum is **Kenilworth Aquatic Gardens**, which has 14 acres of ponds with more than 100,000 water lilies, lotuses, and other plants. It is a good idea to plan a trip early in the day when the blooms are open and before the sun gets too hot. Frogs and turtles can be seen regularly along the footpaths around the ponds. Park naturalists conduct nature walks around the gardens on summer weekends.

One of the most enjoyable ways to spend time outdoors is with a picnic in the park. Visit **Dumbarton Oaks Park** in Georgetown when the wildflowers are in bloom, or visit **Montrose Park**, right next door to Dumbarton Oaks, where you can enjoy the variety of birds and the boxwood maze.

DIRECTORY

SPECTATOR SPORTS

FedEx Field
Arena Drive, Landover, MD.
Tel (301) 276-6000.
www.redskins.com

Georgetown Hoyas
Tel 687-4692.
www.guhoyas.com

Maryland Terrapins
Tel (800) 462-8377.
www.umterps.com

Nationals Park Stadium
1500 South Capitol St, SE.
Tel (202) 675-6287.

RFK Stadium
2400 East Capitol St, SE.
Tel 547-9077.

Verizon Center
601 F St, NW. **Map** 4 D3.
Tel 628-3200.

FISHING AND BOATING

Fletcher's Boat House
4940 Canal Rd, NW.
Map 1 A2. *Tel 244-0037.*

Jack's Boat House
3500 K St, NW.
Map 2 D2. *Tel 337-9642.*

Thompson Boat Center
Rock Creek Parkway & Virginia Ave, NW. **Map** 2 D3. *Tel 333-9543.* www. thompsonboatcenter.com

CYCLING

Big Wheel Bikes
1034 33rd St, NW. **Map** 1 C2. *Tel 337-0254.*
www.bigwheelbikes.com

Bike and Roll
1100 Pennsylvania Ave, NW.
Map 3 C3.
Tel 842-BIKE (2453).
www.bikethesites.com

Washington Area Bicyclist Association
2599 Ontario Rd, NW.
Tel 518-0524.
www.waba.org

TENNIS, GOLF, AND RIDING

East Potomac Golf Course
972 Ohio Drive, SW at Hains Point. **Map** 3 A5.
Tel 554-7660.

East Potomac Tennis Center
1090 Ohio Drive, SW at Hains Point. **Map** 3 A5.
Tel 554-5962. www. eastpotomactennis.com

Langston Golf Course
26th St & Benning Rd, NE.
Tel 397-8638.

Rock Creek Golf Course
1600 Rittenhouse St, NW.
Tel 882-7332.

Rock Creek Park Horse Center
Military & Glover Rds, NW.
Tel 362-0117 (ext 0).
www.rockcreekhorse center.com

Rock Creek Tennis Center
16th & Kennedy Sts, NW.
Tel 722-5949. www. rockcreektennis.com

EXPLORING NATURE

Dumbarton Oaks Park
Entrance on Lovers Lane, off R & 31st Sts, NW.
Map 1 C1.

Kenilworth Park & Aquatic Gardens
1550 Anacostia Ave, NE.
Tel 426-6905.

Montrose Park
R & 32nd Sts, NW.
Map 2 D1.

National Arboretum
24th & R Sts, NE.
Tel 245-2726.

Children's Washington, DC

Visiting the city's monuments can be one of the favorite and most memorable activities for children in DC. Book online in advance to arrange a tour with a park ranger, during which you take a trip in the elevator to the top of the Washington Monument, then walk down the steps. Young children will like feeding the ducks at the Reflecting Pool or Constitution Gardens. You can view the Jefferson Memorial from a paddleboat on the Tidal Basin, and before you leave Washington be sure to see the monuments lit up against the night-time sky.

PRACTICAL ADVICE

One of the best sources of comprehensive information on specific events for children can be found in the "Saturday's Child" page which is in the Weekend section of Friday's *Washington Post*.

As you would expect in a major city, food is widely available in DC, whether it is hot dogs from a seller along the Mall or even strange space food (such as freeze-dried ice cream) from the **National Air and Space Museum** gift shop *(see pp62–5)*.

Sea lion at the National Zoo

OUTDOOR FUN

For a trip into the past, take a ride on *The Georgetown*, a mule-drawn barge on the C&O Canal from April to mid-October (contact the **C&O Canal Visitor Center** for details). Park Service rangers dressed in 19th-century costumes add to the experience.

The beautiful wooded park of the **National Zoo** *(see pp138–9)* is a good place for a walk, and you can also enjoy watching elephant training, panda feeding, and sea lion demonstrations.

For a break from the Mall museums, take a ride on the **Carousel on the Mall** (open in summer only), in front of the Arts and Industries Building. Also worth a visit is the carousel in **Glen Echo Park** (open in summer only), built in 1921. From December to March, ice skaters can head for the outdoor rink at the **National Gallery of Art Sculpture Garden**. Or try **Pershing Park Ice Rink**, located on Pennsylvania Avenue, across from the Willard Hotel. Skate rentals are available.

MUSEUMS

The Discovery Center, a vast educational complex with an IMAX® theater, is housed in the **National Museum of Natural History** *(see pp70–71)*.

Children in front of the National Museum of Natural History

If you want to experience outer space, then see "To Fly!" and the Albert Einstein Planetarium at the **National Air and Space Museum**. A series of children's films and family programs are run by the **National Gallery of Art** *(see pp58–61)*. Children can discuss paintings and take part in a whole range of hands-on activities.

The **National Museum of the American Indian** *(see pp68–9)* has many events, workshops, films and demonstrations designed for the family. Similarly, the **National Museum of African Art** *(see p67)* hosts educative music and storytelling events.

Children are always fascinated by the **National Postal Museum** *(see p53)*, with its many intriguing hands-on activities.

CHILDREN'S THEATER

The Ripley Center of the Smithsonian houses the **Discovery Theater**, which stages puppet shows and plays. See a puppet show or fairytale production at the **Adventure Theatre** in Glen Echo Park. The theater company **Imagination Stage**, located north of Washington in Bethesda, Maryland, presents lively theater productions for children.

The **Kennedy Center** *(see pp118–19)* and **Wolf Trap Farm Park for the Performing Arts** also provide information on all sorts of children's events in the city.

Children's tour in Cedar Hill, the historic home of Frederick Douglass

A LITTLE BIT OF HISTORY

Children studying American history will be fascinated by a visit to Cedar Hill, once the home of Frederick Douglass, in Anacostia. The video in the visitors' center helps to tell the amazing story of this American hero.

You can take a tour of **Ford's Theatre** *(see p96)* where President Lincoln was shot and the house across the street where he died.

The **Washington National Cathedral** *(see pp142–3)* provides a free brochure to take children on a self guided scavenger hunt seeking carvings, specific images in stained-glass windows, and gargoyles. The National Building Museum *(see p103)* runs special programs for children on Saturdays.

SHOPPING

The **National Museum of Natural History** *(see pp70–71)* shops stock a wide variety of goods that will keep children enthralled. Favorites include books, natural history toys, games related to sea life, dinosaurs, and nature, as well as science kits which allow children to reproduce at home some of the wonders of the natural world on display in the museum.

Dinosaur Hall in the National Museum of Natural History

DIRECTORY

PRACTICAL ADVICE

National Air and Space Museum
6th St & Independence Ave, SW.
Map 4 D4.
Tel 633-1000.

National Museum of American History
Constitution Ave between 12th & 14th Sts, NW.
Map 3 B4.
Tel 633-1000.

OUTDOOR FUN

C&O Canal Visitor Center
1057 Thomas Jefferson St, NW. **Map** 2 D3.
Tel 653-5190.

Carousel on the Mall
Arts and Industries Blg, 900 Jefferson Drive, SW.
Map 3 B4.
Tel 633-1000.

Glen Echo Park Carousel
7300 MacArthur Blvd, Glen Echo, MD.
Tel (301) 320-1400 or (301) 634-2222.
www.glenechopark.org

National Gallery of Art Sculpture Garden Rink
7th St & Constitution Ave, NW. **Map** 4 D4.
Tel 842-1310.

National Zoo
3001 Connecticut Ave.
Tel 633-4888.

Pershing Park Ice Rink
Pennsylvania Ave & 14th St, NW.
Map 3 B3. *Tel 737-6938.*

MUSEUMS

National Air and Space Museum
6th St & Independence Ave, SW. **Map** 4 D4.
Tel 633-4629 (IMAX® film schedule).

National Gallery of Art
Constitution Ave between 3rd & 7th Sts, NW.
Map 4 D3.
Tel 789-4995 (children's film program).
Tel 789-3030 (family program).

National Museum of African Art
950 Independence Ave, SW. **Map** 3 C4.
Tel 633-1000.
www.nmafa.si.edu

National Museum of American History
Constitution Ave between 12th & 14th Sts, NW. **Map** 3 B4.
Tel 633-1000.

National Museum of the American Indian
4th St & Independence Ave, SW. **Map** 4 D4.
Tel 633-1000.
www.americanindian.si.edu

National Museum of Natural History
10th St & Constitution Ave, NW. **Map** 3 C4.
Tel 633-1000 (general information).
Tel 633-4629 (IMAX® film schedule).

National Postal Museum
2 Massachusetts Ave, NE.
Map 4 E3.
Tel 633-1000.

CHILDREN'S THEATER

Adventure Theatre
7300 MacArthur Blvd, Glen Echo Park, Md.
Tel (301) 634-2270.

Discovery Theater
1100 Jefferson Drive, SW.
Map 3 C4.
Tel 633-8700.
www.discoverytheater.org

Imagination Stage
4908 Auburn Ave, Bethesda, MD
Tel (301) 718-9521.
www.imaginationstage.org

Wolf Trap Farm Park for the Performing Arts
1551 Trap Rd, Vienna, VA.
Tel (703) 255-1900.
www.wolftrap.org

A LITTLE BIT OF HISTORY

Ford's Theatre
511 10th St, NW.
Map 3 C3.
Tel 347-4833.
www.fordstheatre.org

Frederick Douglass National Historic Site
1411 W St, SE.
Tel 426-5961.

Washington National Cathedral
Massachusetts & Wisconsin Aves, NW.
Tel 537-2934 (Gargoyle tour).
www.cathedral.org

SHOPPING

National Museum of Natural History Shops
Constitution Ave between 12th and 14th Sts, NW.
Map 3 C4.
Tel 633-2060.

SURVIVAL
GUIDE

PRACTICAL INFORMATION

Destination
DC logo

Washington, DC is the heart of the American political world. It is a visitor-friendly place, especially for children and the disabled, since wheelchair accessibility is required almost everywhere, and most museums (including all under the Smithsonian umbrella *see pp98–101*) are free. The whole city shuts down on federal holidays, as well as anytime the government requires it to. With the US President and other world leaders coming and going, unexpected delays and closures can occur. Spring and fall are the best times to visit as the summers can be very hot and winters very cold.

Entrance to the White House Visitor Center

VISAS AND PASSPORTS

Citizens of the UK, most western European countries, Canada, Japan, Australia, and New Zealand, need a valid passport and a return ticket to enter the US, and must register with the online Electronic System of Travel Authorization (ESTA) before departure. Visit https://esta.cbp.dhs.gov to obtain the ESTA; there is a small charge but it is valid for two years. Entry requirements may change – be sure to check before you travel. Citizens of all other countries require a valid passport and a tourist visa. Be aware that anyone entering the US on a visa will be photographed and have their fingerprints checked.

All visitors should carry photo identification at all times. Expect that your possessions will be checked before entering museums and some places, like the Library of Congress, have metal detectors.

TOURIST INFORMATION

The Washington area is very welcoming to tourists. Visitor information desks at the airports will provide guides and maps, and staff will be able to answer questions. Major hotels usually have a knowledgeable guest services desk. Before you travel it may be worth contacting the **Destination DC** tourist office. The website provides information on special offers, local events, and free things to do.

OPENING HOURS

Most banks and offices in DC are open from 9am to 5pm, Monday through Friday. Some banks are also open on a Saturday morning *(see p214)*. Malls or department stores are open daily and have extended hours on a certain day of the week. Stores rarely close for federal holidays; in fact, many federal holidays are big shopping days with special sales.

All Smithsonian Museums are open on federal holidays. Some private museums, like the Phillips Collection, are closed on Mondays. Many gas stations, convenience stores and select pharmacies *(see p213)* stay open 24 hours.

TAXES AND TIPPING

Taxes will be added to hotel and restaurant charges, theater tickets, some grocery and store sales, and most other purchases. Be sure to ask whether the tax is included in the price displayed. Sales tax is 5.75 percent, hotel tax is 14.5 percent, with 10 percent tax on food and beverages.

Tipping is expected for most services: in restaurants tip 15–20 percent of the bill, give $2 per bag to airport and hotel porters, and $2 to valet parking attendants. Bartenders expect 50 cents to $1 per drink; if you visit a hair salon or barbershop, 15 to 20 percent of the bill should suffice.

ALCOHOL AND CIGARETTES

The legal minimum age for drinking alcohol in Washington is 21, and you will need photo identification (I.D.) as proof of your age in order to purchase alcohol and be allowed into bars. It is illegal to drink alcohol in public parks or to carry an open container of alcohol in your car, and penalties for driving under the influence of alcohol are severe. Cigarettes can be purchased by those over 18 years old; proof of age will be required. Smoking is prohibited in all public buildings, bars, restaurants, and stores.

Standard US
two-prong plug

ELECTRICITY

Electricity flows at the standard US 110–120 volts, and a two-prong plug is required. For non-US appliances you will need a plug adapter and a voltage converter.

International Student Identity Card, accepted as I.D. in America

STUDENT TRAVELERS

While students from abroad should purchase an International Student Identiy Card (**ISIC**) before traveling to Washington, they may not use it often as many sights have free entry. Paying museums such as the Phillips Collection give a $2 discount on their regular admission. The ISIC handbook lists places and services in the US that offer discounts to card holders, including accommodations, museums, and theaters. The **Student Advantage Card** is available to all American college undergraduates and offers a range of discounts.

SENIOR TRAVELERS

Senior citizens are eligible for certain discounts with the appropriate proof of age. Amtrak gives a discount of 15 percent for persons over 62 on most trains (not valid for business or first class). Many movie theaters give reduced admission (usually $1 off the regular price) to those aged 60 or over. Most private museums offer a senior's discount similar to the student discount.

The **American Association of Retired Persons** is open to the over-50s. Members qualify for discounts of 5–30 percent on tours, hotels, and travel.

DISABLED TRAVELERS

Washington is a model of accessibility and almost all public buildings, including most hotels and restaurants, are required to be wheelchair accessible. Streets have curb cuts and there are elevators at all Metro stations. The exceptions are historic areas like Georgetown, where 18th-century buildings and cobblestone streets make using a wheelchair problematic. For general advice, contact the **Society for Accessible Travel and Hospitality**.

GAY AND LESBIAN TRAVELERS

In 2009, Washington, DC passed a gay marriage act – one of the few places in the US to recognize same-sex union. The city's lively gay scene centers around Dupont Circle and the adjacent 17th, 14th, and P Streets. The **Human Rights Campaign Headquarters** is home to the national organization for gay rights.

RESPONSIBLE TOURISM

Like many places in the US, Washington, DC is increasingly aware of environmental issues. Visitors can be assured that most public organizations and many restaurants recycle their trash and, in 2009, the city enacted a law charging 5 cents for every plastic and paper bag given at grocery stores.

Local and organic produce are widely available, especially at weekend markets such as the Eastern Market on Capitol Hill (10am–5pm Sat & Sun) and the Dupont Circle Farmers' Market (9am–1pm Sun). The mother of the organic food movement in eastern USA is Nora's *(see p192)*.

Many hotel chains touting their green credentials have representatives in DC, including Fairmont Hotels *(see p176)*, cited as the best hotel chain by treehugger.com.

Local produce on sale at the Eastern Market

DIRECTORY

EMBASSIES

Australia
1601 Massachusetts Ave, NW. **Map** 2 F2
Tel 797-3000.
www.usa.embassy.gov.au

Canada
501 Pennsylvania Ave, NW.
Map 4 D3.
Tel 682-1740.
www.canadainternational.gc.ca/washington

Ireland
2234 Massachusetts Ave, NW. **Map** 3 A1.
Tel 462-3939.
www.irelandemb.org

New Zealand
37 Observatory Circle, NW.
Tel 328-4800.
www.nzembassy.com/usa

United Kingdom
3100 Massachusetts Ave, NW. *Tel* 588-6500.
www.britainusa.com

TOURIST INFORMATION

Destination DC
901 7th Street, NW.
Map 4 D2.
Tel (202) 289-7000.
www.washington.org

STUDENT TRAVELERS

ISIC
www.isic.org

Student Advantage Card
www.studentadvantage.com

SENIOR TRAVELERS

American Association for Retired Persons
601 E St. NW. **Map** 4 D3.
Tel 888-687-2277.
www.aarp.org

DISABLED TRAVELERS

Society for Accessible Travel and Hospitality
Tel (212) 447-7284.
www.sath.org

GAY AND LESBIAN TRAVELERS

Human Rights Campaign Headquarters
1640 Rhode Island Ave, NW.
www.hrc.org

Personal Security and Health

Park police badge

Although as in any major city there is crime, Washington has made great efforts in reducing problems and cleaning up its streets, and with success. If you stick to the tourist areas and avoid straying into outlying areas, you should not run into any trouble. The main sights are located in safe areas where there are lots of people, and serious crime is rare. When visiting sights off the beaten track, take a taxi to and from the destination. Most importantly, pay attention to your surroundings.

LAW ENFORCEMENT

There are nine different police forces in Washington, including the secret service, S.W.A.T. (Special Weapons and Tactics) teams, and the more typical M.P.D.C. (Metropolitan Police, Washington, DC) police.

Because the city is home to the President, whenever he travels, members of the law enforcement agencies follow. When foreign political leaders visit, the police are even more visible than usual: you will see them on horseback, on bicycles, in cars, and even on top of buildings.

As a visitor, should you encounter any trouble, approach any of the blue-uniformed M.P.D.C. officers that regularly patrol the city streets. All M.P.D.C officers carry weapons.

The DC police are well-known for their strict interpretation of the law. In other words: don't talk back, don't argue and never offer money in the form of a bribe; this could land you in jail.

At monuments you will see green-uniformed Park Rangers. Their role is largely crowd control and as a source of information; many are trained historians.

WHAT TO BE AWARE OF

Serious crime is rarely witnessed in the main sightseeing areas of Washington. However, avoid wandering into areas that you have no reason to visit, either during the day or at night. Pickpockets do operate in the city and will target anyone who looks like a tourist. Police officers regularly patrol the tourist areas, but it is still advisable to prepare the day's itinerary in advance, use common sense, and stay alert. Try not to advertise that you are a tourist; study your map before you set off, avoid wearing expensive jewellery, and carry your camera or camcorder securely. Carry small amounts of cash; credit cards are a more secure option. Keep these close to your body in a money belt or inside pocket.

Before you leave home, make a photocopy of your important documents, including your passport and visa, and keep them with you, though separate from the originals. Also make a note of your credit card numbers, in case of theft or loss. Keep an eye on your belongings at all times, whether you are checking into or out of a hotel, standing in the airport, or sitting in a restaurant. It is a good idea to put any valuables in the hotel safe – do not carry them around with you. Most hotels will

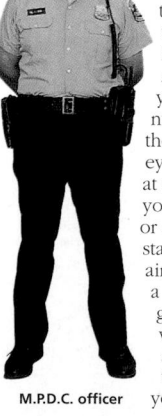

M.P.D.C. officer

not guarantee the security of any belongings that you leave in your room.

IN AN EMERGENCY

Call 911 for police or fire assistance. If you are involved in a medical emergency, go to a hospital emergency room. Should you need an ambulance, call 911 and one will be sent.

LOST AND STOLEN PROPERTY

Although the chances of retrieving lost or stolen property are slim, you should report all stolen items to the police. Call the **Police Non-Emergency Line** for guidance. Make sure you keep a copy of the police report, which you will need when making your insurance claim.

In case of loss, it is useful to have a list of serial numbers or a photocopy of all documents; keep these separate as proof of possession. If you can remember to do so, it is useful to make a mental note of the taxi company or bus route you use; it might make it easier to retrieve lost items.

If your passport is lost or stolen, get in touch with your country's embassy or consulate *(see p211)*. If you lose your credit card, most card companies have toll-free numbers for reporting a loss or theft *(see p215)*.

Hospital sign

HOSPITALS AND PHARMACIES

It is possible to visit a doctor or dentist without being regis-tered with them, but you will be asked to pay in advance. Keep all receipts for medical costs to make a claim on your insurance later. Depending on the limitations of your insur-ance, it is better to avoid the overcrowded city-owned hospitals and opt instead for one of the private hospitals. If taken by ambulance, however, drivers are required to take you to the nearest hospital. If you require a dentist you can

Police Car

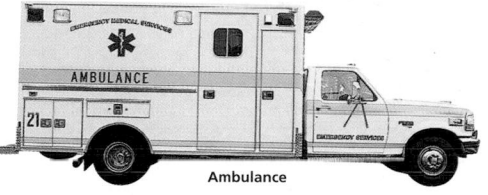

Ambulance

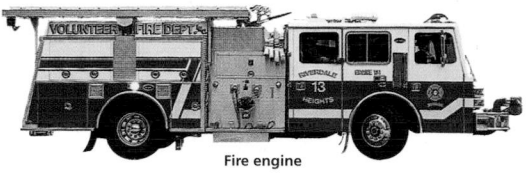

Fire engine

call the **District of Columbia Dental Society**, which provides a free referral service.

Pharmacists are usually able to offer basic medical advice and there are some pharmacies with clinics attached to treat common illnesses and small injuries. Patients are seen by nurse practitioners or physician assistants. One such clinic is the **CVS Minute Clinic**, which has one location in DC, and several in the Virginia and Maryland suburbs.

If you need a prescription dispensed, there are plenty of pharmacies in and around the city, some staying open 24 hours. Ask your hotel for the nearest one. CVS is the most common pharmacy chain.

TRAVEL AND HEALTH INSURANCE

It is strongly recommended to obtain travel insurance before traveling to the United States. It is particularly important to have insurance for emergency medical and dental care, which can be very expensive in the States. Even with medical cover you may have to pay for the services, then make a claim for reimbursement with your insurance company. Should you go to a hospital or seek medical assistance take proof of insurance with you. If you take medication, bring a back-up prescription.

It is advisable to make sure your personal property is insured and to obtain cover for lost or stolen baggage and travel documents, as well as trip cancellation fees, legal advice, and accidental death or injury.

LEGAL ASSISTANCE

Non-US citizens requiring legal assistance should call their embassy *(see p211)*. Embassies will not lend you money but can help with advice on legal matters in emergencies. Should you be arrested for any reason, it is advisable to be cooperative, but you have the right to remain silent.

RESTROOMS

Washington, DC does not have public restrooms. There are free bathrooms available in all visitor's centers, museums, and galleries, and all hotels and restaurants also have restrooms, but they may only be available to paying customers.

DIRECTORY

IN AN EMERGENCY

Police, Fire, Medical (all emergencies)
Tel Call 911,
or dial 0 for the operator.

LOST AND STOLEN PROPERTY

Police Non-Emergency Line
Tel 311.

HOSPITALS AND PHARMACIES

Area Hospitals
Tel Call 411 for directory assistance.

CVS 24-Hour Pharmacy
1199 Vermont Ave, NW.
Map 3 B2.
Tel 628-0720.
6 Dupont Circle, NW.
Map 2 F2.
Tel 785-1466.

CVS Minute Clinic
845 Bladensburg Road, NE.
Tel (020) 397-2600.

DC Dental Society
Tel 547-7613
www.dcdental.org

George Washington University Hospital
(Private.) 900 23rd Street, NW.
Map 2 E3.
Tel (202) 715-4000

Georgetown University Hospital
(Private.) 3800 Reservoir Road, NW. **Map** 1 B2.
Tel (202) 444-2000
Medical Referral Services
Tel 342-2400.

Washington Hospital Center
(Private.) 110 Irving Street, NW.
Tel (202) 877-7000

Logo for CVS pharmacies, a common pharmacy chain in Washington, DC

Banking and Currency

Throughout Washington there are various places to access and exchange your money, from banks to cash machines to bureaux de change. The most important thing to remember is not to carry all your money and credit cards with you at once, and to be prepared to use ATM machines on Sunday when most banks and currency exchange offices are closed.

DIRECTORY

MAIN BANKS

Bank of America
700 13th Street, NW.
Map 3 B3. **Tel** *(202) 624-5090.*
www.bankofamerica.com

Chevy Chase Bank
701 Pennsylvania Avenue, NW.
Map 3 C3. **Tel** *(202) 737-4950.*
www.chevychasebank.com

Sun Trust Bank
1445 New York Ave, NW.
Map 3 B3. **Tel** *879-6000.*
Tel *(888) 786 8787.*
www.suntrust.com

TD Bank
1753 Connecticut Ave, NW.
Tel *888-751-9000*
www.tdbank.com

FOREIGN EXCHANGE

American Express Travel Service
1501 K St, NW. **Map** 2 F2.
Tel *457-1300.*

Thomas Cook/Travelex
Tel *872-1233 (general information.)*
www.travelex.com
Branch at:
1800 K St, NW.
Map 3 A2. **Tel** *872-1428.*

LOST OR STOLEN CARDS

American Express
Tel *800-528-4800.*

MasterCard
Tel *800-826-2181.*

Visa
Tel *800-847-2911.*

WIRING MONEY

MoneyGram
Tel *(202) 547-5197.*
www.moneygram.com

Western Union
Tel *800-325-6000.*
www.westernunion.com

BANKS AND FOREIGN EXCHANGE

Generally, most banks are open Monday through Friday from 9am to 3pm, although some may close later, and Saturday mornings from 9am to noon or 1pm. Most banks are closed on Sundays and federal holidays *(see p39)*. The exception is **TD Bank**, which has many branches with Sunday hours and is open on federal holidays.

Always ask if there are any special fees before you make your transaction. At most banks, traveler's checks in US dollars can be cashed with any photo identification, although passports are usually required to exchange foreign currency.

Foreign currency exchange is available at the main branches of large banks or at independent exchange offices. Among the best known are **American Express Travel Service** and **Thomas Cook/Travelex**, both of which have branches in and around DC. Exchange offices are

American Express credit cards

ATMS

Automated teller machines (ATMs) are found all over the Washington area, usually near the entrance to banks, or inside many convenience stores and supermarkets. Widely accepted bank cards include Cirrus, Plus, Maestro, NYCE, and credit cards such as VISA or MasterCard. Note that a fee may be levied on your withdrawal (a pop-up screen should tell you the fee and ask if you want the transaction to continue). To minimize the risk of robbery, use ATMs in well-lit, populated areas only. Avoid withdrawing money at night or in isolated areas, and be aware of the people around you.

CREDIT AND DEBIT CARDS

American Express, VISA, MasterCard/Maestro, and most international debit cards are widely accepted almost everywhere in Washington,

generally open weekdays from 9am to 5pm. Most exchange offices charge a fee or commission, so it is worth looking around to get the best value rates. Many major hotels can also change currency, but they often charge a higher rate of exchange or commission.

ATM for Chevy Chase Bank, one of the popular banks in DC

from theaters and hotels to restaurants and shops. Indeed, it is advisable to carry a credit card when visiting Washington as it may be required to reserve a hotel or rental car and to pay for gasoline (petrol), especially at self-service stations.

If your credit card is lost or stolen, contact your card company immediately.

CARD SECURITY

Because of the increasing problem of identity theft and card cloning, merchants may ask for photo identification when making a purchase.

If you are traveling overseas, alert your bank of your plans, or they may put a hold on your account if they see untoward charges.

EMERGENCY FUNDS (WIRING MONEY)

MoneyGram and **Western Union** both offer immediate money transfer for a fee. Both sender and recipient will need to locate an agent to set up the transfer and collect the funds (Western Union also has an online facility for sending funds.)

Coins

American coins come in 1-dollar, 50-, 25-, 10-, 5-, and 1-cent pieces. There are also goldtone $1 coins in circulation and State quarters, which feature an historical scene on one side. Each coin has a popular name: 25-cent pieces are called quarters, 10-cent pieces are called dimes, 5-cent pieces are called nickels, and 1-cent pieces called pennies.

1-cent coin
(a penny)

5-cent coin
(a nickel)

10-cent coin
(a dime)

25-cent coin
(a quarter)

An American Eagle
on a $1 gold coin

Bills (Bank Notes)

The units of currency in the United States are dollars and cents. There are 100 cents to a dollar. Bank notes come in the following denominations: $1, $5, $10, $20, $50, and $100. Security features include subtle color hues and improved color-shifting ink in the lower right hand corner of the face of each note.

1-dollar bill ($1)

5-dollar bill ($5)

10-dollar bill ($10)

20-dollar bill ($20)

50 dollar bill ($50)

100-dollar bill ($100)

Communications and Media

US Mail stamp

The almost universal use of cell phones has caused the demise of coin-operated pay phones. It is now difficult to find a public pay phone in the street, although they are still available at main stations. Like most major cities, Washington, DC is thoroughly wired for Internet access. Free Wi-Fi is provided in many public places and there are several other ways to get online. Since Washington, DC is the political capital of the United States, news is readily available from newspapers, magazines, television, and radio.

CELL PHONES

Cell phone service in Washington is generally excellent. If you are coming from overseas and want to guarantee that your cell phone will work, make sure you have a quad-band phone. Tri-band phones from outside the US are also usually compatible but, because the US uses two frequency bands itself, it is recommended to contact your service provider for clarification before you travel; you may also need to activate the "roaming" facility.

Other options include buying a prepaid cell phone in the US or a SIM chip for a US carrier. Many car rental companies also rent cell phones for customers (see p223).

PUBLIC TELEPHONES

In the last decade, the number of public pay phones in the United States has decreased by half and Washington is no exception. However, public pay phones are still available at Union Station, the Smithsonian Museums, and some Metro stations, and occasionally on the street. The area code for Washington is 202. When dialing within the district, omit the code. When dialing outside the district from within DC, you will need to use the appropriate area code. The area code for the Maryland suburbs is 301 and for the Virginia suburbs, 703.

Credit card calls can be made by calling 1-800-CALL-ATT. Directory Assistance is 411 and calls are charged at the local rate. Phone cards of various values can be purchased from most supermarkets, 24-hour stores, newspaper stands, and some branches of Western Union.

TELEPHONE CHARGES

Local calls cost around 50 cents for 3 minutes from pay phones. Calls made from hotel rooms will cost much more, so it is a good idea to locate a pay phone or use your cell. Operator assistance can also be used to help you connect your call, but again, this will cost more.

INTERNET ACCESS

Although Internet cafés are rare in Washington, many public places – such as book-stores, cafés, and airports – have a free wireless service. Most hotels in the city have wireless Internet throughout their rooms and many also have a dedicated business center (with computers) within the hotel. For those without their own laptop, computers (with Internet) are available for use in public libraries and in stores such as FedEx, DHL, and UPS.

Using the Internet in the reading room of a Washington public library

POSTAL SERVICE

Post offices are open from 9am to 5pm, Mondays through Fridays, and have limited Saturday service, usually 9am to noon. Post offices are closed on all federal holidays. Stamps can also be bought from most major supermarkets such as Giant and Safeway.

If the correct postage is affixed, you can send a letter by putting it in one of the blue mailboxes found on street corners all over Washington. Times of mail pickup are written inside the mailbox's lid; there are usually several collections a day. It is mandatory to use a five-digit zip code when sending mail. Be aware that small packages may not be posted in mailboxes for security reasons; they must be taken to a post office.

> ### USEFUL DIALING CODES
>
> - To make a direct-dial call outside the local area code, but within the US and Canada, dial 1 before the area code. Useful area codes for DC and the surrounding area include: Baltimore 410; MD 301, 240; Delaware 302; Northern Virginia 703; West Virginia 304.
> - For international direct-dial calls, dial 011 followed by the appropriate country code. Then dial the area code, omitting the first 0, and the local number.
> - To make an international call via the operator, dial 00; note that the call will be charged at a higher rate.
> - For international operator assistance, dial 01.
> - For local operator assistance, dial 0.
> - For international directory inquiries, dial 00.
> - For local directory inquiries, dial 411.
> - For emergency police, fire, or ambulance services, dial 911.
> - 1-800 and 888 indicate a toll-free number.

Depending on how far the mail needs to travel in the US, it can take from one to five days to arrive at its destination. The most economical way to send international mail is First Class International at less than $1 per ounce, depending on the destination. Express and Priority mail are also available at the post office for a faster, though more expensive, service. If you are a visitor to the city and you wish to receive mail, poste restante, you can have it sent to you by addressing it care of "General Delivery" at the **Main Post Office**, or any other main post office, quoting the city name. They will hold the mail for 30 days for you to collect.

It is worth noting that USPS refers to the United States Postal Service, while UPS is a private courier company.

US mailbox

COURIER SERVICES

Courier services are a popular, if more expensive, alternative to the postal service. Many hotels will arrange for your packages and letters to be shipped either by Federal Express (**FedEx**), **DHL**, a division of Deutsche Poste, or **UPS**. DHL only operates internationally while Federal Express and UPS handle both national

Newspaper vendor

and international letters and packages. FedEx services are available at Fedex Office Centers (easily recognizable by the FedEx arrow logo); DHL is offered at independent office storefront locations like Parcel Plus. FedEx and UPS also have self-service kiosks throughout the city for letters and flat packages. Registration for self-service packages is completed online, and a label downloaded to attach to the package.

TELEVISION AND RADIO

Televisions are everywhere in the United States, from bars and restaurants to hotels and stores. Most have cable hook-up, allowing access to more than 60 different channels. Some of the best to view are CBS, NBC, CNN, ABC, and Fox. For those interested in the political goings-on in the city, tune in to channels C Span 1 and C-Span 2 to watch the proceedings in Congress as they are broadcast live.

Radios can be found in most hotel rooms, as well as in rental cars, and offer a wide range of music, from country through classical and jazz to rock. Popular radio stations include National Public Radio (WAMU at 88.5), modern rock on WHFS (99.1), and soft rock on Easy 101 (101).

NEWSPAPERS

The most widely read newspaper in the DC area is the *Washington Post*, which is also one of the best newspapers published in the country. The local *Washington Times* is widely available as are *USA Today*, *The Wall Street Journal*, and *The New York Times*. Newspapers can be bought from street dispensers (boxes on the sidewalk that dispense newspapers), newsstands, gas stations, convenience stores, hotel lobbies, and bookstores. They are also all available online. Newsstands and some bookstores carry newspapers from most large US cities and many foreign countries.

DIRECTORY

POSTAL SERVICES

Georgetown Station
3050 K St, NW.
Map 2 D2

Main Post Office
Brentwood Station, 900 Brentwood Road, NE, Washington, DC 20066.

Martin Luther King Jr. Station
1400 L St, NW.
Map 2 F3

National Capitol Station
2 Massachusetts Ave, NE.
Map 4 E3.

Temple Heights Station
1921 Florida Ave, NW.
Map 2 E1.

COURIER SERVICES

DHL
Branches all over the DC area.
For customer services call:
Tel (800) 225-5345.
www.dhl.com

FedEx
Branches all over the DC area.
For customer services call:
Tel (800) 463-3339.
www.fedex.com

UPS
Branches all over the DC area.
For the nearest branch call:
Tel (800) 275-8777.
www.ups.com

WASHINGTON TIME

Washington is on Eastern Standard Time. Daylight Saving Time begins on the second Sunday in March, when clocks are set ahead 1 hour, and ends on the first Sunday in November, when clocks go back 1 hour.

City and Country	Hours + or – EST	City and Country	Hours + or – EST
Chicago (US)	−1	Moscow (Russia)	+8
Dublin (Ireland)	+5	Paris (France)	+6
London (UK)	+5	Sydney (Australia)	+15
Los Angeles (US)	−3	Tokyo (Japan)	+14
Madrid (Spain)	+6	Vancouver (Canada)	−3

TRAVEL INFORMATION

Washington is easy to get to via any mode of transportation. Three airports serve the DC area; they are used by most major airlines for domestic and international flights. Two major bus lines also operate to the city,

United Airlines plane

as do Amtrak trains, which arrive at and depart from Union Station, right in the center of Washington. Visitors often tend to travel first to DC, base themselves in the city, and then arrange day or weekend trips into Maryland and Virginia.

Glass-walled interior of Reagan National Airport

ARRIVING BY AIR

There are three main airports in the Washington, DC area: **Dulles International Airport**, **Reagan National Airport**, and Baltimore-Washington International Thurgood Marshall Airport (known as **BWI**). Most of the major carriers, including American Airlines, British Airways, Air France, and United Airlines, fly to at least one of these airports. The majority of international and overseas flights land at Dulles International, 26 miles (42 km) west of Washington in Virginia. Dulles is not directly served by a Metro but there is a connecting shuttle service, the **Washington Flyer Coach**

Service, to take new arrivals to West Falls Church Metro. Between the coach service and the Metro, expect to spend up to an hour-and-a-half to reach the city center. Alternatively, the **SuperShuttle** share-ride bus service runs every hour and will drop passengers at their door. It is a cheaper option than a taxi but journey times depend on detours made to drop off the other passengers. Taxis are plentiful and are the quickest but most expensive option. Make sure the fare is negotiated before departure.

Located about 5 miles (8 km) outside the city in Arlington County, Virginia, the Reagan National Airport is the most convenient airport for central Washington. The city is easily accessible using the Metro, or by taking the SuperShuttle (every 30 minutes), or a taxi.

BWI Airport, which is situated 30 miles (48 km) northeast of DC, tends to be used by low-cost airlines. The Maryland Rail Commuter Service (**MARC**) is the cheapest way to get from the airport to the city, but it runs only on

weekdays. Amtrak *(see p219)* offers the next-best train service for just a few dollars more. The SuperShuttle is also available from BWI, but it is more costly and takes longer than a train ride. The taxi fare from BWI into central DC is rather expensive.

For security reasons, anyone arriving in the US on a visa is now photographed, and will have their fingerprints taken, before being allowed into the country *(see p210)*.

AIR FARES

The busiest season for travel to the US is March through June and September through early November. Christmas and Thanksgiving are also busy. Flights will be at their most expensive during these periods. Flights in June and July are usually the most expensive but there are many discounted accommodations at this time. Weekend flights are usually less expensive than weekdays, while Apex tickets are often the best deal. Apex tickets must be booked at least one week in advance, and

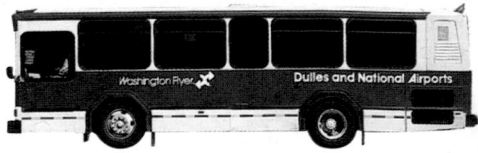

The Washington Flyer, shuttling from Dulles to West Falls Church Metro

AIRPORT	ℹ INFORMATION	DISTANCE/TIME TO WASHINGTON, DC	TAXI FARE	SUPERSHUTTLE
Dulles	(703) 572-2700	26 miles (42 km) 40 minutes	$50–5	$26–35
Reagan National	(703) 417-8000	5 miles (8 km) 15 minutes	$15–20	$13–23
BWI	(800) 435-9294	30 miles (48 km) 50 minutes	$62–5	$32–42

Main concourse at Union Station

your visit must include a Saturday night. Cheap air fares can be obtained by shopping around, so it is worth checking with the airlines and websites such as **Expedia**, **Kayak**, and **Priceline**.

ARRIVING BY TRAIN

Amtrak is one of the best ways to travel to the DC area. Trains from other cities arrive in Washington at Union Station. Trains are also available from Union Station to Baltimore, Philadelphia, Richmond, and Williamsburg. Amtrak offers a deluxe train service to New York City, called the Acela, which travels slightly faster and more comfortably than the regular train, but is more expensive. Trains (either the Acela or the slower Northeast Regional) to New York leave every hour. Another rail service is **MARC**, Maryland's commuter train, which departs on weekdays to Baltimore.

ARRIVING BY CAR

The center of Washington, DC is surrounded by Interstates I-95 and I-495, which together form the congested Capital Beltway. Driving on the Beltway, especially during rush hour, can be intimidating for the inexperienced driver. Interstate I-66 connects Washington to West Virginia, and Interstate I-50 heads east from DC to Annapolis, Maryland, and the surrounding areas. Beyond the Beltway, Interstate I-95 goes north toward Baltimore, Philadelphia, and New York. Interstate I-270 heads north to Frederick, Maryland.

ARRIVING BY BUS

Intercity buses are a great, economical way to get to Washington. As well as the traditional **Greyhound** buses, there are half a dozen bus companies serving DC, including **Megabus**, **Bolt Bus**, **Vamoose**, and the **Washington Deluxe**. Many are equipped with restrooms, free Wi-Fi, power outlets, and even DVD players. Tickets are sold on a scale – one-way to New York is generally about $25, but may be as little as $1 with advance purchase.

Greyhound buses depart from the bus terminal near Union Station, but many of the other bus companies leave from more central locations.

Greyhound bus, an inexpensive way to see the whole country

DIRECTORY

ARRIVING BY AIR

BWI Airport
Linthicum, MD.
Tel (410) 859-7111 or (800) I-FLY-BWI.
Lost & Found
Tel (410) 859-7387
www.bwiairport.com

Dulles International Airport
Chantilly, VA.
Tel (703) 572-2700.
Lost & Found
Tel (703) 572-8479
www.metwash airports.com

Reagan National Airport
Arlington, VA.
Tel (703) 417-8000.
Lost & Found
Tel (703) 417-8560

www.metwash airports.com

SuperShuttle
Tel (800) 258-3826 or (800) BLUE-VAN.
www.supershuttle.com

Washington Flyer Coach Service
Tel (888) 927-4359 or (888) WASH-FLY.
www.washfly.com

AIR FARES

Expedia
Tel (800) 551 2534.
www.Expedia.com

Kayak
www.kayak.com

Priceline
Tel (800) 774-2354.
www.priceline.com

ARRIVING BY TRAIN

Amtrak
Union Station,
50 Massachusetts Ave, NE.
Tel 906-3000 or (800) USA-RAIL.
www.amtrak.com

MARC
Tel (410) 539-5000 or (866) RIDE-MTA.
www.mtamaryland.com

ARRIVING BY BUS

2000 New Century Travel
Tel (202) 798-8222
www.2000coach.com

Bolt Bus
Tel 1-877-265-8287.
www.boltbus.com

C2NY
Tel (202) 332-2691
www.dc2ny.com

Greyhound Busline
Tel (800) 231-2222 or (800) 289-5160.
www.greyhound.com

Megabus
Tel 1-877-462-6342
www.megabus.com

Vamoose
Tel 1-877-393-2828
www.vamoosebus.com

Washington Deluxe
Tel 1-866-287-6932 or 1-718-387-7523
www.washny.com

Getting Around Washington, DC

Washington has a very comprehensive public transportation system. Visitors and locals alike find that it is easier to get around by public transportation than by car, especially as they do not then have the aggravation of finding a much-coveted parking space. All the major tourist attractions in the capital are accessible on foot, by Metrorail, by Metrobus, or by taxi.

Busy night-time traffic in central Washington, DC

GREEN TRAVEL

With such an excellent public transportation system, it is easy to get around Washington, DC without causing undue harm to the environment. Almost every tourist sight is accessible via public transportation. Furthermore, Metrobus runs a fleet of buses powered by Compressed Natural Gas (CNG), a cleaner alternative to gasoline (petrol).

Cycling has become an increasingly popular way to travel in Washington and there is an excellent network of cycle lanes throughout the center. Cycling has been further encouraged with the introduction of the SmartBike self-hire scheme *(see p221)*.

If it is necessary to use a taxi, visitors can encourage green practices by requesting a "hybrid" taxi, powered by a combination of battery and gasoline, although these cabs are not always available. If using a taxi in the Virginia suburbs, **Envirocab** runs an all-hybrid fleet. They are not licensed to operate in the District, however.

All car rental companies offer hybrid cars, but with limited availability. Book ahead to make sure your request is considered.

GETTING YOUR BEARINGS

It is important to know that the city is made up of four quadrants: northeast (NE), northwest (NW), southeast (SE), and southwest (SW), with the US Capitol at the central point. Every address in DC includes the quadrant code (NE, and so on) and, with building numbers running into the thousands on the same street in each quadrant, its use is necessary to distinguish the location.

A useful tip for when you are first trying to find your way around the city is to remember that most numbered streets run North and South, and most lettered streets run East and West. However, be aware that there is no "J," "X," "Y," or "Z" Street, and that "I" Street is often written as "Eye" Street.

WALKING

Washington is a terrific city for walking, as long as you wear comfortable shoes and keep your wits about you. Many of the main sights are clustered around the Mall. In Georgetown, walking is the best way to soak up the atmosphere.

METRORAIL

A map of the Metrorail *(see back endpaper and City Map)* is one of the most important pieces of information visitors will need when trying to get around DC. The system takes some getting used to, and the instructions are in English only, so allow plenty of time when first using the Metrorail (or "Metro," as it is also called.)

The cost of the fare depends on the time and distance you wish to travel, and ranges from $1.35 to $3.90. Tickets, or "farecards," for single or multiple trips can be bought from vending machines. Coins and bills (but no bills over $20) can be used to pay the exact fare; or add more money if you wish to use the farecard again. Passengers need to swipe their farecards through the turnstile at the beginning and end of the trip. If there is any unused fare left at the final destination the ticket will be returned to you; if not, the ticket will be retained. You can top up tickets for further trips. Metrorail passes are on offer for one day ($8.40) and seven days' ($40.50) travel. These can be used to transfer from Metro to bus. For convenience, it may be worth purchasing a SmarTrip card. This is a plastic rechargeable farecard which can also be used on other modes of public transportation in DC.

Five Metrorail lines operate in downtown DC, with frequent services: the Orange Line; Blue Line; Red Line; Yellow Line; and Green Line. Trains run from 5:30am to midnight Monday through Thursday, from 5:30am to 3am on Friday and 7am to 3am on Saturday, and from 7am to midnight on Sunday. Trains run frequently (less than 10 minutes' wait) and, on board, stops are announced at every station. The entire system is accessible for wheelchairs. One warning: eating, drinking smoking or littering, on the Metro is grounds for arrest.

Metro sign

Washington, DC Metrobus

METROBUS

Metrobus is a fast, inexpensive way to get around. Fares can be paid either with exact change on boarding, with a SmarTrip card, or a Metrorail farecard pass (*see* Metrorail.) The standard, off-peak fare is $1.45 (or $1.35 with SmarTrip). If paying with cash, there is a 25 cent charge for bus-to-bus transfers; if using SmarTrip, transfers are free within a 3-hour period. Up to two children under five can travel for free with a fare-paying passenger and there are discounts for disabled travelers and senior citizens. The **Circulator** bus links the main sights in the center and runs every 10 minutes. Fares are $1 for adults and 50 cents for kids.

Maps of all the bus routes are available in Metrorail stations, and maps of specific lines are posted at each bus stop.

Many Metrobuses are wheelchair accessible with a "kneeling" feature that lowers the bus for the disabled rider.

TAXIS

Taxis can usually be hailed from the street corner of major arteries, but if you need to be somewhere at a specific time it is advisable to book. The DC Taxi Cab Commission will provide names of cab companies. Taxi fares in DC are operated using time and distance meters. Passengers should expect to pay a starting "drop" rate of $3, and then 25 cents for every one-sixth of a mile. Luggage, rush hour travel, and gas prices can all incur surcharges from 50 cents to $2, and each extra passenger costs $1.50. Be aware that drivers do not always know the way to addresses beyond the tourist center.

DRIVING AND PARKING IN THE CITY

Driving in DC need not be stressful as long as you avoid the rush hour (between 6:30 and 9:30am, and 4 and 7pm on weekdays.) During these times the direction of traffic flow can change, some roads become one way, and left turns may be forbidden to ease congestion. These changes are usually marked, but always pay close attention to the road. Curbside parking is hard to find at the more popular locations, and is illegal at rush hour in many areas. If using metered parking, it is important to keep within

the time limit; you could otherwise face a fine or risk being clamped. Parking restrictions on Sundays and public holidays are different from other days, so read the parking signs carefully.

Road sign

CYCLING

There is a great network of cycle paths in DC. Bike shops rent out bikes, and will be able to suggest routes. They can usually provide route maps. **Better Bikes** will deliver a rental bike to you for a cost of $25–50 per day. The city also has a pioneer **SmartBike** program, a self-service hire scheme where bikes can be rented from stations around the city. Users need to subscribe for an annual charge of $40 and are issued with a SmartBike user card.

GUIDED TOURS

There are many city bus tours available in DC. **Tourmobile Sightseeing** and **DC Tours** both offer a hop-on-hop-off sightseeing service with numerous pick-up points and extensive routes. For something a bit different, **Old Town Trolley Tours** offers a ride around the main sites in an old-fashioned trolley bus.

The company **Bike and Roll** offers a selection of bike tours in and around the city, including a 1-hour Early Bird Fun Ride and a 10-mile (16-km) Capital Sites Ride.

DIRECTORY

GREEN TRAVEL

Envirocab
Tel (703) 920-3333.
www.envirotaxicab.com

METRORAIL AND METROBUS

Metrorail and Metrobus
600 5th St, NW,
Washington, DC 20001.
Tel 637-7000.
Tel 638-3780 TTY.
www.wmata.com

Circulator
Tel 962-1423.
www.dccirculator.com

TAXIS

DC Taxi Cab Commission
Tel 645-6018.
http://dctaxi.dc.gov

Diamond Cab
Tel 387-6200.

Yellow Cab
Tel 544-1212.

CYCLING

Better Bikes
Tel 293-2080.
www.betterbikesinc.com

SmartBike
Tel 800-899-4449.
www.smartbikedc.com

GUIDED TOURS

Bike and Roll
Tel 866-736-8224.
www.bikeandroll.com

DC Tours
Tel 888-878-9870
www.dctours.us

Old Town Trolley Tours
Tel 888-910-8687.
www.trolleytours.com

Tourmobile Sightseeing
Union Station. **Map** 4 E3.
Tel (202) 554-5100.
www.tourmobile.com

Exploring Beyond Washington, DC

There is much to see beyond Washington's city limits, and traveling by car is easy with a good map. Many of the sights are reachable by public transportation, but it is generally easier and quicker to drive. Car rental is widely available but often expensive. Buses and trains are a cheaper alternative, but your choice of destinations may be more limited.

Driving along the scenic Skyline Drive *(see p165)*, Virginia

CAR RENTAL

To rent a car in the United States you must usually be at least 25 years old with a valid driving license and a clean driving record. All agencies require a major credit card. Damage and liability insurance is recommended just in case something unexpected should happen. It is advisable always to return the car with a full tank of gas; otherwise you will be required to pay the inflated fuel prices charged by the rental agencies. Most rental cars have automatic transmissions and power steering but you should confirm this in avance. Also, check for any pre-existing damage to the car and note this on your contract.

It is often less expensive to rent a vehicle at an airport, as car rental taxes are $2 a day more in the city. It is worth checking the offers of more than one company. Agencies with offices at the Washington airports include **Alamo**, **Avis**, **Budget**, and **Hertz**.

Road sign

RULES OF THE ROAD

The highway speed limit in the DC area is 55 mph (88 km/h) – much lower than in many European countries. In residential areas the speed limit ranges from 20 to 35 mph (32–48 km/h), and near schools it can be as low as 15 mph (24 km/h).

Roads are generally well-signed but it is still wise to plan your route ahead. It is important to obey the signs, especially "No U-turn" signs, or you risk getting a ticket. If you are pulled over by the police, be courteous or you risk facing an even greater fine.

In addition, all drivers are required to carry a valid drivers' license and be able to produce registration documents and insurance for their vehicle. Most foreign licenses are valid, but if your license is not in English, or does not have a photo ID, you must get an international driver's license. Many roads are surveyed by cameras that will issue a ticket even if you

are going just a few miles per hour over the speed limit. This is not limited to major arteries.

Interstate highways are abreviated on signs with a capital "I" followed by a number. Avoid the Capital Beltway (I-495) at rush hour.

GASOLINE (PETROL)

Gas comes in three grades – regular, super, and premium. There is an extra charge if an attendant serves you, but patrons can fill their own tanks at self-service pumps without incurring an extra fee. Most stations are exclusively self-service and only accept credit cards. Gas is generally cheap in the US.

BREAKDOWNS

In the unlucky event of a breakdown, the best course of action is to pull completely off the road and put on the hazard lights to alert other drivers that you are stationary. There are emergency phones along some of the major interstate highways, but in other situations breakdown services or even the police can be contacted from mobile phones. In case of breakdown, drivers of rental cars should contact their car rental company first.

Members of the American Automobile Association (AAA) can have their vehicle towed to the nearest service station to be fixed. For simple problems like a flat tire or a dead battery, the AAA will fix it or sell and install a new battery on site.

PARKING

Most of the major sights that lie beyond Washington have adequate parking for visitors, but there may be a charge to use the facility. In general it is good practice to read all parking notices carefully to avoid fines, being clamped, or being towed away. Do not park beside a fire hydrant, or you risk the car being towed.

Parking sign

TIPS AND SAFETY FOR DRIVERS

- Traffic drives on the right-hand side of the road.
- Seat belts are compulsory in front seats and suggested in the back; children under three must ride in a child seat in back.
- You can turn right at a red light as long as you first come to a complete stop, and if there are no signs that prohibit it. Be aware, however, that turning right on a red light is illegal in Virginia and will incur a fine.
- A flashing yellow light at an intersection means slow down, look for oncoming traffic, and proceed with caution.
- Passing (overtaking) is allowed on any multi-lane road, and you must pass on the left. On smaller roads safe passing places are indicated with a broken yellow line on your side of the double yellow line.
- Crossing a double-yellow line, either by U-turn or by passing the car in front, is illegal, and you will be charged a fine if caught.
- If a school bus stops, all traffic from both sides must stop completely and wait for the bus to drive off.

- Driving while intoxicated (DWI) is a punishable offense that incurs heavy fines or even a jail sentence. Do not drink if you plan to drive.
- Avoid driving at night if unfamiliar with the area. Washington's streets change from safe to dangerous in a single block, so it is better to take a taxi than your own car if you do not know where you are going.
- Single women should be especially careful driving in unfamiliar territory, day or night.
- Keep all doors locked when driving around.
- Do not stop in a rural area, or on an unlit block, if someone tries to get your attention. If a fellow driver points at your car, suggesting something is wrong, drive to the nearest gas station and get help. Do not get out of your car.
- Avoid sleeping in your car.
- Avoid short cuts and stay on well-traveled roads.
- Avoid looking at a map in a dark, unpopulated place. Drive to the nearest open store or gas station before pulling over.

BUS TOURS

Although Greyhound buses *(see p218)* do serve some towns beyond DC (such as Charlottesville and Richmond, with serveral departures daily), the easiest and most enjoyable way to see the sights by bus is on a private tour. Several companies offer bus tours of DC's historic surroundings. **Gray Line** takes you on the Black Heritage tour, to Gettysburg, Colonial Williamsburg, or Monticello;

Tourmobile's *(see p221)* destinations include Mount Vernon, the Frederick Douglass House, and Arlington Cemetery; DC Tours *(see p221)* organizes combination day trips covering Gettysburg, Mount Vernon, Arlington Cemetery, Alexandria Old Town, and Charlottesville. Most bus tours depart from Union Station.

TRAINS

Amtrak trains *(see p219)* travel from DC's central Union Station to New York City and most of the surrounding area, including Williamsburg, Richmond, and Baltimore. The MARC *(see p219)*, Maryland's commuter rail, also runs from DC to Baltimore on weekdays for a few dollars less.

DIRECTORY

CAR RENTAL

Alamo
Tel (877) 222-9075.
www.alamo.com

Avis
Tel (800) 331-1212.
www.avis.com

Budget
Tel (800) 527-0700.
www.budget.com

Hertz
Tel (800) 654-3131.
www.hertz.com

BREAKDOWNS

American Automobile Association (AAA)
701–15th St, NW,
Washington, DC 20005.
Washington office
Tel 481-6811
General breakdown assistance for members
Tel (800) 222-4357
www.aaa.com

BUS TOURS

Gray Line
Union Station,
50 Massachusetts Ave, NW.
Tel 289-1995 or 862-1400.
www.graylinedc.com

Tourmobile bus, one of many sightseeing tour buses available in DC

Street Finder Index

KEY TO THE STREET FINDER

Major sight	P Main parking lot	Synagogue
Minor sight	Tourist information office	Post office
Place of interest	Hospital with emergency room	Pedestrian street
Railroad station	Police station	Ferry terminal
M Metrorail station	Church	State boundary
Bus station	Mosque	DC quadrant boundary

KEY TO ABBREVIATIONS USED IN THE STREET FINDER

Ave	Avenue	NE	Northeast	SE	Southeast
DC	District of	NW	Northwest	St	Street/Saint
	Columbia	Pkwy	Parkway	SW	Southwest
Dr	Drive	Pl	Place	VA	Virginia

0 meters 300
0 yards 300
1:19,100

1st Street NE	4E4	14th Street NW	3B3	44th Street NW	1A2
1st Street NW	4E3	14th Street SW	3B5	45th Street NW	1A2
1st Street SE	4E5	15th Street NW	3B3		
1st Street SW	4E4	15th Street SW	3B4	**A**	
2nd Street NE	4F4	16th Road	1B4	A Street NE	4F4
2nd Street NW	4D3	16th Street North	1A4	A Street SE	4F4
2nd Street SE	4F5	16th Street NW	2F3	Arlington Boulevard	1A5
2nd Street SW	4D5	17th Street North	1A4	Arlington Memorial	
2nd Street SW	4E4	17th Street NW	2F3	Bridge SW	2D5
2nd Street SW	4E5	17th Street NW	3B2	Arlington Ridge Road	1C4
3rd Street NE	4F4	18th Street North	1B4	Avon Place NW	2D1
3rd Street NW	4D3	18th Street NW	2F4		
3rd Street SW	4D5	18th Street NW	3A3	**B**	
4th Street NE	4F1	19th Street NW	2F4		
4th Street NW	4D3	19th Street NW	3A3	Bancroft Street NW	2E1
4th Street SE	4F5	19th Street	1B4	Bates Street NW	4D1
4th Street SW	4D5	20th Road	1A4	Belmont Road NW	2D1
5th Street NE	4F1	20th Street NW	2E4	Brentwood NE	4F2
5th Street NW	4D3	20th Street NW	3A3		
5th Street SE	4F4	21st Road	1A3	**C**	
6th Street NE	4F4	21st Street North	1A3	C Street NE	4E3
6th Street NW	4F4	21st Street NW	2E4	C Street NW	3A3
6th Street SE	4F5	21st Street NW	3A3	C Street SE	4E5
6th Street SW	4D5	21st Street	1A3	C Street SW	3B5
7th Street NE	4F4	22nd Street NW	2E4	California Street NW	2D1
7th Street NW	3C3	22nd Street	1A3	Cambridge Place NW	2D2
7th Street SE	4F5	23rd Street NW	2E5	Canal Road NW	1A2
7th Street SW	3C5	24th Street NW	2E3	Canal Street NW	1C3
8th Street NE	4F4	25th Street NW	2D3	Cecil Place NW	1C3
8th Street NW	3C3	26th Street NW	2D3	Church Street NW	2F2
8th Street SE	4F5	27th Street NW	2D3	Church Street NW	3A1
9th Street NW	3C3	28th Street NW	2D2	Colonial Terrace	1B4
9th Street SW	3C5	29th Street NW	2D2	Columbia Road NW	2E1
10th Street NW	3C3	30th Street NW	2D2	Columbia Street NW	3C1
10th Street SW	3C5	31st Street NW	1C1	Connecticut	
11th Street NW	3C3	31st Street NW	2D2	Avenue NW	2E1
12th Street North	1B5	32nd Street NW	1C1	Connecticut	
12th Street NW	3C2	33rd Street NW	1C2	Avenue NW	3A1
12th Street SW	3C5	34th Street NW	1C2	Constitution	
13th Street SW	3C5	35th Street NW	1C2	Avenue NE	4F4
13th Street NW	3C3	36th Street NW	1B2	Constitution	
13th Street	1A5	37th Street NW	1B2	Avenue NW	2E4
14th St Bridge SW	3B5	38th Street NW	1B1	Corcoran Street NW	2F2
14th Street North	1A5	39th Street NW	1B1	Custer Road	1A5

D

D Street NE	4F3
D Street NW	4D3
D Street SE	4F5
D Street SW	4F5
Daniel French Dr SW	2E5
Decatur Street NW	2E1
Delaware Avenue NE	E4
Dent Place NW	1C2
Desales Street NW	2F3
Duddington Pl SE	4F5
Dumbarton Street NW	2D2
Dupont Circle	2F2

E

E Street NW	2E4
E Street SE	4F5
E Street SW	4D5
East Basin Drive SW	2F5
East Basin Drive SW	3B4
East Capitol Street	4E4
East Place NW	2D2
Eckington Place NE	4E1
Ellipse Road NW	2F4
Ellipse Road NW	3B3
Executive Avenue NW	2F4
Executive Avenue NW	3B3

F

F Street NE	4F3
F Street NW	2E4
F Street NW	3A3
F Street SE	4E5
Fairfax Drive	1A5
Farragut Square	3A2
Florida Avenue NE	4F1
Florida Avenue NW	2E1
Florida Avenue NW	4D1
Folger Square	4F5
Fort Myer Drive	1B4

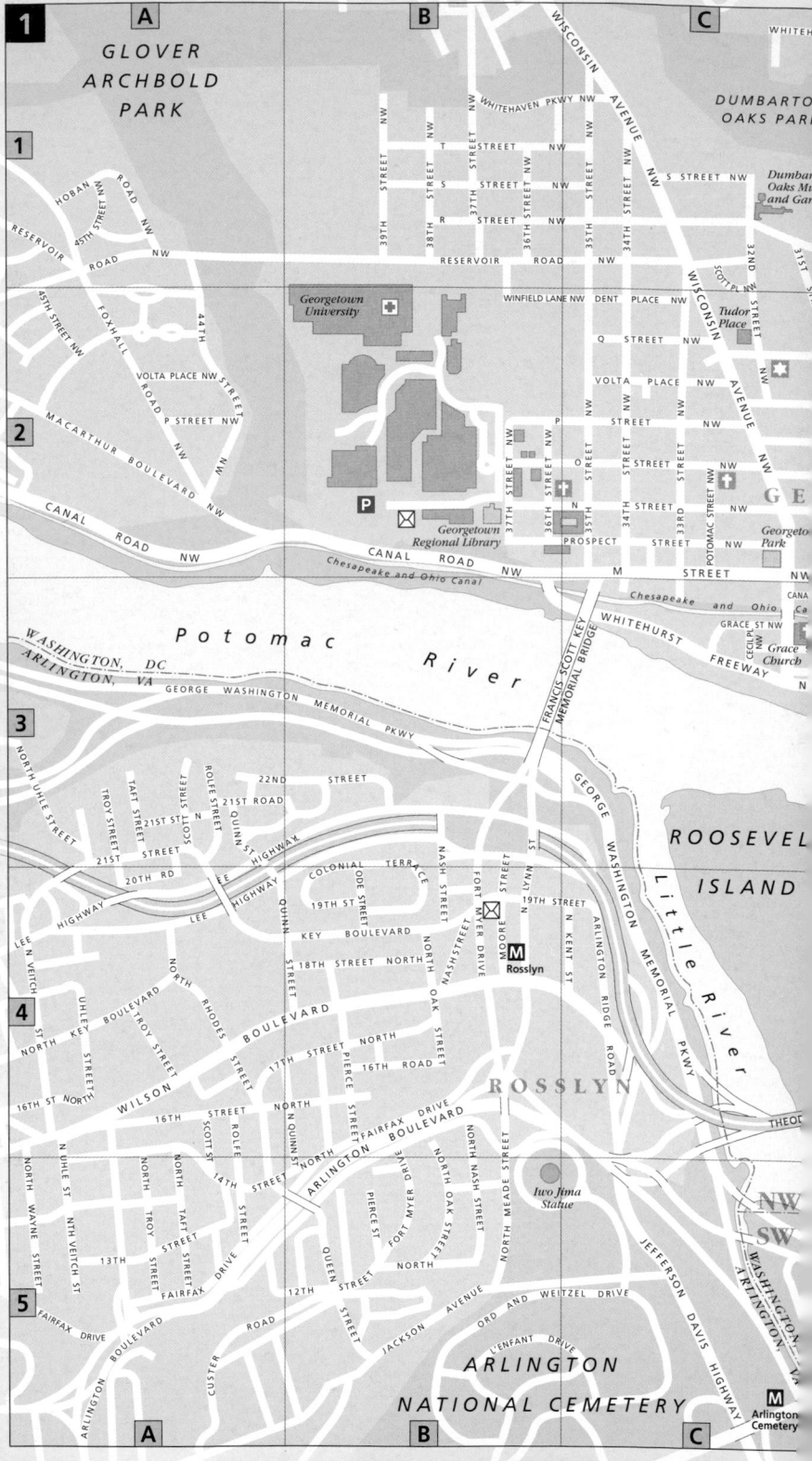

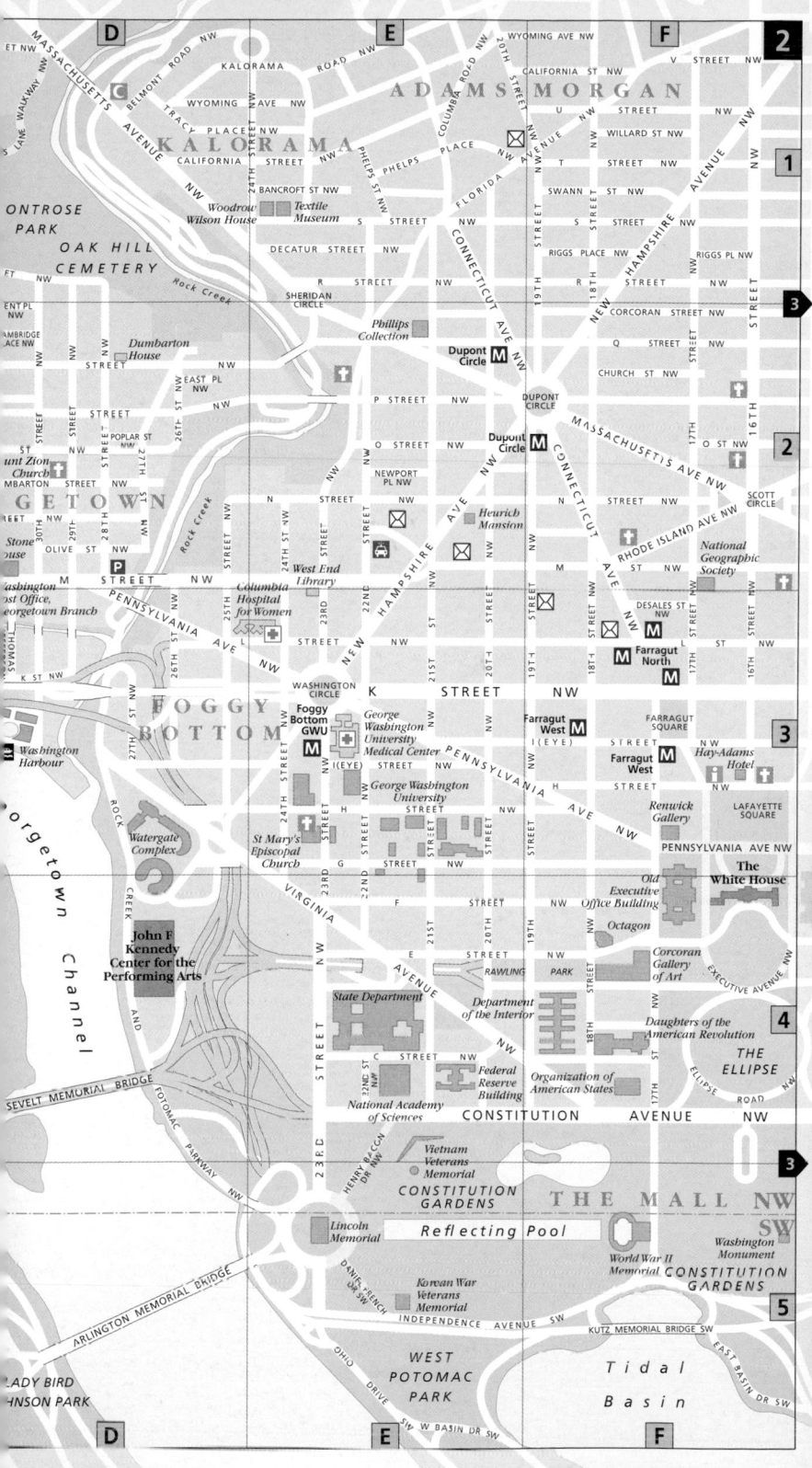

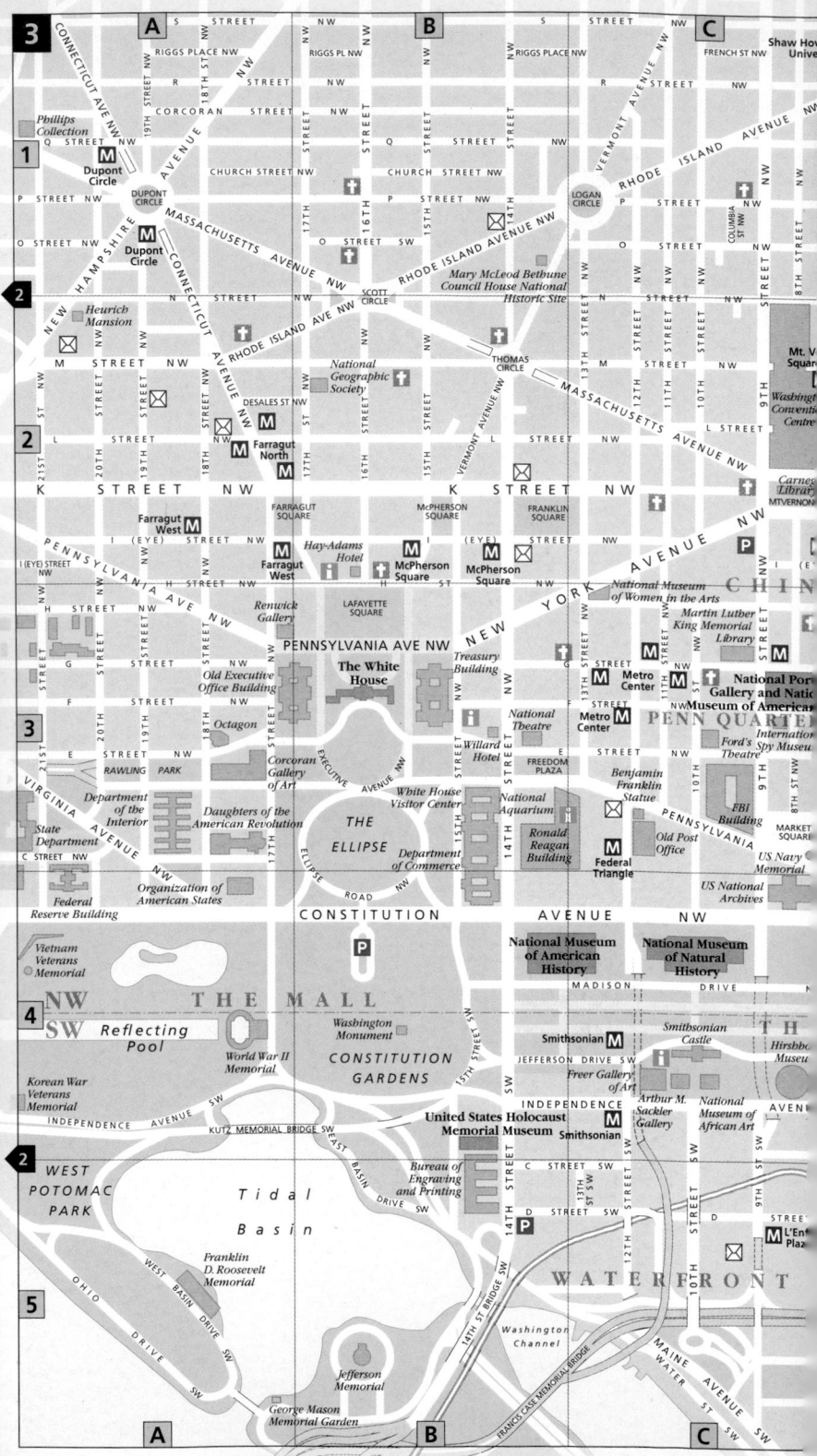

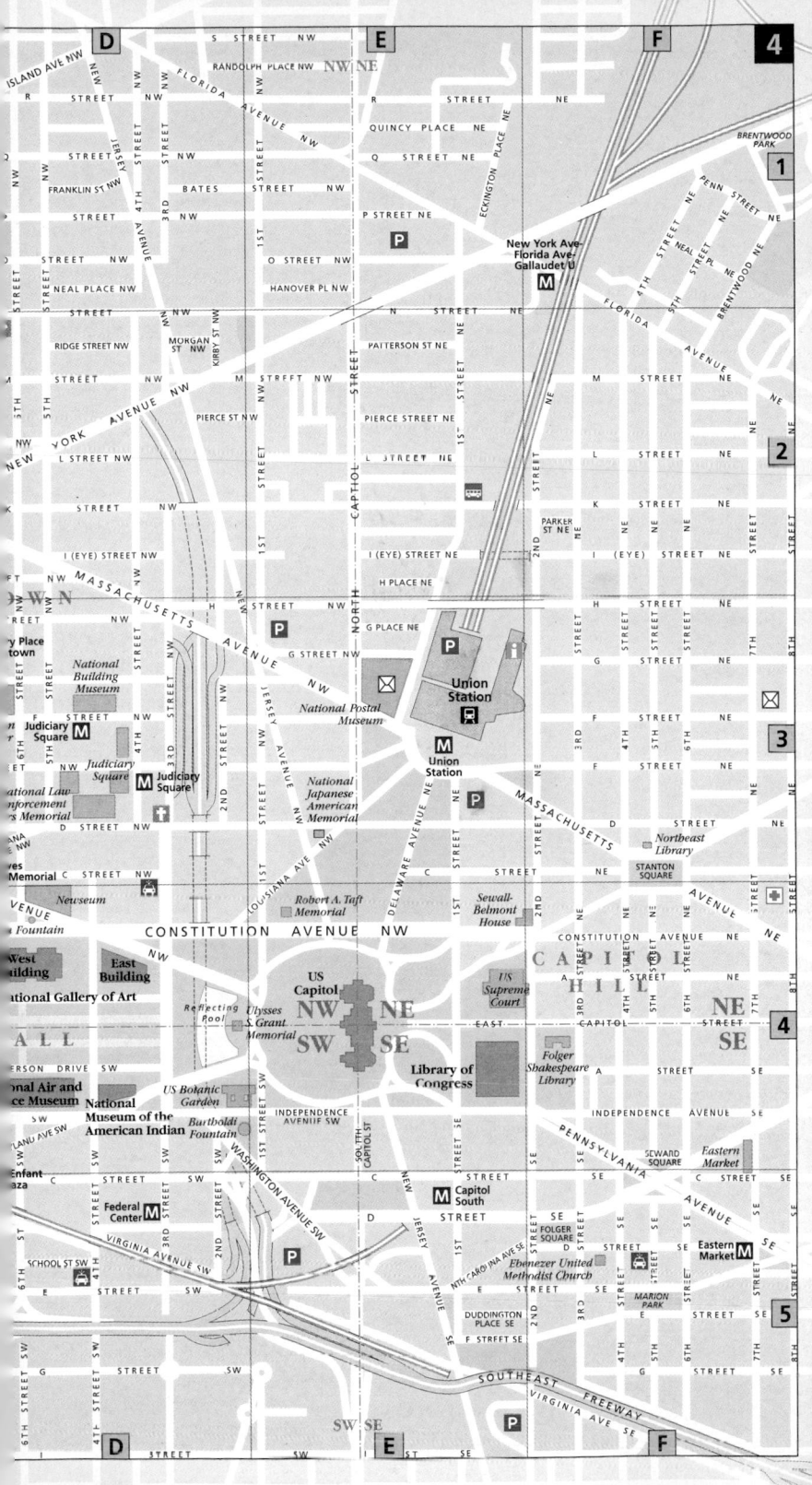

General Index

Acknowledgments

Dorling Kindersley would like to thank the following people whose contributions and assistance have made the preparation of this book possible.

Main Contributors

Susan Burke lives in Virginia and works as an editor for the Air Line Pilots Association. She has taught creative writing for many years and has been a freelance editor of a number of books and journals primarily in the fields of sociology, economics, and politics.

Alice Powers is a freelance writer living in Washington, DC. She has written many articles for the Washington Post and other newspapers. She has also written several literary anthologies and teaches writing at the Corcoran College of Art and Design.

Jennifer Quasha lives in New York City but has a long association with Washington. She has written many articles on subjects ranging from travel to health, and has worked on other Dorling Kindersley books, including *Walking With Dinosaurs*.

Kem Sawyer has lived in Washington for over 20 years and has written children's books, feature articles and book reviews. She particularly enjoys writing about local history.

Managing Editor
Louise Lang

Factchecker
Litta W. Sanderson

Art Director
Gillian Allan

Design and Editorial Assistance
Sue Megginson, Johnny Pau, Hugh Thompson.

Proofreader
Stewart Wild

Indexer
Hilary Bird

Researcher
Sarah Miers

Special Assistance

Particular thanks go to Kathleen Brooks at the National Air and Space Museum, Jessie Cohen and Leah Overstreet at the National Zoological Park, Julie Heizer at the Washington, DC Convention and Visitors' Association, Sarah Petty and Brennan Rash at the National Museum of American Art, Shannon Roberts at the National Gallery of Art and Morgan Zinsmeister at the National Museum of American Art. Thanks also to Dumbarton House, National Headquarters of The National Society of The Colonial Dames of America.

Additional Photography: Max Alexander, Frank Greenaway, Dave King courtesy of Natural History Museum, Tim Mann, Ian O'Leary, Rough Guides/Angus Osborn, Jon Sawyer, Kim Sayer, Giles Stokoe, Clive Streeter, Scott Suchman, Matthew Ward, Stephen Whitehorn.

Additional Illustration: Arun K. Pottirayil.

Additional Cartography: Uma Bhattacharya

Additional Contributions: Emma Anacootee, Tessa Bindloss, Vandana Bhagra, Sherry Collins, Anne Coombes, Anna Freiberger, Rose Hudson, Esther Labi, Hayley Maher, Sam Merrell, Susan Millership, Sangita Patel, Catherine Palmi, Pollyanna Poulter, Alice Powers, Pamposh Raina, Litta W. Sanderson, Sands Publishing Solutions, Kem Sawyer, Susana Smith, Alka Thakur, Lauren Thomas, Conrad Van Dyk, Ros Walford, Dora Whitaker, Hugo Wilkinson.

Additional Picture Research: Marta Bescos.

Photography Permissions
Dorling Kindersley would like to thank the following for their assistance and kind permission to photograph at their

establishments, as well as all the cathedrals, churches, museums, restaurants, hotels, shops, galleries and other sights too numerous to thank individually.

Picture Credits

t-top; tl-top left; tlc-top left center; tc-top center; trc-top right center; tr-top right; cla-center left above; ca-center above; cra-center right above; cl-center left; c-center; cr-center right; clb-center left below; cb-center below; crb-center right below; bl-bottom left; b-bottom; bc-bottom center; bcl-bottom center left; br-bottom right; d-detail

Works of art have been reproduced with the permission of the following copyright holders:

ROBERT HARDING PICTURE LIBRARY: Schuster 2–3; CAPITOL HILTON HOTEL: 172; HIRSHHORN MUSEUM AND SCULPTURE GARDEN: "The Burghers of Calais" (1884-1889) by Auguste Rodin 66tl.

IMAGE BANK: Archive Photos 97b; Andrea Pistolesi 50cl, 78bl;

KIPLINGER WASHINGTON COLLECTION: 78tl; LIBRARY OF CONGRESS: Carol M. Highsmith 46b.

MATISSE RESTAURANT: 182cl; Courtesy Mount Vernon Ladies' Association: 160tl, 160cla.

NATIONAL AIR AND SPACE MUSEUM © SMITHSONIAN INSTITUTION: SI Neg. No. 99-15240-7–31tl; NATIONAL GALLERY OF ART, WASHINGTON, DC: Samuel H. Kress Collection, Photo: Philip A. Charles *Bust of Lorenzo de' Medici* 57tl; Ailsa Mellon Bruce Fund, Photo: Bob Grove *Ginevra de' Benci* c. 1474 by Leonardo da Vinci 58tr; Samuel H. Kress Collection *A Young Man With His Tutor* by Nicolas de Largilliere, 1685–58clb; Samuel H. Kress Collection *Christ Cleansing the Temple* (d), pre-1570, by El Greco 60t, Samuel H. Kress Collection *Madonna and Child*, 1320–1330 by Giotto 60cl; Collection of Mr. and Mrs. Paul Mellon *Woman with a Parasol*, 1875, by Claude Monet 59t; Harris Whittemore Collection *Symphony in White, No. 1: The White Girl*, 1862, by James McNeill Whistler 59cr; Timken Collection *Diana and Endymion*, c. 1753, by Jean-Honore Fragonard 60b; Chester Dale Collection *Miss Mary Ellison*, 1880, by Mary Cassatt 61b; John Russell Pope (architect) 201; .

NATIONAL MUSEUM OF AMERICAN ART/© SMITHSONIAN INSTITUTION: 98tr, Gift of Mr. and Mrs. Joseph Harrison *Old Bear, a Medicine Man*, 1832, by George Catlin 98br; *Achelous and Hercules*, 1947, © T. H. Benton and R. P. Benton Testamentary Trusts/VAGA, New York/DACS, London 2006 – 98-99c; Bequest of Helen Huntington Hull, granddaughter of William Brown Dinsmore who acquired the painting in 1873 for "The Locusts," the family estate in Dutchess County, New York *Among the Sierra Nevada, California* 1868 by Albert Bierstadt 98bl; Gift of John Gellatly *In the Garden (Celia Thaxter in Her Garden)*, 1892, by Childe Hassam 99bl; Gift of Herbert Waide Hemphill, Jr. and Museum purchase made possible by Ralph Cross Johnson, *Bottlecap Giraffe* by an unidentified Artist, completed after 1966–100tl; © Untitled Press, Inc/VAGA, New York and DACS, London 2006 *Reservoir*, 1961, by Robert Raus-chenberg 100cr; Gift of Anonymous Donors *The Throne of the Third Heaven of the Nations Millenium General Assembly*, c. 1950–1954, by James Hampton 100bl. Gift of the Georgia O'Keeffe Foundation *Manhattan* 1932 by Georgia O'Keeffe 99cb; NATIONAL MUSEUM OF AMERICAN history/© SMITHSONIAN INSTITUTION: 74b, 74c, 74tl, 75br, 75cr, 75t, 76br, 77br, 77c, 77tl; NATIONAL MUSEUM OF THE AMERICAN INDIAN: 68tl, 68tr, 68bl, 68br, 69tl, 69cr, 69b; NATIONAL MUSEUM OF NATURAL HISTORY/© SMITHSONIAN INSTITUTION: 70b, 70br; Dane Penland 71t; NATIONAL PARK SERVICE: J. Fenney 111t, 210cla; Richard Freer 165bl; Rick Latoff, courtesy www.Parkphotos.com 67b; Mary McLeod Bethune Council House NHS, Washington D.C. 140c.

NATIONAL PORTRAIT GALLERY/© SMITHSONIAN INSTITUTION: Gift of The Morris and Gwendolyn Cafritz Foundation and Smithsonian Institution Trust Fund *Selfportrait*, 1780–1784, by John Singleton Copley 99ca; Gift of Friends of President and Mrs. Reagan, *Ronald Wilson Reagan*, 1989, © Henry C. Casselli 101c; *Diana Ross and the Supremes*, 1965, © Bruce Davidson/Magnum 101b; Transfer from the National Gallery of Art, Gift of Andrew W. Mellon, 1942, *Pocahontas*, Unidentified artist, English school,

after the 1616 engraving by Simon van de Passe, after 1616 – 101tl; Gift of the Morris and Gwendolyn Cafritz Foundation and the Regents' Major Acquisitions Fund, Smithsonian Institution *Mary Cassatt*, 1880–1884, by Edgar Degas 99tl; Courtesy National Portrait Gallery *"Casey" Stengel*, 1981 cast after 1965 plaster by © Rhoda Sherbell 99tr.

NATIONAL POSTAL MUSEUM/ © SMITHSONIAN INSTITUTION: Jim O'Donnell 53c.

NATIONAL ZOOLOGICAL PARK/© SMITHSONIAN INSTITUTION: Jessie Cohen 138–9; PETER NEWARK'S AMERICAN PICTURES: 28tl.

NEWSEUM: 93tl; DAVID NOBLE: 1, 54.

RICHARD T. NOWITZ: 63b, 81crb; Abe Nowitz 37c.

OCTAGON MUSEUM/AMERICAN ARCHITECTURAL FOUNDATION, WASHINGTON DC: 115b.

PHILLIPS COLLECTION: 135br, 135c; POPPERFOTO: Reuters 28cl, 28cr; PRIVATE COLLECTION: Kevin Ryan 196t.

REX FEATURES: 27tc; SIPA Press/Trippett 27cb.

MAE SCANLAN: 31cla, 32t, 36b, 62bl, 77t, 104, 206t, 206tr; SCIENCE PHOTO LIBRARY: US Geological Survey 10; SMITH-SONIAN NATIONAL AIR AND SPACE MUSEUM: 64br, LEN SPODEN PHOTOGRAPHY: 147tl, 147tr, 148br, 149tl, 151br, 151t; FRANK SPOONER PICTURES: Markel-Liaison 91br; COURTESY OF THE SPY MUSEUM: 102tl, 102c; STA TRAVEL GROUP: 211tl.

TEXTILE MUSEUM: Gift of Mrs. Charles Putnam 136t.

TOPHAM PICTUREPOINT: 125clb.

TRH PICTURES: National Air and Space Museum 63t, 64t.

UNITED AIRLINES: 218t; UNIVERSITY OF VIRGINIA: Library Special Collections Department, Manuscript Print Collection 127tl; UNITED STATES HOLOCAUST MEMORIAL MUSEUM: 81cra.

WHITE HOUSE COLLECTION, COURTESY WHITE HOUSE HISTORICAL ASSOCIATION: 108cl/b, 109t/c/bl/br, 110b, Peter Vitale 111bl; Bruce White 111cr.

Front Endpaper: All special photography except David Noble br; Mae Scanlan tl.

Back Endpaper: © 1998 Washington Metropolitan Area Transit Authority.

Map Cover: - PHOTOLIBRARY: Imagestate RM/Tony Sweet.

Jacket: Front - PHOTOLIBRARY: Imagestate RM/Tony Sweet. Back - ALAMY IMAGES: A Cnoncc tl; Rob Crandall bl; Alex Segre - Iwo Jima Memorial 1995 ©Felix DeWeldon cla; Michael Ventura clb. Spine - PHOTOLIBRARY: Imagestate RM/Tony Sweet t.

All other images © Dorling Kindersley. See www.dkimages.com for more information.

ⓜ System Map
metro

Station in Service ⊙

Transfer Station ◉

Commuter Rail
◆ Virginia Railway Express · Ⓜ MARC

Bus to Airport 🚌

Parking 🅿

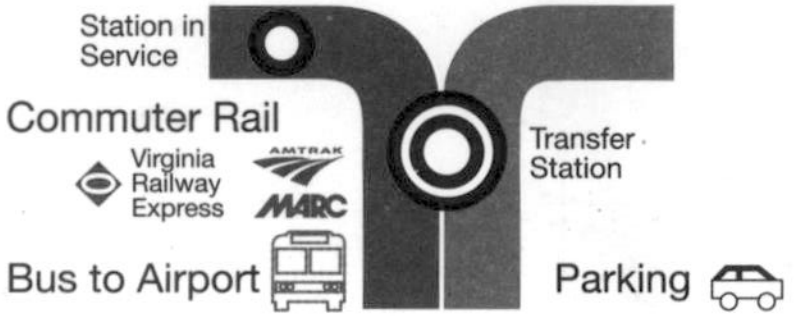

Legend

- 🔴 Red Line • Glenmont to Shady Grove
- 🟠 Orange Line • New Carrollton to Vienna/Fairfax-GMU
- 🔵 Blue Line • Franconia-Springfield to Largo Town Center
- 🟢 Green Line • Branch Avenue to Greenbelt
- 🟡 Yellow Line • Huntington to Fort Totten

MetroOpensDoors.com
Customer Information Service: 202/637-6000
TTY Phone: 202/638-3780

RED LINE

Shady Grove · Rockville · Twinbrook · White Flint · Grosvenor-Strathmore · Medical Center · Bethesda · Friendship Heights · Tenleytown-AU · Van Ness-UDC · Cleveland Park · Woodley Park-Zoo/Adams Morgan · Dupont Circle

GREEN LINE

Greenbelt · College Park-U of Md · Prince George's Plaza · West Hyattsville · Fort Totten · Brookland-CUA

Glenmont · Wheaton · Forest Glen · Silver Spring · Takoma · Georgia Ave-Petworth · Columbia Heights · U St/African-Amer Civil War Memorial/Cardozo

Yellow Line service operates between Mt Vernon Sq/7th St-Convention Center and Fort Totten stations except Weekdays 5:00 to 9:30 a.m. and 3:00 to 7:00 p.m.

B30 to BWI Thurgood Marshall Airport

Every other outbound Red Line train terminates at Grosvenor-Strathmore station Weekdays 7:00 to 9:30 a.m. and 4:00 to 6:30 p.m.

Montgomery County / Prince George's County

District of Columbia / Montgomery County

Capital Beltway

New Carrollton

R.C.L.

MAI 2011

G

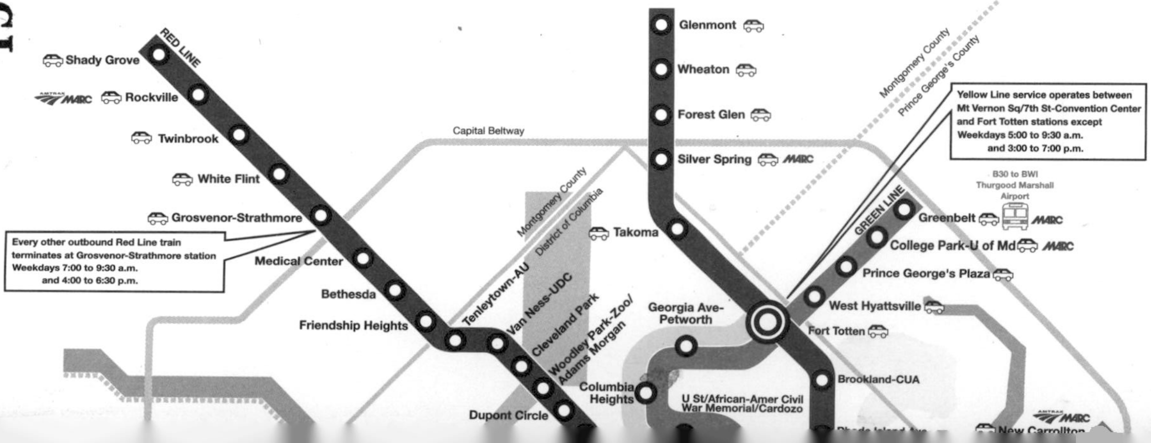